Dedication

To the memory of Guy D. Jordan, co-founder
and Fellow of the American Cichlid Association
and to Ethelwyn Trewavas, inspiration, mentor
and friend.

ISBN 1-56465-146-0

© 1994
Tetra-Press
Tetra Werke Dr. rer. nat. Ulrich Baensch GmbH
P.O.Box 1580, D-49304 Melle, Germany
All rights reserved, incl. film, broadcasting,
television as well as the reprinting

Printed and bound in Spain by Egedsa, Sabadell
Printed in Spain
Distributed in U.S.A. by
Tetra Second nature (Division of Warner-Lambert)
Blacksburg, VA 24060-6671
WL-Code: 16077
D.L.B.: 20.861-94

Contents

THE CICHLID AQUARIUM

Introduction

No group of ornamental fishes arouses such strong emotions among aquarists as do the cichlids. Their many partisans praise their intelligence, brilliant coloration, ease of maintenance and highly evolved parental behavior. The family's equally numerous detractors regard cichlids as ferocious predators that divide their waking hours between destructive manipulation of their physical environment and gratuitous battery of any fish in the immediate vicinity too large to make a convenient mouthful. As a dedicated cichlid keeper of over twenty years' standing, I naturally have a positive view of the Cichlidae as aquarium residents.

Yet the sad truth is that the pejorative judgement embodied in the conventional view of cichlids has a basis in fact. Many cichlids are specialized predators.

No few species are destructive of rooted plants or otherwise given to rearranging their tank's decor. Finally, the overwhelming majority defend a territory against all comers as an integral part of their reproductive pattern, often with unpleasant consequences to their tankmates.

However, the Cichlidae are a large and astonishingly diverse group of fishes. If one can find among its over twelve hundred species a number that fit the negative profile of the family to perfection, a comparable effort will turn up at least as many cichlids that are neither predatory, given to massive earthmoving nor inordinately aggressive towards other fishes even during periods of reproductive activity. Furthermore, much of the seemingly sociopathic behavior attributed to cichlids is due less to any inherent and invincible bellicosity than to their prospective keepers' ignorance of their maintenance requirements.

As in other areas of the aquarium hobby, failures in cichlid keeping arise primarily because aquarists lack reliable information on both the biology of these fishes and the techniques of keeping and breeding them in captivity.

The aim of this book is to provide such a primer of cichlid biology and maintenance. It is written for the hobbyist of some prior fishkeeping experience who either contemplates the acquisition of his first cichlids or else has already taken the first steps in that direction.

A working knowledge of the basics of aquarium maintenance is thus assumed, as is a degree of familiarity with the anatomy and natural history of fishes.

The initial chapter is an overview of cichlid biology that seeks to answer the apparently simple question: "What is a cichlid?". Its objective is to provide the reader with an appreciation of the enormous diversity of the Family Cichlidae and some notion of its fascinating natural history.

Subsequent chapters relate the behavior of cichlids to their management in captivity, offer specific recommendations on how set up a cichlid aquarium and discuss approaches to the maintenance of cichlids in captivity. Feeding, nitrogen cycle management, water chemistry and treatment of commonly encountered management and medical problems are specifically addressed.

The seventh chapter deals with breeding cichlids under aquarium conditions. The eight through eleventh introduce the reader to the major groups of cichlids available to aquarists, while the last explores alternative approaches to learning more about cichlids and includes suggestions for further reading.

This book would not have been possible without the assistance of far more people than can be individually acknowledged herein. In recognizing the contributions of my informants, I must also absolve them of responsibility for any of my positions regarding the biology or aquarium husbandry of cichlids. I am confident that they share my hope that this book will serve the reader as a trustworthy guide to the often challenging, always rewarding and never boring pastime of cichlid keeping.

Introduction to the Second Edition

The past decade has witnessed major advances in our understanding of cichlid biology. On one hand, the ongoing exploration of the world's fresh waters continues to multiply the number of cichlid taxa known to science. On the other, the publication of major revisionary studies drawing upon the full spectrum of investigative techniques has clarified our understanding of cichlid evolutionary relationships. Both trends have led to substantial changes in the nomenclature of both Paleotropical and Neotropical cichlids. Our understanding of how cichlids relate to their often highly complex environments has been enormously broadened by long-term field studies of the ichthyofaunas of Lakes Malawi and Tanganyika, the Amazon basin and Middle America undertaken during this period. Meanwhile, laboratory research has revealed many of the physiological and behavioral mechanisms that underlie these successful adaptations.

Concurrently with this information explosion has come an unprecedented expansion of the number of cichlid species available to aquarists. This agreeable state of affairs arises from the interaction of a number of trends in the aquarium hobby. In the case of cichlids from the southern tributaries of the Amazon, it is due to the opening up of new areas to the commercial exportation of ornamental fishes. In the case of the Malawian and Tanganyikan cichlid faunas, it follows the more intensive exploration of an already important focus of fish exportation. The remarkable increase in the selection of Mesoamerican cichlid species commercially available is due largely to systematic efforts to bring these fish into commercial production in Florida. West African cichlids, on the other hand, have been the beneficiaries of a less structured but equally effective effort undertaken by numerous determined and highly dedicated European hobbyists. Unfortunately, not all the trends of the past decade have been positive. Since the first edition of this book went to press, cichlid enthusiasts have witnessed the collapse of the Lake Victoria ecosystem, triggered by the extirpation of roughly two thirds of its endemic cichlid species by an introduced predator, the Nile perch. The clock is ticking inexorably towards the final midnight of extinction for the cichlids of Madagascar. Here the one-two punch of habitat degradation and impact of exotic predators and competitors threatens to exterminate the living representatives of an icthyofauna that survived the demise of the dinosaurs. West African habitats thought secure thirty years ago are now seriously compromised by massive deforestation. This development bodes ill for many forest-associated species, among them cichlids whose ready availability aquarists have come to take for granted. Closer to home, the unsustainable pumping of groundwater in the desert regions of northern Mexico and the rapid spread of chemically dependent export agriculture in the remainder of Middle America pose immediate threats to the integrity of a regional ichthyofauna dominated by cichlids.

The information explosion generated by a decade of productive research clearly mandated substantial changes in the text. These are intended to embody to the fullest extent practical current views of cichlid taxonomy, but given the dynamic state of this field of endeavor, readers would do well not to take them as definitive pronouncements. The dramatic increase in available cichlid species has motivated both an expansion of the catalog section and the inclusion of additional illustrations. However, a less obvious but equally important reason for preparing this updated version of **The Cichlid Aquarium** has been the need to alert readers to the threats facing cichlids and indeed, all tropical freshwater fishes in nature.

Barring a most improbable reversal of existing trends, it is quite likely that by the turn of the century, a significant number of cichlid species will exist only under some sort of active management. Public aquaria, zoos, and government agencies will play a key role in implementing such programs. However, the enthusiasm and expertise of amateur aquarists affords them an opportunity to make meaningful contributions to the conservation of threatened cichlids, while the limitation of existing institutional resources makes their involvement absolutely essential to the success of such programs. If the readers of this book come away with an awareness of the scope of the problem, a realization that they can contribute to its solution, and firm resolve to involve themselves in such conservation efforts, the labor entailed in this revision will have been amply rewarded.

CHAPTER I

WHAT IS A CICHLID?

Diagnosis and Relationships of the Family Cichlidae

The obvious and necessary starting point of any discussion of cichlid biology is a clear understanding of what makes a cichlid a cichlid.

From the perspective of the systematic ichthyologist, the Family Cichlidae is easily defined. From that of the average aquarist, the dividing line between cichlid and non-cichlid often seems less sharply drawn.

For instance, one often sees the chameleon perch, *Badis badis,* offered for sale as a dwarf cichlid, notwithstanding that it is a member of the Family Badidae, whose closest relatives are the anabantoid fishes, not the Cichlidae [Figure 1]. Aquarists sometimes fall into the error of regarding cichlids as the tropical representatives of the North American sunfishes and basses.

In fact, those important sport fish belong to a quite different and only distantly related group, the Family Centrarchidae. Some cichlids display a remarkable external similarity to centrarchids.

However, this merely reflects the fact that they make their living in much the same manner [Figures 2 & 3]. In such instances, identical forces of natural selection operate to produce superficially similar body plans. Such convergence in morphology may offer insights into the ecology of the species in question, but are useless in assessing their evolutionary relationships.

Were this not difficulty enough, the family's remarkable morphological diversity deceives many inexperienced hobbyists about the true affinities of such popular aquarium residents as the freshwater angelfish [Figure 4], *Pterophyllum scalare* (LICHTENSTEIN 1823) and the magnificent discus fishes [Figure 5] of the genus *Symphysodon.*

Fig. 1: Though superficially similar to many dwarf cichlids, the chameleon perch, *Badis badis,* is more closely related to the labyrinth fishes than to the Family Cichlidae.

Fig. 2: The green sunfish, *Leopmis cyanellus,* a piscivorous sunfish of the North American Family Centrarchidae.

Fig. 3: This piscivorous Middle American cichlid *Nandopsis friedrichsthalii,* Heckel 1840, is an ecological analog of the green sunfish.

Hence, the importance of defining the family as unambiguously as possible and placing it in its proper relationship to other groups of fishes.

As a quick glance at Figure 7 reveals, cichlids are representatives of the largest group of fishes, the advanced bony fishes of the Infraclass Teleostei. They are spiny-finned fishes of the Superorder Acanthopterygii belonging to the enormous Order Perciformes, or perch-like fishes. Together with the related Families Labridae (wrasses), Embiotocidae (viviparous surfperches) and Pomacentridae (damselfishes) of the Suborder Percoidei, cichlids are characterized by **the fusion of the lower pharyngeal bones into a single triangular tooth-bearing structure.** In all four of these families, the upper and lower pharyngeal bones are enabled by means of a complex musculature to function as **a second set of jaws in the processing of food** [Figure 6].

The shape of the lower pharyngeal bone and its associated dentition varies dramatically within the family. These features so closely reflect the **trophic**, or feeding pattern of the species in question that a quick glance at the lower pharyngeal bone tells an ichthyologist a good deal about the ecology of the fish from which it was taken. This arrangement frees the true jaws from a primary role in processing foodstuffs. This opens the way for natural selection to make them more efficient structures for prey capture or manipulation of the physical environment. The remarkable diversity embodied in the Family Cichlidae no less than the undesirable ability of many cichlids to outcompete species native to regions where they have been introduced owe much to the simple fact that cichlids possess such efficient **pharyngeal jaws.**

Cichlids further have but **a single pair of nostrils** [Figure 8], a feature that unequivocally distinguishes them from wrasses and surfperches. Taken in combination with **moderately to highly protrusible jaws, toothless palates, an anal fin with three or more spines** and **a single dorsal fin containing both spiny and soft elements**, this feature immediately sets them apart from all other freshwater fishes.

The only **skeletal characteristics** that unfailingly set cichlids apart from the very similar marine damselfishes are **the absence of a bony shelf beneath the orbit**, or eye socket of the skull and **the presence of an obvious suture line at the point of fusion of the two halves of the lower pharyngeal bone** [Figures 9 & 10].

Additionally, most, though not all, cichlids have a **divided lateral line,** another feature that sets them apart from the damselfishes.

Fig. 4: Many newcomers to the tropical fish hobby are surprised to learn that the angelfishes of the genus *Pterophyllum*, such as these lovely marble angels, are members in good standing of the Family Cichlidae!

Fig. 5: The extreme lateral compression and retiring disposition of the discusfishes of the genus *Symphysodon* make it difficult for many aquarists to accept them as real cichlids.

Finally, the two families differ quite dramatically in important details of their reproductive biology, not the least striking of which is the mechanism by which the eggs are attached to the substratum upon which they have been deposited.

While these features enable an ichthyologist to unerringly diagnose a preserved specimen as a representative of the Family Cichlidae, they are only peripherally significant to the aquarist. Of considerably greater interest is the fact that cichlids are **secondary division freshwater fishes**. This category comprises families whose ancestors evolved under marine conditions, then successfully invaded and colonized freshwater biotopes, such as the Cyprinodontidae (killifishes), Poeciliidae (livebearing topminnows) [Figure 11], Melanotaeniidae (Australasian rainbowfishes) and, of course, the Cichli-dae. In contrast, **primary division freshwater fishes** comprise families whose entire evolutionary career has taken place in freshwater, such as the Osteoglossidae (bony-tongued fishes), Mormyridae (elephant-noses), and the numerous lineages of the order Cypriniformes.

This enormous assemblage includes such important ornamental fishes as the characoids, of which the Family Characidae (true characins) is most familiar to aquarists, the gymnotoids (Neotropical knifefishes), the Cyprinidae (true carps and minnows) [Figure 12], the Cobitidae (loaches) and all save two families of siluroids (catfishes).

Primary division freshwater fishes are sensitive to dissolved sodium chloride. Secondary division fishes, on the other hand, are usually quite salt tolerant.

6 a—e & 7 a—e: A representative selection of cichlid species [Figure 6] and their lower pharyngeal bones and associated dentition [Figure 7] (a) *Nimbochromis venustus* (Boulenger 1908), a piscivorous cichlid; (b) *Lamprologus tretocephalus* Boulenger 1899, a malacophagous, or mollusk-eating cichlid; (c) an undescribed zooplankton-feeding cichlid of the genus *Copadichromis*; (d) *Oreochromis* cf. *spilurus* (Gunther 1894), a microphagous cichlid; (e) *Geophagus brachybranchus* Nijssen & Kullander 1991, a substratum-sifting invertebrate-feeding cichlid.

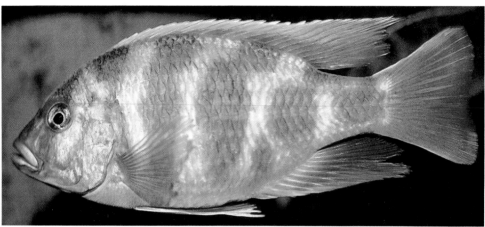

a)

b)

c)

d)

e)

In extreme cases, representatives of this group can live and breed successfully even under marine conditions [Figure 13]. The implications of such salt tolerance as a determinant of cichlid distribution will become evident when the family's evolutionary history is considered.

Of greater concern to aquarists is the fact that most cichlids share the characteristic tolerance of secondary division fishes for a wide range of water conditions.

Most can be expected to prosper under all save the most extreme pH and hardness values in captivity.

Of equal importance, secondary division freshwater fishes have **an essentially opportunistic reproductive pattern.** In most primary division fishes, reproductive activity is markedly **seasonal.**

These fishes typically depend upon **highly specific environmental stimuli** to trigger gonadal maturation and subsequent spawning. However, cichlids will breed **whenever their reserves of stored food are sufficient to per-**mit the maturation of eggs and the **implementation of species-typical parental behavior.**

The only environmental factor that operates in a proximate way to inhibit or encourage breeding in cichlids is water temperature. These life history characteristics make cichlids among the most easily maintained and bred of all aquarium residents.

Of comparable importance, cichlid reproductive patterns are characterized by **sophisticated parental care of the eggs and eleuthroembryos, or yolk-sac fry** which in the majority of species **also extends to the mobile fry.**

While parental care of the eggs and eleuthroembryos is not uncommon in fishes, extension of such protection to the mobile fry is quite unusual [Figure 14].

The marine damselfishes, for example, vigilantly defend their eggs until they hatch, but only one species, *Acanthochromis polyacanthus*, is known to extend such protection to its mobile fry.

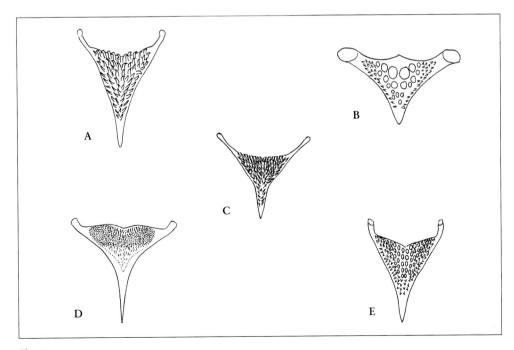

Fig. 7.

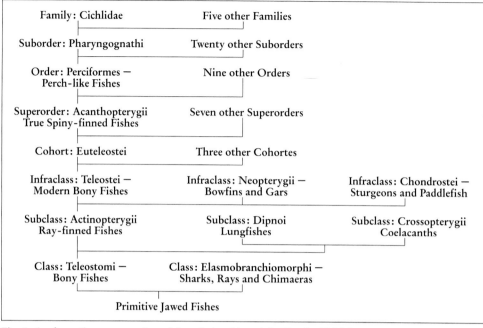

Family: Cichlidae	Five other Families	
Suborder: Pharyngognathi	Twenty other Suborders	
Order: Perciformes — Perch-like Fishes	Nine other Orders	
Superorder: Acanthopterygii True Spiny-finned Fishes	Seven other Superorders	
Cohort: Euteleostei	Three other Cohortes	
Infraclass: Teleostei — Modern Bony Fishes	Infraclass: Neopterygii — Bowfins and Gars	Infraclass: Chondrostei — Sturgeons and Paddlefish
Subclass: Actinopterygii Ray-finned Fishes	Subclass: Dipnoi Lungfishes	Subclass: Crossopterygii Coelacanths
Class: Teleostomi — Bony Fishes	Class: Elasmobranchiomorphi — Sharks, Rays and Chimaeras	
	Primitive Jawed Fishes	

Fig. 8: A schematic representation of the relationships of the Family Cichlidae.

The pelagic larvae of the remaining species are strictly on their own.

Cichlids are also unusual in that the female plays an important parental role, either in conjunction with the male or as the sole custodian of the spawn [Figure 15]. The usual rule among externally fertilizing egg-laying bony fishes is for the male alone to undertake the parental role.

The consequent complexity of cichlid parental behavior is one of the family's most aquaristically appealing features. Its expression is aesthetically pleasing to most human observers, and effectively frees the aquarist from the most burdensome duties associated with successful captive breeding of egg laying fishes.

The other side of this coin is that parental behavior is often synonymous with acute intolerance of other fishes and extremely effective measures aimed at excluding such potential fry predators from the immediate vicinity [Figure 16].

Much of the behavior deemed undesirable in these fishes relates in some manner to reproduction.

Fig 9: The single pair of external nares characteristic of the family is clearly visible in this close-up of the head of a female *Nandopsis motaguensis* (Gunther 1866).

This factor must be considered carefully when setting up the cichlid aquarium.

Finally, cichlids are **highly intelligent** fishes. Their responses to the environment are **more varied** and their behavior **less rigidly stereotyped** than those of most other fishes.

Fig. 10 & 11: Note the overall similarity between *Archocentrus spilurus* (Gunther 1862), a small Central American cichlid (9) and this damselfish, *Glyphidotontops cyaneus*. In this instance, superficial similarity reflects close relationship between the Families Cichlidae and Pomacentridae.

Fig. 12: The ability of the green sailfin molly, *Poecilia latipinna,* to live and breed in sea water is characteristic of many secondary division freshwater fishes.

Fig. 13: The diminutive *Barbus jae*, an African representative of the true minnows. The Cyprindae are the most species-rich family of primary division freshwater fishes.

Fig. 14: Like many secondary division freshwater fishes, *Oreochromis mossambicus* (Peters 1852) can live and breed successfully under marine conditions. This is a male of the golden color variety of this important food fish.

This trait manifests itself most obviously in the way cichlids respond to novel stimuli in captivity, but can also be seen in their responses to unexpected circumstances in nature. Perhaps its most obvious manifestation is the undeniable fact that cichlids not only breed but breed readily in captivity, where conditions are utterly different from those in nature. Behavioral scientists have long appreciated the ease with which cichlids respond to many standard conditioning paradigms.

This is one reason the family has endeared itself to students of animal behavior [Figure 17].

On a more intimate level, the complexity of interactions between individual large cichlids and their keepers is proverbial.

Cichlids have no difficulty relating to conspecifics as individuals and readily extend such recognition of individual differences to the human beings with which they come into contact.

Such behavior quite often earns them promotion to the status enjoyed by such traditional animal companions as dogs or cats.

This is not to deny intrafamilial differences in behavioral complexity. These exist and correlate well with differences in feeding ecology, predators necessarily being quicker on the uptake than plankton feeders or herbivores. They are also related to the type of parental care a given species practices. Maternally mouthbrooding *Haplochromis* species, for instance, seem notably more stereotyped in their behavior than biparentally cus-todial *Cichlasoma* or *Hemichromis* species. This should come as no surprise given the complexity of the problems faced by the guardians of a swarm of several thousand mobile fry. But even taking these differences into account, cichlids tower above the generality of freshwater aquarium fishes with regard to behavioral sophistication. This feature of cichlid biology may very well be at least as important as the trophic flexibility previously alluded to in explaining the family's success in colonizing new habitats.

Fig. 15: The vigilant care of this pair of *Herichthys carpintis* (Jordan & Snyder 1899) for their mobile fry is common among cichlids, but very unusual among fishes as a whole.

Fig. 16: The careful attention given her clutch by this female *Nanochromis minor* Roberts & Stewart 1976 illustrates another feature that sets cichlids apart from the generality of parental bony fishes: female involvement in caring for the zygotes.

Fig. 17: Cichlids are fearless in the defense of their progeny. This female *Hemichromis fasciatus* (Peters 1858) responds aggressively to the approach of a magnetized glass cleaning pad.

Fig. 18: Behavioral researches as done by this aquarist find cichlids to be excellent experimental subjects.

An Introduction to Cichlid Diversity

The Family Cichlidae is extremely speciose.

When the faunas of the Great Lakes of Africa are fully inventoried, the final tally of cichlids will probably exceed two thousand species.

To put this figure in perspective, of the entire order Perciformes, which comprises sixty-five families, only the Family Gobiidae boasts more species.

On the level of morphological diversity, cichlids have few rivals among perciform fishes and compare favorably with any single family of ostariophysan fishes, such as the Characidae or Cyprinidae. Cichlids range in size from the Neotropical *Apistogramma borelli* (REGAN 1906) [Figure 18] and the diminutive snail-dwelling *Lamprologus multifasciatus* BOULENGER 1906 [Figure 19] of Lake Tanganyika that barely attain 2" SL to such giants as *Cichla monoculus* SPIX 1831 of the Amazonian region and *Boulengerochromis microlepis* (BOULENGER 1899) [Figure 20], another Tanganyikan endemic, that can attain lengths of almost a yard.

Confronted with fish as different in appearance as *Aequidens tetramerus* (HECKEL 1840) [Figure 21], *Geophagus steindachneri* EIGENMANN and HILDEBRAND 1910 [Figure 22], *Theraps bifasciatus* (GUNTHER 1864) [Figure 23], *Astatoreochromis vanderhorsti* (GREENWOOD 1954) [Figure 24] and *Labeotro-*

Fig. 19: *Apistogramma borellii* is one of the smallest known cichlids. Large males such as this measure barely 2" SL!

Fig. 20: The largest known cichlid is *Boulengerochromis microlepis*, an open-water predator from Lake Tanganyika.

17

Fig. 21: *Aequidens tetramerus* Heckel 1840 is typical of the genus in body form. This male was collected from the Rio Nanay in Peru.

pheus trewavasae FRYER 1956 [Figure 25], an inexperienced observer could be forgiven a reluctance to attribute all five to the same Family! As the accompanying montage of photographs makes clear, this remarkable range of phenotypes reflects the fact that cichlids have exploited virtually every means of making a living tropical freshwaters offer a fish.

In *Pungu maclareni* (TREWAVAS 1962), a cichlid endemic to Barombi-Mbo, a volcanic crater lake in the Cameroons, the family can even claim representation among the hand-ful of fish, marine or freshwater, that feed on sponges. Two quite distinct cichlid lineages have evolved adaptations that allow them to feed upon the fins and scales of other fishes. Such **dermal grazers** have been identified in the cichlid faunas of Lakes Victoria, Tanganyika and Malawi and their eventual discovery elswhere in Africa and in the Neotropics is highly likely.

Analysis of their stomach contents taken with the distinctive shape of their jaw teeth suggests that at least two species of haplo-

Fig. 22: *Geophagus steindachneri* (Eigenmann & Hildebrand 1910) comes honestly by its common name of red-hump eartheater, though few specimens are as well endowed in this respect as the male herein depicted?

Fig. 23: A male *Theraps bifasciatus* (Gunther 1864), a recently introduced herbivorous cichlid from Middle America.

chromines native to Lake Victoria fed in large part upon the ectoparasites of other fishes, while such cleaning behavior has been observed in the Malawian species *Pseudotropheus crabro* (RIBBINK and LEWIS 1982) and *Docimodus evelynae* (RIBBINK and LEWIS 1982). Cichlids native to Lakes Edward, George, Victoria and Malawi have even evolved a feeding strategy absolutely unique to the family, **paedophagy**, in which the embryos of maternal mouthbrooding cichlids are the exploited food resource [Figure 26].

As remarkable as their success in utilizing a wide range of food resources is the sophistication cichlids display in the exploitation of a particular trophic niche. By rough estimate, about a quarter of the known cichlid species depend upon other fishes as a food source. Though most are solitary predators, pack hunters such as the Tanganyikan *Lamprologus callipterus* BOULENGER 1906 [Figure 27], that collaborate in the capture and dismemberment of their prey, can be found among these specialized piscivores.

The former include small prey specialists, such as *Hemichromis fasciatus* PETERS 1858 [Figure 28], and many small predatory haplochromine species endemic to the East African lakes [Figure 29].

Other predatory species, among them the Central American *Petenia splendida* GUNTHER 1862 [Figure 30] and the Malawian *Serranochromis robustus* (GUNTHER 1864), take fishes a third to half of their standard length as a matter of course.

This category comprises both **cruise predators**, such as the streamlined *Ramphochromis* of Lake Malawi [Figure 31] that actively chase down prey, and hunters that await the approach of potential victims in ambush, such as the Neotropical pike cichlids of the genus *Crenicichla* [Figure 32].

One such **ambush predator**, the Malawian *Dimidiochromis compressiceps* (BOULENGER 1908) [Figure 33], exploits coloration that mimics the leaves of the *Vallisneria* thickets within which it hunts, while *Nimbochromis livingstoni* (GUNTHER 1893) [Figure 34], like-

19

Fig. 24: Native to the basin of the Malagarazi, Lake Tanganyika's major inflowing river, *Astatoreochromis vanderhorsti* is a mollusc-feeding haplochromine cichlid.

Fig. 25: This male of the red dorsal morph of *Labeotropheus trewavasae* is representative of the mbuna, a group of specialized haplochromine cichlids endemic to Lake Malawi. Like most members of this group it is adapted to take algae from rocky surface.

Fig. 26: A male *Haplochromis (Lipochromis) maxillaris* Trewavas 1928, a paedophage, or embryo-eating cichlid endemic to Lake Victoria.

Fig. 27: A male *Lamprologus callipterus,* a pack-hunting piscivorous cichlid native to Lake Tanganyika.

Fig. 28: The West African *Hemichromis fasciatus* feeds in large measure upon the fry of sympatrically occurring tilapias.

Fig. 29: The outsized, pointed head and large mouth of this male *Sciaenochromis fryeri* Konings 1993 betray a piscivorous feeding pattern. Lake Malawi boasts an unusually large number of such small but highly efficient piscivores.

Fig. 30: The highly piscivorous *Petenia splendida* has the largest gape of any Mesoamerican cichlid. Adults can take prey up to 6″ SL with ease.

wise endemic to Lake Malawi, has evolved a combination of behavior and color pattern that allows it to ambush fish without benefit of any sort of cover by mimicking a decomposing cadaver. Hungry fish approaching the dead *N. livingstoni* in the expectation of making an easy meal wind up becoming one themselves!

Equally impressive is the way different cichlid lineages have independently evolved the morphological and behavioral features that allow them to exploit the same food source. As their generic names imply, the South American genera *Geophagus* and *Gymnogeophagus* are "earth eaters", cichlids that sift through the substratum in search of buried aquatic insect larvae and snails. These fish have long snouts, elevated eyes, a buccopharyngeal apparatus that facilitates separation of edible from inedible items, and a color pattern based upon a profusion of iridescent spangling highly cryptic when viewed from above against the reflective bottoms over which they forage [Figure 35]. In the New World tropics, *Geophagus* analogues with essentially identical adaptations to this lifestyle can be found in two Central American genera, *Amphilophus* [Figure 36] and *Thorichthys*.

Among the Paleotropical cichlids, practitioners of this life style include the West African genera *Chromidotilapia* [Figure 37] and *Tylochromis*, the endemic Tanganyikan genera *Xenotilapia* and *Callochromis*, [Figure 38], such Malawian cichlids as *Fossorochromis rostratus* (BOULENGER 1899) and numerous species of *Lethrinops* and *Taeniolethrinops* [Figure 39] and the Malagasy *Ptychochromis*

Fig. 31: The pelagic, barracuda-like *Ramphochromis* species of Lake Malawi actively chase down the smaller fishes upon which they prey.

Fig. 32: The pike cichlid *Crenicichla lepidota* Heckel 1840 is an ambush predator that awaits the approach of prey in hiding.

Fig. 33: The distinctive body shape and color pattern of *Dimidiochromis compressiceps* (Boulenger 1908) allow it to effectively vanish in Lake Malawi's Vallisneria beds.

Fig. 34: The blotched color pattern of *Nimbochromis livingstonii* (Gunther 1893) allows it to lure small fish into striking distnace by mimicking a rotting cadaver. This may be the most unusual hunting strategy practiced by any piscivorous fish!

Fig. 35: True eartheaters such as this *Satanoperca leucostictus* Muller & Troschel 1849 are superbly adapted to sift through the substratum in search of aquatic invertebrates. Compare this species with the following ecologically analogous but unrelated cichlids.

Fig. 36: *Amphilophus altifrons* (Kner & Steindachner 1863), a substratum-sifting cichlid from the Pacific slope of Costa Rica and Panama bears an uncanny resemblance to the foregoing species.

oligoacanthus (BLEEKER 1875). Notwithstanding their superficially similar appearance, these cichlids are not closely related. Comparable examples of evolutionary convergence can be found among cichlids specialized for piscivory, for selective browsing of invertebrates from rocky surfaces or for feeding on attached algae, vascular aquatic plants, mollusks or zooplankton.

To a certain extent, cichlid diversity reflects the family's success in colonizing a wide range of habitats in both the Old and New World tropics.

However, I must emphasize that as a group, cichlids are effectively limited in their ability to survive and prosper in a given biotope by intolerance of low water temperatures.

While few species immediately succumb when the mercury drops below 70 °F., none is immune to the long-term effects of low temperatures. These range from increased susceptibility to attack by ectoparasites and pathogenic bacteria to steady deterioration of motor abilities and sensory acuity. Such victims are both at a disadvantage relative to cool

water adapted competitors and increasingly vulnerable to predation. The majority of cichlids are thus found in the lowland tropics [Figure 40].

The farther north or south one moves from the Tropics of Cancer and Capricorn, the fewer cichlids are present in the fauna [Figure 41] and the greater their dependence upon specialized environmental features for the thermally favorable microclimates essential to their survival.

For example, the presence of cichlids in the lower reaches of the Nile and the Rio Parana, which enter the sea well outside the tropical zone, depends largely upon the fact that their watersheds lie mostly within the tropics.

The temperature profile of their lower courses sufficiently reflects this state of affairs to permit survival of tropical forms therein even during the coldest months of the year [Figure 43].

Inability to adapt to cold also accounts for the family's limited success in colonizing tropical highland environments.

Fig. 37: This pair of *Chromidotilapia finleyi* from the Mungo River in the Cameroons is representative of the most widespread genus of West African *Geophagus* analogs.

Fig. 38: A pair of *Xenotilapia flavipinnis* Poll 1985, an attractive representative of this genus of substratum-sifting cichlids endemic to Lake Tanganyika.

Fig. 39: The larger representatives of the genus *Taeniolethrinops* such as this male *T. furcicauda* (Trewavas 1931) are easily the most *Geophagus*-like of all the Malawian cichlids.

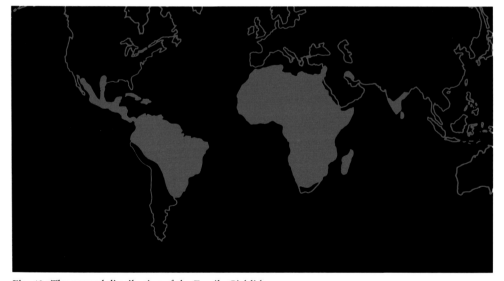

Fig. 40: The natural distribution of the Family Cichlidae.

Fig. 41: While the majority of cichlids are to be found in lowland tropical habitats, extratropical outriders exist in both the Old and New Worlds. The range of *Nandopsis beani* (Jordan 1888), for example, extends to the Rio Yaqui on the west coast of Mexico. Only the Texas cichlid naturally ranges farther north in the New World.

Fig. 42: *Gymnogeophagus setequedas* Reis, Malabarba & Pavanelli 1992, another extratropically distributed cichlid. This small eartheater can be collected in the vicinity of Buenos Aires, Argentina, well south of the Tropic of Capricorn.

27

Fig. 43: Native to the Pacific slope of southwestern Costa Rica and northern Panama, *Theraps sieboldii* (Kner & Steindachner 1864) is one of the few cichlids regularly found above the 1500' contour.

Isolated specimens of *Theraps sieboldii*, KNER and STEINDACHNER 1864 [Figure 44], *Archocentrus nigrofasciatus* (GUNTHER 1866) and *Amphilophus alfari* (MEEK 1907) have been taken from the upper reaches of Central American rivers at an altitude of 5000 feet. For the most part, however, the 1500 foot contour effectively defines the border between the lowland biotopes congenial to the Cichlidae and the highland biotopes that are not. No cichlid is native to the Plateau of Mexico or to the Andean highlands of Bolivia, Peru and Ecuador, though the family is well represented in the lower reaches of the rivers rising thereupon.

A single tilapia, *Oreochromis niloticus* (LINNAEUS 1757), is reported from the Ethiopian Plateau. This highland area is otherwise devoid of cichlids.

The family's absence from the Arabian Peninsula, where they might be expected given the current distribution of its Near Eastern outriders, can probably also be ascribed to an inability to prosper in highland biotopes, for the few permanent streams remaining in that arid part of the world are a feature of montane environments.

This caveat aside, cichlids can be found in virtually any body of water within their range that supports fish life. Morphologically specialized forms with vestigial swim bladders such as *Steatocranus,* which prosper in the extensive rapids of the lower Zaire and Volta Rivers in Africa [Figures 44 & 45], have their counterparts in the *Teleocichla* and *Retroculus* species of Brazil's Rio Tocantins and Rio Xingu.

The cichlid fauna of the lower Zaire rapids also includes the only sightless member of the family, *Lamprologus lethops* RIBBINKBERTS and STEWART 1976. Cichlids with similarly modified swim bladders also live among the pebbles of Lake Tanganyika's surge zone [Figures 46 & 47]. Together with Lake Malawi, this enormous freshwater sea also boasts cichlids adapted for life in the perpetual twilight of depths in excess of 100 feet and in the open waters of the pelagic zone [Figures 48 & 49].

Fig. 44: A turbulent stretch of the Volta River below the Akosombo Dam in Ghana.

Fig. 45: A pair of *Steatocranus irvinei* (Trewavas 1943), a specialized rheophilous cichlid endemic to the Volta River basin.

Fig. 46: A typical rocky shoreline habitat in Lake Tanganyika.

Fig. 47: Goby cichlids such as this *Eretmodus cyanostictus* Boulenger 1901 are characteristic inhabitants of Lake Tanganyika's turbulent surge zone.

Fig. 48: Male *Cyprichromis microlepidotus* (Poll 1956), a specialized pelagic zooplankton feeder endemic to Lake Tanganyika.

Fig. 49: The open waters of Lake Tanganyika.

Fig. 50: Male *Apistogramma iniridae* Kullander 1979, a dwarf cichlid characteristic of blackwater biotopes in Venezuela.

Fig. 51: A typical black-water habitat in Amazonia.

Fig. 52: A highly eutrophic remnant pool on the floodplain of the Rio Zapote, a tributary of the Rio San Juan in northern Costa Rica.

Fig. 53: Male *Herotilapia multispinossa*, a cichlid native to the Atlantic slope of Nicaragua and Costa Rica that thrives in such habitats.

Fig. 54: Cast net fishermen on Lake Togo, a brackish water coastal lagoon in West Africa. *Tilapias* comprise the bulk of their catch.

Fig. 55: A male black-chin tilapia, *Sarotherodon melanotheron* Ruppel 1854, the dominant fish of coastal lagoons in much of West Africa. This species has colonized the upper reaches of Tampa Bay, a similar biotope in Florida.

Fig. 56: A female *Oreochromis grahami* (Boulenger 1912). This distinctive tilapia is endemics to Lake Magadi, a small, geothermal soda lake in Kenya whose waters are more saline than those of the sea.

Cichlids can be found in highly acidic, calcium deficient, biologically unproductive "blackwater" habitats in both Africa and South America [Figures 50 & 51] as well as in stagnant backwaters so eutrophic that they verge on the polluted [Figures 52 & 53]. The Asian *Etroplus suratensis* (BLOCH 1790) as well as several *Sarotherodon* and *Oreochromis* species are native to brackish water habitats [Figures 54 & 55] and can function as fully marine fishes when circumstances require. A number of tilapias have also managed to colonize highly mineralized hot springs in the Rift Valley of East Africa, prospering in an environment that would not seem out of place in the pages of Dante's *Inferno!* [Figure 56]

The only other fishes that live so close to their upper lethal temperature limit are some of the North American pupfishes of the genus *Cyprinodon.*

Distribution and Evolutionary History of Cichlids

The natural distribution of the Family Cichlidae is both extensive and interesting. A glance at the range map discloses cichlids to be the dominant percoid group in Africa, South America and Middle America up to the Rio Conchos-Rio Grande basin of northeastern Mexico.

Four insular endemics, two each native to Cuba and Hispaniola, round out the distribution of the Neotropical Cichlidae.

A handful of cichlid species is native to the Near East, a distinctive assemblage is endemic to the island of Madagascar, and three species are native to Sri Lanka and extreme southern India.

No native representatives of the family occur farther east in Asia nor are cichlids a natural component of the distinctive Australasian freshwater fish fauna.

This state of affairs is certainly not due to the rigors of an inherently hostile environment. Feral populations of cichlids are now established in both areas, often prospering to a degree unanticipated by those responsible for their introduction!

Cichlid distribution poses an interesting challenge to students of historical •biogeography.

Until relatively recently, the prevailing hypothesis envisaged cichlids evolving initially in Africa, dispersing eastward across Asia, entering the New World via the Bering land bridge during one of the several intervals when Siberia and Alaska were so linked, then moving southward into South America. Once established in the Neotropics, cichlids underwent a secondary radiation, giving rise to the distinctive assemblage of species native to the New World. Following the logic of this model, the two *Etroplus* species would be regarded as relics of transcontinental dispersal, while the presence of cichlids on Madagascar could be explained by a successful crossing of the Mozambique Channel by one or two ancestral African species whose descendants again underwent an independent evolutionary radiation.

An alternative scenario envisages ancestral cichlids island-hopping from Africa to South America across a hypothetical archipelago of South Atlantic islands, Archihellenis. This model likewise postulates colonization of Madagascar via direct crossing of the Mozambique Channel and regards the Indian cichlids as the easternmost outriders of an unsuccessful attempt to invade tropical Asia from the family's African center of dispersal.

Both models assume the positions of the continents have remained unchanged from the beginning of the Tertiary Era to the present. Each relies strongly on the known tolerance of cichlids for marine conditions to explain the family's contemporary distribution. However, each has major problems.

The first, or **overland dispersal model**, must explain how a family noted for its colonizing abilities managed to move from Africa into the Neotropics without leaving any trace of its passage in the ichthyofaunas of tropical southeast Asia and North America above the Rio Grande.

One can always invoke the Pleistocene Ice Ages to account for the absence of cichlids from the Mississippi.

However, such climatic changes do not satisfactorily explain their absence from the Mekong, or any other southeast Asian river of from the northern two-thirds of the Indian subcontinent.

Introduced cichlids find that part of the world very much to their liking and there are no paleoclimatological data to suggest that it has ever enjoyed other than a tropical climate.

The pattern of cichlid diversity in the Neotropics also argues against an entry into South America from the north.

The Middle American cichlid fauna comprises ten genera.

Eight of these belong to the *Heros* lineage [Figure 57].

The exceptions are *Aequidens coeruleopunctatus* (KNER and STEINDACHNER 1863) [Figure 58], an acara whose range extends into the Pacific slope rivers of southeastern Costa Rica, and two *Geophagus* species, neither of which is found north of the Rio Chagres drainage in Central Panama.

Fig. 57: A parental pair of *Neetroplus nematopus*, one of the several Heros-derived genera endemic to Central America.

Fig. 58: An essentially Panamanian species, *Aequidens coeruleopunctatus* (Kner & Steindachner) barely squeaks across the border into extreme southern Costa Rica. Its nearest relatives are the Colombian *Ae. latifrons* and the Venezuelan *Ae. pulcher.*

The South American cichlid fauna, on the other hand, comprises thirty-eight genera pertaining to five quite distinct lineages. Three of these are so distinctive that they arguably merit subfamilial recognition.

This state of affairs admits of two possible explanations. Either these lineages were already well differentiated at the time that cichlids entered South America or, alternatively, the family has been present in the Neotropics long enough for a single ancestral stock to have given rise to as many as four distinct subfamilies.

If the first obtains, the overland dispersal model must explain the absence of all save one of these lineages from the region through which all must have passed to enter South America as well as the evolution of ecologically equivalent *Heros*-derived taxa that fill niches in Mesoamerica occupied by representatives of other lineages in South America.

The second demands a protracted presence in South America that cannot be reconciled with the chronology of overland links between Eurasia and North America on one hand and North and South America on the other.

Furthermore, nothing known of the interrelationships of Neotropical cichlids suggests that the *Heros* lineage represents a likely ancestral stock for three of these five lineages.

Hence this lineage's dominance in Mesoamerica cannot be explained plausibly as the persistence of the common ancestor of all South American cichlids in this critical corridor, which such overland dispersal would otherwise imply.

The second, or **island-hopping model**, posits cichlid dispersal across major oceanic barriers in their movement from Africa to South America.

Indeed, both models invoke such a capacity to explain the family's presence on Madagascar.

Unfortunately, what is known of the relationships of the Malagasy cichlids provides scant support for either hypothesis.

Had Madagascar been colonized by venturesome cichlids that managed successfully to traverse the Mozambique Channel, one would expect to find the nearest relatives of the endemics that sprang from the event among the species of the immediately opposite mainland.

In fact, the Cichlidae of Madagascar have no obvious affinities with any African cichlids.

The nearest relatives of the most species-rich Malagasy genus, *Paretroplus*, are the *Etroplus* species of southern India and Sri Lanka. The remaining Malagasy cichlids have no obvious sister group on the African mainland and appear to share a distant common ancestor with the etroplines.

A capacity to cross oceanic barriers is assumed to follow from the demonstrated ability of many cichlids to survive and breed under marine conditions.

As noted, this is not unusual in secondary division freshwater fishes [Figures 59 & 60]. However, the ability to traverse extensive stretches of open ocean requires more than physiological tolerance of dissolved sodium chloride and elevated pH values. It requires a whole suite of morphological and behavioral adaptations for openwater living notably lacking in the Cichlidae as a whole. Indeed, there is no evidence cichlids are proficient at crossing major oceanic barriers and a good deal to suggest their dispersal is quite effectively blocked by them.

The Antillean species *Nandopsis tetracanthus* (CUVIER and VALENCIENES 1831) and *N. haitiensis* (TEE-VAN 1935) are markedly salt tolerant, while Cuba and Hispaniola are separated from Florida and Puerto Rico respectively by narrow channels. Their width was further reduced during the Ice Ages, when ocean levels were dramatically lowered by the massive amounts of water locked up in glaciers. Yet no cichlid is native to either Florida or Puerto Rico.

The rapidity with which recently introduced cichlids have attained dominant positions in the freshwater fish faunas of both areas certainly argues neither is lacking as a suitable cichlid habitat. The only explanation for the failure of *N. tetracanthus* to colonize Florida and *N. haitiensis* Puerto Rico is that neither possesses the capacity to disperse actively across the narrow straits that separate them from these eminently hospitable and formerly virgin biotopes.

Fig. 59: The mangrove belt of such barrier islands as St. George's Key in Belize is home to *Amphilophus troscheli* (Steindachner 1867).

Fig. 60: *Amphilophus troscheli,* a Mesoamerican cichlid that can live and breed under marine conditions.

These arguments against both models, while convincing to anyone familiar with cichlid natural history, suffer from the fact that the pertinent biological evidence is circumstantial in nature. This criticism does not apply to the most telling argument against their validity, which comes from the realm of geology. Recall that the underlying premise of both models is that the position and orientation of the continents have been invariant over geological time.

This reflected mainstream thinking in geomorphology in the late nineteenth and first half of the twentieth century, when these models were elaborated. However, the last three decades have seen a major revolution in geological thinking in favor of the ideas of the turn-of-the-century Austrian geologist Alfred WEGENER.

WEGENER argued that the continents had formerly been united in two enormous land masses, Laurasia in the northern hemisphere, and Gondwanaland in the southern.

According to this view of **continental drift**, the southern supercontinent's fragmentation gave rise to Antarctica, Australia, the Indian subcontinent, Madagascar, Africa and South America.

Geologists are not only certain of the sequence of these events, but can even date these episodes of continental fission with accuracy.

This revolution in geological thinking not only invalidates the previous two models but simultaneously suggests an alternative and far more satisfactory explanation of contemporary cichlid distribution. It even offers some insight into the age of the family and its constituent lineages.

The depauperate freshwater fish fauna of Australia includes only two primary division freshwater fishes, a lungfish and an osteoglossid, and of course, no cichlids. Living representatives of the first two groups are also found in Africa and South America, areas where primary division freshwater fishes such as characoids and catfishes and the secondary division cichlids are major components of freshwater ichthyofaunas.

The simplest explanation for this pattern is that both lungfish and osteoglossids were pre-

sent in the common pool of Gondwanan freshwater fishes at the time of Australia's fission, between 180 and 120 million years ago, while cichlids and the other primary division groups were not.

The splitting off of the fragment that gave rise to the Indian subcontinent occurred between 100 and 65 million years ago. The presence of closely related cichlids in southern India and on Madagascar is clear evidence that the *Etroplus* lineage was extant and present on the IndoMalagasy precursor fragment when it split from proto-Africa.

Note only one of the genera present on Madagascar has close relatives in southern India and on Sri Lanka and that no Malagasy cichlid has close relatives on the African mainland.

This suggests in both Africa and on the Indian subcontinent, these ancient cichlids succumbed to more effective competitors with the passage of time. The villains of the piece in Africa were probably more advanced cichlids. In the Indian region competition from invading cyprinids may have ultimately eliminated all aboriginal cichlids from the ichthyofauna save the euryhaline *Etroplus*, whose salt tolerance allows them to thrive in brackish water habitats closed to primary division competitors.

The most satisfying feature of this **vicariance model** is that it explains the presence of cichlids in Africa and South America without recourse to either traceless dispersal across Eurasia and North America or movement across oceanic barriers. In fact, studies of the South Atlantic basin that contributed to acceptance of continental drift by geologists have put paid to the notion that the hypothetical Archihellenis ever could have existed in that ocean!

The opening of the South Atlantic following fission of proto-South America from proto-Africa began some 160 million years ago, in the middle of the Jurassic epoch and was complete by the end of the Cretaceous, some 65 million years ago.

Until the evolutionary relationships of the cichlid subfamilies have been worked out in greater detail, there is no way of knowing how many ancestral lineages were present on

Fig. 61: Male *Oreochromis aureus* (Steindachner 1864), a West African species whose range extends into Palestine. Widely employed in commercial aquaculture, it has established feral populations in many parts of the world.

Fig. 62: A male *Nandopsis tetracanthus* (Cuvier & Valenciennes 1831) one of the two cichlids endemic to Cuba.

proto-South America when it began its inexorable drift to the west. It is clear this sequence of events allows the Cichlidae ample time for extensive evolutionary radiation in the Neotropics irrespective of the number of basal stocks initially present in South America.

The handful of cichlids native to the Jordanian region and the Persian Gulf either comprise species that also occur in the Nile basin, such as *Tilapia zillii* (GERVAIS 1848), *Sarotherodon galilaeus* (ARTEDI 1757) and *Oreochromis aureus* (STEINDACHNER 1864) [Figure 61] or endemics whose nearest relatives are of Nilotic provenance, such as *Haplochromis flaviijo sephi* (LORTET 1883), *Iranocichla hormuzensis* (COAD 1982) and the various *Tristamella* species. It is thus likely cichlids dispersed into the Near East from the Nile region fairly recently during a period of warmer, wetter climate.

The history of cichlids in Mesoamerica is less easily explained. That they entered from South America appears incontestable.

However, the number of species present, the diversity of morphotypes comprised therein and patterns of intraregional distribution suggest that cichlids have been in Middle America for a very long time and that the

region has supported at least two independent centers of evolutionary activity, centered respectively on the Rio San Juan basin in southern Nicaragua and northern Costa Rica, and the Rio Usumacinta basin in southeastern Mexico and northern Guatemala. The presence of multiple centers of radiation is consistent with the region's complex geological history.

However, the view that the family first entered Mesoamerica when the Isthmus of Panama arose in the late Pliocene, some three million years ago, cannot be reconciled with either the impressive morphological diversity of the Mesoamerican cichlid fauna or its present distribution.

Such a late entry simply would not have afforded a limited number of colonizing species sufficient time to evolve so many distinctive phenotypes unrepresented among the *Heros* lineage's South American representatives.

Yet the only way to get ancestral cichlids into nuclear Central America early enough to account for the present diverse fauna would seem to require invoking the putative ability to actively cross major oceanic barriers. An elegant solution draws upon data suggesting the Greater Antilles and parts of nuclear Central

Fig. 63: Male *Nandopsis managuensis* (Gunther 1866) a close mainland relative of the Cuban *H. tetracanthus*.

America are actually fragments of northwestern South America that have drifted northeastward, carried by complex crustal plate movements whose continued motion contributes significantly to the seismic and volcanic activity that typifies the Caribbean Basin. This scenario envisages passive transport of cichlids into Middle America by the beginning of the Paleocene, some 60 million years ago. It thus affords them ample time to evolve along the lines required to produce the present fauna. Whether representatives of the *Heros* lineage were the only cichlids so shanghaied or whether only they survived the vicissitudes of life in a severely restricted environment during the slow northward drift may never be known. Contemporary fossils could establish the presence of other lineages in that region of South America at the onset of fission. However, freshwater fish fossils are rarely encountered in areas of active mountain building such as northwestern South America. Nor are cichlids well represented in the few fossil ichthyofaunas to date found and studied in the Neotropics.

This vicariance model was originally invoked to explain the derivation of the freshwater fish fauna of the Greater Antilles. It has the advantage of getting cichlids to Cuba and Hispaniola without recourse to bouts of long-distance swimming. Regrettably, neither the relationships of the Antillean cichlids nor their sparse representation in the ichthyofaunas of those islands support the notion that they reached their present homes in this fashion.

If the Antillean cichlids are the products of long independent evolution under insular conditions, one would not expect them to be closely related to any contemporary mainland species.

One would also expect such similarities as do exist to point to the probable South American ancestors of both Mesoamerican and Antillean cichlids, rather than to any species presently native to Central America.

As it happens, all four Antillean cichlids are "dwarf" representatives of the predatory genus *Nandopsis*.

Both the morphology and color pattern of the Cuban cichlid, *N. tetracanthus* [Figure 62],

and the odo, *N. hatiensis*, suggest that their nearest relative is *Nandopsis managuensis* (GUNTHER 1866) [Figure 63], a species native to the Atlantic slope of Central America from southern Costa Rica to northern Honduras. Furthermore, the genus *Nandopsis* is not represented among either the *Heros* lineage species of western South America or those native to the eastward-draining rivers of that continent.

Given the length of time cichlids would have been present on Cuba and Hispaniola under the vicariance model, one might reasonably expect a repetition under insular conditions of the family's extensive mainland radiation.

That such a large land mass as Cuba possesses only two cichlids when mainland areas of far more restricted extent such Belize or Costa Rica boast seven and ten times as many species respectively also strongly suggests that the family is a relative newcomer to the Greater Antilles. Though it seems something of a biogeographical *deus ex machina*, passive transport via tropical cyclonic storms explains the presence of cichlids on Cuba and Hispaniola better than any alternative hypothesis advanced to date.

The Role of Cichlids in Tropical Freshwater Communities

Given the family's extensive range, great morphological diversity and success in colonizing a wide range of lowland tropical biotopes, it is not surprising that many people overestimate the role cichlids play in these fish communities.

The accompanying figure [Figure 64] should put matters into proper perspective.

In the mature riverine fish communities of both Africa and South America, cichlids have an important but by no means preeminent place.

In fact, the dominant groups as determined by number of species present in the fauna are primary freshwater representatives of the Order Cypriniformes. These include characoid fishes in both Africa and the Neotropics; gymnotoid knifefishes; cyprinoid fishes, of which only true minnows, by virtue of their African sympatry with cichlids, are germane to this discussion; and numerous catfish families. The same pattern emerges if one takes number of individuals in a given habitat as a measure of dominance. A seine haul from any small African stream will consist mostly of assorted characoids, the majority representatives of the Family Alestidae, and small cyprinids of the genus *Barbus*. A comparable South American sample will yield an overwhelming preponderance of characoids, the smaller species of the Family Characidae predominating. Cichlids are likely to be present in both samples, but never in the numbers of their cypriniform neighbors.

Cichlids do play a dominant role in the fish faunas of the African Great Lakes and in Middle America. In the latter case, cichlid preponderance has come about as a result of historical accident.

Cichlids appear to have entered the area well ahead of potential cypriniform colonists from South America and underwent an impressive evolutionary radiation in an environment devoid of serious primary division competitors.

Whether the family will retain its dominant position in the face of more recently arrived South American characins is an interesting question. Regrettably, this natural experiment in evolutionary ecology will require several million years to run its course, so no contem-

Fig. 65: The elaborate hygienic behavior of cichlids, as exemplified by this parental female *Nandopsis salvini* (Gunther 1862) frees them from dependence upon seasonally available spawning sites.

porary ichthyologist is likely to be around to witness its outcome!

The family's success in the African Great Lakes appears due to life history features that put cichlids at an advantage relative to cypriniform fishes under lacustrine conditions. To understand this, it is necessary to review some elementary features of fish reproductive biology. Unlike the shelled eggs of reptiles and birds, fish eggs interpose no effective barriers between the developing embryo and a potentially hostile environment. Fish embryos are thus vulnerable to attack by parasitic microorganisms.

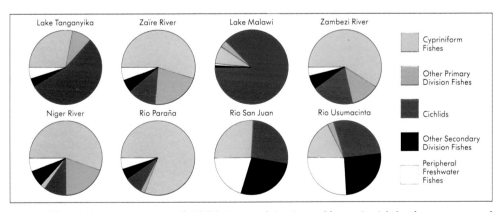

Fig. 64: The relative representation of cichlids in several riverine and lacustrine ichthyofaunas, expressed as percentage of the total number of species present.

Fish have two options for minimizing this risk. Most seek out microhabitats with recently disturbed or inherently depauperate microbial communities, such as stream beds scoured by a recent spate or newly inundated zones of a riverine floodplain to spawn. Alternatively, they rely upon hygienic behavior towards the zygotes to minimize this obstacle to reproductive success.

The majority of tropical cypriniform fishes fall into the former category. In the tropics, the availability of such spawning sites is highly correlated with the onset of the rainy season; so, for many fishes, is the availability of abundant food.

With few exceptions, cypriniform fishes have thus evolved life history patterns that allow them to channel their reproductive effort into one or two massive bursts of spawning activity whose timing is triggered by specific environmental cues associated with the arrival of the rains.

Such an arrangement guarantees access to suitable spawning sites and assures that both adults and fry will be able to make optimal use of abundant but ephemerally available food.

Cichlids, as noted earlier, are opportunistic breeders whose parental behavior comprises both hygienic and custodial elements [Figure 65]. This frees them from dependence upon spawning areas created by the action of external forces as well as from the necessity to correlate reproductive effort with specific environmental changes.

While such a reproductive pattern confers no special advantages upon cichlids vis-a-vis primary division freshwater fishes under riverine conditions, it does give them a real edge in colonizing lacustrine biotopes.

Because most cannot breed successfully in the lake proper, the normally dominant cypriniform fishes can maintain themselves in a lacustrine fauna only if they can migrate upriver to suitable spawning grounds. Where such movements are impossible, disappearance of those species dependent upon them is inevitable.

This leads to greatly diminished primary division representation in the ichthyofauna of the developing lake, leaving cichlids, who suffer from no such reproductive constraint, free

to become the dominant element in the evolving lacustrine fish community.

The cichlid dominated faunas of Lakes Victoria, Tanganyika and Malawi represent the final result of such a process on a large scale. As the youngest of these faunas is many thousand years old, it might seem unlikely, given the lifespan of human observers, that any experimental evidence bearing upon such a hypothesis could ever be forthcoming.

As it happens, human efforts at economic development in Africa have produced a number of unplanned but apposite experiments whose results have been quite illuminating.

The construction of hydroelectric dams on several African rivers has provided dramatic evidence of how rapidly a mature riverine fish fauna can change when suddenly confronted with lacustrine conditions. Wherever these have been studied, the same pattern emerges. The number of species present decreases markedly, due to the disappearance of primary division fishes incapable of breeding under lacustrine conditions, while cichlids increase their absolute numerical representation in the new community. Impoundments such as Lake Volta and Lake Kariba will silt up and disappear too quickly for their suddenly dominant cichlids ever to undergo anything remotely resembling the evolutionary explosions that ultimately took place in the much longer-lived Great Lakes.

They do, however, suggest how the earliest stanzas of those epics of cichlid evolution must have read.

Cichlid Power Out of Place

I have referred in passing to the establishment of breeding cichlid populations in areas outside the family's natural range.

Such range extensions have come about through human activity and fall into two categories.

The first consists of the establishment of localized breeding populations in thermally favorable microhabitats far outside the tropics.

Fig. 66: Since its accidental introduction two decades ago, the black acara, *Cichlasoma bimaculatum* has become the most abundant mid-sized percoid fish in the canals of southern Florida.

Fig. 67: The West African *Tilapia mariae* is now the dominant large percoid in southern Florida. Extreme reproductive precocity. Highly efficient parental behavior and an ability to prosper in environments disturbed by human activity explain the success of such exotics.

43

Fig. 68: The introduction of *Tilapia zillii* into the Salton Sea basin appears to have been the result of a poorly designed experiment in the biological control of aquatic weeds.

Fig. 69: An abrupt decline in the numbers of the Salton Sea pupfish, *Cyprinodon macularius*, the basin's only native fish species, coincided with the establishment of *T. zillii* in the Coachella Valley.

Examples are the presence of *Tilapia mariae* BOULENGER 1899, *Pseudotropheus zebra* (BOULENGER 1899) and *Archocenrus nigrofasciatus* in Rogers Springs, a constant temperature artesian springflow in southern Nevada, or the naturalization of *Hemichromis guttatus* GUNTHER 1862 in Banf Hot Springs in Alberta. While their effect upon fishes native to these thermal sanctuaries can be devastating, ecological impact of such localized introductions is likely to remain limited. Inability to survive winter temperatures restricts the ability of such naturalized cichlids to disperse outward into the remainder of the drainage in question. This minimizes the intensity of their interactions, competitive or exploitative, with the areas's indigenous fishes. Because the number of suitable microhabitats are accessible to persons desiring to perpetrate such introductions is limited, range extensions of this sort have been and are likely to remain rare.

Those of the second type entail establishment of feral cichlid populations in areas where climatic conditions place minimal restraints upon their ability to disperse into suitable habitats. Under such circumstances, the indigenous fish community is abruptly exposed to the full impact of the invader's activities. The greater aggressiveness of many cichlids often gives them an edge in competitive interactions with native fishes, be the resource contested food or access to breeding sites. The physiological plasticity of most species frequently allows them to exploit environments disturbed by human activity more effectively than any indigenous species. Finally, their sophisticated and efficient parental behavior often allows cichlids to outreproduce otherwise efficient native competitors by a wide margin. Consequently, dramatic changes in the composition of the local fish fauna frequently follow a cichlid's successful naturalization.

The inadvertent introduction of the predatory peacock bass, *Cichla monoculus* SPIX 1831, into Lake Gatun, the impoundment that occupies the midportion of the Panama Canal, was followed by the dramatic reduction in numbers or virtual disappearance from the lake

Fig. 70: A sexually active female *Nandopsis haitiensis* (Tee-Van 1935). This Hispaniolan endemic appears not to have been harmed and may have even benefitted from the naturalization of two tilapia species in its habitat.

45

proper of ten of the fourteen species formerly found therein.

In the two decades since their discovery in the canals of Dade County, the black acara, *Cichlasoma bimaculatum* (LINNAEUS 1757) [Figure 66] and *Tilapia mariae*, [Figure 67] have become the dominant percoid fishes of southern Florida, successfully penetrating even the relatively undisturbed waters of Everglades National Park.

The establishment of *Tilapia zillii* [Figure 68] in the Salton Sea basin of southern California went hand in hand with an abrupt decline in the numbers of the Coachella Valley's only indigenous fish, the Salton Sea pupfish, *Cyprinodon macularius* [Figure 69]. On Taiwan, Sri Lanka and Hispaniola, the Mozambique mouthbrooder, *Oreochromis mossambicus* (PETERS 1852) has proliferated explosively, becoming one of the commonest freshwater fishes within a short time of its entry into natural waters.

The effects of such introductions vary from one case to the next. In the Hawaiian Islands, whose fresh waters were devoid of indigenous true freshwater fishes, the only objections to the naturalization of five tilapias and *Cichla monoculus* are aesthetic. The introduction of any cichlid to an extant fish community with no evolutionary experience of the family is quite another matter when native species of commercial or scientific interest are adversely affected. The abrupt decline in the numbers of the Salton Sea pupfish cited earlier is an excellent example of the adverse consequences of cichlid naturalization. This said, the fact remains that such data as exist on the effect that exotic cichlids have had upon most impacted tropical fish communities are ambiguous. The presence of exotic predators and potential non-cichlid competitors complicates attempts to determine the role introduced tilapias have played in the well-documented decline of Madagascar's native fishes. At the other extreme, the impact of the Mozambique mouthbrooder and blue tilapia on the indigenous freshwater fishes of Hispaniola appears to have been minimal.

Here these African exotics coexist with substantial populations of numerous poeciliid

Fig. 71: Exact predictions of the impact of introduced tilapia species on such endemic New Guinea fishes as this *Chilatherina bleheri* may not be possible, but the past history of these widely disseminated aquaculture subjects in other parts of the world provides little basis for optimism in this instance.

species of the genera *Gambusia* and *Limia* and of the native *odo, N. haitiensis* [Figure 70]. However, the absence of reliable baseline data on the composition of Hispaniolan freshwater fish communities prior to the introduction of tilapias should inspire a cautious assessment of any assertions that they have been unaffected by the establishment of these African exotics.

Fig. 72: The ability to survive periods of cool weather inherent in its extratropical distribution in southern Brazil, Uruguay and Argentina doubtless explains the success the chanchito, *Heros facetus*, has enjoyed in colonizing the fresh waters of Portugal.

Fig. 73: A male *Archocentrus nigrofasciatus* (Gunther 1866) from Guanacaste Province, on the Pacific slope of Costa Rica. The population of this species established in Rogers Spring, Nevada, owes its existence to a well-meaning but poorly informed aquarist seeking a home for unwanted pets.

Ecologists now regard as axiomatic that mature ecosystems contain no empty niches. The logical corollary of this premise is that invaders succeed at the expense of one or more of a community's established residents. Data from terrestrial ecosystems supporting this position are both unambiguous and distressingly abundant. While the mechanisms involved in these interactions are poorly understood, to assert that the explosive population growth of introduced cichlid populations in locales as far apart as Florida, the lower Colorado River, the Philippines and Papua New Guinea [Figure 71] has not had deleterious effects upon native fishes would be unrealistic in the extreme. In short, discovery of any cichlid in a body of water to which it is not native should — and usually does — immediately set alarm bells ringing in those quarters with an interest in wildlife conservation and sound fisheries management.

Aquarists and ornamental fish farmers have received considerable criticism from conservationists and regulatory agencies for their role in extending the range of many cichlid species.

The establishment of the chanchito, *Heros facetus* (JENNYNS 1842) [Figure 72] in Portugal, the introduction of most of Florida's thriving feral cichlids and such localized phenomena as Rogers Springs [Figure 73] can certainly be blamed upon thoughtless hobbyists or fish farmers. However, the record shows that the responsibility for the overwhelming majority of cichlid introductions falls upon a broad spectrum of governmental agencies. The establishment of *Tilapia zillii* in the Coachella Valley can be traced back to an improperly designed experiment in the biological control of aquatic weeds, and that of *Oreochromis mossambicus* in the coastal waters of southern California to the mistaken use of that species as a biological control agent by a local mosquito abatement district. The fisheries establishment of the Mexican government has assiduously introduced *Oreochromis aureus* into the standing waters of the Sonoran and Chihuahuan deserts, often with catastrophic consequences for the endemic fishes of those areas, while the King of Thailand himself takes credit for having brought the first specimens of

Fig. 74: A male *ngege*, *Oreochromis esculentus* (Graham 1928). Once the basis of an important regional fishery, this species is now gone from Lake Victoria proper.

O. mossambicus to his country and making fry available to all interested parties.

The agency primarily responsible for spreading tilapias throughout the tropics is the Food and Agriculture Organization of the United Nations. The F.A.O. aggressively promoted their use as aquaculture subjects even where native species would have profitably repaid efforts to rear them for human consumption.

Largely due to its efforts, the fisheries services of many Third World countries have adopted a similar position with regard to tilapia introductions, which continue apace in countries as far apart as Ecuador and Indonesia.

The object of this exercise is not to absolve the aquarium hobby in its broadest sense from its documented responsibility for the naturalization of many cichlids in Florida and elsewhere.

It is rather to point out that by virtue of their greater resources, immunity from effective oversight and ability to influence public perception of these introductions, such governmental and paragovernmental agencies are much more efficient vectors of potentially harmful exotic fishes than any private person could ever be.

The tragedy of such experiments in evolutionary ecology is that they are irreversible. Once an exotic is established in a river system, there is no means of eradicating the newcomer and returning to the *status quo ante*.

The desirability of cichlids as both ornamental and food fishes makes their transport worldwide understandable and their large-scale culture inevitable. One can only urge aquarists and fish farmers alike to absolutely refrain from practices that result in the entry of living specimens of **any** cichlid species into waters to which it is not native. Governmental and international development agencies, on the other hand, should carefully consider the possible negative impact feral cichlids can have upon an indigenous fish fauna before advocating the use of tilapias for aquaculture or the introduction of large predators such as *Cichla monoculus* as game fish in yet another tropical country.

Cichlids in Peril

Given their demonstrated ability to wreak havoc outside of their original range, it may seem ironic to close this chapter with an overview of threats to the future survival of cichlids in their home waters.

This topic was not covered in the first edition of this book for the simple reason that when it was written, very few cichlid species could have been described as endangered or threatened.

The impact of a broad array of exotics on the endemic cichlid fauna of Madagascar had been documented, some concern had been expressed over the eventual effect of the introduced Nile perch on the haplochromine cichlids of Lake Victoria and there was a general feeling of unease over the effects of groundwater extraction on the cichlids native to the desert regions of northern Mexico. The last decade has seen the situation of these three cichlid faunas deteriorate dramatically and highlighted new areas of concern in other parts of the world. Cichlids have now joined the long list of plants and animals whose survival is threatened by the increasingly disruptive environmental effects of human activity on the planetary ecosystem.

The ongoing collapse of Lake Victoria's ecosystem following the extermination of most of its endemic cichlids by the Nile perch is without a doubt the single most spectacular manifestation of this trend. The introduction of this giant predator was originally suggested in the 1950s as a fisheries management measure. The traditional fishery in Lake Victoria was based upon gill net harvesting of an open-water phytoplankton-feeding tilapia, the *ngege, Oreochromis esculentus* (GRAHAM 1928) [Figure 74].

Declining yields due to ineffective management of tilapia stocks led to the suggestion that a large piscivore be introduced to convert the substantial numbers of the lake's small haplochromine cichlids into fish large enough to support a gill net fishery.

The introduction was made in spite of warnings of adverse impacts upon both Lake Victoria's haplochromines and the existing tilapia fishery.

49

Fig. 75.: A male *Haplochromis (Astatotiapia) piceatus* Greenwood & Gee 1969. The elimination of this species and other deepwater insectivores may well account for the enormous lake fly emergencies that have followed the naturalization of the Nile perch in Lake Victoria.

These predictions of disaster have proven uncannily accurate. By a conservative estimate, three out of every five of Lake Victoria's endemic haplochromine cichlids have literally been eaten out of existence by the Nile perch.

We will never know exactly how many cichlid species Lake Victoria supported, but based upon the work of the *Haplochromis* Ecology Study Team of the University of Leiden, an estimate of 500 species is not unreasonable.

Lake Victoria thus enjoys the dubious distinction of having hosted the largest single vertebrate extinction since the Cretaceous terminal event that put paid to the dinosaurs. Because their habitat preferences or life styles placed some species at greater risk than others, the impact of the Nile perch has not been the same on all members of the Lake Victoria species flock.

Some feeding guilds, notably the open-bottom deep water insectivores [Figure 75], piscivores [Figure 76] and paedophages [Figure 77], have been totally obliterated.

Others, such as rock-scraping algae eaters [Figure 78] and omnivores [Figure 79] closely associated with extensive stands of marginal vegetation, have managed to maintain substantial populations despite the presence of *Lates* in the Lake.

Regrettably, the future of these survivors remains in doubt. While they seem safe enough from Nile perch predation, they are not immune   from its indirect effects on Lake Victoria's ecosystem.

As predicted, *Lates* proved to be an equal opportunity predator, devouring tilapias and haplochromines with equal enthusiasm. The immediate effect of the Nile perch's unselective appetite was the collapse of the traditional tilapia fishery, which at its peak saw between 20,000 and 30,000 metric tons of fish landed yearly. The long-term consequences of the extirpation of the *ngege* are more subtle and in the long run, far more serious.

Tanganyika and Malawi are deep rift lakes, whose permanently stratified waters are devoid

Fig. 76: A female *Haplochromis (Pyxichromis) orthostoma* Regan 1922. Competition from juvenile Nile perch as well as predation upon them by adults have caused the disappearance of large piscivorous species such as this from Lake Victoria.

of oxygen at depths in excess of 200 feet and in consequence support a limited benthic fauna. Lake Victoria, a much shallower body of water, formerly supported aerobic conditions even at its deepest points.

This state of affairs permitted the evolution of an extensive assemblage of endemic deep-water haplochromines.

Oreochromis esculentus is one of the very few tilapias that feeds by straining phytoplankton from the water.

Most ostensibly phytoplankton-feeding tilapias harvest this resource after it has died and sunk to the bottom to form organic detritus. With the *ngege* no longer present to harvest them, the lake's massive phytoplankton blooms die and drift to the bottom, where they fuel explosive proliferation of saprophytic bacteria.

This has rendered the waters of Lake Victoria devoid of dissolved oxygen below a depth of 75 feet.

This anoxic zone continues to rise towards the surface.

It is at the moment an open question whether this process will stop short of obliterating both *Lates* and those native fish species that have to date survived its depredations. The doubts surrounding the long-term viability of the Lake Victoria ecosystem certainly argue forcefully that those cichlid species not beneficiaries of organized captive breeding efforts represent very poor candidates for a long-term life insurance policy.

The future prospects of the Malagasy cichlid fauna are also grim. The island's freshwater fishes must cope with both the habitat changes consequent upon massive deforestation and an astonishing array of exotic competitors and predators, most far better adapted to habitats modified by human activity. Colonial fisheries personnel successfully naturalized carp, goldfish, four different species of tilapia, four species of poeciliids, among them *Gambusia affinis*, several anabantoid fishes, and black bass.

In a stunning falsification of the hypothesis that ecological insensitivity is exclusively characteristic of colonial administrations, the Malagasys have since independence added the banded snakehead to the roster of successfully established exotics. Predation by black bass has resulted in the extinction of one Malagasy cichlid, *Ptychochromoides betsilianus* (BOULENGER 1899) from Lake Itasy and its surrounding satellites and the virtual elimination of the formerly widespread *Paratilapia polleni* BLEEKER 1868 [Figure 80] and *Ptychochromis oligoacanthus* (BLEEKER 1868) from the central highlands of the island.

The tropical lowlands have provided Malagasy cichlids a secure haven from the black bass, which cannot breed successfully unless it experiences a period of cool weather each year to mature its gonads.

As snakeheads operate under no such disadvantage, native fishes no longer enjoy the protection of a thermal refuge from exotic predators, a state of affairs that augurs poorly for their long-term survival.

Fisheries formerly based on one or more *dambas* of the genus *Paretroplus* are now dominated by naturalized tilapias.

The decline of the partially herbivorous *dambas,* which are restricted to the coastal lowlands of Madagascar, cannot be attributed to black bass predation and began long before the introduction of the snakehead. That it has been paralleled by progressive deforestation and the explosive proliferation of four introduced and essentially herbivorous tilapias of the genera *Tilapia* and *Oreochromis* is, to say the least, highly suggestive.

The salt tolerance of species such as *Paretroplus polyactis* BLEEKER 1868 affords them some degree of protection from both the predatory snakehead and the competitive pressures of their distant African relatives. The future survival of such strictly freshwater *dambas* as *Paretroplus petiti* PELLEGRIN 1929 and *P. maculatus* KEINER and MAUGE 1966 is much less certain.

Having evolved in isolation from the selective pressures operating in the outside world, the cichlid dominated faunas of other African lakes are equally vulnerable to disruption and eventual extirpation by translocated exotics.

Fig. 77: A pair of *Platytaeniodus degeni* Boulenger 1906. The extirpation of mollusk-eating cichlids such as this facilitates the spread of schistosomiasis, a debilitating disease caused by a parasite that uses freshwater snails as a secondary host.

Fig. 78: Rockfrequenting haplochromine cichlids such as this male of the Mwanza Gulf population of an undescribed insectivore known as *Haplochromis* sp. "Rock Kribensis" have not been as severely impacted by the Nile perch as the generality of Lake Victoria cichlids.

It is tempting but highly misleading to visualize this threat in terms of macropredators like the black bass or the Nile perch. Given its role as a predator on cichlid fry, its reproductive output, its presence in adjacent streams and the ease with which it can be transported, *Hemichromis elongatus* (GUICHENOT 1861) represents a far greater threat than the Nile perch to the cichlids endemic to the Cameroons' Lakes Barombi Mbo, Ejagham and Bermin.

Neither of Lake Tanganyika's freshwater sardine species grows large enough to pose a direct threat to any cichlid native to Lake Malawi.

However, the successful establishment of these efficient pelagic plankton feeders would certainly have a negative impact on any native species that feed upon zooplankton at some point in their life cycle.

While relatively few Malawian cichlids are plankton feeders as adults, virtually all species depend upon this resource to some extent as fry.

The scale of the Lake Victoria debacle has — at least temporarily — derailed the Malawian Fishery Department's proposed introduction of either species of *ndangala* into Lake Malawi.

How long this state of salutary apprehension will persist remains to be seen.

While tilapias have been freely introduced into the fresh waters of both Middle and South America, the impact upon the fishes indigenous to these regions of these attempts to undo the fission of Gondwanaland by homogenizing the cichlid fauna of its daughter continents has been relatively limited.

Tilapias do not always naturalize successfully in the Neotropics and do not appear to inevitably displace native cichlids when they do.

Translocations of Neotropical cichlids into drainages outside their aboriginal ranges, such as the introduction *Cichla monoculus* into the Rio Chagres drainage in Panama, are another matter altogether.

As the invasion of the formerly isolated Laguna Medialuna in the Mexican state of San Luis Potosi by *Herichthys carpintis* (JORDAN and SNYDER 1899) has demonstrated, the risk they pose to endemic species goes beyond predation and competition. Such invaders are potentially more dangerous, for they often have the potential to hybridize with native cichlids.

Seen in this light, the recent interest shown by Mexican fisheries biologists in the aquaculture potential of their native cichlids may not, from the perspective of the conservation biologist, prove an unmitigated blessing.

However, the real threat to the desert fishes of northern Mexico comes from the reckless pumping of groundwater.

Agribusiness interests out for a quick profit are "mining" fossil water, removing water from the region's aquifers at a rate that exceeds the potential for replenishment by orders of magnitude.

The drastic lowering of the water table that follows such exploitation greatly reduces or altogether stops the artesian spring flows that sustain surface water habitats such as marshes and sinkhole lakes.

When these disappear, so do their associated fish populations. The few people aware of the existence of desert fishes usually associate the term with pupfishes of the genus *Cyprinodon*.

However, cichlids are included among the half dozen families represented in this freshwater biota.

Since the appearance of the first edition of this book, aquarists have made the acquaintance of the dentally polymorphic *Nandopsis minckleyi* (KORNFIELD and TAYLOR 1983), restricted to the Cuatro Cienegas basin of Coahuila and enjoyed the opportunity of working with two strikingly colored cichlids endemic to Laguna Medialuna, *Nandopsis bartoni* (BEAN 1892) [Figure 81] and *N. labridens* (PELLEGRIN 1903). However, there are at least half a dozen isolated populations of distinctive *Herichthys* nominally ascribed to *H. cyanoguttatus* [Figures 82] scattered over northern Mexico whose biological status has yet to be ascertained.

Given the current rate of aquatic habitat loss in this part of the world, nothing short of a concerted effort to establish captive popula-

Fig. 79: The ongoing eutrophication of Lake Victoria threatens the survival of such cichlids as this male *Haplochromis* sp. "Thick-skin", whose preference for densely planted habitats affords it a degree of protection from the Nile perch.

Fig. 80: A male *Paratilapia polleni* Bleeker 1868, the most primitive living cichlid species. Competition from and predation by the black bass have virtually exterminated the *marakely* from the central highlands of Madagascar.

Fig. 81: Introgressive hybridization with introduced cichlids from the lower reaches of the Rio Panuco drainage poses a threat to such endemic Laguna Medialuna species as *Nandopsis bartoni* (Bean 1892).)

Fig. 82: A sexually active female *Herichthys* sp. from Ocampo in the Mexican state of Coahuila. Non-sustainable pumping of water from the aquifers that supply their habitats poses the greatest threat to the survival of such desert cichlids.

tions of these cichlids is likely to keep them from becoming extinct before they have been properly studied.

Two potential threats to the survival of both Neotropical and African cichlids whose magnitude remains to be assessed are deforestation and the expanding use of agrochemicals in the Third World.

While the cutting of tropical forests is a world-wide phenomenon, such activity is potentially most threatening to the cichlids of West Africa.

Since the first edition of this book was published, West Africa has lost nearly three-quarters of its lowland rain forests.

The continuous belt of trees that extended from Zaire to Benin in the east and Ghana to Senegal in the west has been reduced to isolated fragments.

The persistence of these remnants in the face of an expanding human population's need for firewood and agricultural land is highly unlikely. The effects of forest loss on such

fishes as characoids and cyprinodonts that feed directly upon the continuous stream of insects and plant matter that drops from the canopy is predictable.

Its effects upon forest-associated cichlids is not.

However, the fact that many West African genera are restricted to streams flowing under forest canopy strongly suggests that the noted ecological plasticity of cichlids may not be up to coping with such drastic environmental change.

Research in this area is desperately needed before realistic efforts to conserve these cichlids can be undertaken.

For the moment, however, aquarists should give serious thought to organizing captive breeding programs for such West African genera as *Anomalochromis, Nanochromis, Pelvicachromis* [Figure 83] and *Thysochromis* as well as for obligate forest-dwelling representatives of more ecologically plastic genera, such as *Hemichromis cristatus* LOISELLE 1979 and

Tilapia brevimanus BOULENGER 1911 [Figure 84].

The last two decades have witnessed a substantial increase in the use of pesticides and herbicides in Third World countries. A recognized problem in Central America, the pollution of aquatic ecosystems in the tropics by agrochemicals is by no means restricted to that quarter of the world. As far back as the mid-1960s, inappropriate use of insecticides intended to control cocoa capsids caused the extermination of the only population of the killifish *Epiplatys chaperi* known to occur east of the Volta River.

The German collector Heiko BLEHER's repeated failure to secure specimens of *Limbochromis robertsi* (THYS and LOISELLE 1971) from headwaters streams of the Birim River flowing through cocoa plantations near the Ghanaian town of Kibi strongly suggests that a similar mischance extirpated this cichlid from its type locality.

In Central America, bananas are the *raison d'etre* of extensive pesticide use. Although not native to the Neotropics, bananas are susceptible to many of the pests that attack the closely related native plants of the genus *Heliconia*.

Repeated applications of pesticides, nematicides and fungicides are thus an integral feature of bananas culture for export. The chemical plume generated by either a cropdusting plane's missed approach or a heavy rain immediately following the routine application of these chemicals can provoke massive fish kills that extend kilometers downstream of the focus of contamination.

Streams subjected to repeated outrages of this sort are easily recognized, for they contain only adult cichlids and characins. Such large fish can swim fast enough to stay ahead of the toxic plume as it is carried downstream and will do so until they find refuge in an unpolluted tributary.

Small fish, such as young of the year cichlids and characins, cannot outrun the wave of contamination and perish. Characins rely on seasonal cues to trigger breeding, while cichlids are usually precluded by energetic constraints from respawning immediately after such a disaster, unlike poeciliids, which give birth every four weeks.

Fig. 83: Extensive deforestation threatens the survival of many Nigerian cichlids whose present commercial availability aquarists have come to take for granted, such as these *Pelvicachromis* cf. *subocellatus*.

It may thus take anywhere from six months to a year for the size distribution of the fishes in a devastated stream to return to pre-spill values.

The distribution patterns of Central American riverine cichlids are sufficiently broad to preclude "one-shot" extirpation of any given species by a chemical spill.

The long-term effects of repeated outrages of this sort on both the invertebrates that support the aquatic food web and on the genetic structure of fish populations subjected to such periodic mass mortality are poorly understood.

However, what is known does not augur well for the long-term stability of these communities or the persistence of many of their component species [Figure 85].

Barring major — and unanticipated — changes in present agricultural practices, aquatic habitats in areas devoted to large-scale banana culture, such as the lowlands of Belize, Costa Rica and Panama must be considered at risk.

At many points in its turbulent geological history, Central America has been a much less agreeable home for freshwater fishes than it is at present.

Coping with these vicissitudes may explain why Mesoamerican cichlids are an adaptable lot even by the family's impressive standards.

The chemical warfare they are presently experiencing is, however, another matter altogether.

However outrageous the suggestion might seem, these cichlids should also be considered prime candidates for an organized captive breeding effort by serious aquarists.

The preservation of viable populations of any species in a secure portion of their natural habitat must always be the desired goal of any conservation effort. However, for many freshwater fishes, this option is simply not realistic.

In the near term, these species will either survive under some sort of management or go extinct.

Fig. 84: A male *Tilapia brevimanus* Boulenger 1911, an obligate forest-dwelling species from Guinee, Sierra Leone and Liberia.

Conservationists have long appreciated that captive breeding programs can play a crucial role in assuring the survival of terrestrial animals. The realization is finally dawning that they will prove equally crucial to the continued existence of a large — and rapidly increasing — number of freshwater fishes. Serious aquarists, by virtue of their fish breeding expertise, can play an important role in the implementation of such programs.

Those interested in participating in such hands-on conservation efforts are referred to the last chapter for more detailed information.

My object in this chapter has been to bring cichlid enthusiasts a fuller appreciation of the place their favorite aquarium fish occupy in the complex web of life.

The reader should now have some idea of what makes a cichlid a cichlid, of the great diversity comprised within the Family Cichlidae and where it stands in relation to other groups of fishes.

He should have a clear picture of where cichlids occur in nature, as well as an appreciation of the most current views on how they got there, together with some understanding of the family's role in fish communities where it is native.

He will hopefully understand why it is important to prevent naturalization of cichlids in congenial habitats outside of their natural range and shape his actions accordingly. Finally, it is hoped that he will begin to think of himself as a participant in an unfolding attempt to save as much as possible of our planet's wonderful array of life forms and of his hobby as a means to that end.

The next chapter builds on this background in discussing cichlid behavior and how it must influence any approach to setting up the cichlid aquarium.

Fig. 85: The spread of commercial banana culture, with its associated largescale use of toxic agrochemicals poses a significant threat to Central American cichlids such as this pair of *Archocentrus septemfasciatus* (Regan 1908) from the vicinity of Limon, Costa Rica.

CHAPTER 2

CICHLIDS AS AQUARIUM RESIDENTS

Introduction

As noted in the Introduction, cichlids have the reputation of being the terrorists of the aquarium world.

Conventional wisdom depicts them as highly predatory fishes that divide their waking hours between the demolition of their immediate surroundings and the persecution of their tankmates.

It should be evident from the preceding chapter that the Family Cichlidae is too diverse for such a blanket indictment to stand unchallenged.

Cichlids vary as much in temperament as in size or morphology.

However, in its intense focus upon **cichlid behavior,** the conventional wisdom encapsulates a very important truth.

Quite simply, no attempt to maintain and breed cichlids in captivity can succeed unless their prospective keeper has some understanding of why these fish behave as they do.

In setting up quarters for other fishes, it is necessary to anticipate their physical requirements carefully.

When dealing with cichlids, equal weight must be given to behavioral considerations. Cichlids stand accused of three classes of aquaristically undesirable behavior.

First and foremost, cichlids supposedly kill other fishes, regardless of species, with which they are housed.

Second, they are viewed as implacable enemies of rooted aquatic plants.

Third and last, cichlids are believed to be tireless manipulators of their environment.

This class of behaviors includes massive excavation and movement of gravel, toppling of rockwork, destruction of heaters and ejection of filter siphons from the aquarium.

Some of these behaviors can be modified or ameliorated.

Others are intractable.

Before setting up a cichlid aquarium, the prudent aquarist must learn to distinguish between them in order to avoid costly and potentially discouraging errors in his selection of tanks, equipment, furnishings and companions for the new-found objects of his enthusiasm.

Cichlid Behavior Towards Other Fish: Predation and Aggression

Different motivations underlie destructive behavior by cichlids towards other fishes.

Predatory behavior, defined as the capture and subsequent consumption of smaller fishes, is motivated by hunger.

Its elaboration is essentially a function of a given species position in the food web of its native waters.

A good many cichlids do feed exclusively upon smaller fishes in nature, occupying much the same role in the rivers and lakes of Africa and the Neotropics as black basses of the genus *Micropterus* do in the fish communities of North America [Figure 86]. These cichlids are appallingly efficient piscivores under any circumstances.

Many more cichlids are **opportunistic piscivores.**

They feed on smaller fishes whenever they can, but lack the behavioral and morphological specializations that allow them to indulge their appetite for fresh fish with any regularity in nature [Figure 87].

Such behavior is hardly restricted to cichlids, as anyone who has watched neon tetras or tiger barbs devour newly dropped guppy fry in a community aquarium will attest.

Under aquarium conditions, the distinction between specialized and opportunistic predators effectively disappears. The limits upon prey movement imposed by tank walls guarantee that cichlids otherwise hopelessly incompetent as predators have a good shot at capturing and devouring smaller fish in an aquarium. Such predatory behavior is not amenable to modification in captivity.

With few exceptions, cichlids will eat any fish they can catch small enough to swallow conveniently.

The only way to prevent such distressing occurrences is to exercise common sense in selecting their tankmates.

The question of suitable companions for cichlids will be considered subsequently in greater depth.

Suffice for the present that as a rule of thumb, any fish **less than half the total length** of the largest cichlid present in a given community stands a good chance of being treated as a prospective meal.

Such factors as body depth and the presence or absence of fin spines and/or armor plating also influence the outcome of such interactions.

However, the novice cichlid keeper is better off erring on the side of caution in this respect.

Fortunately, there are plenty of cichlids whose modest adult size makes them safe additions to a community tank housing representatives of other families. Aggressive interactions account for most of the undesirable behavior attributed to cichlids.

To the uninformed aquarist, such behavior often appears gratuitous. However, aggression is costly to its practitioners in terms of the risk of injury it entails and the degree to which it preempts time required to carry out other important activities.

Thus, it is hardly surprising that a tight correlation exists between aggression and access to or control of such critical resources as shelter, food, breeding sites or mates; nor, given that evolution can be viewed as a game in which victory goes to the individual producing the largest number of descendants, is it unexpected that the aggressive defense of offspring characterizes the reproductive behavior of many animals, cichlids included.

Among cichlids, serious aggression occurs chiefly in the context of **territorial behavior,** the defense of a discrete space against intrusion by other fishes.

In nature, few cichlids practice persistent territorial defense, a hallmark of many of their distant marine relatives, the damselfishes.

Fig. 86: The large mouth and highly protrusible jaws of *Caquetaia myersi* (Schultz 1944) are the marks of the specialized piscivorous cichlid.

Fig. 87: Though it will eat smaller fish in captivity, *Nandopsis octofasciatus* Regan 1903, the Jack Dempsey, rarely does so in nature. Like most large Heros species, it lacks the morphological and behavioral specializations essential to a piscivorous lifestyle.

Fig. 88: The Malawian *Pseudotropheus elongatus* Fryer 1956 is unusual in that both sexes exclude other fishes from a feeding territory. A number of mbuna resemble some of the herbivorous damselfishes in both their dependence upon an algal garden and its defense against both conspecific and heterospecific intruders.

The exceptions are the several *Julidoch-romis* species, a number of sedentary rock- and shell-dwelling Tanganyikan species of the related genus *Lamprologus* and a few representatives of the Malawian genus *Pseudotropheus* [Figure 88].

There is strong circumstantial evidence it also typifies the rapids-dwelling worm cichlids of the Zairian genus *Teleogramma*. Some mechanism operates to space out individuals of the larger predatory cichlids such as the **guapotes** of the genus *Nandopsis* and such specialized invertebrate feeders as the snail-eating *Tilapia buettifokeri* (HUBRECHT 1881) in nature.

However, it is unclear whether these large cichlids actively exclude conspecifics from a given area or whether such spacing is passive, arising from strong mutual antipathy.

In the first two genera, the resource defended is shelter against predators and a suitable spawning site; in the case of *Teleogramma*, shelter against the powerful current of the Zairian rapids for individuals of both sexes that also serves as the female's spawning site.

In a few persistently territorial *Pseudotropheus* species that cultivate algae gardens, both sexes exclude potential competitors for the available algal resource.

In most cases, however, only males are territorial. This suggests the primary resource defended is a suitable display and breeding site.

The behavior of the larger cichlids cited is related to their feeding patterns. It may serve to assure each individual access to an adequate food supply.

In all cases, territorial defense is directed principally against conspecifics [Figure 89], which represent an individual's most serious competitors for any critical resource.

However, heterospecifics with similar living requirements may be excluded from the defended area as well.

The majority of cichlids restrict territoriality to periods of sexual activity.

However surprising it might seem to persons unfamiliar with cichlids in nature, most

Fig. 89: Intraspecific aggression manifests itself at an early age among guapotes of the subgenus *Nandopsis*. Such behavior seves to disperse such young *Nandopsis managuensis* more or less uniformly through their environment.

species are actually rather social when not breeding!

In captivity, a combination of abundant, high protein food and favorable water temperatures allows cichlids to remain in a state of continual reproductive readiness.

This in turn results in persistent manifestation of some form of territoriality even by species that defend a breeding site only a few weeks each year in the wild.

During the prespawning period, conspecifics are the chief targets of the resident fish's (or fishes') attacks, for their identical breeding site requirements make them obvious competitors.

Intolerance of other fishes broadens markedly after spawning in species that practice long-term defense of the mobile fry. This reflects the simple fact that all other fish represent a serious threat to the young and must be dealt with accordingly.

Grim as this picture of cichlid behavior may seem, territorially based aggressive behavior can be manipulated in a manner that minimizes its negative effects under aquarium conditions.

One can, for example, totally eliminate aggression associated with breeding by maintaining a community display tank of solitary male specimens of several different species.

Most aquarists prefer not to so preclude the possibility of spawning. They thus seek to keep cichlids in a somewhat less restrictive situation.

Success in this endeavor depends largely upon understanding the basis of a given species behavior.

If the critical resource is shelter, conflict can be minimized by providing suitable retreats for all potential contestants.

The same holds for spawning sites. **It is, however, impossible to overemphasize the importance of providing cichlids with living quarters large enough to allow them a reasonably normal expression of species-specific territorial behavior.** Nine times out of ten, unacceptable levels of aggression in captivity arise from mistaken efforts to house cichlids in aquaria that do not afford them adequate living space. I will return to this aspect of cichlid keeping when I discuss tank selection.

However, I must emphasize that aquarists with limited tank space are not thereby automatically debarred from the pleasure of keeping and breeding cichlids.

The tremendous size range encompassed by the family extends to species that live and breed successfully in tanks as small as 15 gallons. Information on the space requirements of individual cichlid species can be found in Chapters 8 through 11.

Cichlid Behavior Towards Aquatic Plants

A comparable distinction with respect to motivation is in order when considering cichlid behavior towards plants. Many cichlids, among them the popular *Heros severus* (HECKEL 1840) and *Uaru amphiacanthoides* (HECKEL 1840) [Figure 90] are markedly **herbivorous** in the wild. They can — and do — consume fair quantities of animal food, but the bulk of their diet consists of the leaves, fruits and seeds of vascular plants, both aquatic and terrestrial.

Other species, such as the majority of the popular **mbuna** of Lake Malawi, [Figure 91]

Fig. 90: Even subadult *Uaru amphiacanthoides* like this 3″ specimen are partial to vegetable food. An adult can demolish several leaves of Romaine lettuce in a matter of hours.

Fig. 91: Like many mbuna, this orange morph female *Labeotropheus trewavasae* will eat rooted aquatic plants in captivity, notwithstanding morphological adaptions for rasping algae from solid surfaces.

Fig. 92: Like most mid-sized acaras, these *Aequidens pulcher* (Gill 1858) pose no threat to rooted aquatic plants outside periods of sexual activity.

65

Fig. 93: Though not herbivores, male *Callochromis pleurospilus* (Boulenger 1906) dig such massive spawning pits that their activities risk dislodging any rooted plants in their tank.

or the several *Sarotherodon* species are algae grazers or detritivores that do not feed upon higher plants in nature but do so with gusto in captivity.

Such cichlids naturally treat a planted aquarium as a self-service salad bar. Nor do they draw a distinction between rooted and floating plants.

Not even generous provision of vegetable food in their diet will alter such behavior.

Reference is made to the presence of herbivorous tendencies in the species covered in the Catalog section. Note again there are many cichlids totally devoid of tendencies to graze on the aquascaping [Figure 92]. A bit of discrimination in his choice of subjects allows the prudent aquarist the pleasure of enjoying cichlids in a planted setting.

Most cichlids are indifferent to plants as a food source. The damage they inflict upon rooted plants arises in consequence of other activities.

Substratum-sifting cichlids often uproot shallowly rooted plants in the course of their normal foraging.

Most cichlids dig extensively in association with breeding [Figure 93]. This behavior poses obvious risks to any rooted plants in the immediate vicinity of such excavation.

Strongly rooted plants, such as the various swordplants of the genus *Echinodorus,* as well as representatives of the genera *Anubias* and *Cryptocoryne,* are relatively resistant to casual disruption.

Growing plants in discrete containers inserted into the gravel also affords them a measure of protection.

However, one often encounters individuals that appear to deracinate plants for no apparent reason.

Such behavior is characteristic of specimens maintained in isolation. It is of a piece with other abnormal behaviors that arise when cichlids are so maintained and will be considered in that context.

Note that floating plants are not molested by these species.

Indeed, most cichlids regardless of size appreciate the cover afforded by a screen of such vegetation [Figure 94].

Fig. 94: The extreme shyness of *Crenicara filamentosa* can be reduced by providing it with a layer of floating plants.

Environmental Manipulation by Cichlids

The final class of undesirable behaviors of which cichlids stand accused falls under the catch-all phrase of destructive modification of the environment.

Most aquarists think immediately of massive excavation in this context, but this by no means exhausts the list.

There are reliable reports of cichlids pushing over rockwork, with disastrous results to the glass walls or bottoms of their quarters, of cichlids disassembling interior filters and scattering their contents across the tank bottom, and of cichlids flipping the intake siphons of power filters right out of their aquarium.

A few really belligerent cichlids will "kill" thermostatic heaters by the exercise of such ingenious expedients as ramming the pilot light head on or seizing the offending unit in their jaws and slamming it a few times against the nearest solid object [Figure 95]. Here again, the aquarist is faced with a mixed bag of motivations which must be sorted out before he attempts to devise workable means of coping with such behavior.

Digging under natural conditions can be motivated by hunger, by the necessity of maintaining a shelter or by reproductive activity.

Substratum-sifting for food [Figure 96] and maintenance of shelter [Figure 97] are markedly species-specific.

Little can be done to influence their expression in captivity beyond housing their practitioners over substrata coarse enough to impede any efforts to move individual particles.

Digging in conjunction with spawning is practically universal within the family [Figures 98]. Indeed, it is one of the more interesting aspects of the cichlid reproductive cycle.

What renders such behavior frustrating to most aquarists is its almost continuous expression in captivity. This again stems from the fact that under aquarium conditions, cichlids exist in an ongoing state of low-level rut.

Thus males of the various *Haplochromis* [Figures 99] and *Sarotherodon* species, whose digging in nature is restricted to a few weeks yearly seem to devote most of their waking hours to the excavation of massive craters in captivity.

Most disruption of rockwork occurs as a side effect of such activity. Again, little can be done to prevent such behavior, although intelligent selection of substratum and furnishings for the cichlid aquarium can go far towards minimizing its impact.

The remaining behaviors in this class, to which can be added the apparently gratuitous destruction of rooted plants noted earlier, are essentially aberrant in character.

They are usually encountered in cichlids maintained in isolation and simply comprise a predictable response to a most atypical environment.

Cichlids are intelligent animals whose intelligence has evolved in response to the demands of a complex environment. Zookeepers are well aware when such an animal is placed in a much simplified environment, it commonly behaves in an abnormal or even pathological manner.

The repetitive pacing of large carnivores housed in isolation is an excellent example of such behavior.

Self-plucking by psittacine birds is another.

In the case of cichlids, absence of normal interactions with other fish lowers the threshold level for aggression-eliciting stimuli to the point where **anything** elicits a violent response from the isolated fish. This can be an object in the aquarium, such as a plant or flashing pilot light, or some stimulus beyond its confines, such as a person's entry into the room containing its quarters.

Lacking such stimulation, isolated fish often engage in massive digging efforts, shift-

Fig. 95: Like many of its large congeners, *Amphilophus trimaculatus* (Gunther 1866) sometimes attacks filter intake siphons and heaters with great persistence and often unforunate results.

Fig. 96: While they constantly shift the substratum in search of food, eartheaters such as this *Satanoperca daemon* Heckel 1840 seldom displace gravel during the course of their foraging.

Fig. 97: Though they rarely exceed 2″ SL, the dwarf shell-dwelling *Lamprologus* such as this female *L. ocellatus* (Steindachner 1909) often displace substantial volumes of gravel in the process of maintaining their shelters.

ing their tank's gravel layer from one end of the aquarium to the other.

Clearly cichlids do best in the company of other fishes. Thus, the obvious remedy for aberrant behavior is to move the isolated fish into a community setting.

When this cannot be done — and I appreciate the difficulties inherent in applying such advice to a large oscar or **guapote** — measures must be taken both to protect aquarium appliances from assault and provide the isolated fish a less boring environment. Approaches to safeguarding equipment will be considered later.

Environmental enrichment requires a bit more imagination. but is by no means impossible.

Placing its tank in a location that allows an isolated cichlid to observe human activity in its vicinity goes far in this direction, though I refuse to speculate upon how the fish interprets such goings on in its neighborhood!

Situating the tank immediately adjacent to another aquarium affords both residents an opportunity to interact without risk of injury.

Finally, providing the fish with alternative targets for its aggressive tendencies often works well in such cases. Ping-pong balls are ideal for this purpose. Intact, balls float at the surface, while those punctured with a needle in two or three places take on water and sink to the bottom. Isolated cichlids derive great satisfaction out of pushing them around the aquarium.

Some individuals learn rapidly that balls flipped **out** of their tank are usually tossed back **in** again by human beings.

This sets the stage for hours of mutually diverting activity!

I hope the forgoing has dispelled the notion that cichlids are hopelessly intractable aquarium residents. Some cichlid behavior, notably that related to feeding, is essentially unmodifiable. It must simply taken into account when selecting companions and tank furnishings.

Fig. 98: Like most other cichlids, this female *Geophagus brasiliensis* (Quoy & Gaimard 1824) restricts earthmoving to the preparation of a spawning site.

Fig. 99: Male *Protomelas* cf. *kirkii*, like many of their Malawian congeners, construct truly enormous spawning pits in nature. Seen in this light, their substratum-shifting activities in captivity assume modest proportions indeed!

Most of the remaining behavior aquarists condemn in the family is neither gratuitous nor malicious.

It rather represents a complex set of adaptations to the demands of an often rigorous environment.

Its expression in captivity leads to undesirable consequences because of spatial constraints imposed upon the movement of other fishes by aquarium conditions. The impact of such behavior is greatly influenced by the environment in which cichlids find themselves.

Hence the next two chapters will consider the equipment and furnishings required to make the cichlid aquarium an environment that promotes the physical well being of these fish and with which they can interact with minimal risk to themselves, their companions and surroundings.

CHAPTER 3

SETTING UP THE CICHLID AQUARIUM

Introduction

As already stated, this book assumes its readers are already reasonably proficient aquarists. It would thus be superfluous to consider the mechanics of setting up an aquarium for cichlids in great detail.

However, cichlids, by virtue of both their size and behavior, make some unique demands upon aquarium hardware. The novice cichlidophile will tread a smoother path if he selects his equipment with no illusions in this regard.

My object is thus to focus upon the equipment essential for success in keeping and breeding cichlids in captivity.

Choosing a Suitable Tank for Cichlids

Choice of an appropriate tank is absolutely essential to success with cichlids.

The best advice to the prospective cichlid keeper is to **invest in the largest tank that will fit in his available space.**

If his object is a display of single specimens of the larger Neotropical cichlids or an exclusively male assortment of colorful Malawian cichlids, a workable rule of thumb allows **one inch of adult fish body length for each two and a half gallons of tank volume.** This may seem overly generous, but in reality water displacement by tank furnishings brings the ratio closer to one inch of fish per two gallons of water. This is not unreasonable given both the demands medium-sized to large cichlids place upon filtration systems and their requirements for living space. The aquarist who maintains both sexes of a given species in a community setting must accept the virtual inevitability of spawning attempts.

The fact that cichlids will spawn freely in a community tank means both their requirements for a breeding territory and those of their tankmates for a secure refuge beyond its limits must be considered when choosing their tank. Information on spawning territory sizes

for the species discussed in Chapters 8 through 11 will suggest **minimum** tank sizes for the major cichlid groups.

A tank whose bottom area is twice that of a given species' breeding territory will usually house six to eight cichlids comfortably, assuming that no more than a single pair is sexually active at any given moment.

Once again, if practical to purchase a tank larger than the suggested minimum value, never hesitate to do so. Please note it is possible to induce many — though by no means all — cichlids to spawn as isolated pairs. In such cases, one can make do with a smaller tank. However, this approach has its own shortcomings, to which I will return in Chapter 7. Interested readers are referred to that chapter for a discussion of apposite techniques. Such large tanks require careful attention to their placement.

Stresses consequent upon being set upon an uneven surface can cause the universally available frameless glass tanks to loose their structural integrity.

This can lead to anything from a slow leak to the aquaristic version of Noah's flood in the living room, with disagreeable consequences to fish and furnishings alike. Both the likelihood and magnitude of such a disaster increase with the volume of the tank.

It is therefore essential that the surface upon which such a tank rests be ABSOLUTELY LEVEL BEFORE it is filled with water! It is much easier to assure a level surface for a large tank, not to mention support its considerable weight when filled, if its intended resting place is a stand specifically designed for such a purpose rather than a piece of furniture already in place. Such stands are available in wood or metal in a wide range of styles. It is thus fairly simple to find one compatible with a room's decor.

Where aesthetic considerations do not enter the picture, as is usually the case when setting up a separate fish room, equally satisfactory racks can be assembled from cinder or

Fig. 100: A deep tank is a good investment only if it is intended to house such species as *Pterophyllum altum*.

concrete construction blocks and lumber or from slotted angle iron.

Two final considerations should enter into the selection of a suitable cichlid tank.

First, most cichlids are bottom-oriented fish that spend little time in the upper half of the water column. The extent of a tank's **bottom area** is thus more relevant to the well being of its residents than is its **depth.**

So unless one intends to keep angelfish or similar deep-bodied species [Figure 100] or pelagic plankton feeders like the *Cyprichromis* species of Lake Tanganyika, little is to be gained from the purchase of the so-called show style tanks that increase depth at the expense of length and/or width. These tend to be more expensive than standard design tanks of the same volume, yet actually provide less usable living space for the generality of cichlids.

Second, it is absolutely essential that a cichlid tank either come equipped with a secure glass cover as part of its original equipment or that it be capable of having such a cover retrofitted. Most cichlids are adroit and powerful jumpers whose response to disagreeable stimuli is an attempt to escape from their immediate vicinity with a flying leap [Figure 101].

However useful this tactic may be in nature, it rarely proves so in captivity.

The despondency provoked by the sight of the desiccated cadaver of a prized specimen on the floor is heightened only by the realization that such fatalities, unlike many others that may befall an aquarium fish, are totally preventable by the use of secure tank covers.

Fig. 101: Like many lamprologine cichlids, *Julidochromis ornatus* Boulenger 1898 is an accomplished jumper that must be kept in a tightly covered tank.

Equipping the Cichlid Aquarium

Temperature Control and Illumination

A suitable tank selected, the cichlid enthusiast must next consider accessory equipment. As noted in the preceding chapter, cichlids are warm-water fishes.

A thermostatic heater is thus essential to their successful maintenance.

The larger than average volume of most cichlid tanks requires the use of high wattage units to maintain suitable water temperatures. Be guided by performance rather than price in selecting a heater.

Cheap heaters **inevitably** malfunction.

It is simply a matter of how soon after purchase the contacts of their bimetallic strip thermostats will weld themselves closed.

This condition makes it impossible for the heater to shut itself off. Unless such a malfunction is quickly noticed, the result is a tank of cichlid *bouillabaisse*. Solid-state thermistor regulated heaters pose least risk of accidental malfunction.

Sealed unit heaters are the most reliable of those that rely upon a bimetallic thermostat to regulate their activity. As with any other electrical appliance, warranty strength is a good measure of reliability.

An accurate thermometer is another essential piece of equipment.

No commercially available unit is without shortcomings.

Those that must be placed within the tank typically end up jammed in some obscure corner at an angle that makes it impossible to read them, targets of the cichlid passion for rearranging their surroundings.

Liquid crystal display (LCD) units that are attached to the outside of the tank obviously remain where they can be easily read.

However, all are influenced to a greater or lesser degree by the temperature of the tank's surroundings. To make the best of an unsatisfactory situation, invest in an accurate photographic darkroom thermometer and use it as a standard against which each LCD stick-on unit can be calibrated. That unit's correction factor can be noted on a strip of self-adhesive plastic label tape attached to one side of the tank for easy reference thereafter.

Illumination is best provided by fluorescent bulbs.

Incandescent lighting produces considerable heat, thereby complicating the problem of minimizing temperature fluctuations. The type and wattage of bulbs used will depend upon which cichlids are kept.

If one's preference permits cultivation of live aquatic plants, their culture requirements will necessarily determine the amount and type of illumination provided.

Otherwise, be guided by aesthetic considerations. Cichlids prefer moderate light levels.

They do **not** look their best under either cool white or warm white fluorescent lighting.

Tubes that radiate strongly in the red and blue wavelengths sold specifically as aquarium lights do illuminate cichlids to advantage.

Though touted as enhancing the growth of vascular aquatic plants, their spectrum is not ideal for this purpose. It does greatly encourage proliferation of blue-green algae, whose growth is always a problem in a cichlid aquarium's nutrient-rich water.

Fluorescent tubes manufactured specifically for the indoor culture of house plants radiate a spectrum that favors growth of vascular aquatic plants and does a creditable job of showing cichlid colors off in the bargain.

Such tubes can be obtained from any nursery or garden supply store if unavailable at local retail aquarium shops.

Filtration Systems

The one decision to which the prospective cichlid keeper **must** devote careful thought is choice of filtration system. Effective filtration simultaneously maintains water clarity and provides favorable living conditions for a tank's inhabitants by promoting the breakdown of organic waste products.

Every filtration system relies to a greater or lesser degree upon two separate processes.

Mechanical filtration refers to removal of particulate matter from suspension. The usual

74

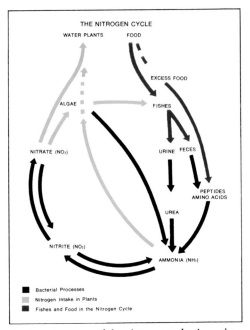

Fig. 102: Diagram of the nitrogen cycle. Aquarists are chiefly concerned with its catabolic aspect, in which complex nitrogen-bearing organic compounds are sequentially broken down into simpler substances.

approach entails passing water through a porous medium that retains suspended material.

Biological filtration refers to degradation of nitrogenous organic waste into simpler inorganic compounds by bacterial activity. This process is summarized in the accompanying figure [Figure 102]. Management of the nitrogen cycle is the most important aspect of successful fish keeping.

The object is to keep the level of toxic metabolites from rising to harmful levels. Efficient filtration plays an important role in nitrogen cycle management and thus influences the effort that must be devoted to water changing.

It is no exaggeration to state that the well-being of any ornamental fish no less than the aquarist's enjoyment of his hobby largely depend upon selection of an efficient, low maintenance filtration system.

Fortunately, filtration technology has experienced several revolutions in the last quarter of a century.

Their cumulative effect has greatly broadened the options available to the cichlid keeper. These differ chiefly in the relative importance they accord to mechanical or biological filtration.

It is helpful to distinguish between essentially mechanical approaches, in which organic matter is trapped with the object of removing most of it from the system **before** it is broken down by bacterial action, and biological approaches, which encourage the progressive degradation of such waste into simpler inorganic compounds within the aquarium.

Each has its advantages and disadvantages when applied to the cichlid aquarium.

Intelligent selection among available alternatives requires an understanding of the demands cichlids place on a filtration system and the strengths and limitations of each approach in responding to them.

Cichlids pose a major challenge to any filtration system on two fronts.

First of all, the **waste load**, or quantity of metabolic by-products a fish adds to a filtration system is directly proportional to the amount of food it eats.

Most cichlids are medium-sized to large fish with heavy appetites. This in itself complicates nitrogen cycle management in their quarters. The problem is further compounded by the fact that many cichlids are messy eaters.

Their food processing unavoidably releases a cloud of fine particles into the environment whenever they feed.

This constitutes an additional organic nitrogen input that the filter must somehow handle. Second, the propensity of many cichlids to rearrange the substratum to their liking greatly increases the amount of suspended particulate matter a filter must cope with.

It also effectively precludes employment of the most widely used biological filtration systems, because their functional core is an under-gravel filter whose operation is gravely impaired by such behavior. Given the family's diversity, no single approach to filtration will work satisfactorily for all cichlids under all conditions.

A primarily biological approach gives satisfactory results in lightly stocked tanks up to

50 gallons capacity housing cichlids in the dwarf to middle-sized range.

If stocking density is increased, or species that dig actively or have messy feeding behavior are maintained, supplementary mechanical filtration will prove necessary.

In aquaria larger than 50 gallons, the relative importance of mechanical filtration increases proportionately with tank volume regardless of the fish maintained.

Finally, effective mechanical filtration is absolutely essential when very large cichlids such as the more robust *Heros*-lineage genera, haplochromines and tilapia are kept, for the sheer volume of their waste load will swamp even the most efficient biological filter.

Workable approaches to filtration will be suggested for the major cichlid groups in Chapters 8 through 11.

Given the selection of motor-driven outside filters currently available it is relatively simple to arrange effective mechanical filtration for a cichlid tank

A unit that turns the tank volume over once an hour serves quite well, notwithstanding the generally held view that equates filter effectiveness with turnover rate.

While appreciative of some water movement, most cichlids do not relish living in the equivalent of a soda fountain in full play! These filters are of two types that differ in their mode of operation.

Passive intake units rely upon siphon action to carry tank water into the filter box, whence it is returned to the tank by a pump.

Powered intake units rely on a rotary impeller to pull water into the filter box, whence it overflows back into the aquarium after passing through the filter media.

Each has its strengths and weaknesses, which the cichlid keeper should understand before making his final selection.

Passive intake units are not self-priming. Once interrupted, the siphon flow will not restart itself automatically. The pump consequently will empty the filter box, then continue to run dry.

This can have disastrous consequences for both fish and filter unless promptly detected. Unfortunately, most high capacity power filters are of this type.

Their use is mandatory on any tank housing robust cichlids, whose behavior towards the intake siphons frequently threatens maintenance of water flow into the filter box.

To avoid such problems, block access to these or other appliances by installing a sliding screen a few inches short of one or both ends of the aquarium [Figure 103]. This is easily done. Simply cut a piece of plastic egg crate diffuser grating a bit smaller than the interior dimensions of the tank. Then mount guard rails cut from 0.25" X 0.75" plastic stripping along the inside of the front and rear panels with silicone elastic sealant.

Once the sealant has dried, the screen or screens slide easily into place, creating a protected end space for siphons and heaters beyond the reach of even the most bellicose cichlid.

Powered intake units move less water through the filter box over a given time than do passive intake units. This is because the rate of flow is constrained by the number and diameter of the inflow tubes, not the capacity of the impeller.

Powered intake units have one, or at most two inflow tubes, of lesser diameter than those of passive intake filters, which can be fed by half a dozen siphons.

This limits their utility in tanks larger than 75 gallons capacity and in those housing the larger, messier cichlid species.

They enjoy two great advantages.

Their intakes are immune to frontal attacks by large cichlids and they will restart themselves automatically if stopped by a power outage. Finally, they are noticeably quieter than most passive intake filters. This is important when choosing a filter for an aquarium to be set up in a residential area such as a den or living room.

The foam fractionator, or protein skimmer, represents a very different approach to removing metabolic wastes from an aquarium before they can undergo mineralization.

Such units exploit the fact that air bubbles have a weak electrical surface charge that attracts and holds protein fragments and free amino acids.

In salty or heavily mineralized fresh water, the foam thus generated will remove a signifi-

Fig. 103: The male *Amphilophus astromaculatus* (Regan 1912) is prevented from interfering with aquarium appliances by the plastic diffuser grating barrier visible in the background.

cant volume of the soluble organic waste produced by a tank's residents before it can be attacked by nitrifiers.

A protein skimmer directs a heavy stream of such bubbles through a plastic tube to produce a froth that can be directed into an outside receptacle. This is then emptied of its metabolite-laden contents as necessity dictates.

A high-tech variant of the protein skimmer introduced ozone into the airstream to increase the unit's efficiency.

Because it is much easier to generate a stiff head of foam in sea water, protein skimmers have a greater following among marine aquarists than among their freshwater counterparts.

However, they remain useful adjuncts to nitrogen cycle management in tanks housing cichlids with a preference for hard, alkaline water.

The aquarist opting for a primarily biological approach has a choice of four different types of filter.

Each relies upon the activity of a community of **aerobic**, or oxygen-dependent saprophytic bacteria to break down complex nitrogenous organic wastes into simple inorganic nitrogen compounds. The terms **nitrification** and **mineralization** are interchangeably applied to this stepwise process. However, they have little else in common.

Hence, the prospective buyer requires a clear notion of each filter's particular strengths and weaknesses before deciding which to employ.

Properly utilized, each will perform effectively in a cichlid aquarium, and all can be successfully paired with outside power filters when circumstances dictate a two-tier approach to filtration. The most familiar such unit is the undergravel filter, which uses the tank's substratum as the matrix within which particulate matter is trapped and degraded by bacterial activity.

Its effectiveness depends upon the rate of water flow through the filter bed.

This in turn depends on the geometry of the plastic filter plate, particle diameter and relative homogeneity of the substratum and the strength of the filter's motive force.

The simplest such units draw particulate waste directly into the gravel bed.

Until relatively recently, undergravel filters relied upon the airlift principle to pull water through the filter bed.

A readily available design innovation allows such units to be mated with rotary impeller driven power heads.

This greatly accelerates water movement through the substratum and with it filter efficiency.

Such units heads are particularly useful in assuring effective filtration of tanks of 75 gallons capacity and larger.

In heavily stocked tanks, the gravel bed of such a filter will quickly become clogged with particulate waste.

Regular purging is thus an essential aspect of proper filter maintenance and is best carried out in conjunction with scheduled water changes.

The so-called reverse flow undergravel filter minimizes this problem by drawing the tank's water through a mechanical prefilter, then pushing it up through the tank's gravel bed.

This allows its associated flora of nitrifying bacteria to work exclusively on dissolved metabolites.

The efficiency of such units is limited by the rapidity with which water flow through the prefilter is impeded by mechanical blockage of its media.

As the canister filters that usually serve this purpose are not easily serviced, the utility of reverse flow undergravel filters in tanks whose residents generate a heavy waste load is limited, however persuasive the arguments may be for installing such units in lightly stocked aquaria.

Undergravel filters suffer two serious shortcomings in the cichlid aquarium. One can be mitigated with the exercise of a bit of ingenuity; the other is inherent in their design.

As noted, cichlid digging effectively sabotages their operation by exposing large areas of the bottom plate. This can be easily prevented.

Cover the filter plate with half inch sheet sponge cut to fit the interior dimensions of the tank bottom. Then place a piece of egg crate diffuser grating over the sponge. It is advisable to fasten the grating to the filter plate with monofilament fishing line to preclude any possibility of disassembly.

Finally, add a layer of gravel deep enough to cover the sheet of grating. This system employs both the gravel layer and the sponge sheet as a filter bed. The rigid plastic grating limits the amount of gravel the fish can remove during the course of their excavations and protects the sponge from their potentially disruptive attentions.

Their absolute immobility combined with the vulnerability of their nitrifier flora to the action of antibiotics and a number of other commonly used therapeutic agents such as methylene blue and formalin is the unavoidable shortcoming of all such filters. Many of these medications destroy the benign bacterial community of the filter bed as efficiently as they kill pathogens. Abrupt cessation of biological filtration in a heavily stocked tank can be disastrous.

This state of affairs puts the cichlid fancier on the horns of a nasty dilemma when he is faced with systemic bacterial infections that can be treated only with antibiotics.

Fortunately, there are less vulnerable alternatives to the undergravel filter.

Sponge filters, as their name implies, employ a sponge matrix rather than a bed of gravel to support the microbial community upon which biological filtration depends [Figure 104]. They combine the efficiency of undergravel filters with a high versatility.

Not least of their advantages is that they can be removed to a holding jar or another aquarium whenever their tank is being medicated, then returned with functional efficiency unimpaired once treatment is completed.

Their effectiveness depends upon the geometry of the filter mass and the rate at which water is drawn through the biologically active sponge. The Tetra line of sponge filters is superior to its competitors with respect to the former. Their cylindrical filter elements can be so positioned that their **entire** surface area is functional.

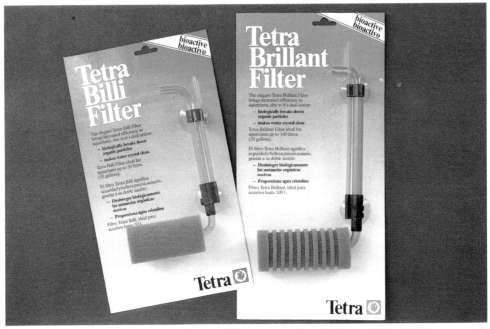

Fig. 104: The Tetra Brillant- and Billi-Filters are the most versatile and efficient biological filters currently available.

Sponge filters that rest directly on the bottom, on the other hand, draw water over only a fraction of their surface area.

Sponge filters require a bit more by way of ongoing maintenance than do undergravel systems.

The filter mass periodically should be rinsed out under luke-warm running water.

If filter activity and waste load are in rough balance, this should not be necessary more than twice monthly.

If the sponge becomes clogged with particulate matter more often than this, the waste load in the tank is more than the filter can handle.

If it is not practical to reduce the tank's stocking rate, addition of another sponge filter or of a supplementary mechanical filter should put an end to this problem.

Simple airlift driven units can successfully filter tanks of up to 35 gallons capacity. They are the filter of choice for rearing tanks, where their biologically active surfaces provide a rich source of supplementary food for growing fry and are ideal for use in heavily planted aquaria. As noted, they do not handle heavy waste loads well. This precludes their use in tanks containing the larger, messier cichlids.

Units of the Tetra PHAS line are designed to permit the facile mating of a high speed rotary impeller driven power head to a sponge filter.

The resulting unit can handle large tank volumes and heavy waste loads most effectively.

It is also possible to mate a sponge filter to a powered intake outside filter.

In such an arrangement, the sponge filter serves as a mechanical prefilter with biological capacity.

This allows the outside unit to be charged with chemically active media whose efficiency would otherwise be compromised if they were overlain with organic detritus.

Such an hybrid system is particularly useful when one wishes to raise or lower the tank pH by passing its water through a calcareous matrix such as coral gravel or oyster shell or through strongly acidic peat.

A particular shortcoming of these filters is that some cichlids find the biologically active sponges quite tasty.

They will bite sizeable chunks out of them until only a few ragged patches are left attached to the filter stem!

Tilapia buttikoferi, T. mariae, Uaru amphiacanthoides, Heros appendiculatus (CAS-TELNAU 1855), *H. severus* and a number of *Theraps* species [Figure 105] stand accused of such behavior.

Short of moving the filter behind a protective screen, as already recommended for intake siphons and heaters, little can be done to prevent this *contretemps* once a large cichlid develops such a bizarre appetite.

Canister filters sidestep the problem of cichlid interference with biological filtration by pumping particle-laden water through a filter bed housed **outside** the aquarium.

Such units share the advantages of sponge filters with respect to protection of their biological activity in the face of antibiotics.

They offer the further advantage of allowing the user a choice of media for the filter bed, as they can accommodate sponge pads, gravel or specially crafted ceramic rings with equal ease.

Their chief shortcomings are cost, which is substantially greater than that of either undergravel or sponge filters, the ease with which they are blocked by heavy waste loads, and the unavoidable difficulties associated with clearing such blockages when they occur.

Notwithstanding these disadvantages, they remain a practical alternative to biological filtration available to the keeper of large cichlids.

The problem of frequent blockage due to waste overload can be mitigated considerably if these units are used in conjunction with an easily serviced high performance power filter or connected to a mechanical prefilter.

Withal, the security canister filters offer against interruption of biological filtration makes them a good investment for cichlid aquaria of 50 gallons capacity or larger.

These units are available in a wide range of sizes, so there is little difficulty in finding one whose capacity is suited to a given tank.

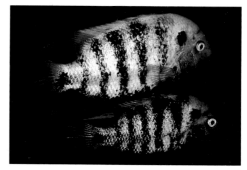

Fig. 105: Herbivorous cichlids like these *Theraps fenestratus* (Gunther 1860) often develop a taste for biologically active sponges. This limits the utility of sponge filters in their quarters.

The trickle filter is the latest development in the field of biological filtration.

Such units move waste-laden water through a mechanical prefilter, then allow it to trickle slowly over a bed of biologically active plastic filter media.

Treated water gathers in a reservoir whence it is pumped back to the tank.

Concentrations of dissolved oxygen in this film of water are at the saturation mark.

As the efficiency of nitrifying bacteria is very much a function of the amount of oxygen available to them, mineralization of metabolic wastes takes place very rapidly in such units, which offer the additional advantage of a highly oxygenated return flow.

The first feature recommends the trickle filter for heavily stocked tanks or those housing notably messy species. The second makes it the unit of choice for tanks housing cichlids native to well-oxygenated biotopes, such as river rapids or the surge and pelagic zones of large lakes [Figure 106]. Trickle filters, while highly effective, are not inexpensive.

The fiscally prudent aquarist may thus find more labor intensive approaches to maintaining water quality in his tanks, such as an accelerated schedule of water changes a more cost effective approach to sound nitrogen cycle management.

When setting up biological filtration in a cichlid tank, remember that it tkes time for the filter bed to reach full waste handling capacity.

To avoid possible losses, initially add only a few expendable fish to the tank.

If these are still alive and prospering a week later, it is safe to begin adding additional fish every five to seven days.

One can track the filter's progress by following daily changes in ammonia, nitrite and nitrate concentrations in the tank subsequent to its installation with commercially available test kits, as is done in marine aquaria.

Successive peaks of dissolved ammonia, nitrite and nitrate, followed by a steady nitrate concentration mark the progress of the filter's microbial community towards full maturity.

However, such precision is not as critical in the cichlid as it is in the marine aquarium.

Ammonia is a problem only in the hard, alkaline water demanded by Malawian and Tanganyikan cichlids, while most extralacustrine cichlids can tolerate brief exposures to high nitrite levels without coming to harm. Hence disaster is unlikely to strike if one or two specimens are added to the tank a day or two earlier than they ought to be.

At all costs the novice cichlid keeper must avoid the common practice of adding a full complement of fish to a freshly set-up tank.

This is an invitation to all manner of complications. These can range from immediate loss of fish to ammonia and/or nitrite poisoning to an epidemic of bacterial infections due to erosion of normal resistance levels following exposure to such a physiologically stressful environment.

However frustrating the step by step approach may be, it is clearly best to make haste slowly when stocking a new cichlid tank.

It is prudent to provide supplementary aeration in heavily stocked aquaria serviced exclusively by outside power and/or canister filters.

As noted, there is a slight but omnipresent risk that water flow through such units will be interrupted through accidental blockage, behavioral disturbance or mechanical failure.

When power filters are in normal operation, they do an admirable job of aerating the tanks they serve.

However, sudden interruption of normal filter operation can have a negative effect upon the rate at which carbon dioxide leaves the aquarium. The result is often acute respiratory distress for its inhabitants.

Fig. 106: Because of their extreme sensitivity to nitrite, rapids-dwelling cichlids such as *Steatocranus mpozoensis* Roberts & Stewart 1976 should never be introduced to an aquarium until its biological filter is fully run in.

The consequences can swiftly be lethal during spells of hot summer weather.

Even a single airstone can spell the difference between life and death in such an emergency.

Large cichlids represent a considerable investment in both time and money well worth the modest price of a small diaphragm-type air pump to protect.

Incidental Accessories

Several other pieces of equipment are essential adjuncts to the cichlid aquarium.

The following list itemizes these accessories.

Some items are marked with an asterisk. Their use will be considered subsequently. The rest of this chapter will be devoted to that of the remainder.

1. Water test kits (pH, hardness, chlorine, ammonia, nitrite, nitrate) *
2. Flexible tubing (3/8" — 5/8" internal diameter) *
3. Plastic buckets
4. Dip nets
5. Clear plastic specimen holding box
6. Net breeding traps *
7. Jeweller's loupe or other hand magnifying lens *
8. Kitchen baster
9. Set of plastic measuring spoons
10. Measuring cup calibrated in both metric and Anglo-American units
11. Notebook

Plastic buckets serve a multitude of uses.

They can be utilized as receptacles for dirty water, vessels for carrying fresh water or as fish transport containers.

They can even serve as emergency quarters for a fish in need of temporary isolation or a biological filter removed from a tank undergoing medication with antibiotics. **Never use for aquaristic purposes buckets that have previously contained detergent or solutions of other household chemicals.**

Calibrated vessels are necessary to precisely measure out water conditioners or medications, some of which are moderately corro-
sive — hence the admonition to use plastic rather than metal spoons.

A kitchen baster is a useful instrument for dispensing food and medication. It is perfectly safe to borrow such utensils from the kitchen. However, in the interest of domestic harmony it is advisable to purchase a separate set for aquarium use!

Dipnets intended for the cichlid aquarium should have an opening at least two inches wider than the **total length** of its largest resident and measure half again as deep.

Commercially available aquarium dipnets that meet these requirements for cichlids up to 8" (c. 20.0 cm) SL are readily available.

Suitable nets for robust cichlids are harder to find.

Aquatic entomological dipnets serve this purpose admirably for larger species. These nets can be ordered from scientific supply houses or firms that specialize in the sale of commercial fishing gear. They are expensive but extremely durable, which makes them a defensible investment.

Landing nets used by sport fishermen are not suitable for use with aquarium fish.

Captured specimens can become easily tangled in their larger meshes and suffer serious injuries as they struggle to escape. Apropos of this, cichlids thrash about more vigorously when netted than other aquarium fish of comparable size. It is therefore essential to use only stoutly constructed nets to capture and handle them.

Last but by no means least, the novice cichlid enthusiast should invest in an inexpensive notebook. To its pages should be committed such information as purchase date and source of newly acquired fish, observations on their preferred foods, behavior towards other fishes and reproductive biology, onset and symptoms of medical problems and success of measures employed to treat them.

Such a record makes it much easier for the aquarist to learn from his experiences no less than to share them with others who enjoy his interests.

The presence or absence of a regularly kept notebook near an aquarium tells the knowledgeable observer a great deal about a cichlid keeper's commitment to his hobby.

CHAPTER 4

FURNISHING THE CICHLID AQUARIUM

Introduction

The necessary equipment to keep cichlids alive and well in hand, the aquarist faces the task of suitably furnishing their tanks. As any visitor to the facilities of a commercial angelfish or **mbuna** breeder can attest, it is feasible to keep and breed cichlids in tanks devoid of any furnishings beyond the equipment necessary to maintain their residents in good health. [Figure 107.) However, most cichlid enthusiasts prefer to house their charges in a setting at once psychologically reassuring to the fish and aesthetically pleasing to human observers [Figure 108]. In view of their more-or-less well developed tendency to rearrange tank decor to **their** liking, efforts at aquascaping the cichlid aquarium must be planned more carefully than would be the case were the tank to house other inhabitants.

While their behavior necessarily imposes certain constraints upon furnishing their quarters, it is still possible to decorate a cichlid aquarium in a manner equally satisfying to parties on either side of the glass.

Fig. 107: Mbuna are commercially bred in large, bare concrete vats such as these used by Don Conkel's Tropicals, a major producer of African cichlids located in Odessa, Florida.

Fig. 108: Most aquarists prefer to house Malawian cichlids in a more a esthetically pleasing environment, as exemplified by this attractively aquascaped tank.

Selecting a Suitable Substratum for the Cichlid Aquarium

The first concern in furnishing the cichlid aquarium is the choice of a suitable substratum. Cichlids are acutely uncomfortable in an environment that reflects light **upwards** from the bottom. They never look their best under such conditions.

Many otherwise outgoing species become reclusive, while timid species may refuse to eat until this source of stress is eliminated. Furthermore, the excavation of either shelter pits for their newly hatched fry or of a spawning site is an important element in the reproductive pattern of most cichlids.

Many species will adapt to an environment that does not allow them to express such behavior, but even behaviorally flexible species spawn more freely in one that does. Some sort of bottom covering is therefore essential in the cichlid aquarium.

What substratum and how much is to be employed depend largely upon the cichlids to be kept.

Substratum depth in a cichlid tank hinges upon whether the fish maintained therein will coexist uneventfully with rooted aquatic plants and/or an undergravel filter.

If their behavior allows aquascaping with live plants or the use of undergravel filtration, both depth of the substratum as well as its chemical makeup and particle size must be dictated by their requirements.

A minimum substratum depth of 1.5" over the filter plate is recommended when setting up an undergravel filter, while most strongly rooted aquatic plants do best planted in a bed at least 2" deep.

If, on the other hand, it is impractical to keep plants or run an undergravel filter in the cichlid aquarium, one need only to provide enough gravel to cover its reflective bottom. A layer 0.5" to 1.0" deep answers this requirement admirably. A shallow substratum minimizes the likelihood that organic matter can accumulate out of contact with oxygen-bearing water to undergo dangerous anaerobic decomposition.

The hydrogen sulfide gas produced by this process is toxic to fish at low concentrations.

Its accidental release when such a pocket is disturbed accounts for many otherwise inexplicable fish deaths reported by aquarists unaware of its lethal potential.

The aquarist must continually be alert to this hazard when cichlids — **particularly large cichlids** — are maintained over deep substrata in tanks without undergravel filtration.

As most cichlids dig to a greater or lesser degree, whatever substratum their keeper chooses for their aquarium should be free of sharp edges or abrasive surfaces. Otherwise the fish may injure their mouths and pharyngeal regions.

This automatically eliminates both crushed coral and black slag glass from consideration in this context.

River or beach gravel of a suitable grade is the best choice of substratum for most cichlid tanks.

The red flint gravel available throughout most of the Mississippi basin makes a particularly pleasing substratum, but any non-toxic gravel of appropriate particle size will suffice.

Bear in mind that regardless of its source, **gravel intended for aquarium use must be**

Fig. 109: When individual particles are fairly large, even accomplished diggers like this female *Herichthys cyanoguttatus* Baird & Girard 1854 find moving gravel too difficult to be undertaken without good reason.

washed under running water until the overflow comes off perfectly clear.

The designation **washed gravel** simply means the particles have been freed from their original soil or clay matrix. It does not mean the gravel is free from either dust or coarse particles of organic matter that can complicate the management of the nitrogen cycle in a newly established cichlid aquarium.

Where tap water is naturally soft, it may prove advantageous to employ a calcium-rich substratum of moderate chemical activity as the bed of an undergravel filter.

This provides some buffering capacity to the water of Malawian, Tanganyikan and Mesoamerican cichlid tanks. The preferred substratum in such instances is Philippine coral gravel.

This naturally wavesmoothed material answers the need for an effective buffering agent admirably while posing minimum hazard to rooting cichlids. Crushed dolomite is a poor second choice.

Many aquarists opt for dolomitic gravel because it is less expensive than the Philippine product.

However, its chemical composition is not appropriate to this task, while its texture hardly recommends it as the medium for an effective undergravel filter bed.

Aquarists who wish to keep cichlids with a preference for soft acid water confront the opposite challenge of finding a substratum incapable of releasing calcium into the aquarium. Epoxy coated gravels represent a costly but effective solution to this problem. These products come in a wide range of painfully intense colors as well as in a series of very pleasing clear coated natural mix.

Efforts to incorporate such artificially colored gravels into the decor of a cichlid aquarium range from mildly repellent to positively nauseating.

However inexplicably, tastes in such matters do differ, and readers without my aesthetic scruples can stand assured that all coated gravels are equally inert — and thus equally safe — under aquarium conditions.

The smooth surface of coated gravels does not provide optimal attachment for nitrifying bacteria.

They thus make a poor bed for an undergravel filter. Gravel to be used as a filter bed or a substratum for rooted plants should have an average particle size roughly that of an upper case printed "O". Some variation in particle size poses no difficulties to the culture of rooted plants.

However, as smaller particles tend to settle out with time, it is worth the trouble to obtain as homogenous a product as possible if the gravel is intended as the bed for an undergravel filter. Otherwise the smaller particles will sift down and block the openings in the filter plate, to the detriment of its efficiency.

If neither function enters into substratum selection, one can manipulate particle size with the aim of modifying the digging behavior of the tank's residents.

The effort cichlids put into digging is strongly influenced by substratum particle size.

Fish that dig constantly when kept over a relatively fine substratum restrict excavation to periods of reproductive activity when confronted with a coarser bottom [Figure 109].

Gravel particles 0.25" to 0.50" in diameter will inhibit even the larger *Heros* lineage and tilapia species to a marked degree.

Of course, the aquarist risks missing a great deal of interesting behavior if he keeps cichlids over too coarse a substratum.

The fascinating shelter-burying behavior of the dwarf **ostracophil** or shell-dwelling *Lamprologus* species of Lake Tanganyika is a case in point.

These diminutive cichlids find even relatively fine aquarium gravel more of a mouthful than they can easily handle.

They must be kept over a silica sand bottom if they are to behave as they would in nature.

Finally, there is an alternative to the use of particulate substrata in the cichlid aquarium. This entails resting a piece of paving sandstone or flagstone cut ½" smaller on all sides than the internal dimensions of the tank on a C-shaped frame made of CPVC pipe.

This lifts the slab high enough off the bottom to allow free water movement, which effectively precludes anaerobic breakdown of trapped waste.

The space beneath provides a hiding place of last resort for harassed adults or fry.

The slab furnishes a solid surface for the erection of rockwork structures, is easily kept free of detritus and is pleasing to the eye in the bargain. Such an arrangement is particularly suitable for tanks housing **mbuna** or their ecological analogues from Lake Tanganyika.

It inarguably represents the only substratum totally beyond the ability of a tankful of cichlids to manipulate!

Live Aquatic Plants in the Cichlid Aquarium

As I have already pointed out, the belief that all cichlids are incapable of coexisting with aquatic plants is unfounded.

The Neotropical and West African dwarf cichlids, as well as most of the smaller representatives of the *Aequidens* lineage are frequently found in well planted biotopes in nature. They invariably do better when an attempt is made to recreate such conditions in captivity.

One can keep and even breed angelfish and discus in bare tanks, but these popular cichlids never seem truly comfortable in such severely functional surroundings and show to best advantage only in well planted aquaria [Figure 110].

The same holds true for the numerous *Haplochromis* species native to Lake Victoria and many African river systems.

If he exercises a modicum of foresight in selecting the species he wishes to keep, there is no reason why the cichlid enthusiast cannot simultaneously exercise a bent for aquatic horticulture. Not that all plants do well in a cichlid aquarium even if its inhabitants are neither herbivorous nor given to wholesale deracination of the aquascaping.

Cichlids are warm water fishes whose well-being demands minimum temperatures in the low 70 °F. range. Plants that require cooler water for part or all of the year cannot be expected to prosper in such an environment.

Cichlids also produce strongly eutrophic water conditions.

Plants intolerant of high nitrate levels are thus unlikely to find conditions in a cichlid tank congenial.

Finally, medium-sized and large cichlids require well aerated aquaria to prosper.

Many plants do not care for strong water movement and do poorly under such conditions.

It is therefore prudent to consult a reference on aquarium plants before attempting to culture a given species in a cichlid aquarium.

In general, crown plants are a better choice for the cichlid aquarium than bunch plants.

The latter, while easier of culture, are more susceptible to accidental dislodgement than the former. Furthermore, they often respond to the nutrient-rich environment by running rampant.

Some even grow right out of the water and develop the emergent form of their species where circumstances permit. Their maintenance entails much pruning and replanting which fish find disturbing and aquarists inconvenient.

Crown plants root more securely and their response to well fertilized waters is to spread laterally rather than grow vertically.

It may eventually become necessary to thin out a stand of *Vallisneria* or *Cryptocoryne*, but never with the frequency that bunch plants must be pruned back and replanted.

The numerous species of *Hygrophila* are probably the most suitable bunch plants for use in a cichlid aquarium. They root quite strongly, which makes them less vulnerable to casual dislodgement than other plants of this sort.

They are no less given to rampant growth than the generality of bunch plants, however and will become leggy and unattractive unless pinched back frequently.

The several *Vallisneria* species are the best all-around choice for a cichlid aquarium. They come in a wide range of sizes suitable for use in tanks of 15 gallons capacity on up, thrive under trophic conditions and tolerate water movement well. As a rule, *Vallisneria* do best in moderately hard, slightly alkaline water, but it is often possible to obtain local cultivars of several species adapted to prevailing pH and hardness values.

Fig. 110: Both discus and angelfish do best when kept in a planted tank.

All *Vallisneria* require strong light to prosper.

This limits their utility in tanks housing cichlids that prefer subdued illumination.

Swordplants of the genus *Echinodorus* also do well in the cichlid aquarium, though the dimensions of the more robust species restrict their use to tanks of 50 gallons or larger [Figures 111 & 112]. Discus and angelfish particularly relish their presence, to the extent of spawning preferentially upon their leaves.

Swordplants require intense light, a rich substratum and frequent feeding, and not all species appreciate strong water motion. As these are costly plants, the prudent aquarist will determine beforehand which species are most likely to respond favorably to his growing conditions.

The larger *Echinodorus* have a distinctive emergent form, but this is rarely seen under indoor conditions.

Many swordplants flower under aquarium conditions and set seeds that will begin to germinate while still attached to the flower stalk. Most aquarists exploit this fact to propagate these highly desirable plants, which do not reproduce asexually by runners in the manner of *Vallisneria.*

Compared to the preceding two genera, the remaining crown plants are slow growing, but compensate for this by tolerating more subdued lighting.

They do well under a screen of floating plants, which makes them ideal for use with the light shy Neotropical and West African dwarf cichlids. The large Asian genus *Cryptocoryne* comprises species that range from dwarfs rarely exceeding 2" in height to robust species reminiscent of the middle-sized swordplants in appearance [Figures 113 & 114]. Not all species do well under eutrophic conditions, but most of those generally available adapt satisfactorily to such environments. Their major shortcoming is a tendency to loose all their leaves when transplanted into a new environment.

The temptation to discard such unprepossessing specimens should be resisted. They will eventually grow back their foliage.

When pleased with their surroundings, *Cryptocoryne* propagate asexually by crown division and runners, eventually producing dense thickets whose shelter is relished by such timid cichlids as *Cleithracara maronii* (STEINDACHNER 1882) or *Dicrossus filamentosus* (LADIGES 1959).

Fig. 111 & 112: Both the Amazon swortplant, *Echinodorus bleheri* (left), and the ruffled swortplant, *E. major* (right), are excellent choices for the cichlid aquarium.

Fig. 113 & 114: *Cryptocoryne ciliata* (left) and *C. undulatum* (right) illustrate the diversity of habit and foilage type characteristic of this large genus. Their ability to grow in dim light makes crypts good choices for the dwarf cichlid aquarium.

Fig. 115 & 116: The West African *Anubias udulatus* (left) and *A. nana* (right) are ideal plants for the cichlid aquarium. Their rather slow growth is their only real disadvantage.

89

Fig. 117 & 118: Both *Microsorium pteropus (left) and Bolbitis heudelotii* (right) are true ferns. Their ability to cling to solid surfaces such as driftwood makes them extremely useful in aquascaping a cichlid aquarium.

They sometimes flower when grown submerged, but this is more likely to occur when they are grown emerged in a terrarium.

The numerous African *Anubias* species are also excellent plants for the cichlid aquarium. The genus comprises both dwarf and tall-growing forms [Figures 115 & 116], though it cannot match *Cryptocoryne* in diversity of foliage types.

Though slow growers, *Anubias* are extremely tough leafed plants that can be housed safely even with casually herbivorous cichlids.

The same is true of two aquatic ferns, *Microsorium pteropus,* the Java or sword fern [Figure 117], and *Bolbitis heudelotii,* the African water fern [Figure 118]. Their leaves are not notably tough, but they do seem highly distasteful to plant eating fishes.

These ferns should not be planted in the substratum. Offer them instead a solid surface for the attachment of their roots.

Waterlogged driftwood is an excellent choice.

Unfortunately, both species grow slowly, which complicates commercial propagation. Hence, it is not as easy to find a source of these water ferns as for other aquatic plants.

Retail dealers often stock bare-root specimens of such house plants as *Aglaonema* (Chinese Evergreen), *Spathiphyllum* (Panama Crypt), *Dieffenbachia* (Mother-in-Law Plant), *Croton* and *Dracaena.*

Their use in the cichlid aquarium is recommended on the grounds that their tough leaves render them immune to the attentions of its inhabitants.

This is true enough, but it must be remembered that these are not true aquatic plants.

They are incapable of taking root and growing in the aquarium, where their ultimate fate is to decompose slowly, polluting the water as they do so.

Such substantial sources of decaying organic matter simply introduce an additional complicating factor in the proper management of the nitrogen cycle, a task which the cichlids render sufficiently challenging unaided!

They are thus best omitted from the furnishings of a cichlid aquarium.

It advisable to maintain a layer of floating plants in cichlid tanks. Cichlids are easily frightened by overhead movement.

A floating screen of plants largely eliminates this source of stress. Furthermore, a healthy growth of floating plants serves to minimize algal growth, always a problem in cichlid tanks.

Floating plants compete with algae for available nutrients. This aspect of their biology also facilitates management of the nitrogen cycle. They also screen out the light necessary to fuel algal proliferation.

Of the generally available floating plants, *Azolla* and *Salvinia* require stronger light to prosper than is generally available under aquarium conditions. *Riccia* is devoured so enthusiastically by many cichlids that it is best regarded as a source of supplementary vegetable food than a viable alternative to providing surface cover.

Common duckweed, *Lemna minor,* floating fern, *Ceratopteris thalictroides,* and hornwort, *Ceratophylum submersum,* are the usual choices available to the cichlid keeper.

Hornwort provides a rather open screen, allowing enough light penetration to support growth of such rooted plants as *Vallisneria.*

Floating fern and duckweed can form mats that shade out any rooted plants beneath them.

These differences should be taken into account when selecting a floating cover.

Hornwort and floating fern are distasteful to fishes. Even markedly herbivorous cichlids have to be very hungry to consider eating them.

Floating fern tolerates salinities of up to 10 % that of sea water as well as a wide range of pH and hardness values.

All floating plants require periodic thinning out. This aside, their maintenance poses few problems.

Duckweed is a partial exception to this rule. It frequently proliferates so rapidly that it becomes a nuisance, clogging filters and interfering with aeration.

It is a mercy that duckweed is enthusiastically eaten by many herbivorous fishes.

It can be fed fresh or frozen for subsequent use as a valuable dietary supplement.

Infrastructure for the Cichlid Aquarium

The importance of providing cichlids with adequate shelter has already been noted.

The tolerance of some species for rooted plants notwithstanding, many desirable cichlids do behave destructively towards aquatic vegetation.

Thus the cichlid enthusiast must rely extensively upon the basic infrastructure of aquascaping when furnishing his tanks.

Rockwork and driftwood spring immediately to mind because of their aesthetic qualities.

However, from a strictly functional standpoint, a wide range of man-made objects are equally useful in providing cichlids with necessary living space.

Many of these artifacts also enjoy some decorative value.

The aquarist can thus exploit a wide range of possibilities when furnishing the cichlid aquarium.The choice of furnishings is largely influenced by the purpose of the aquarium in question.

The aquascaping of a display aquarium aims at providing a visually pleasing setting for its inhabitants. This objective is generally realized most successfully by the use of natural materials.

In aquaria intended for a strictly functional role, such considerations as ease of maintenance and cost often dictate use of man-made objects to provide shelter or spawning sites. Overall, cichlids seem quite indifferent about how their quarters are decorated as long as the furnishings are functionally serviceable.

The aquarist can thus allow his approach to aquascaping be dictated by his circumstances.

Rockwork

Rockwork is more extensively used in decorating cichlid aquaria than any other material.

It is generally available, relatively inexpensive and offers a wide range of sizes, colors, shapes and textures.

It is also bulky and, with few exceptions, very heavy.

It is thus a poor choice to furnish a tank from which fish must be regularly caught, an operation that invariably requires manipulation or removal of its infrastructure.

Nor are all rocks safe for use in aquaria. Some contain soluble minerals that can release toxic substances into the water.

It is therefore advisable to be very conservative about introducing unfamiliar rocks into any aquarium. When in doubt, leave it out!

Granite, feldspar, basalt and quartz can be safely used in a cichlid tank. They are attractive but very heavy.

Slab sandstone and shale are particularly useful in constructing the overhangs and caves that are an essential feature of any cichlid tank, though the former may eventually crumble over long exposure to water.

Pumice rock is extremely desirable because its sponge-like structure makes it easily worked.

It can be cut or chipped readily into a wide range of shapes as well as drilled using a concrete bit.

The aquarist can thus place caves wherever he wills in a large boulder. Finally, it is extremely light.

This facilitates the construction of elaborate structures with minimum risk of disaster should they collapse.

The availability and price of these rocks vary dramatically from one part of the country to the next, depending upon the local abundance of the species in question. Rockwork is most inexpensively purchased from building supply or landscaping firms, whose selection is also broader than that available in retail aquarium shops.

Fig. 120: The Rio Ciruella, a typical stream on the Pacific slope of Costa Rica. Reproducing this cichlid habitat in the home aquarium would be quite simple. Whether the end result would prove aesthetically satisfying is quite another matter!

Stored outside, rockwork can become heavily encrusted with soil and organic material.

Rocks intended for aquarium use should thus be thoroughly hosed down with a high pressure water stream before being placed in the tank. If rocks are encrusted with algae, an overnight soak in a 15% solution of chlorine bleach followed by a brisk scrub with a stiff brush is recommended before introducing them to an aquarium. Novice cichlid keepers often try to recreate as faithfully as possible the natural surroundings of their fish.

As a rule, attempt to replicate cichlid biotopes in captivity are foiled by the scale with which nature disposes of available materials [Figure 119]. A typical talus slope in Lake Malawi comprises individual boulders that range from watermelon to small automobile in size. Other rocky biotopes can be duplicated in an aquarium, but are unlikely to win resounding approval on aesthetic grounds.

The lower reaches of many large Central American rivers are characterized by channels bestrewn with rounded rocks of apple to cantaloupe size interspersed with patches of coarse gravel.

The local cichlids find such environment much to their liking, but it is doubtful many

Fig. 119: A typical rocky biotope in Lake Malawi, Note the size of its constituent rocks.

aquarists would concur in this judgment! [Figure 120]

The aquarist should aim at producing an environment that satisfies the basic needs of his fish in a visually satisfying manner [Figure 121]. Rockwork should be arranged to provide a series of caves or overhangs along the sides and rear of the tank while leaving the center as a common swimming space for its inhabitants.

In tanks housing biparentally custodial substratum-spawning cichlids, it is wise to arrange rockwork so that the bottom area is broken up into several discrete, easily defended territories, each centered on a potential spawning site.

In tanks intended for the strongly **petricolous**, or rock-loving cichlids of either Lake Tanganyika or Lake Malawi, it is advisable to run the rockwork almost to the surface of the water along at least one side of the tank. Such an arrangement is both visually pleasing and highly functional, for it multiplies the number of refuges available to fry or subordinate adults.

I cannot overemphasize the importance of basing such structures on secure foundations. Because cichlids are proficient diggers, it is only a matter of time before rockwork erected upon the surface of a particulate substratum is undermined and collapses.

Over and above any risk such a collapse poses to its author, disastrous consequences can follow if any of the falling rocks crack the sides or bottom of the aquarium.

The foundations of all rockwork in a cichlid aquarium MUST rest securely upon a solid surface!

Unless he has opted for the elevated slab bottom previously mentioned, the aquarist should emplace the infrastructure of the tank **prior** to adding gravel.

Wood

Waterlogged wood is widely used to decorate the cichlid aquarium.

This material is ubiquitous in tropical riverine habitats, so it is hardly surprising that many cichlids utilize it for cover.

The deeper-bodied species of the *Heros* lineage, *Uaru amphiacanthoides* and the several *Pterophyllum* and *Symphysodon* species seem particularly at ease housed in a tank so furnished. Branches can be suspended from the rim of a tank to hang downwards into the water, in imitation of the submerged brush piles beloved of many cichlids.

Fig. 121: An attractive example of an aquarium designed to house Tanganyikan rock-dwelling cichlids.

Large stumps may be employed in the same manner as rockwork.

It is even easier to drill a system of holes and tunnels into a piece of wood than it is to work a piece of pumice rock, and the final result is just as satisfying from the standpoint of its ultimate users.

Driftwood has some serious disadvantages, however. First is the rather limited availability of larger pieces, which goes far to explain the stiff prices they command even in the Pacific-Northwest and the Great Lakes region, where driftwood can usually be collected in quantity. Second, wood requires careful preparation before it can be used in an aquarium. Its superficial layers can absorb any toxic chemicals to which it has been exposed during its immersion.

The first step in preparing a piece of driftwood for aquarium use thus entails sanding away these superficial layers.

This has customarily been done to driftwood intended for aquarium use, but such treatment is not always given to wood sold for landscaping or interior decorating purposes. It is obviously a necessary preliminary in preparing any pieces the aquarist might have collected himself.

Finally, dry driftwood floats. Smaller pieces are often sold bolted to a piece of slate. These can be added directly to the tank.

However, this approach does not guarantee success when applied to larger chunks, for the weight of the slate is seldom sufficient to cancel out the wood's inherent buoyancy! It may be possible to hold such pieces underwater by placing rocks on the corners of the slate, but even this alternative is impractical if the piece of wood has not been so modified. In most instances, driftwood must be waterlogged before it can be used in a tank.

This is a slow process, the interval required depending upon the volume and geometry of the piece in question. Solid chunks, for example, absorb water more slowly than slender branches.

Routing out as extensive a series of cavities and tunnels from larger pieces as possible speeds the process up to a degree.

However, it is still unusual to saturate a large piece of driftwood in less than six months.

To accomplish this, immerse the wood in a large plastic trash can and let nature take its course. It may be necessary to hold the wood down with large stones to keep the piece entirely submerged. Change the water in the curing container several times during this process.

Some woods, such as cypress and oak contain large concentrations of tannins and lignins that can leach out and give the water a peaty color. This is harmless to most fish, but can be unsightly.

Water changes accelerate the leaching process, which reduces the likelihood that the cured driftwood will discolor the water in the tank to which it will eventually be added.

Should it prove necessary to remove the wood from the water for any length of time, it must not be allowed to dry out.

Otherwise, the soaking process will have to be repeated.

Between uses, waterlogged wood should be sealed in a large plastic trash bag and kept therein until needed again.

Decoratively shaped pieces of several very dense tropical woods are readily available through commercial channels.

Sold under such trade names as "Asian ironwood" or "Mopani wood", this material is heavier than water and hence does not require the pre-use soaking recommended for other types of wood.

All of these woods have a very high tannin-lignin content.

It is therefore prudent to bleach larger pieces thoroughly before introducing them into an aquarium. Otherwise, untreated pieces will severely stain aquarium water and in areas where with very soft tapwater, depress the tank pH significantly. An overnight soak in a 10 % solution of laundry bleach repeated several times will effectively forestall this problem.

Artificial Shelters

Where aesthetic considerations are not paramount, man-made objects can be used to provide necessary shelter for cichlids [Figure 122]. Plastic plants and plastic simulacra of driftwood are both functional and attractive enough to use in display as well as working aquaria.

However, neither clay flowerpots, sectioned CPVC pipe, cinder block nor slate strips are likely to be chosen as tank furnishings for their visual appeal.

These materials are most commonly employed as artificial shelters in cichlid aquaria.

Cinder block is chiefly used to furnish the quarters of very large cichlids. It provides modular caves beyond even the ability of these highly persistent environmental manipulators to push around.

Slate strips or sheets provide easily removed vertical spawning surfaces for species with a preference for such breeding sites.

Clay flowerpots and plastic pipe are the most generally favored artificial shelters, however. Available in a wide range of lengths and diameters, they are capable of comfortably accommodating cichlids of any size. They can be modified with minimal effort using simple tools.

An essentially modular character allows their use in either small or large tanks with equal success. They are lightweight, and hence easily manipulated. Finally, and perhaps most important, cichlids accept them readily.

There is little to choose between the two as shelters. However, cichlid eggs adhere more readily to the rather rough surface of clay pots, which gives them the advantage as spawning sites.

Plastic pipe is more costly than are clay pots, but its greater durability somewhat compensates for this.

Bear in mind whatever the materials used to furnish a cichlid tank, it is essential to provide shelter in abundance.

The presence or absence of sufficient cover has a significant effect upon the level of aggression manifested by its inhabitants.

Fig. 122: The functional approach to furnishing a tank for large cichlids. Male *Nandopsis motaquensis* sheltering in ceramic pipe.

Choosing Other Residents for the Cichlid Aquarium

As noted in Chapter 2, most cichlids can be successfully maintained in a community setting. A visit to a public aquarium provides ample testimony of the ease with which cichlids can be incorporated into a display of other fishes.

However, such displays also confirm the importance of adequate living space and careful selection of companions in achieving such an effect.

Little more need be said on the subject of suitable quarters, but it is worth considering the question of suitable companions in greater detail.

An obvious reason for housing cichlids with other fishes is aesthetic. The coloration, habitat preferences and behavior of many fishes complement those of cichlids in a manner many find pleasing.

For the present, however, there is merit in a more explicitly functional approach to this matter.

Other residents of a cichlid tank can be regarded as **dither fish**, as **target fish** or as **scavengers**.

These categories are not mutually exclusive, notwithstanding that from the aquarist's viewpoint, a given addition to a cichlid tank may be chosen to perform one primary function.

Dither Fish

Dither fish are active, midwater-dwelling species used to overcome the tendency of many cichlids to hide in captivity. They generate the behavioral equivalent of white noise by providing a sense of reassurance for such retiring subjects as dwarf cichlids, angelfish and discus. Schooling fishes are ideal for this purpose. They derive a sense of reassurance primarily from their numbers.

Hence they swim freely about, indifferent to such environmental factors as level of illumination, human activity in the vicinity of the aquarium or the presence or absence of shelter.

Fig. 123: *Leporinus fasciatus* feeds in large measure upon the scales and fins of other fishes. It is thus a poor choice of dither fish for a tankful of cichlids.

Fig. 124: *Danio malabaricus* is too large and active to make suitable dither for dwarf cichlids, although there is no objection to using it with mid-sized cichlids such as the various acaras.

Fig. 125: Small schooling cyprinids such as *Brachydanio frankei* make excellent dither fish for riverine dwarf cichlids.

Cichlids use the behavior of such fishes as an indicator of potential danger and respond to their high activity level by coming out of hiding and engaging in the full range of their species-typical behavior. A wide selection of fishes can be used as dither in a cichlid tank. Obviously, they must be too large to make a convenient mouthful. It is equally important that dither fish be neither given to fin-nipping nor themselves behave in so boisterous a fashion that they either intimidate the cichlids with which they are housed or outcompete them at feeding time.

The former caveat excludes a number of characoid fishes from consideration.

The several *Leporinus, Anostomus* and *Roeboides* species feed upon the fins and scales of other fishes [Figure 123]. They are thus unsuited for use as dither with cichlids regardless of size.

The numerous *Astyanax* species and the larger representatives of the genera *Hemigrammus* and *Moenkhausia* are too boisterous for use with dwarf cichlids, though they make excellent dither for medium-sized representatives of the family.

The same qualifications apply to cyprinids of the genera *Danio* [Figure 124], *Raiamas* and *Hampala*, as well as to the larger *Barbus* species.

Poeciliids and melanotaeniids make good dither fish also.

However, the former may proliferate embarrassingly if the cichlids with which they are housed are too inept as predators to make serious inroads on the number of young dropped monthly.

Suitable dither fish must be able to prosper under the same environmental conditions as the cichlids whose tanks they share.

Characoids and cyprinids [Figure 125] provide the best dither for cichlids that prefer soft, acid to neutral water conditions, while livebearers and Australasian rainbowfishes [Figures 126 & 127] are good choices for species that require hard, alkaline water.

Representatives of the Family Goodeidae also do well in hard alkaline water, but many species of these Mexican livebearers are simply too aggressive to be kept with small to medium-sized cichlids [Figure 128].

Finally, remember that their beneficial effects on cichlid behavior depend upon the expression of **normal schooling behavior** by the dither fish.

It is thus essential to introduce sufficient individuals to elicit such behavior.

Half a dozen specimens appears the minimum number necessary to evoke normal schooling behavior in most of these species.

Fig. 126

Fig. 126 & 127:
Poeciliids such as the
merry widow, *Phallich-
thys amates* (above),
and Australasian rain-
bowfishes, such as
*Melanotaenia macculo-
chi* (left), make excel-
lent dither fish for Tan-
ganyikan dwarf cich-
lids, for they also pros-
per in hard, alkaline
water.

Fig. 127

Fig. 128: Although hardy and colorful, such
goodeids as *Xenotoca eiseni* are so aggressive
as to function as "anti-dither" for most small
Tanganyikan cichlids.

99

Target Fish

As their name implies, **target fish** provide a focus for the aggression associated with reproduction in biparentally custodial cichlids [Figure 129]. Essentially, all the tankmates of a pair of reproductively active cichlids function as target fish, more or less in despite of any specific intent on the part of their keeper to so employ them. This largely explains the family's lurid reputation for thuggery in captivity.

The use of target fish to promote pair formation and/or normal parental behavior will be considered at greater length as an adjunct to the breeding of biparentally custodial cichlids.

Suffice for the moment to note other cichlids are more likely to survive such an experience with minimal damage than the generality of aquarium fishes. This is due to the fact that given sufficient maneuvering room, they can usually be counted upon to give as good as they get in their aggressive interactions with the incipient breeding pair.

The intensity of such interactions can be considerably moderated if care is taken in selecting which cichlids will share quarters.

When one speaks of a compatible community, this is often assumed to mean one comprising cichlids that occur together in nature.

Though much may be said for this approach to keeping cichlids from both the practical and the aesthetic viewpoints, such an interpretation of compatibility is needlessly restrictive.

More critical is selection of species with comparable levels of aggressiveness and whose signalling systems are sufficiently similar to minimize likelihood of fighting due to failure of communication.

As a rule, species with the same mating system and mode of parental care have less difficulty communicating their behavioral state to one another than do those that differ in these regards.

Presumably such similarities reflect common selection pressures associated with a given reproductive pattern. It is otherwise difficult to explain the degree of overlap in the signal repertories of cichlids such as the West African jewel fish, *Hemichromis paynei* LOISELLE 1979 [Figure 130] and the Central American

Fig. 129: Many large characoids, like the silver dollars of the genus *Mylosoma*, make good target fish for such medium-sized cichlids as the acaras and smaller species of the *Heros* lineage. In a large tank, their superior speed and maneuverability preserves them from serious danger.

Nandopsis salvini GUNTHER 1864 [Figure 131], who last shared a common ancestor prior to the separation of South America and Africa at the beginning of the Cretaceous epoch.

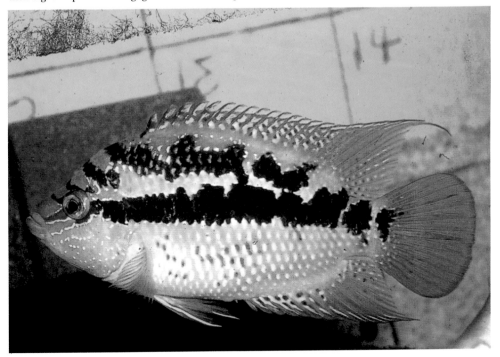

Fig. 130 & 131: Though only distantly related, such West African jewel fishes as these *Hemichromis paynei* (Fig. 130: above) and the Middle American *Nandopsis salvini* (Fig. 131: down) share sufficient elements of their signal repetoire to engage in effective interspecific comunication.

Scavengers

Scavangers can be defined as any organisms whose activities either reduce the risk of anaerobic decay of organic matter in an aquarium's substratum or help control algal growth upon its sides, bottom and furnishings.

These tasks are usually assigned to catfishes and snails, with loaches of the Family Cobitidae and the large cyprinids referred to colloquially as "sharks" sometimes coming in for consideration as well.

Unfortunately, the behavior of cichlids towards such bottom-dwelling animals places serious constraints upon the choice of scavengers.

It must be offered in their defense that many traditional scavengers compete with cichlids for available shelter and all represent a serious threat to the eggs and fry of substratum spawning species. Their well developed chemosensory abilities allow catfishes to forage efficiently at night, when darkness totally incapacitates parental cichlids.

The cichlid response to this threat is an effort to banish any and all catfish from their breeding territory **before** spawning and to keep them as far away as possible afterwards.

In the confines of an aquarium, catfish and other scavengers cannot always move beyond the reach of the irate cichlids, which often leads to unpleasant consequences.

With the exception of the African mochokid catfishes of the genus *Synodontis*, smooth-skinned catfishes are not recommended for the cichlid aquarium.

The smaller representatives of the Families Bagridae, Pimelodidae, Auchenipteridae and Ageniosidae come in for serious harassment and may well be killed.

The larger representatives of these essentially predatory groups, on the other hand, eventually grow large enough to pose a threat to the cichlids! [Figure 132] Other smooth-skinned catfish families pursue lifestyles that make them useless as scavengers (Amphiliidae, Schilbeidae, Trichomycteridae, Malapteruridae

Fig. 132: The red-tailed catfish, *Phractocephalus hemioliopterus*, grows large enough to prey on the most robust cichlids in nature.

Fig. 133: Upsidedown catfish of the genus Synodontis, such as *S. flavitaeniatus* are the only smooth-skinned siluroids that function as effective scavengers in the cichlid aquarium.

and Chacidae). *Synodontis* combine a tough skin, formidable fin spines and teeth and a decidedly Mosaic commitment to repaying transgressions against their persons in kind [Figure 133]. Cichlids quickly discover that it does not pay to harass them.

For their part, the catfish seem to learn from experience it does not pay to intrude upon a pair of reproductively active cichlids.

Thus, a state of armed truce prevails so long as the aquarium affords sufficient shelter for both parties. *Synodontis* are moderately efficient scavengers when properly motivated, *i. e.,* when hungry. This is seldom enough in captivity, as these catfish are almost as skilled

in training their keepers to feed them on demand as cichlids are!

Of the armored catfishes, the Family *Callichthyidae*, whose best known representatives are the droll little *Corydoras* catfishes, are too easily bullied and killed to make suitable scavengers in most cichlid tanks [Figure 134].

Even dwarf cichlids such as *Nannacara anomala* REGAN 1905 can eliminate these inoffensive little catfish by biting off their barbels and plucking out their eyes.

The banjo catfishes of the Family Bunocephalidae are equally vulnerable.

The spiny armored catfishes of the Family Doradidae are effectively cichlid-proof, but

Fig. 134: The popular armored catfishes of the genus Corydoras, such as these *C. arcuatus*, are too small and inoffensive to survive in most cichlid aquaria.

Fig. 135: The larger loricariid carfishes, such as this unidentified *Hypostomus* serve a useful role as scavengers in the cichlid aquarium. Their heavy armor renders them impervious to attack by even very large cichlids.

like the banjo catfishes, their usefulness as scavengers is minimal.

The more robust armored suckermouth catfishes of the Family Loricariidae, on the other hand, make excellent additions to the cichlid aquarium [Figure 135]. They do a reasonable job of keeping algae under control, no mean feat given the eutrophic conditions that cichlids so effortlessly produce in their quarters, and have little difficulty holding their own in the process. This is largely because they are so thoroughly armored as to be proof against anything short of a depth charge attack, in part to the fact that most species share the *Synodontis* approach to cichlid bullying.

No cichlid once chased by a large *Panaque* or *Hypostomus* seems inclined to provoke a repeat performance! Like their distant African relatives, these South American catfishes insist on access to individual shelters. If this requirement is met, they too will coexist satisfactorily with a tankful of cichlids.

Loaches represent a mixed bag from the standpoint of suitability for a cichlid tank. The genera *Acanthopthalmus*, *Misgurnus* and *Nemacheilus* usually fare poorly in such an environment.

The loaches of the genus *Botia*, on the other hand, do quite nicely when housed with cichlids of the same general size [Figure 136]. They have a rather *Synodontis*-like attitude towards life, while their well-developed retractable subocular spines allow them to effectively indulge it under most circumstances. They also insist upon access to suitable shelter and will fight ferociously in its defense.

The horsefaced loach, *Acanthopsis choirorhynchus*, does exceedingly well in any cichlid tank with sufficient depth of gravel to allow it to burrow [Figure 137]. As its generic name implies, this species too is equipped with a pair of subocular switchblades, but rarely has to use them its defense.

Even large predatory cichlids give up on the horse-faced loach after having their target literally vanish beneath the gravel before they are close enough to do any damage.

Both of these loach genera do an excellent job of keeping the gravel stirred up, earning their place far better than most catfishes.

The "sharks" of the genera *Balantocheilus*, *Labeo*, *Epalzeorhynchus* and *Morulius*, on the other hand, cannot match the efficiency of loricariid catfishes in the control of algae.

Fig. 136: The larger *Botia* species, such as this clown loach, *B. macarantha*, have little difficulty holding their own in the cichlid aquarium.

They can be expected to battle constantly with the resident cichlids over access to shelter and foraging space [Figure 138]. There is something to be said for their use as target fish for some of the larger, more bellicose cichlids, but they do not earn their keep as scavengers.

The only snail that can maintain its numbers in the company of most adult cichlids is the Malaysian livebearing snail, *Melanoides tuberculata* [Figure 139].

The burrowing habits and thick shell of this active species afford it a degree of protection even against the attentions of such specialized snail eaters as the red devil, *Heros labiatus* GUNTHER 1864 and *Tilapia buttikoferi*.

Very small individuals are sometimes swallowed whole by large cichlids, but *M. tuberculata* is sufficiently prolific to maintain itself in the face of such episodic predation.

This is fortunate, as a thriving colony of these snails is the best possible guarantee against pockets of anaerobic decomposition developing in the gravel. Like most snails, this species is extremely prolific and in the absence

Fig. 137: The horsefaced loach, *Acanthopsis choirorhynchus*, is another good scavenger for the cichlid aquarium.

Fig. 138: The red-tailed shark, *Epalzeorhynchus bicolor,* is an inefficient scavenger. Its strongly territorial behavior almost guarantees conflict with cichlids over available shelters if they are housed together.

of effective predation, its population can quickly increase to nuisance levels.

Fortunately, it is an easy matter to trap large numbers by placing a few food tablets in a glass bottle and leaving the baited receptacle in place over night.

Other kinds of snails are useful scavengers in fry rearing tanks until such time as the young cichlids grow large enough to begin picking them off.

The reader should now have some idea of what to expect from cichlids under aquarium conditions.

He should have a clear notion of what they require by way of living space and life support equipment as well as an appreciation of workable approaches to aquascaping the cichlid aquarium.

Certain facets of their behavior must be taken as they come, but if prudence is exercised in selecting tank furnishings and companions, it is possible to maintain cichlids successfully in an aesthetically pleasing community environment. The novice cichlid fancier must next confront the challenge of keeping a tankful of cichlids in good health.

The next chapter will address itself to the task of maintaining the cichlid aquarium.

Fig. 139: The constant activity of *Melanoides tuberculata* serves to aerate the substratum of a cichlid aquarium.

CHAPTER 5

MAINTAINING THE CICHLID AQUARIUM

Introduction

The preceding chapters considered the particular needs of cichlids as aquarium residents and made specific recommendations about the equipment necessary to meet them satisfactorily. As noted in the Introduction, this book assumes its readers to have a working knowledge of freshwater aquarium keeping, hence its scanty treatment of the mechanics of setting up a cichlid tank.

Readers without such a practical background should refer to Tetra's **Digest for the Successful Aquarium** before proceeding any further in that direction.

Cichlid maintenance has much in common with that of any established aquarium.

Appliances should be checked regularly for proper functioning, water losses from evaporation replaced and the front glass kept free of algae in the cichlid aquarium as in any other.

However, the family's biological peculiarities facilitate the aquarist's task of keeping them in good health in certain respects while complicating it in others; hence, the need to emphasize specific aspects of good technique when considering a maintenance program for the cichlid aquarium. Be it noted that in comparison with many other ornamental fishes, cichlids are very hardy aquarium residents.

However, they do make certain demands upon their keeper which he must understand **before** he undertakes to work with them.

This chapter addresses those demands as well as ways of meeting them successfully.

Feeding Cichlids

Healthy cichlids have healthy appetites.

In fact, a cichlid's general condition is so faithfully mirrored in its appetite that sudden refusal to eat in any context save that of paren-

tal behavior should be interpreted as a signal of severe stress, as might arise from the initial stages of a systemic bacterial infection or serious deterioration of environmental quality.

The aquarist is thus rarely faced with the problem of inducing cichlids to eat. His concern instead centers on assuring them a nutritionally adequate diet.

Due to revolutionary developments in the area of fish nutrition, this is much easier today than it was a few decades ago.

Contemporary prepared foods supply a balanced, highly palatable diet for cichlids.

Flaked foods are readily taken by cichlids of all sizes [Figure 140], although because of their heavy appetites and rather messy eating habits, larger cichlids are best offered prepared foods in another form.

Pelletized foods, such as Tetra's DoroMin, DoroGreen and DoroRed are ideal for all large cichlids [Figure 141]. Many brands of prepared foods are available commercially. These vary in nutritional value, palatability and in their contribution to the waste load of the tank where they are fed.

There is a widely held but erroneous notion that the only relevant measure of a food's value is its crude protein assay. In fact, few cichlids have a digestive system that allows them to process such high protein formulations as trout pellets efficiently. Furthermore, foods with an elevated protein content can seriously complicate nitrogen cycle management when they are fed as a staple.

Far more important to the well being of most cichlids is the proportion of roughage to protein in the diet. In nature, the food of most cichlids comprises 50% to 85% roughage by weight, yet few food manufacturers take this into account in their formulations.

Presence of the full complement of vitamins and trace elements in the formula is even more important.

Fig. 140: Like most other small to medium-sized cichlids, this female *Hemichromis paynei* (Loiselle 1979) thrives on a diet based upon Tetra Cichlid Food.

Laboratory studies have shown the presence or absence of minute amounts of these substances can have a dramatic effect upon the efficiency with which cichlids utilize available food.

The Tetra line of flake foods combines excellent nutritional characteristics, high palatability and a good selection of special formulations that facilitate meeting the trophic needs of such specialized feeders as the primarily algivorous mbuna of Lake Malawi [Figure 142].

Tetra's DoroMin, DoroGreen and DoroRed are an ideal choice for larger cichlids as they combine high palatability and excellent nutritional value.

Tetra Flake foods and the Doro line of food sticks are available in bulk.

This is an important consideration to cichlid keepers, who must supply high quality food in vast quantity to satisfy the robust appetites of their charges. Most cichlids can be kept in good condition on an exclusive diet of prepared foods and may even spawn freely on such a regime.

However, all do better when regularly offered live and fresh food [Figure 143]. This is particularly true when conditioning fish for breeding.

It is not the superior nutritional value of such foods as much as their superior palatability that makes them so valuable.

The fish eat more because they prefer the taste of these foods. In doing so, they rapidly accumulate the metabolic reserves necessary to mature eggs and undertake species-typical reproductive behavior.

Thus the wise cichlid keeper varies his fishes' diet with such offerings as frequently as their availability and his pocketbook permit.

The choice of live foods is obviously dictated by the size of the cichlid to be fed.

It is futile to offer newly hatched brine shrimp to an adult oscar or feeder goldfish to dwarf cichlids! Knowledge of a given cichlid's feeding pattern in nature simplifies the selection of appropriate live foods in captivity.

Not all cichlids, for example, can manage snails unaided [Figure 144], though most happily nibble at the meat exposed when their shells have been crushed beforehand.

Many excellent live foods are only seasonally available, such as *Daphnia*, or else available only in certain geographical areas, such as glassworms, aquatic larvae of the midge genus *Chaoborus*.

These foods should be utilized whenever available, though it is obviously impractical to rely exclusively upon them when planning a conditioning program. The only live food whose use I do **not** recommend is *Tubifex*.

There is a strong and persistent correlation between regular feeding of these worms and the outbreak of systemic bacterial infections among their consumers [Figure 145]. Conventional wisdom notwithstanding, there is no simple means of ridding these worms of their impressive flora of associated bacteria and thereby rendering them safe as a fish food.

Given the numerous alternatives available, there is no point in exposing valued cichlids to this completely avoidable disease risk.

Fortunately, a number of versatile live foods can be cultured easily and on a year-round basis. One of the most useful is *Artemis salina*, the brine shrimp.

The simply hatched nauplii of this remarkable crustacean are an essential first food for newly mobile cichlids, but they are equally appreciated by adults of dwarf and even many middle-sized cichlids. Grindal worms (*Enchytraeus* sp.) are also appreciated by small to mid-sized cichlids. Though a bit smaller than their near relative, the white worm, they are more easily cultured, for they can better survive the summer in an unrefrigerated environment.

These worms must be offered to small cichlids in moderation.

When fed to excess, they can bring on fatty degeneration of the gonads.

A third easily cultured live food appreciated by most cichlids is the vestigial-winged mutant of *Drosophila melanogaster*, the common fruitfly.

Fig. 141: Very large cichlids such as this *Hoplarchus psittacus* (Heckel 1849) do best on a diet of pelletized food.

Many cichlids feed regularly upon stranded terrestrial insects in nature and find these cultured fruitflies an acceptable addition to their menu.

Finally, newly mobile fry of extremely prolific cichlids such as *Herotilapia multispinosa* are eagerly taken by all cichlids in this size range and easily produced in quantity.

When feeding cichlid fry, take care to utilize them **before** their fin spines harden sufficiently to make them a prickly mouthful, a point usually attained by the fourth week post-spawning for most substratum spawning species. It is easier to accommodate the taste of large cichlids for live food throughout the year, for feeder goldfish and guppies are always available at most retail establishments [Figure 146]. However, there are many robust species that either have little taste for small fish or else are pathetically inept at capturing them even in the restricted space of an aquarium [Figure 147]. These cichlids eagerly take both dwarf red earthworms and mealworms, actually the larvae of a tenebrionid beetle.

These foods can also be fed to smaller cichlids, though many aquarists find the necessary maceration involved in the process too disagreeable to so employ them. Even strongly piscivorous cichlids will eat such invertebrate foods readily.

Indeed, the keeper of such gluttons often finds the main advantage to raising these highly nutritious foods is primarily economic!

Indoor culture of dwarf red earthworms requires a basement or garage corner, but mealworms can be cultured in quantity in a few square feet of closet shelf space. This is not the place to recount in detail the culture methods required to produce these foods. Interested readers are referred to pertinent references cited in the recommended reading list following the Index.

Most cichlids relish fresh frozen almost as much as they do live foods. Regrettably, not all live foods respond equally well to freezing.

Brine shrimp and *Daphnia* undergo exoskeletal bursting during freezing. This greatly reduces their nutritional value when subsequently thawed. Both chrinonomid larvae (bloodworms) and glassworms withstand freezing well, as do the mysid shrimp and krill sold as food for marine fishes.

All are relished by cichlids, though not all species possess the jaw capacity to handle the last two easily.

Seafood intended for human consumption is also appreciated by cichlids.

Frozen lean white-fleshed fish, shrimp, crab, clams and scallops, finely shaved with a

Fig. 142: The *mbuna* of Lake Malawi require a stable diet rich in vegetable matter and high in roughage. Many species, like this male red morph *Labeotorpheus fuelleborni* Ahl 1927 also require continuous access to pigment precursor substances to maintain the full intensity of their coloration in captivity.

hand-held grater or in a food processor, are a nutritious addition to the diet of captive cichlids.

Beef heart is often suggested as a protein source in cichlid diets. There is disagreement over its suitability as a staple food, particularly for markedly herbivorous cichlids [Figure 148]. If care is taken to trim away **all** indigestible fat and circulatory tissue from the heart muscle before feeding, there seems no reason not to offer it as an occasional dietary supplement.

Failure to trim the meat carefully introduces the risk that a piece of indigestible tissue

will cause a potentially fatal intestinal blockage in one of its consumers.

Many cichlids require fresh vegetable food to maintain the full intensity of their coloration as well as for their general well being. This requirement is easily met, for a wide range of such foods is readily available.

As previously noted, duckweed, either fresh or frozen, is relished by many cichlids.

Bunch plants such as *Anacharis* are viewed with favor by herbivorous cichlids, a fact novice cichlid keepers often discover the hard way! So are most leaf vegetables grown for human consumption.

Fig. 143: Dwarf cichlids, like this pair of *Nanochromis minor*, spawn more frequently when their diet contains substantial amounts of live food.

Romaine or other leaf lettuce varieties and spinach are particular favorites.

Many cichlids are quite fond of cooked green peas, though their high starch content dictates that they be fed sparingly.

Thinly sliced young zucchini or other marrow squashes are a superb food.

Many cichlids greedily devour the immature seeds as well as the pulp and skin [Figure 149]. These foods should be blanched by brief contact with boiling water, or frozen, then thawed before being offered to the fish.

Many herbivorous cichlids are uneasy about feeding near the surface. Hence it is best to fasten blanched vegetables to a small rock with a rubber band and let it sink to the bottom with its edible burden. There the fish can feed at their leisure.

Bear in mind it may take cichlids a while to learn to eat an unfamiliar food. Feed only small quantities of these vegetables until the fish develop a taste for them. It is easy to succumb to temptation and overfeed cichlids.

Keep in mind that the frantic posturings of a group of cichlids are not symptoms of incipient starvation.

These are intelligent fishes.

They come to associate the appearance of their keeper with that of food and swiftly learn that certain behavior is predictably followed by the introduction of something edible into their tank [Figure 150]. Large cichlids should be fed twice daily.

Mid-sized and dwarf species appreciate three or four small feedings daily but can make do with two.

The tried and tested rule that fish should be fed **no more than they can consume in five minutes** applies quite well to cichlids.

Adherence to these guidelines may not always be easy, given the persistent and persuasive begging of a tankful of cichlids, but it greatly simplifies nitrogen cycle management therein.

One sometimes hears of large cichlids becoming extremely picky about their diet.

Fig. 144: Like most mollusc-eaters, *Tilapia buttikoferi* boasts a powerful pharyngeal mill that makes short work of snail shells.

Fig. 145: Though dwarf cichlids like this female *Apistogramma borellii* are very fond of Tubifex worms, their regular use as fish food poses a serious risk of systemic bacterial infection to their consumers.

Fig 146: Juveniles of such specialized piscivorous species as *Cichla temensis* require regular feedings of smaller live fishes to grow at their optimum rate in captivity.

113

Fig. 147: Though it grows to a large size, the chocolate cichlid, *Hypselacara temporalis* Gunther 1862 is not an accomplished piscivore, preferring earthworms and mealworms to feeder goldfish in captivity.

The oscar that eats only feeder goldfish of a certain color is the classic example of such behavior.

These reports attest more cogently to the trainability of some aquarists than they do to any tendency towards dietary specialization by their fish.

These fish have learned their keepers can be conditioned to provide a specific food if they refuse to eat other items offered them. This is the piscine equivalent of a child threatening to hold its breath until the adults around him give in to his demands.

Altering such behavior requires a certain resolution on the aquarist's part but otherwise is easily accomplished.

It entails nothing more than raising the tank temperature by four or five degrees Fahrenheit and not feeding its inhabitants for a few days.

Appetite, as the saying goes, makes the best sauce.

Managing the Nitrogen Cycle in the Cichlid Aquarium

Keeping dissolved metabolic wastes at a safe level dominates the maintenance routine for a cichlid aquarium.

It is not that cichlids are any more susceptible to nitrite and ammonia poisoning than other fish.

Indeed, sensitivity to such intoxication varies sharply within the family.

Species endemic to the African Great Lakes, for instance, display less tolerance for these substances than many of their counterparts from riverine environments characterized by dramatic seasonal changes in water quality.

It is simply that cichlids fall at the large end of the size distribution for ornamental fishes, hence, their waste output is also higher than that of smaller species.

This results in a much faster buildup of toxic substances in their tanks.

Unless ongoing measures to prevent this are implemented, the inevitable result is the loss of prized fish. This can be the direct result of nitrite poisoning.

More commonly, such losses are due to bacterial infections that result from the erosion of normal resistance to these pathogens caused by prolonged exposure to sublethal but stressful metabolite levels. The ability to measure dissolved metabolite concentrations in the aquarium is essential to successfully managing the nitrogen cycle.

Simple to use, accurate commercial test kits for dissolved ammonia (NH_3), nitrite (NO_{2-}) and nitrate (NO_{3-}) are available at reasonable prices. Though nitrite is the chief offender in freshwater aquaria, it is useful be able to test for all these substances.

As noted earlier, it takes time for a biological filter to attain full operating capacity.

This process is characterized by peaking of each metabolite in turn, followed by stable low nitrate readings and the virtual disappearance of the other two chemical species.

With experience, aquarists develop some sense of the time involved in filter bed maturation.

It is easier to develop such an appreciation if these changes in concentration are initially followed in a quantitative manner.

The ability to test for dissolved ammonia is also essential when treating water to eliminate chloramines, a point to which I will subsequently return.

Always test for dissolved ammonia and nitrite whenever fish display respiratory distress, following the onset of obvious disease symptoms or after the loss of a specimen.

Such events often signal a breakdown of the normal operation of the nitrogen cycle.

This can be verified only by testing for these substances.

Finally, spot testing the nitrite level in an aquarium gives the novice cichlid keeper a handle on the effectiveness of his maintenance routine. Eventually he will learn to diagnose the onset of nitrite stress from subtle changes in his fishes' behavior.

However, until he attains such expertise, periodic testing is the essential means of tracing concentrations of this dangerous substance.

Fig. 148: It is unwise to employ beef heart as dietary staple for such specialized herbivorous cichlids as these individuals of the golden rainbow morph of *Tropheus moori*.

Fig. 149: As it feeds extensively upon terrestrial plant seeds in nature, the fondness of *Theraps nicaraguensis* (Gunther 1864) for thinly sliced blanched zucchini in captivity is hardly surprising.

The first step towards an effective maintenance program for the cichlid aquarium entails the selection of an appropriate filtration system.

Hence the considerable space devoted to the subject in Chapter 3.

Given an efficient biological filter, dense planting and extremely low stocking rates, it is possible **in theory** to set up an aquarium that requires no more than twice yearly cleaning of the filter bed to maintain dissolved nitrite concentrations at safe levels. The catch is that not all cichlids can be maintained in this manner. Some are intolerant of plants, while others must be maintained at high densities to keep aggression at acceptable levels.

More to the point, few aquarists will accept the same stocking rates for a cichlid aquarium that allow biological filtration to operate effectively in the marine aquarium. Under these circumstances **no** filtration system can maintain toxic metabolite concentrations at safe levels unaided.

However, a properly chosen system can enormously reduce the amount of supplementary effort necessary to attain this objective. The filter is therefore the most important piece of supporting equipment the cichlid enthusiast will purchase for his tank.

Regardless of the system chosen, no filter will perform effectively unless properly serviced. A regular schedule of filter care is thus essential to a successful maintenance program. Mechanical filters must have their media replaced or purged whenever they become clogged with waste.

The frequency depends upon both the number of fish present and their size.

In a heavily stocked cichlid tank, this can be as often as twice weekly.

Therefore select an easily cleaned filter and employ reusable media such as Eheim's Ehfi-Fix©.

This plastic medium relies upon electrostatic precipitation of particulate waste as well as simple mechanical entrapment.

Fig. 150: Large specimens of the popular oscar, *Astronotus ocellatus* are accomplished beggars that quickly learn to manipulate their keeper to best advantage.

It can be flushed clean in seconds under a strong stream of water and reused *ad libitum*. It is more expensive than that of non-reusable media such as dacron floss. However, the frequency with which floss must be replaced in cichlid tanks quickly equalizes the cost differential.

Cleaning a powered-intake outside filter charged with EhfiFix© requires no more than five minutes.

Replacing a saturated dacron pad or wad of floss takes no longer. There is thus no excuse for neglecting this essential facet of cichlid maintenance.

Undergravel filters also require periodic cleaning. However, this is best carried out in conjunction with water changes and will be considered in that context.

Sponge filters likewise require purging when they become clogged.

Such attention should not be required frequently unless the tank is seriously overstocked.

If it is not possible to thin out its population of fish, either an additional sponge filter or a supplementary mechanical filter should be added to the system.

Dirty sponges are easily cleaned by repeatedly squeezing them under a strong stream of lukewarm water.

Again, this task rarely requires more than a few minutes.

The frequently expressed fear that the chlorine level of most municipal water supplies will compromise their flora of nitrifying bacteria is unfounded, so there is no excuse for ignoring clogged sponges. The frequency with which a canister filter must be cleaned depends on both the waste load it must handle and the medium with which it is charged. Exposed to comparable waste loads, dacron or sponge pads clog more rapidly than EhfiFix© or ceramic rings.

Because disassembling these units is something of a project, it is worth investing in the more expensive — and durable — ceramic or plastic media.

The frequency with which canister filters must be cleaned can be further reduced if they are fitted with an easily purged mechanical pre-filter.

Fig. 151: Cleaning the gravel of an aquarium is a simple matter with a Tetra HydroClean©.

The second step entails carrying out a regular schedule of partial water changes. This serves two important purposes.

The first is to remove dissolved wastes and toxic nitrogen cycle products from the aquarium.

Second, if properly carried out, water changes will also remove solid wastes that have settled into the substratum.

This automatically serves to clean an undergravel filter bed should such a unit be in use.

Tetra's Hydro-Clean© aquarium gravel washer performs both functions admirably.

When thus purging the substratum, work the base of any rockwork thoroughly, as waste buildup occurs very rapidly in such areas. In fact, it is good idea to re-arrange the rockwork in a cichlid tank several times yearly in conjunction with a major water change.

This both simplifies management of the nitrogen cycle and tends to break up established patterns of social interactions between its residents, often with beneficial effects.

The Hydro-Clean© works by siphon action and is the gravel cleaner of choice for fry tanks or small aquaria.

The volume of water involved in making large-scale water changing tends to discourage proper maintenance if one must rely on the bucket brigade approach, however. Most of the mess and inconvenience associated with these essential maintenance activities can be eliminated if the aquarist invests in a Python No Spill Clean and Fill©.

This ingenious device allows one to clean the substratum, remove old water and refill an aquarium without ever lifting a bucket.

Powered by a simple venturi attached to a faucet, it consists of a length of flexible tubing mated to a wider tube of rigid plastic tube.

Water flow through the tubing is regulated by a simple, easily manipulated ball valve.

The partial vacuum created when water flows through the open venturi sucks both water and detritus from the tank being serviced. A No Spill Clean and Fill© can purge a bed of gravel up to 8" deep with no difficulty.

Assuming the water flow through the faucet to which it has been attached is powerful enough, one of these units can service a tank as far as 75 feet distant with no loss of efficiency.

Once the desired area of tank bottom has been purged of wastes or sufficient water has been removed, it is a simple matter to set the temperature of the stream flowing from the open tap at the appropriate temperature, close the venturi and refill the tank. Aquarists with many tanks to maintain may find one of the several automatic water changers on the market the simplest means of coping with this task.

Fig 152: Frequent large-scale water changes are essential to the well-being of such robust cichlids as *Oreochromis tanganyikae* (Gunther 1894) in captivity.

Fig. 153: Like most Tanganyikan endemics, *Julidochromis r. regani* Poll 1942 does not appreciate large-scale water changes. This dictates reliance upon alternative approaches to nitrogen cycle management in their aquaria.

Remember these devices are designed only to remove and replace water.

Their use must thus be accompanied by regular purging of the tank's substratum with a Hydro-Clean© or a No Spill Clean and Fill© to avoid dangerous accumulation of solid waste.

The frequency of water changes and the volume replaced per change depend upon the filtration system in use and the nature and number of fish housed in a given tank. A 75 gallon tank containing eight to twelve large tilapias, *Heros*-lineage species or robust Malawian haplochromines and equipped solely with a high capacity mechanical filter can require weekly changes of half its volume to keep its inhabitants in good health [Figure 152]. Heavily stocked fry tanks likewise demand equally frequent major water changes to promote optimal growth.

At the other extreme, a well planted 29 gallon tank equipped with a pair of sponge filters and housing a trio of *Apistogramma* and a half dozen small dither fish can typically manage with a 10% water change every month. A useful rule of thumb is to replace 25% – 30% of a tank's volume with new water every ten to fourteen days.

Certain Tanganyikan cichlids are an important exception to this pattern. The popular substratumspawning genera *Lamprologus*, *Chalinochromis*, *Telmatochromis* and *Julidochromis* in particular are sensitive to water changes on such a scale [Figure 153]. To avoid seriously traumatizing these cichlids, replace no more than 10% of their tank's volume at any one time.

Fortunately, the persistent pair bonding of these species makes it feasible to house them as single pairs in tanks large enough to exploit the full potential of biological filtration in managing the nitrogen cycle.

Under such conditions, large-scale water changes are unnecessary.

The Problems of Chloramine Intoxication and Gas Embolism in the Cichlid Aquarium

Fresh water must be of the same chemical makeup and at about the same temperature as that it is intended to replace. Equally important, it must be free of additives likely to harm the fish.

Aquarists have long appreciated the need to neutralize chlorine added to municipal water supplies as a disinfectant.

In the past, cichlid keepers have been less troubled by this problem than most of their fellow hobbyists.

Most adult cichlids are not noticeably upset by the chlorine concentrations in most water supplies, while use of proprietary dechlorinating agents sufficed to prevent any problems incident upon changing water for fry or adults of sensitive species.

This situation is changing rapidly due to a widespread shift from chlorine to **chloramines** for water treatment.

Unlike free chlorine, these nitrogen-chlorine compounds do not combine with dissolved organic compounds to form cancer causing trihalomethanes.

From a medical perspective, they are thus far superior as disinfectants to the traditional chlorine.

From the aquarist's standpoint, however, they are a disaster, for they combine extreme toxicity with great environmental persistence. Chloramine concentrations between 0.05 and 0.40 ppm are fatal to a wide range of fish. Concentrations in municipal water supplies usually range from 1.0 to 1.5 ppm.

Chloramines are very stable compounds that neither break down readily nor dissipate from a closed system.

Unlike gaseous chlorine, they cannot be neutralized by the addition of commercial dechlorinating agents to the aquarium at the manufacturers' recommended dosage.

Sodium thiosulfate, their active ingredient, will break down chloramines, albeit at higher concentrations than those required to neutralize free chlorine.

However, this simply replaces one toxic substance with another equally dangerous to

fish, for free ammonia is a chloramine decomposition product.

Any method of eliminating dissolved chloramines must neutralize both chlorine and residual ammonia to be fully acceptable for aquarium use.

If a tank has a functional biological filter, its associated bacterial flora should be able to degrade ammonia produced by chloramine breakdown to harmless nitrate without any assistance from the aquarist provided water changes are done on a **moderate** scale, *i. e.,* no more than 10% of the tank volume at a time.

However, one cannot rely upon this process in a newly established aquarium or in a tank that relies primarily on mechanical filtration. Under these circumstances, direct intervention by the aquarist is necessary.

Fortunately, there are a number of proprietary products on the market that will detoxify chloramines by breaking the chlorine-amino bond, neutralizing the free chlorine and forming an organic complex with the residual ammonia that is harmless to fish while it is being metabolized by the filter's flora of nitrifying bacteria [Figure 154].

Used according to the manufacturer's instructions, these products will eliminate any threat chloramine poses to ornamantal fish.

There are other approaches to the neutralization of chloramine. The first entails employing **sodium thiosulfate** to decompose the chloramine and neutralize the free chlorine thus produced, and a **chemically active medium** in the filter to remove residual ammonia from solution. Either PolyBio-Marine's PolyFilter©, an easily handled bonded pad, or one of a number of granular preparations that rely upon zeolites will serve this purpose. Please note that the amount of dechlorinating agent necessary to accomplish this will vary with the pH of the water and the chloramine concentration present. It may thus be necessary to experiment with the dosage before finding one appropriate to local conditions.

Prudence dictates doing this with a known volume of freshly drawn water **before** starting the water changing process! Residual chlorine concentrations are easily measured using any of the test kits available commercially.

A negative reading for residual chlorine indicates that all the chloramine originally present has been eliminated from solution.

The second approach entails adding **fresh activated carbon** to the filter immediately before adding newly drawn water to the tank. Note that only **high grade activated carbon** removes chloramines from solution.

Inexpensive aquarium grade charcoal is totally ineffective for this purpose. Nor will even high quality carbon do the trick if it has been previously used to remove dissolved organics from the water.

It must be absolutely fresh to perform efficiently!

The manufacturer's instructions should initially determine the amount of carbon added to the filter. New water can then be added and the filter allowed to function.

The first time this procedure is utilized, test the water for dissolved ammonia fifteen minutes later.

A positive result is to be expected. Repeat the test an hour later.

At this time, no ammonia or only trace amounts should be detectable.

Next test for residual chlorine. If the results are positive, add a quantity of carbon to the filter equal to half the original amount and repeat the test in an hour.

In the unlikely event that detectable amounts of chlorine are still present, repeat the procedure.

The final quantity of carbon required to remove all the chloramine from the system should be employed subsequently when making water changes.

Once all the chloramine is gone, the carbon should be removed from the filter. It is best discarded.

There is no means of measuring its residual chloramine adsorbing activity and its subsequent use for other purposes is not advisable.

During the winter, aquarists in areas that suffer protracted low temperatures are often confronted with the problem of "gas bubble disease" in their fish after large-scale water changes.

The solubility of any gas is a function of temperature. Hence, during the cold months, tap water picks up large volumes of dissolved air that must leave solution as the water temperature increases.

Under aquarium conditions, the escaping gas forms a myriad of tiny bubbles in the fins and superficial body tissues of its inhabitants.

This can result in impairment of gill function, with attendant respiratory distress, locomotor malfunction due to swimbladder damage and widespread skin damage, often followed by dangerous secondary bacterial and fungal infections. Small fish are proportionately more vulnerable to this condition, but even robust cichlids can die from the effects of severe gas embolism.

Fortunately, it is possible to prevent gas embolism losses if a bit of foresight is exercised in making winter water changes.

First, it is a simple matter to determine whether the water supply poses any risk to the fish. Draw a glass of cold water from the tap and allow it to stand at room temperature for an hour or so.

Fig. 154: When used according to the manufacturer's instructions, dechloraminating agents such as Tetra's Aquasafe/NH₄Cl will efficiently neutralize any chloramines present in tap water.

If by this time the inside of the glass is covered with fine bubbles, the potential for "gas bubble disease" is present.

Suitable precautions must thus be taken whenever water is changed. The most obvious is to draw water a day ahead of time and encourage dissolved gas to dissipate by running an airstone in the storage vessel during the interval.

This approach is practical only if small volumes are involved, for the logistic problems involved in preconditioning more than a few buckets of water at a time are formidable. They can be overcome, but at a cost difficult to justify for any operation smaller than a full-scale fish room.

An alternative approach entails making smaller changes — on the order of 10% of the tank volume — at more frequent intervals and using a mist nozzle to replace water thus removed. These are used by serious gardeners to provide the extremely fine mist appreciated by many tropical plants. By breaking a stream of water into such minute droplets, such a nozzle accelerates the departure of dissolved gases from solution.

The rate of flow through such nozzles is a good deal less than through an unhindered hose. This slows down the whole water changing process dramatically and is another reason for minimizing the volume replaced per change.

Use of selectively active media to extend the interval between water changes during the winter may also prove a helpful means of minimizing the problems encountered during this season.

For obvious reason, gas embolism is less likely to be a problem in tanks serviced by trickle filters, a factor that should be taken into account when assessing the cost effectiveness of investing in such a unit. As noted, an alternative approach to keeping dissolved metabolite levels at acceptable levels entails the use of chemically active filter media capable of selectively removing ammonia and nitrite from solution.

Mention has already been made of these media as adjuncts to dechloramination. Though quite effective, they have some obvious drawbacks.

They must be removed from the filter of any tank that is undergoing medication, as they remove therapeutic agents from solution as efficiently as they do ammonia or nitrite. Furthermore, their capacity is finite and they cannot be regenerated.

Finally, these media are by no means inexpensive. Hence the question of cost effectiveness arises in any consideration of their use in nitrogen cycle management.

Use of these media is certainly defensible whenever it is impractical to make frequent major water changes.

This situation can arises when an aquarist maintains cichlids whose particulat pH and hardness requirements cannot be met using tap water.

The extreme sensitivity of many Tanganyikan cichlids to substantial water changes represents another such instance.

Chemically active media are also useful in extending the interval between necessary water changes.

I always place such media in the outside filters of my tanks before going on a long trip. This prevents dissolved nitrite concentrations from rising to dangerous levels due to interruption of my normal maintenance routine or in the event of an unanticipated mortality in my absence.

They also provide effective insurance against catastrophe in newly set-up aquaria.

However, where there is no constraint upon regular water changes, the rapidity with which these media are saturated in a cichlid tank makes their regular use economically unattractive.

Water Chemistry in the Cichlid Aquarium: pH, Hardness and Trace Elements

Cichlids inhabit such a broad spectrum of environments that it is possible to find species that prosper under any water conditions available to an aquarist. The accompanying figures present in schematic form the range of preferred pH [Figure 155] and hardness [Figure 156] values for the major groups of

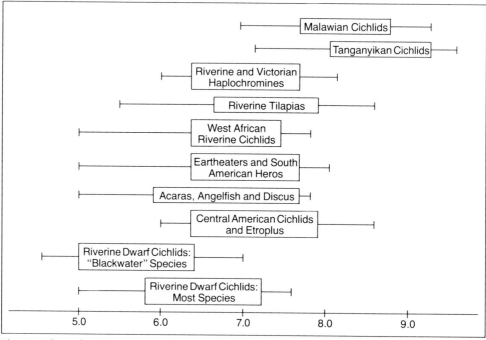

Fig. 155: The preferred pH-ranges of several major cichlid groups.

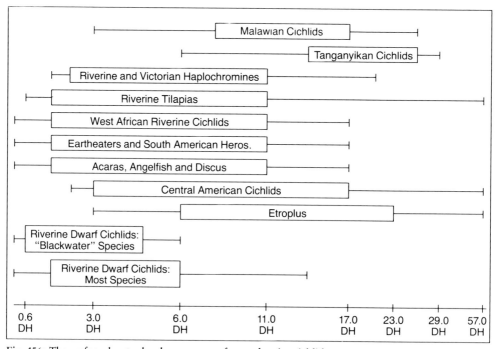

Fig. 156: The preferred water hardness ranges of several major cichlid groups.

cichlids as well as the limits within which survival, if not normal reproduction, is possible. Note that with few exceptions, the breadth of the preferred range is impressive.

Most cichlids are quite undemanding about the precise pH and hardness of their water.

The aquarist who exercises a bit of common sense in matching his choice of cichlids to the chemical make-up of his tap water is thus spared the necessity of agonizing over minute adjustments of its pH and hardness in order to assure the well-being and reproductive success of his fish.

As one might expect in so diverse a family, however, there are some exceptions to this pattern. As a rule, cichlids simply refuse to breed when maintained at pH values that fall outside of their optimal range.

However, a number of taxa, notably the various *Pelvicachromis* species [Figure 158] and a number of Malawian haplochromines may breed quite freely under such conditions

but invariably produce broods with skewed sex ratios.

In the most extreme instance, all the young so produced are of the same sex. From the standpoint of the breeder attempting to establish an aquarium strain, such a "success" is no improvement over complete failure to induce a spawning!

Careful attention to matching the pH and hardness values prevalent in the native habitat of these species is obviously essential when setting up their spawning tank.

A cichlid fancier's life is much easier if he elects to keep species that prosper in his unmodified tap water. However, it often transpires that the fish he yearns to possess will not thrive without modification of its chemical make-up.

This entails the ability to measure both pH and hardness reliably.

Hence the first step in this direction is the purchase of accurate water test kits. Traditio-

Fig. 157: The giant krib *Pelvicachromis sacramontis* Linke & Staeck 1981, is one of a number of West African dwarf cichlids whose broods enjoy a balanced sex ratio only if spawning occurs within a fairly narrow pH and hardness range.

Fig. 158: No attempt to modify either the pH or hardness of aquarium water should be undertaken unless one has the means at hand to measure these parameters accurately.

nally, the problem has been viewed as one of modifying the pH to suit the needs of a given species.

In actuality, efforts to change pH without taking into account the water's natural buffering capacity, essentially a function of its hardness, rarely produce the desired effect. Exposing fish to repeated short-term fluctuations in acidity or alkalinity actually does more harm than good.

The essential problem in this situation is that of modifying hardness. In areas of high carbonate hardness (over 5°dH) the pH will usually remain stable in the face of any attempts to lower it.

This type of water is desirable for African Rift Lake cichlids. In areas of lower carbonate hardness (less than 3°dH), the pH is less stable.

While such water is more easily made either more acidic or more basic, keeping the pH from dropping to dangerously low levels can often be a serious problem.

It is far easier to make soft water hard than hard water soft.

The sodium exchange units used to soften water for domestic use do not produce water acceptable to cichlids from soft water biotopes.

These species require the almost total removal of **all** dissolved salts from the water, not the substitution of sodium and chloride ions for the cathodes and anodes naturally present in solution, such as calcium or magnesium and carbonate or sulfate.

The technology of large-scale demineralization of tap water using strong cation/anion exchange resins is well developed. However, the cost of connecting a commercial deionizing unit to a domestic water supply together with that of its ongoing maintenance represents a considerable overhead cost for any hobby.

Small, reasonably priced reverse osmosis (RO) units are a readily available alternative to ion-exchangers.

These units demineralize water by passing it through a membrane impermeable to dissolved substances, representing a more practical alternative for most aquarists. However, these units have their drawbacks as well. The ratio of bypass to treated water is very high for RO units — on the order of seven gallons of water down the drain for each gallon of demineralized water produced.

In many areas, such profligate use of water cannot be defended on either environmental or economic grounds.

A third alternative entails using already demineralized water as the basis of these operations.

Deionized water can be purchased in bulk and its price is usually low enough to make purchase an acceptable option when first setting up tanks of up to thirty gallons capacity.

Whatever its source, the demineralized water should be mixed with tap water until the desired hardness level is attained. The pH can then be adjusted downwards to the desired value. Water can be acidified either by direct addition of a strong acid or by running a peat filter in the tank until the desired pH value is attained.

Each approach has its disadvantages. Adding strong acids directly to an established aquarium is dangerous to its inhabitants and likely to have unpredictable results.

This approach is not recommended, as a rapid pH drop to dangerously low values and/or rapid liberation of excess CO_2 may well result.

The commonly suggested alternative to the strong acids entails the use of sodium biphosphate in their stead. This is a much safer chemical.

However, its use increases the concentration of sodium ions in solution, which may not be desirable for other reasons.

Fig. 159: Like all Tanganyikan endemics, *Triglachromis otostigma* (Regan 1920) must be kept in hard alkaline water to prosper.

127

Furthermore, the sudden increase in dissolved phosphate, an important plant nutrient, can have unpredictable — and often undesirable — effects upon algal growth.

Filtering softened water through peat replicates the natural acidification process. The pH of the water is lowered, while beneficial organic compounds are simultaneously released into the aquarium. Unfortunately, not all peats possess the desired level of chemical activity, and those that do are not always readily obtainable.

A further difficulty arises from the tendency of peat to compress into an impermeable mat in a filter. This slows the acidification process by reducing the total reactive area in contact with the water. It is usually necessary to continue running a peat filter after fish have been added to the aquarium, if for no other reason than to provide a buffer against shifts in pH following water changes.

This further complicates matters, for organic matter trapped in a peat mat undergoes anaerobic decay. This can lead to release of toxic substances into the tank if the mat is disturbed.

Regular use of Tetra's Blackwater Extract is a convenient alternative to peat filtration. Blackwater Extract© further adds to the aquarium water important trace elements, essential iodine and vitamins. Used as instructed, it is safe for fish while posing no danger to the aquarist should a bottle inadvertently be spilled or smashed.

Remember, to maintain a steady pH and hardness value in a soft water aquarium, only deionized water should be used to make up losses due to evaporation.

A regular schedule of partial water changes is also very important. Nitrate ion tends to acidify soft water.

Elevated nitrate levels can cause abrupt pH drops.

As I can attest from personal experience, missing a scheduled water change in a heavily stocked but poorly buffered fry tank can cause

Fig. 160: Even in hard, alkaline water, Tanganyikan mouthbrooders such as this *Simochromis diagramma* Boulenger 1898 cannot breed successfully unless dissolved potassium and magnesium levels are above a certain critical threshold.

its pH to plunge from 6.8 to 3.8 overnight, to the considerable distress of its residents!

Replacement water must have the same chemical makeup as that removed from the tank.

Unless the aquarist lives in an area where tap water is naturally soft, this entails an ongoing investment in deionized water as well as considerable effort to mix up the necessary volume of fresh water prior to each change. Given these circumstances, water changing can become an onerous and costly proposition. Hence the use of chemically active filter media as a mainstay in nitrogen cycle management in such tanks is usually economically defensible.

The aquarist wishing to keep hard water cichlids in a soft water area has an easier time of it, as his task entails adding salts to the water supply rather than removing them [Figure 158]. In areas of moderate hardness, no more may be required to provide suitable conditions than the addition of Philippine coral gravel or crushed oyster shell to the filter.

This is customarily done by using it as an undergravel filter bed.

However, the same hardening effect can be had by enclosing a quantity in a net bag and placing it in an outside power or canister filter. In areas with extremely soft tap water, I recommend the use of commercial salt mixes that reproduce the chemical makeup of water from Lake Malawi or Lake Tanganyika. They satisfactorily replicate the pH and hardness conditions these cichlids require to prosper, when used according to manufacturer's instructions. The addition of 10 g (c. 1 tbsp.) of commercial marine salt mix per ten gallons of water serves the same purpose for Central American cichlids. Tap water can be used to top up tanks that have been treated in this manner.

However, don't forget to replace dissolved salts that are removed from the tank by a water change with an equivalent quantity of salt mix. Otherwise, the tank water will grow progressively softer and less alkaline, a change unlikely to benefit its inhabitants. Many naturally

Fig. 161: Dwarf Tanganyikan cichlids like this female *Lamprologus brevis* Boulenger 1899 are particularly susceptible to goiter.

Fig. 162: Mesoamerican cichlids such as this male *Thorichthys affinis* (Gunther 1862) also benefit from regular use of Tetra's African Vital© in their tanks.

rally hard water supplies are deficient in dissolved potassium and magnesium.

The presence of these elements seems essential for reproductive success in many mouthbrooding cichlids from Lakes Malawi and Tanganyika.

These fish spawn freely in such deficient waters, but fertilization of the eggs does not occur.

This results in an aborted incubation sequence a few days after spawning [Figure 160]. Breeders who experience persistent failures of this sort should obtain a complete chemical analysis of their tap water from the local authority. If values for dissolved potassium and magnesium are lower than 18.0 ppm and 77.0 ppm respectively, supplementation is called for.

Addition of one level tsp. of commercial salt substitute (potassium chloride) per ten gallons of tank water brings dissolved potassium values up to acceptable levels even in areas where the local water supply is devoid of this element. Two level tablespoons of Epsom salts (magnesium sulfate) per ten gallons does likewise for magnesium ion.

Water supplies in some regions are iodine deficient. Unless supplementary iodine is added to the environment of fishes maintained in such water, this situation may result in goiter, a massive thyroid gland enlargement that can lead to severe respiratory impairment and eventual death. Dwarf cichlids seem particularly vulnerable to this condition, possibly due to their small adult size.

Tanganyikan cichlids regardless of size share this susceptibility [Figure 161]. Regular use of Tetra's AfricanVital©, which contains iodine in a readily absorbed form effectively prevents pathological thyroid enlargement under such water conditions [Figure 162]. Like many deficiency diseases, goiter is a reversible condition. Even extreme cases respond rapidly to treatment with African Vital©.

CHAPTER 6

TROUBLESHOOTING THE CICHLID AQUARIUM

Introduction

The aquarist who has chosen his tank wisely, equipped it properly and taken to heart the previous chapter's advice on good maintenance procedure is well on his way to success with cichlids. However, an established aquarium of any sort is a complex biological system. Experienced hobbyists are well aware that it is impossible to exercise total control over all the variables in such a system.

Faithful adherence to sound maintenance practices minimizes the likelihood that problems requiring outside intervention will arise, but the possibility of trouble can never be eliminated altogether.

This is particularly true in the cichlid aquarium, where the behavioral idiosyncrasies of its inhabitants introduce an additional level of complexity.

Hence the cichlid fancier should learn to spot the first signs of impending difficulties as well as appropriate corrective measures.

Learning to Be a Careful Observer

An experienced cichlid keeper needs only a quick look at a tank to ascertain the condition of its inhabitants.

As aquarists of all persuasions are made, not born, one may dismiss the notion that such skills are innate! They are rather acquired with practice and thus can be learned by anyone with sufficient motivation.

It is much easier to develop observational skills if one has a clear idea of what to look for.

The following checklist should aid the novice to develop a practiced eye:

Is all equipment functioning properly?

Check filters and pumps for normal operation.

Check mechanical filters for media in need of purging or replacement.

Check the thermometer to see if the heater is maintaining the desired water temperature.

Has there been any change in the condition of the tank since it was last examined?

Is the water is cloudy or discolored?

Smell the water. It should have a fresh aroma. A sour or putrescent smell is a clear indication of serious problems.

Has algal growth undergone a sudden spurt?

Check plants (if present) for signs of sudden deterioration and the gravel for discolored patches.

Are all of the tank's inhabitants present?

If a pinch of food doesn't bring everyone to the surface, why not?

Check the cover glass for possible escape routes and the floor for signs of the missing.

Check behind infrastructure, in rear corners and at the surface for reclusive or injured fish or for cadavers. If the missing fish is one of the tank's smaller inhabitants, check the larger fish for signs of a recent heavy meal, such as a bulging stomach and a diminished appetite.

Do the fish look different in any way?

Look for changes in coloration, the sudden appearance of spots or blemishes on the body and fins, missing scales or torn fins, distended gill covers or a sudden bloating of the abdominal region.

Are the fish behaving differently than usual? If so, are all of them or only a few individuals acting strangely?

Note differences in patterns of movement and swimming ability, breathing rate and response to food.

Check behavioral interactions carefully. Note increases or decreases in aggressive behavior as well as sudden shifts in the targets of such behavior.

Some readers will be discouraged by the length of this list.

In practice, it takes about five minutes per tank for an **inexperienced** observer to run through. A practiced aquarist can do it in three.

Anyone unwilling to invest that much time and effort twice daily to assure the well being of his fish should sell his equipment and take up an alternative pastime devoid of responsibility towards living creatures. He clearly has no business as a fish keeper.

Changes in appearance or behavior need not invariably signal that something is amiss.

Sudden changes in coloration coupled with increased aggressive behavior may simply signal the onset of reproductive activity. This can lead to future problems if the tank is not large enough to allow other residents to evacuate the territory claimed by the male or pair in question. However, as a rule it is not cause for immediate concern.

The combination of bulging throat and distended gill covers in a female mouthbrooder usually means she is carrying a clutch rather than suffering respiratory distress.

Obviously baseline information is necessary to properly evaluate changes in coloration or behavior. Reference works such as this are a useful source of baseline data, but the aquarist's own prior experience with the system in question is more valuable still. This is one of the chief reasons for keeping a notebook.

The recording process itself promotes the habit of systematic observation, while the resulting written record is always available for subsequent examination.

Many of the potential problems itemized in this checklist suggest their own solutions.

Nonfunctioning equipment must be restarted, repaired or replaced. Potential exit points need to be covered.

The solutions to others are not necessarily self evident.

The remainder of this chapter will address these problems in turn and suggest appropriate solutions.

Pollution Induced Trauma and Its Treatment

Pollution Induced Trauma (PIT) is a catch-all term for a wide range of symptoms caused by toxic substances in the aquarium. Because it is caused by deterioration of environmental quality, **all** the residents of a contaminated tank will be affected to some degree.

Its milder manifestations include labored breathing, diminished appetite, and often a darkening in color. Unless the underlying cause of the problems is removed, the severity the symptoms will escalate. Gasping at the surface, frantic dashing across the tank, and loss of equilibrium are ultimately followed by death.

Prompt implementation of corrective measures is essential when dealing with PIT.

The sooner the cause of stress is removed from the system, the greater the likelihood affected fish will recover fully.

Correct identification of the toxic substance in question is the first step in countering its effects. In most cases, PIT is due to **nitrite** or, more rarely, **ammonia intoxication.** Test for both substances at the first onset of PIT.

If concentrations of either are over trace levels, inadvertent nitrogen cycle mismanagement is at the root of the problem. Such a mischance is most likely in tanks stocked at or slightly over their maximum capacity.

Under these circumstances, the normal output of metabolic wastes is already pushing the filtration system's capacity close to its limits.

Any sudden input of nitrogenous compounds — by accidental overfeeding, addition of a new fish to the tank, the death of a resident, or decline in the rate at which nitrogen cycle byproducts are degraded or removed from the system, can rapidly result in a dangerous increase in nitrite or, if alkaline water conditions prevail, ammonia concentrations [Figure 163].

The response to such an emergency is to **immediately** make a 75% to 80% water change. Thoroughly purge the substratum as described in the preceding chapter while removing old water from the tank.

Next, add a chemically active medium such as PolyFilter© immediately to the filtration system.

This may entail nothing more than adding a quantity of the material in question to an already operating power filter.

Alternatively, it may require setting up a temporary unit for the duration of the emergency.

The chemically active medium must be on line **before** fresh water is added.

So doing may shift the tank pH from acidic to alkaline.

This in turn can result in a sudden increase in the concentration of toxic ammonia, which exists as harmless ammonium ion in acidic water, but changes into ammonia under basic conditions.

If the ammonia is not removed as fast as it forms, the short-term results of a major water change can be as deadly to fish as total inaction! The initially described symptoms should disappear rapidly once the concentration of toxic substances is reduced. Nevertheless, it is prudent to monitor both ammonia and nitrite concentrations for the next few days and replace the chemically active medium should either begin to rise again. Finally, the source of the problem must be identified and eliminated.

In the short run, this may entail removing a decomposing cadaver from the tank or exercising greater restraint at feeding time. In the long run, it may mean finding a new home for some of its residents and accepting the inescapable fact that there is a finite limit to the number of cichlids a given system can support. The notion that there is always room for one more fish in an established aquarium is seductive but it **invariably** leads to disaster.

The end product of the mineralization of metabolic wastes, nitrate, is not acutely toxic to fish. However, as pointed out in the preceding chapter, elevated nitrate levels can provoke catastrophic drops in pH if a tank's water is poorly buffered [Figure 164].

Fish stressed in this manner typically display clamped fins, respiratory distress, loss of color and appetite and in extreme cases, sloughing off of their body mucus.

If initial tests for ammonia and nitrite yield negative results, the next step should be to check both the pH and nitrate levels of the affected tank.

The immediate response to a nitrate-provoked pH crash should again be a substantial water change, accompanied by a liberal dose of

Fig. 163: Lake Tanganyika cichlids like this *Lamprologus cylindricus* Seegers & Staeck 1986 are particularly susceptible to ammonia poisoning because they must be kept in hard, alkaline water.

one of the proprietary products sold as a "bandage in a bottle" to assist the fish to temporarily cope with the effects of a compromised mucus layer.

If the species under culture can tolerate hard water, enhancing the buffering capacity of the tank's water by adding coral gravel or oyster shell to either the substratum or the filter system should prevent reoccurrence of the problem.

If the tank is devoted to soft water species, the only measures that will work in the long run are to reduce the stocking rate and carry out water changes with scrupulous regularity.

PIT can be caused by substances external to the aquarium. If the water tests previously discussed yield negative results, one must conclude the source of pollution is exogenous. Immediate corrective measures are essentially as recommended in the case of nitrogen cycle breakdown, but one should add the PolyFilter© to the system before making a water change. Given the extreme toxicity of some exogenous pollutants, repeat the water change in 48 hours to be certain all traces are purged from the aquarium.

Regrettably, greater toxicity also means that even prompt implementation of corrective measures may not prevent some losses.

Household insecticides are the most commonly encountered exogenous toxins. Slow release insecticidal strips should **never** be hung in the same room as an aquarium or placed anywhere near its air source.

If aerosol sprays must be used in their vicinity, great care must be taken to prevent any insecticide from drifting into aquaria or being blown into the water via the air supply.

Cover tanks completely with a plastic drop sheet and move the pump outside the room being sprayed for at least an hour. It is vital to prevent activated carbon from coming into contact with insecticides, as it can adsorb considerable quantities of these materials.

When added to a filter unit, such contaminated carbon releases adsorbed insecticide into solution with lethal consequences. To prevent such an occurrence always store activated carbon in a sealed container.

Certain formulations of silicone elastic sealant contain cyanide or arsenic compounds as mold inhibitors. These products are totally unsuited for aquarium use, as they slowly release highly toxic cyanide or arsenic ions into the water.

Only complete replacement of the offending sealant will put an end to the resulting losses.

To prevent this sort of intoxication, employ only silicon elastic formulations certified as safe for aquarium use.

Finally, nicotine is quite toxic to fish. Dwarf cichlids and fry of all species seem particularly sensitive. Fortunately, this source of pollution is easily eliminated.

If it is not feasible to prohibit smoking near aquaria, make some provision to draw the tobacco smoke out of the room that houses them.

Adding a chemically active medium to the filter provides some back-up capacity if the room cannot be properly ventilated.

Physical Injuries and Their Treatment

The spatial limitations of aquarium life taken with the family's well developed aggressive tendencies guarantees that cichlid keepers will eventually have to deal with injuries resulting from tank resident interactions.

This is particularly true of inexperienced cichlid enthusiasts, who are still learning how to manipulate their fishes' behavior in a manner that minimizes serious fighting between or harassment of tankmates.

Expertise in cichlid first aid is worth acquiring, for in their ability to inflict the maximum amount of damage in the minimum amount of time, cichlids yield pride of place only to piranhas among commonly kept aquarium fishes! Fortunately, cichlids also have a remarkable recuperative capacity.

With proper supportive treatment, even apparent candidates for euthanasia have an excellent chance of making a full recovery.

Just as a field surgeon, faced with the problem of best allocating limited medical resources, must practice triage upon the casualties demanding his attention, so must the aquarist learn which injuries warrant the effort of treating.

Swim bladder injuries, manifested by a loss of either equilibrium or neutral buoyancy, are untreatable.

Afflicted fish may well survive for a considerable time if maintained in isolation. Their likelihood of surviving the normal rough and tumble of a community tank is nil, as is their utility as breeding stock. Such fish are best humanely destroyed.

A swift slam against a solid surface is the simplest means of euthanasia available in such cases.

More reticent aquarists will be pleased to learn that a tenfold increase in concentration of commercially available tranquillizing agents kills a terminally ill or incurably damaged fish almost as quickly.

Fig. 164: Fry of Lake Victoria cichlids such as this *Haplochromis* sp. "macula" do not tolerate abrupt drops in pH well.

At the other extreme, major efforts are unnecessary to treat minor injuries.

Split or nipped fins and the odd missing scale or two are simply part and parcel of life in the cichlid aquarium. Indeed, based on my field observations, they are a routine feature of cichlid existence in nature. The aquarist who wishes to institute therapeutic measures should make a partial water change, treat the tank with AfricanVital© at the recommended dosage and raise the temperature a few degrees Fahrenheit.

The water change temporarily lowers the bacterial count, the B-complex vitamins in AfricanVital© promote fin regeneration, and the increase in temperature stimulates the fish's immune system and somewhat speeds up the healing process.

Injuries requiring carefully concerted attention are major losses of fin tissue or scales [Figure 165]. Either or both can occur with appalling swiftness if normally ritualized aggression escalates into serious fighting.

Under normal aquarium conditions, there is simply no way the loser can move far enough away from the winner to escape continued battering.

Few sights are more disheartening than the discovery of a prized specimen hanging just below the surface of the tank, flanks half denuded of scales and fins in shreds.

Partially desiccated specimens rescued from a spell on the floor are comparably unpromising in appearance, for they have likewise suffered serious skin damage.

It may well appear the only humane course of action is to put the fish out of its misery at once.

However, as long as the victim's gill covers are moving and it eventually demonstrates it can swim normally, there is a good chance that it can be saved.

Start by **immediately** isolating the fish in a hospital tank.

The tank's volume should reflect the victim's dimensions and it must be equipped with a functioning filter.

Cover the bottom with a thin layer of gravel to eliminate disturbing reflections and provide some sort of shelter to put the injured fish at its ease.

A clay flowerpot of appropriate diameter placed on its side, opening tilted away from the front glass serves this purpose admirably.

Fill the tank with freshly drawn water of the same temperature and chemical makeup as that of the victim's original home. Hospital tanks should be dimly lit and **must** be tightly covered.

Newly isolated cichlids are often easily frightened by movement in their vicinity and typically respond to them with frantic efforts to escape.

A prolonged stay on the floor does little to enhance the prognosis of an injured cichlid!

The first stages of treatment entail use of antibiotics. Hence it is best to equip the tank initially with a mechanical filter.

Once antibiotics have been phased out, it can be replaced with a matured sponge filter.

Massive skin injuries pose two dangers to their victims.

First, it exposes a massive area to secondary bacterial and/or fungal infection.

Second, electrolyte loss through the injured areas imposes severe physiological stress upon injured fish.

This in turn can lay the victim open to systemic bacterial infection.

Effective therapy must address both hazards as well as promote normal regeneration to the greatest extent possible.

The most effective counter to the threat of secondary infection is immediate treatment with a broad-spectrum antibiotic.The furanring based antibiotics, originally developed for aquaculture use, are my personal preference in such cases, but tetracycline also gives satisfactory results.

Dosage should follow the manufacturer's instructions.

Tetra AquaSafe© is one of several excellent products that treat the problem of electrolyte loss by providing the injured fish with an artificial substitute for its lost body slime.

As noted earlier, AfricanVital© plays an useful role in treating such injuries because of the positive effect of B vitamins on tissue regeneration.

Both products used in accordance with the manufacturer's directions should play an integral part in such therapy.

Continue antibiotic therapy until the first signs of tissue regrowth are noticed. At this point, it can be safely discontinued.

Remember that it is necessary to replace most of the tank's water before redosing with antibiotics. It is also necessary to renew the dosage of Aqua Safe© or its equivalent and of AfricanVital© at the same time. Injured fish should be fed sparingly at first.

The combined traumas of serious skin damage and sudden isolation may depress the appetite. It is prudent to feed only live foods during the early stages of treatment.

Such items are more likely to tempt the patient's appetite and less likely to complicate nitrogen cycle management by fouling the water should they go uneaten.

The duration of the recovery process and the degree of regeneration that occurs therein depend upon the severity of the injuries.

Fins bitten back to the body may regenerate with badly bent rays. If the **fin ray primordia** have been in part or totally destroyed, regeneration will either be incomplete or else fail to occur altogether.

Scale regeneration is automatic, though it may occur slowly if the injuries entailed damage to underlying dermal and muscle tissue.

Whether scales regrow in their original alignment or the replacement scales are normal in shape depends likewise on the injury's severity and to some extent upon the treatment.

The same is true of less catastrophic types of fin damage.

Using such products as AquaSafe© and AfricanVital© reduces considerably the likelihood that fin rays will regrow crooked or that replacement scales will regenerate abnormally, though it is unclear why this should be the case.

Serious injuries are easier to prevent than to treat. A tight cover will keep cichlids inside their tanks and off the floor.

Fig. 165: Highly aggressive cichlids such as *Amphilophus festae* (Boulenger 1899) frequently provide their keeper with opportunities to practice trauma therapy on their tankmates.

Harmony in the cichlid tank is more likely if residents are matched with respect to size and aggressive tendencies.

Careful observation over time of interactions between the residents of a cichlid community will allow the aquarist to spot potential cases of intramural thuggery before they attain serious proportions.

He can then take appropriate corrective measures. These include removal of either aggressor(s) or victim(s) and rearrangement or supplementation of the tank's furnishings.

Finally, misapplication of certain spawning techniques virtually guarantee serious injury to one of the prospective breeders. This issue will be discussed subsequently at greater length.

Suffice for the moment to note that the use of alternative approaches can eliminate this source of risk altogether.

Selected Diseases and Their Treatment

Cichlids are hardy aquarium residents.

If proper attention is given to nitrogen cycle management in their aquaria and they are protected from abrupt temperature fluctuations, they rarely contract the usual afflictions of aquarium fish.

This observation, however, offers little consolation to the aquarist faced with some malady that demands his attention. A comprehensive treatment of fish diseases is beyond the scope of this work.

Readers seeking more information are referred to selected references listed in the final chapter. However, it is appropriate to consider herein some complaints of particular concern to cichlid keepers.

The first stage of disease control is quarantine of newly acquired cichlids for five to ten days. Unless one is absolutely certain they have come directly from a breeder of known competence, this means ALL new arrivals should be so isolated.

Both shipping and the need to adjust to a new environment are stressful to fish. Repeated exposure to stress increases susceptibility to systemic bacterial infections.

Isolating new arrivals minimizes the possibility that any diseases or parasites they may be carrying will spread and enormously simplifies the task of treating any problems that do occur.

The quarantine tank should be set up in the same manner as the hospital tank, but with a functioning biological rather than a mechanical filter.

Sponge filters such as the Tetra Brillant© series serve this purpose extremely well.

Some breeders advocate prophylaxis of freshly imported specimens with a combination of broad spectrum antibiotic and antiparasitical agents.

Such a shotgun approach to medication is unwise.

First, prophylactic antibiotic use has led to the evolution of pathogen strains resistant to several widely used medications in both veterinary and human practice.

This is certainly not to be desired in any sort of fish culture.

Second, many antiparasitical agents are only slightly less dangerous to the fish than to the parasites themselves.

Cichlids should never be stressed in this fashion unless the alternative is eventual death of the afflicted fish.

Medicate cichlids ONLY when their condition clearly indicates that a specific treatment is appropriate and likely to prove beneficial!

Imported or pond-bred cichlids frequently sport small numbers of black spots on their body and fins. This condition, sometimes known as **black spot disease**, is produced by metacercarial cysts of a parasitic trematode worm whose ultimate hosts are such fish-eating birds as herons or kingfishers.

The metacercarial stage is passive, the fish acting as the **phoretic host**, the parasite's means of transport to its ultimate host.

Affected fish rarely sport more than a few metacercariae, which do no harm.

This is more than can be said for some of the products sold to treat this condition.

Unless an aquarist maintains both the snail intermediate host in his aquaria and allows fish-eating birds to forage freely on his premises, this parasite cannot perpetuate itself in captivity.

Fig. 166: Mbuna like this male OB morph *Pseudotropheus zebra* are highly susceptible to such systemic bacterial infections as "Malawi bloat" when maintained under stressful conditions.

In time, the cysts drop off, ending the infestation for good. It is therefore pointless to treat affected fish.

A much more serious parasitic infestation associated with pond-bred cichlids is caused by monogenean worms commonly, though inappropriately, referred to as gill or skin flukes. These monogenetic trematodes are dangerous because they do not require multiple hosts to perpetuate themselves.

Consequently their numbers can increase very rapidly under favorable conditions. The high stocking rates prevalent in ponds and, *pari passu*, home aquaria, afford these parasites just such an opportunity.

Repeated scratching behavior often associated with a slimy appearance to the skin indicates their presence on the body.

Less immediately evident but more serious are gill infestations. Heavy parasite loads can dangerously compromise respiration and often manifest themselves in accelerated movement of the gill covers or a tendency to hang tail down just below the surface and gulp at the oxygen-laden superficial layer of water.

This may not in itself prove lethal, but it requires little additional stress to cause death from acute respiratory failure.

If this were not enough, the injuries caused by both skin and gill monogeneans can open a fish to potentially lethal secondary bacterial infections. The smaller cichlids and fry of all species are particularly vulnerable to such attacks.

Diagnosing gill monogeneans is complicated by the fact that most symptoms of a heavy infestation are identical with those of PIT. Fortunately, even a low-power microscope is sufficient to detect the parasites in a skin scraping.

While microscopic examination provides absolute proof of their presence, such an iron-clad diagnosis is not an essential precondition for instituting therapy.

If testing permits the aquarist to reject intoxication as cause of the observed symptoms, he should next treat the affected tank for monogeneans.

Two genera of monogeneans are responsible for the majority of such infestations. They differ in their mode of reproduction, *Dactylogyrus* laying extremely tough eggs, while *Gyrodactylus* is viviparous. Adults of both types can be readily eradicated.

Four drops of commercial strength (37% solution) formaldehyde per gallon of water will eliminate them with reasonable dispatch; so will several proprietary antiparasitical medications used according to the manufacturer's instructions.

These products irritate the already damaged gill filaments to some extent, reducing their respiratory efficiency still further. Hence the importance of providing supplementary aeration during treatment.

Unless positive which genus of monogenean is attacking the victim, repeat the treatment following a full-scale water change five to seven days later. This kills the parasites that will have hatched out from the medication-resistant *Dactylogyrus* eggs. A final word of warning: skin and gill monogeneans are **extremely** contagious.

Nets and other appliances used in an infested tank should be soaked in a disinfectant bath before being employed in parasite-free aquaria. The aquarist likewise should wash and dry his hands carefully after working therein.

A third problem to which pond-bred cichlids are prone is intestinal hexamitiasis, caused by the ciliate protozoan parasite *Hexamita*. When present in small numbers, these protozoans do not appear to trouble their hosts unduly.

Large-scale infestations, typically provoked by external stresses that depress the infected fish's immune system, are another matter.

When present in large numbers, *Hexamita* can damage the intestinal tract sufficiently to compromise the host's ability to dig its food properly and assimilate necessary nutrients.

This weakens infected fish and greatly increases their susceptibility to attack by pathogenic bacteria. Infected fish typically have an undernourished appearance and tend to behave lethargically.

They are often paler in color than are uninfected conspecifics. Clear, somewhat mucilaginous stringy feces are a certain sign of a heavy infestation.

Once an infested fish's condition has reached this point, cessation of feeding typically follows.

Opportunistic systemic bacterial infections such as "Malawi bloat" usually claim the victim before it can starve to death.

Hexamita is highly susceptible to the antiparasitic drug metronidazole, one of the active ingredients of Tetra's medicated flakes and food sticks.

Fed to fish suspected of harboring the parasite for a week, either product will quickly put paid to this dangerous protozoan. Regrettably, there is no effective way of treating fish that have stopped eating. This drug is not absorbed through the gills, so simply adding it to their aquarium's water is pointless.

Because freshwater fish do not drink significant quantities of water, infested individuals are unlikely to swallow enough medicated water to materially affect the course of this disease. For this reason, it is prudent to put any wild-caught or pond-reared cichlid that has recently undergone a stressful experience, such as shipping, on a regime of medicated food as part of its quarantine process.

One of the most dreaded diseases the cichlid fancier can encounter is "Malawi bloat".

In its classic manifestation, afflicted fish lose their normally heavy appetites, become reclusive and develop a noticeably bloated appearance.

The condition does not respond to treatment with generally available antibiotics. Death occurs from three days to several weeks after the onset of bloating.

As is the case with diseases that resist therapy, a tremendous amount of misinformation has arisen about "Malawi bloat".

As such misinformation gets in the way of both effective prophylaxis and treatment, it must be countered before approaches to either can be considered.

First of all, the disease is misnamed. It is in no sense restricted to Malawian or even

African cichlids [Figure 166]. Indeed, any fish can be attacked, though the symptoms can — and often do — differ between species and even individuals.

Second, the condition is not directly caused by physical blockage of the intestine, improper diet or acidic water conditions, though both preexisting intestinal protozoan infestations and environmental stresses of any sort increase a fish's vulnerability to infection.

The causative organisms are pathogenic bacteria.

Three genera are implicated, *Aeromonas*, *Haemophiles* and *Pseudomonas*.

Several species of each genus appear to be dangerous to fish.

Third, the initially described syndrome is **not** the only manifestation of their activity.

Depending upon what organs are attacked, quite different symptoms can be produced. "Bloat" itself is a manifestation of kidney dysfunction.

Loss of appetite and the appearance of bloody, translucent feces are manifestations of intestinal infection.

The blood-streaked fins and open sores of hemorrhagic septicemia occur when the pathogen attacks skin and muscles [Figures 167].

These symptoms can occur in isolation or in any possible combination. Given that a common suite of causative organisms is responsible for these diverse symptoms, it is more useful to employ the term **systemic bacterial infections** when speaking of these problems rather than attempt to deal with them piecemeal.

The bacteria responsible for these diseases are impossible to exclude from the cichlid aquarium, nor would such a course of action be worth the effort even if possible.

None of these pathogens poses any risk to fish whose resistance to infection is at normal levels.

Only when stress weakens their normal defenses against bacterial invasion do cichlids succumb to these pathogens. Prevention simply requires keeping stress at acceptable levels.

This entails treating pre-existing medical problems that increase their susceptibility to bacterial infection in a timely and efficacious manner, providing cichlids with adequate living space, avoiding situations that lead to persistent harassment of some residents of a community by others, careful nitrogen cycle management and proper attention to diet. In short, good maintenance habits are the best defense against systemic bacterial infections. However, the aquarist has no control over what has befallen a cichlid before it enters his possession and may be unaware of significant sources of stress such as internal parasites.

He may thus have to treat such infections in spite of all efforts to prevent their occurrence.

Many antibiotics effective against gram-negative bacteria are **potentially** capable of destroying these pathogens.

Such qualification is essential because affected fish must ingest these medications if they are to be absorbed into the bloodstream and function effectively. This entails feeding the fish medicated food.

However, loss of appetite and consequent cessation of feeding are among the first symptoms of these infections.

This is why antibiotics usually available to aquarists are largely ineffectual in combating systemic infections.

Successful treatment is possible only by using antibiotics that are absorbed directly into the bloodstream via the gills.

The medication of choice in treating systemic bacterial infections is **minocycline hydrochloride**, at a dose of 250 mg/10 gallons of water. This potent antibiotic is manufactured by the Lederle Laboratories Division of American Cyanamid and sold under the trade name of Minocin©. Repeat this dosage following a complete water change two days later if the victim does not respond to the initial treatment with the resumption of food intake. Do not repeat the treatment a third time, as it is likely to prove lethal.

Minocin© is a relatively new antibiotic, unavailable save by prescription.

It is also expensive.

A sympathetic physician or dentist may help to overcome the obstacle of access, but a drop in price is unlikely until this antibiotic comes into widespread veterinary use.

Hence the advantage of moving afflicted fish into a smaller hospital tank for treatment.

Fig. 167: Dwarf cichlids such as this male *Apistogramma trifasciata* Eigenmann & Kennedy 1903) are vulnerable to hemorrhagic septicemia [Dorland, 1974] if exposed to elevated nitrite levels for any length of time.

Contrary to popular belief, systemic bacterial infections are not highly contagious.

However, the appearance of an infected fish in a given tank should trigger the start of supportive measures. Isolate the diseased fish or fishes, make a major water change **at once**, and pay appropriate attention to the filtration system.

It is an excellent idea to begin feeding Tetra Medicated Fish Food© to the remaining tank residents immediately.

Either in flake or floating pellet form, this formulation, fed over a five day period, will effectively knock out any infections in their initial stages of development.

Finally, aggressive interactions between the tank's residents should be observed for signs that any one fish or group of fish is being persistently harassed.

If such is the case, it will be necessary to change the community's make-up in order to reduce behavioral stress to less dangerous levels.

The preceding chapter outlined approaches to maintaining cichlids in good health; the present addressed itself to correcting the consequences of a breakdown of sound maintenance practices or problems arising from circumstances beyond the aquarist's control. The reader who takes them to heart will quickly discover that cichlids respond to good care with determined attempts to reproduce.

The next chapter will thus consider the reproductive biology of cichlids and suggest approaches to breeding them successfully in captivity.

CHAPTER 7

BREEDING CICHLIDS UNDER AQUARIUM CONDITIONS

Introduction

As already noted, cichlids are reproductive opportunists with highly evolved parental behavior. In practical terms, given the presence of both sexes in the same tank, properly maintained cichlids eventually attempt to breed. As most aquarists keep cichlids largely to observe such behavior, this is all to the good.

Furthermore, cichlids not only spawn freely in captivity, but their progeny are among the most easily reared egglayer fry, thanks largely to the family's well-developed hygienic behavior and the fact that newly mobile fry of most species can initially take *Artemia* nauplii or finely powdered prepared food. Basically, the aquarist provides food, while the parental fish do (or does) everything else!

However, though its parental behavior is among the family's strongest selling points, it does introduce complications into cichlid husbandry. Spawning preliminaries can pose a hazard to prospective partners, while its aftermath is often positively lethal to other fish sharing their aquarium.

Nevertheless, given some understanding of their breeding behavior, one can manage cichlids in ways that make spawning a positive experience for all interested parties. In this chapter, I will outline the basic features of cichlid reproduction biology, point out those that complicate its expression in captivity and suggest ways to overcome these difficulties.

Breeding Techniques for Monogamous Cichlids

Introduction

Most who have dealt with cichlid reproductive biology have focused upon differences in how the fish care for their progeny.

The usual dichotomy encountered in the aquarium literature is between "substratum spawning" versus "mouthbrooding" cichlids.

In fact, the single aspect of cichlid reproductive biology most relevant to the aquarist is not a given species' mode of parental care, but rather its **mating system**.

Cichlids are either **monogamous**, a male and female remaining in association for a single reproductive episode, or **polygamous**, an individual of one sex consorting with several individuals of the opposite sex during a single breeding period.

The presence or absence of a long-term bond between the sexes determines how the fish must be handled before and after spawning, not whether or not the developing embryos are held in the mouth until they are free-swimming. Because monogamous and polygamous cichlids must be handled very differently, it is thus essential to focus first upon its mating system when planning to breed a given species in captivity.

Contrary to popular belief, knowing how a cichlid cares for its young tells one little about its mating system.

This misapprehension has doubtless arisen because the overwhelming majority of polygamous cichlids are also maternal mouthbrooders, while the preponderance of substratum spawning species are characterized by monogamy. These correlations, though strong, are by no means absolute.

Though all biparentally custodial cichlids are monogamous, not all monogamous cichlids are substratum spawners.

For instance, monogamy characterizes a number of both primitive (*Aequidens, Bujurquina, Geophagus, Gymnogeophagus, Satanoperca*) [Figure 168] and advanced (*Chromidotilapia, Eretmodus, Spathodus, Tanganicodus, Perrisodus, Greenwoodochromis*) mouthbrooding cichlids.

142

Fig. 168: *Burjuquina marine* (Eigenmann 1922), a monogamous primitive mouthbrooder. Among cichlids, monogamy is strongly correlated with protracted care of the mobile fry.

Conversely, several substratum spawning cichlid taxa are known to be polygamous in nature (*Acarichthys, Apistogramma, Crenicara, Dicrossus, Guianacara, Nannacara, Teleogramma,* some *Gymnogeophagus, Nanochromis* and many *Lamprologus*) [Figure 169].

The key to spawning monogamous cichlids successfully is obtaining a compatible pair.

During pair formation, two reproductively competent individuals of the opposite sex transform mutual animosity to joint defense of a territory centered on a suitable spawning site.

Fig. 169: *Acarichthys heckeli,* a large eartheater with a polygamous mating system.

This cooperation persists after spawning and ultimately extends to the defense of the mobile fry.

In nature, males and females interact in an exploratory manner until two compatible individuals encounter one another.

There is nothing mystical about the basis of such compatibility.

Quite simply, the gonadal cycles of the two fish must be in synchrony for pairing to occur.

In some species, among them *Aequidens coeruleopunctatus* (KNER and STEINDACHNER 1863), *Theraps maculicauda* (REGAN 1905) [Figure 170], *Theraps melanurus* GUNTHER 1826 and *Amphilophus calobrensis*, (MEEK and HILDEBRAND 1913), males first establish a territory from which they court females.

In others, such as *Hemichromis fasciatus, Amphilophus citrinellus* GUNTHER 1864 [Figure 171] and *Petenia splendida*, courtship involves non-territorial individuals who subsequently establish a jointly defended demesne.

The important point is that pairing is preceded by an often lengthy testing process. Consequently, one cannot just drop a male and female cichlid into a breeding tank and expect connubial bliss automatically to follow. The fish **must** be allowed to interact in an environment that facilitates courtship, or the end result will be mayhem, not matrimony.

Regardless of how courtship is conducted, its successful end result is two strongly territorial individuals living in close proximity.

This situation is inherently unstable because of the tension between territorial and sexual behavior inherent in such an arrangement.

In nature, this tension is easily relieved, for the pair has no lack of suitable targets against which to redirect the aggression engendered in each member by the propinquity of the other.

When pairs lack the opportunity to so redirect their aggressive behavior, which is often the case in captivity, the result can be the disintegration of the pair bond, frequently with

Fig. 170: In nature, male *Theraps maculicauda* (Regan 1905) stake out a territory from which they court passing females.

Fig. 171: Male and female Midas cichlids, *Amphilophus citrinellus* (Gunther 1864) pair prior to the establishment of a breeding territory in nature.

lethal consequences to the female and any off-spring present.

The prospective breeder of monogamous cichlids must thus overcome two problems. First, he must create an environment that allows females to survive long enough to attain gonadal synchrony with their potential mates.

Second, once pairing has occurred, he must somehow duplicate conditions that promote a stable pair bond for however long it takes the fish to spawn and rear their young.

Alternative Approaches to Pair Formation in Captivity

Pair formation is most readily and safely accomplished in an environment that allows prospective mates to interact with other fishes as well as with one another.

The ideal way to provide such a behaviorally enriched environment entails raising six to eight young conspecifics to maturity together in a tank large enough for the expression of species-typical territorial behavior.

Such an environment guarantees both sexes will be present and more or less in reproductive synchrony, provides suitable target fish for incipient pairs but precludes the possibility any single individual will be singled out for potentially damaging harassment, and affords ample maneuvering room for all. Pair formation occurs automatically under these conditions.

If the tank is large enough, the first pair to form simply excludes the remaining fish from a portion of it and settles down to breeding with no further ado. Otherwise, separation of the remaining fish may be necessary to avoid casualties.

A single male and female will also pair up with minimal difficulty if kept in a community of behaviorally compatible heterospecifics. They can, however, be counted upon to spawn successfully therein with minimal risk to its other inhabitants **only** if its dimensions allow them to move beyond the limits of the pair's territory.

145

This **naturalistic approach** to pair formation and breeding depends upon the presence of suitable **target fish** for the pair's aggressive behavior. It is a workable technique only if the fish are housed in a tank large enough to furnish the pair a territory and its other inhabitants with adequate living space beyond its boundaries.

It is thus most useful for small to mid-sized cichlids with relatively modest space requirements.

In a tank too small to satisfy the spatial demands of all its inhabitants, the lives of the target fish will in all likelihood be brief, brutish and nasty.

The ferocity of parental cichlids in defense of their progeny has few equals among aquarium fishes.

Isolating the pair by either removing all other fishes or moving it to a separate tank is often suggested to avoid this difficulty. However, to do so is an invitation to conjugal disharmony.

Elimination of targets for the pair's aggression can lead to disintegration of the pair bond, with predictably unpleasant consequences.

Fortunately, there are three workable alternatives to the naturalistic approach of breeding monogamous cichlids available to aquarists with limited tank space.

The first, and simplest, exploits the fact that target fish need not be physically accessible to discharge their stabilizing function.

A potential spawn predator isolated behind glass is attacked as persistently as it would be were the barrier removed.

There are two ways to exploit this phenomenon.

The first entails partitioning off a portion of the breeding tank with glass pane or plastic egg crate diffuser grating.

The target fish is placed in the smaller, the incipient pair in the larger of the two compartments and nature allowed to take its course. A solitary specimen of any comparably sized cichlid serves this purpose admirably

The second, and more efficient, entails dividing a tank in half and placing a breeding pair on either side of the partition.

If glass rather than a permeable diffuser grating is employed, it will be necessary to operate a filter in each compartment. Take care to keep the glass from becoming overgrown with algae.

If the targets cannot be clearly seen by the pair, they no longer serve their purpose.

Inattention to this chore can lead to the failure of a spawning effort and loss of the female.

The second alternative depends upon the fact that among the majority of monogamous cichlids, males grow larger than do females. Because of this, females can swim through openings impassable to a male.

Implementation of this approach exploits such sexual dimorphism.

It entails dividing the breeding tank with a barrier containing several openings scaled to allow the female free movement from one side to the other, while confining the male to a single compartment [Figures 172 & 173]. The male's quarters should contain the future spawning site, which should be placed as close to the barrier as possible.

As both fish will inhabit it after pairing has occurred, the male's compartment should be larger than the female's.

I refer to this as the **separate bedroom method** of breeding monogamous cichlids. Others call it the hidey-hole method.

By any name, this approach permits potential breeders to synchronize their reproductive cycles with no risk to the female, who simply moves beyond the male's reach should his attentions become overbearing.

The same option is open to her should the pair bond begin to erode at some future time. This approach is particularly valuable when the aquarist must work with only a single pair of large or very aggressive cichlids. It permits the pair to interact directly with minimal risk to the female.

One can thus observe much of the elaborate courtship and parental behavior that makes cichlids such interesting aquarium residents free from worry over the possible loss of valuable breeding stock.

The final approach is the **incomplete divider method**. It depends upon the fact that a male and female cichlid will perform their

Fig. 172 & 173: The openings cut into the plastic partition allow this female *Tilapia buttikoferi* ready access to the male, while affording her a means of escaping from him should his attentions prove overbearing.

respective parts of the spawning act even when physically separated as long as they are in sight of one another.

If the barrier is not watertight and the spawning site located in reasonable proximity to it, enough sperm will diffuse through to fertilize some fraction of the egg plaque.

As initially practiced, this approach entailed no more than inserting a fragment of rockwork or clay flowerpot beneath the lower edge a glass partition and placing the potential spawning site as close as possible to the barrier on the female's side.

To more effectively maximize sperm movement, replace the glass barrier with one of plastic diffuser grating. This method totally eliminates risk to the female. Because the barrier allows fry to move freely between compartments, it also allows both sexes the opportunity to assume a parental role.

Its disadvantages are two-fold.

First it also totally eliminates normal behavioral interactions between male and female. Many aquarists who keep cichlids precisely in order to observe such behavior find this unfortunate.

Second, not all of the eggs deposited by the female will be fertilized, no matter how close the spawning site is to the barrier.

The incomplete divider method is thus best adapted to single pairs of very large cichlids such as the more robust *Heros* species [Figure 171]. These cichlids are so large and aggressive on one hand and so fecund on the other that most aquarists are quite pleased to trade off a percentage of the spawn in order guarantee the safety of hard-to-replace breeding stock.

A complication incidental to any approach involving the use of a single pair of cichlids is that of securing an individual of each sex.

Assuming one has selected a mix of sizes when purchasing six to eight youngsters for rearing to maturity, this problem will not arise. Statistical probability guarantees at least one individual of the limiting sex will be present among half a dozen subadults selected at random.

However, this approach is sometimes precluded by considerations of available space or limited finances [Figure 172]. It is thus helpful

to be able to distinguish between the sexes before purchasing breeding stock.

Family diversity precludes pronouncing any hard and fast rules with regard to such secondary sex characteristics as color or fin development.

When appropriate, such distinctions will be presented for the species covered in the Catalog section.

There are two criteria of broad applicability in sexing cichlids, however.

The first relates to the phenomenon of **male growth superiority.**

Simply put, male cichlids are larger than females of the same age.

Furthermore, this size difference does not wait upon the onset of sexual maturity to manifest itself, hence the injunction to select a mix of sizes from a tank of fry when choosing breeding stock.

Second, as reference to Figure 173 should illustrate, the genital papillae of male and female cichlids differ in appearance when seen under slight magnification.

A jeweler's loupe or field biologist's hand lens allows one to distinguish between the bluntly rounded ovipositor and the pointed male genital papilla even in fish in the 2"–3" SL size range.

A tensor lamp or handheld flashlight provides a suitable concentrated light for such inspections.

Hold the fish firmly in the damp folds of a net during the examination.

Covering their eyes reduces the intensity of their efforts to wriggle free, thus greatly facilitating this operation for all parties concerned.

Postpairing Management of Parental Cichlids and Their Fry

Cichlids require little encouragement to spawn.

Balky pairs often respond favorably to a partial water change, particularly if it is carried out as a low pressure front is moving through the area.

As a rule, however, these fish spawn when they are good and ready, not a moment sooner!

The pair usually signals its intent by a sudden burst of pit digging and nipping off of the future spawning site.

Typically the female undertakes most of the burden of site preparation, but it is not unusual for the male to participate in the actual "scrubbing" of the spawning site. Spawning can be expected within twenty-four hours of the appearance of the female's ovipositor, a conspicuous, blunt-tipped tube that protrudes from her vent [Figures 174–177]. Postspawning behavior comprises efficient custodial and hygienic elements.

Among the advanced mouthbrooding monogamous cichlids, one or both parents hold the developing embryos within their buccal cavities until their development is complete.

Among the remaining monogamous species, the male as a rule defends the spaw-

ning territory against predatory intruders, while the female fans and cleans the egg plaque.

Sex role stereotypy varies considerably between species. At one extreme, among the various *Pelvicachromis* and other cave spawning species, hygienic behavior is carried out exclusively by the female [Figure 178], custodial behavior by the male.

At the other, these duties are divided almost equally between the sexes in the African genus *Hemichromis* and the Mesoamerican genus *Thorichthys* [Figure 179]. Its expression is also influenced by the level of threat posed by potential spawn predators. In the essentially danger-free aquarium environment, the male is much freer to participate in the hygienic aspects of brood care than is usually the case in nature.

At hatching time, the wrigglers are chewed out of their eggshells by the adults. They then are either orally brooded until they are free-swimming (primitive or delayed mouth-brooders) [Figure 180 & 181] or moved to

Fig. 174: Large aggressive cichlids with a monogamous mating system, such as *Amphilophus labiatus* (Gunther 1864) are most safely bred using the incomplete divider method.

Fig. 175: The cost of purchasing a group of expensive Tanganyikan cichlids such as *Lamprologus sexfasciatus* Trewavas & Poll 1952 often makes the group approach to pairing impractical. Hence the importance of being able to ascertain the sex of individuals before selecting potential breeders.

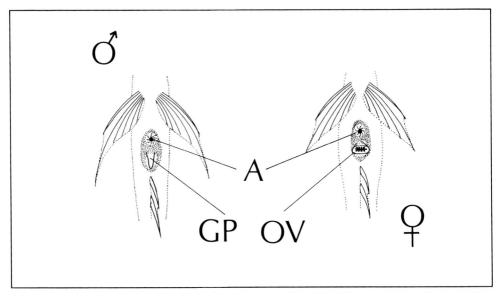

Fig. 176: Diagrammatic representation of the male (GP) and female (OV) urogenital papilae in cichlids. A: anus.

Fig. 177 a

Fig. 177 b   Fig. 177 c

Fig. 177 d

Fig. 177 a–d: Spawning sequences of the Texas cichlid, *Herichthys cyanoguttatus*, whose behavior is representative of other monogamous, substratum spawning cichlids.

151

Fig. 178: Regardless of their mating system, hygienic behavior is carried out exclusively by the female in most cavity spawning species, such as *Lamprologus calliurus* Boulenger 1906, a dwarf species endemic to Lake Tanganyika.

Fig. 179: Both sexes share hygienic responsibilities in the jewelfishes of the genus *Hemichromis*, as the behavior of this parental male *H. cristatus* Loiselle 1979 attests.

Fig. 180 & 181: Primitive mouthbrooders like *Bujurquina vittata* Heckel 1840) chew the zygotes free of their eggshells and carry them in their buccal cavities until they are fully mobile.

Fig. 181

Fig. 182: Fry of substratum spawner such as *Herichthys cyanoguttatus* are chewed free of the egg shells and moved to a pre-dug pit. They may be moved several times before attaining mobility.

Fig. 183: The fry of many cichlids graze mucus from their parents' flanks, but only in the genus *Symphysodon* is such feeding behavior obligatory.

Fig. 184: The eggs of cave-spawning cichlids such as *Steatocranus casuarius* Poll 1939 are light-sensitive and must be artificially incubated in total darkness.

previously prepared receiving areas [Figure 182] where they will be tended until they become mobile (substratum spawners *sensu stricto*).

Both parents actively defend the mobile fry. In some cases, they also stir up the bottom, raising a cloud of detritus within which their progeny can forage, or even masticate large chunks of food and spit out the resulting mouthful of fine particles into the school of fry.

The fry of many species nibble mucus from the flanks of their parents. Such behavior is facultative in many Mesoamerican species and the Asian chromides of the genus *Etroplus*, but is obligatory for discus and *Uaru* fry.

Indeed, these South American cichlids are among the few fishes whose parental care includes a trophic component comparable to that of mammals [Figure 183]. Sometimes this sequence of events breaks down, resulting in loss of the spawn to parental cannibalism.

Such episodes are typical of young pairs and cease once the fish have grown older. The exercise of a bit of patience is usually all that is required in such cases.

Impatient breeders or those unfortunate enough to have a persistent spawn-eating pair have the option of removing the spawn as soon as possible after spawning and hatching it artificially.

This presupposes the fish have spawned on a conveniently removable object, but this caveat aside, the process is straightforward.

Remove the egg plaque to a container filled with freshly drawn water of the same temperature and chemical make-up as that in the breeding tank. Two to five gallon tanks are ideal for this purpose.

Place an airstone next to the plaque and bleed a moderate stream of air into the tank.

The aim is to create a **gentle** current next to the developing embryos that mimics the female's fanning.

Too strong a current can dash newly hatched fry against the tank walls or their former site of attachment, resulting in their death or congenital deformation. As develo-

155

ping embryos are vulnerable to microbial attack, it is prudent to add a bacteriostatic agent to the hatching tank.

Methylene blue, the traditional choice, is oxidized too rapidly to be of much use. Neutral acriflavine, used at half the recommended medicinal dosage, or MarOxy©, a proprietary product based upon stabilized chlorine oxides, used at the manufacturer's recommended dosage, are more effective in controlling harmful bacteria and fungi in the hatching tank.

The developing embryos of cave-spawning cichlids such as the various *Pelvicachromis, Nanochromis* and *Steatocranus* species [Figure 184] are markedly light-sensitive. It is usually necessary to place the substratum upon which they have been deposited in an orientation that exposes them to strong light to assure they are properly aerated.

Hence, if one decides to hatch them artificially, they must be protected against this hazard. It suffices to tape brown wrapping paper to the outside surface of the tank walls and cover glass until the fry are fully mobile. The masking can then be safely removed. Hatching tanks are rarely large enough to house fry for more than a few days before becoming dangerously crowded. During this

period, slowly replace the original medicated water with fresh water from the tank to which the fry will eventually be transferred.

When the time comes to move the fry, carefully siphon off all save a quart or two of the hatching tank's volume, then pour the remaining water and fry into the rearing tank. This is a far safer means of transferring very young fry than netting them. While hatches of up to 90% of the eggs in a given spawn are possible, such intervention is best regarded strictly as a method of last resort when dealing with cichlids. No matter how carefully a spawn is handled, this netting results in a significant percentage of congenitally deformed fry.

Furthermore, the aquarist who takes the burden of postspawning care upon himself misses some of the most fascinating parental behavior in the entire animal kingdom. Unless the species in question is so rare that production of tank-reared fry must take absolute priority over other considerations, he is better advised to let the passage of time rectify any deviations from normal parental behavior by his cichlids. Newly mobile cichlid fry are easily reared.

With very few exceptions, to be noted on the Catalog section, the few species too small

Fig. 185 & 186: Both substratum spawning tilapias such as *Tilapia guineensis* (Bleeker 1863) (above) and mouthbrooders such as *Oreochromis chilwae* (Trewavas 1966) (next page) will abandon their newly mobile progeny in peripheral waters, whose elevated temperatures afford a secure refuge from fry predators.

Fig. 186

to take *Artemia* nauplii and finely powdered prepared foods manage microworms quite nicely.

It is thus seldom necessary to culture infusoria to tide them over until they grow large enough to eat newly hatched brine shrimp.

Remember when feeding live *Artemia* nauplii that adults of even large cichlids species devour them as greedily as their offspring and apportion them accordingly. Cichlid fry are voracious feeders and should be fed at least two and preferably three or four times daily. The schedule of partial water changes in their tank should reflect this fact. Otherwise losses from stress induced bacterial infections or outright nitrite intoxication will surely follow.

Custodial care in nature persists until the young are no longer threatened by whatever fry predators present the greatest hazard to their survival in that habitat. This period averages six to eight weeks for most species, but exceptions either way are known.

Parental tilapias have been observed "dumping" fry less than a week old in the superheated peripheral waters of their chosen habitats [Figures 185 & 186]. This seemingly self-defeating approach actually works very well, because young tilapias thrive at temperatures several degrees Fahrenheit above the upper lethal limits of both their principal predators and their chief trophic competitors.

As long as they stay within these **thermal sanctuaries**, these fry are as safe from predatory fish as they would be under their parents' supervision.

In other instances, parental care persists much longer than average.

Adult orange chromides, *Etroplus maculatus* (BLOCH 1795), have been observed defending young on the verge of sexual maturity, while in the Tanganyikan *Lamprologus brichardi* POLL 1974 and a number of ecologically analogous congeners, fry remain within the parental territory after the pair has respawned and assist their parents in defending their younger sibs! [Figure 187]

Persistence of parental care in nature is a response both to the intensity of predation pressure and to the simple fact that the exigencies of effectively protecting their progeny precludes normal foraging by the adult fish.

The female in particular is thus prevented from garnering sufficient nourishment to yolk up a second batch of eggs as long as she is committed to the defense of her present brood.

In captivity, their keeper's generosity at feeding time removes this **bioenergetic constraint** from parental cichlids.

Thus it is not uncommon for a female to mature another clutch within six weeks of spawning. This can lead to a second spawning attempt well before fry from the first have attained full independence.

It is extremely important to separate parents and offspring as soon as the pair shows persistent signs of respawning. Their behavior

157

towards their older progeny at this point varies from indifference to active hostility.

In the former case, the older fry may well prey upon the eggs or young either before or after hatching. This can lead to serious complications if one member of the pair attempts to defend the older fry against the other's efforts to protect their new offspring from sibling cannibalism. In the latter instance, the pair will attempt to eject the older fry from their territory before respawning.

If the older fry cannot move beyond their erstwhile protectors' reach, they will be killed and eaten [Figure 188]. Removing the young from the breeding tank before the pair begins the preliminaries to respawning can have a serious destabilizing effect upon the pair bond. **Contrary to popular belief, the overwhelming majority of monogamous cichlids do not mate for life.** Persistent pair bonding is documented only for some of the strongly petricolous Tanganyikan cichlids of the genera *Julidochromis* and *Lamprologus*.

In these species, joint defense of a shelter seems to be the basis for the long-term association of male and female.

Among other monogamous cichlids, pairing is for the duration of a single reproductive effort only!

Thus, when the fry are removed, effectively terminating the current episode, the male and female are right back at square one.

Rebonding may be facilitated to some extent by the fact that the gonadal cycles of the two fish are more apt to be in synchrony than those of two individuals thrown together at random. However, it is advisable to monitor the progress of events very carefully at this stage unless the female has the option of moving beyond the reach of her erstwhile consort.

The rate at which cichlid fry grow under aquarium conditions is influenced by both the amount of food they receive and the frequency with which water in the rearing tank is changed. Dissolved metabolites are powerful growth inhibitors and cannot be allowed to accumulate if stunting is to be prevented.

Changes of 75% to 85% of the rearing tank volume every three to five days are by no means excessive. In captivity, most cichlid fry grow rapidly but unevenly. This frequently results in a tendency for growing fry to dine within the family.

The extent of sibling cannibalism varies markedly between species, but such behavior can be expected from most cichlids. Fry not sorted according to size usually cull one another quite efficiently.

The aquarist who must feed a brood of a thousand or more ravenous *Nandopsis* or *Tilapia* fry may regard such behavior as a provident dispensation rather than a serious problem.

Recall, however, that cichlids are characterized by early male growth superiority.

Thus if nature is allowed to take its unmodified course the likely end result will be a strongly male biased sex ratio among the well-fed survivors.

It is rarely in the aquarist's best interest to rear an entire brood of one of these super-

Fig. 187: Pairs of *Lamprologus brichardi* allow older fry to remain within the parental territory after they have respawned. As they grow larger, these fry assist the adults in defending their younger sibs.

Fig. 188: Pairs of *Lamprologus pleuromaculatus* Trewavas and Poll 1952 tolerate fry from a previous spawning within the limits of their territory until the hatching of their current clutch, then drive them away. This pattern of intolerancer is characteristic of most substratum spawning cichlids.

prolific species to a saleable size [Figure 189]. Fry grow more rapidly and evenly if they are not crowded, while the sheer size of the spawn can seriously depress the local market for that species. The optimal course for the amateur breeder is to net out a few hundred fry randomly for future rearing when he separates them from their parents.

The remainder can be used as live food for other large fish. To those who object to such a course of action on aesthetic or humane grounds, I would point out that it merely duplicates the eventual fate of ninety-nine out of every hundred cichlid fry in nature!

Monogamous cichlids have an undeserved reputation of being difficult to breed in captivity. It is more accurate to describe them as less flexible in their space requirements than many other egglaying fishes. Furthermore, the complexity of their reproductive behavior obliges the aquarist to pay more attention to the preliminaries to spawning than with subsequent management of the developing embryos if he wishes his efforts to succeed.

At the risk of seeming to restate the obvious, the key to breeding monogamous cichlids is obtaining a compatible pair. The reader who heeds the foregoing suggestions should encounter few difficulties in playing the successful matchmaker. The truly remarkable reproductive behavior of these fish no less than the fry resulting from it will amply reward his pains.

Fig. 189: *Cichlasoma* sp. Guapole Amarillo. Parental pair with fry

159

Breeding Techniques for Polygamous Cichlids

Introduction

Monogamous cichlids are characterized by the long-term association of a male and female for the duration of a single reproductive effort.

Because for many decades virtually the only cichlids available were characterized by such a mating system, many hobbyists are surprised to discover that there are many cichlids whose mating system is based upon some form of **polygamy**, in which one or both sexes interact with multiple spawning partners during the course of a single reproductive episode.

For aquaristic purposes, it is important to distinguish between **harem polygyny**, in which a single male controls access to and spawns with the same group of females over an extended period, and **open polygamy**, in which the association between the sexes is restricted to the sexual act itself and both male and female may enjoy access to multiple partners during a single spawning effort.

Harem polygyny is based upon a male's defense of an extensive territory containing several potential spawning sites against other males.

Each of these sites in turn serves as the focus of a smaller territory occupied by a female.

Females vigorously exclude other females from their demesnes.

With the onset of ripeness, they respond favorably to the advances of the resident male, who visits all the females regularly and spawns with each in turn.

Once the male has performed his essential function, he is brusquely expelled from her territory by his erstwhile consort.

Parental care is exclusively maternal in its initial stages, although in some species the male may sporadically assist in defending the mobile young.

These cichlids are typically characterized by dramatic sexual dimorphism [Figures 190 & 191]. Males can be up to three times as large as females and frequently have more elaborate finnage.

However, some males of normally dimorphic species remain quite small and never develop the elaborate finnage of their larger counterparts.

Such so-called **sneaker males** have earned their name by their pursuit of an alternative male breeding strategy. They do not engage in territorial defense, but rather exploit their resemblance to females to enter a resident male's demesne and interact with the members of his harem.

If the territorial proprietor is heavily preoccupied with the defense of his borders against his neighbors' incursions or should two females simultaneously be ready to spawn, the odds are good that one of these sneaker males may enjoy a degree of reproductive success.

Aquarists have also observed sneaker males actually joining a couple during the actual spawning act.

Presumably, such behavior affords these female impersonators a further opportunity to enjoy reproductive success at the expense of a territorial proprietor.

Though at least two primitive mouthbrooders of the genus *Gymnogeophagus*, *G. balzanii* (PERUGIA 1891) [Figure 192] and *G. gymnogenys* (HENSEL 1879) are known to practice harem polygyny, this mating system is strongly correlated with cave-spawning.

In both cases, the reproductive pattern of these species allows the exclusively maternal brood care that is a prerequisite for such a mating system to evolve.

Though *Acarichthys heckeli* and the several *Guianacara* species are exceptions to this pattern, most harem polygynists are dwarf cichlids. This greatly facilitates their management under aquarium conditions. Openly polygamous cichlids, on the other hand, exclusively comprise species that practice **maternal mouthbrooding.**

This should come as no surprise, for this mode of parental care allows total male emancipation from any sort of custodial involvement.

Under such circumstances, the best way for a male to maximize his reproductive success entails spawning with as many females as possible during a single reproductive period.

Fig. 190 & 191: The differences between male (above) and female (below) *Apistogramma cacatuoides* Hoedemann 1951 with respect to size, fin development and coloration are representative of the sexual dimorphism characteristic of haremically polygynous cichlids.

Fig. 191

Conversely, a female is under no constraint in her choice of sexual partners.

In nature, females typically exercise the option of maximizing the genetic diversity of their broods by dividing a clutch among several males.

Such polygamous mating has given rise to three different mating systems in nature, based upon the presence or absence of male defense of a display and spawning territory, the duration of its defense and the degree to which territorial males are dispersed.

Aterritorial polygamy is essentially a consort-type mating system, in which a male attempts to sequester a receptive female from other males.

The consorting couple moves about freely and spawning occurs wherever the two fish happen to find themselves when the female expels one or more eggs.

Females can — and often do — change spawning partners, though not without protest from their consort of the moment.

This is not a commonly encountered mating system among cichlids.

It has been reported from two quite different Tanganyikan genera, the rock-dwelling *Tropheus* [Figure 193] and the midwater-dwelling *Cyprichromis* [Figure 195] and from some representatives of the more-or-less pelagic Malawian genus *Copadichromis*.

Of the two territorially based mating systems, **persistent display site polygamy is essentially self-explanatory. It is based upon continued male defense of a multi-purpose territory centered upon a suitable display and spawning site against conspecifics of the same sex, or in some cases, against males of other species with identical territorial requirements.**

This again does not appear a widespread option among cichlids. It is prevalent among the mbuna of Lake Malawi [Figure 195] and a number of their Tanganyikan analogues of the genera *Petrochromis, Simochromis* **and** *Cyphotilapia.*

Fig. 192: As might be expected given its polygamous mating system, males of *Gymnogeophagus balzanii* grow twice as large as females and are more brightly colored.

On the other hand, **lek** or **arena type** mating systems are extremely common among mouthbrooding cichlids.

They are characterized by the short-term male occupation of relatively small, tightly clustered breeding territories, often to such an extent that their boundaries are coterminous [Figure 196].

Arena type mating systems are characteristic of mouthbrooding cichlids that breed over open bottoms.

The greater number of species living in such habitats as much as any other consideration may account for the prevalence of lek behavior in the family.

Be that as it may, lek mating systems characterize most Malawian haplochromine genera as well as the overwhelming majority of riverine haplochromines.

Lek behavior has also been observed among representatives of this lineage endemic to the northern Great Lakes such as Kivu and Victoria.

This mating system characterizes a diverse assemblage of Tanganyikan genera, among them the sand-dwelling genera *Callochromis* [Figure 197], *Enantiopus* and *Xenotilapia* as well as the featherfins of the genera *Cyathopharynx* and *Opthalmotilapia*.

Last but not least, the maternal mouthbrooding tilapias of the genus *Oreochromis* are also arena-breeding cichlids. Though the operation of these three mating systems differs dramatically in nature, they fortunately have enough in common to allow the aquarist to manage their practitioners identically in captivity.

I will thus begin this treatment of polygamous cichlids with a brief consideration of haremically polygynous species, then move on to a more detailed discussion of those with openly polygamous mating systems.

Fig. 193: The male of this spawning pair of *Tropheus duboisi* owes his reproductive success to successful sequestration of the ripe female from rival males rather than to defense of a fixed breeding territory.

Fig. 194: As this photo demonstrates, males of the midwater-spawning *Cyprichromis leptosoma* (Boulenger 1898) are very intolerant of one another's proximity, notwithstanding their aterritorial mating system.

Fig. 195: The persistent defense of a combination display and breeding site is typical of many mbuna such as this male *Pseudotropheus greshakei* Meyer & Foerster 1984.

Fig. 196: The tightly packed spawning pits covering the bottom of this pond are typical of an arena of sexually active male *Sarotherodon mossambicus*. This tight clustering of displaying males characterizes all lek breeding cichlids.

Fig. 197: Males of *Callochromis macrops* (Boulenger 1898) move en masse into the shallow water of Lake Tanganyika to dig the pits from which they court potential spawning partners. Females of arena breeding cichlids typically respond to such a sexual cafeteria by dividing their spawning efforts among several different males.

165

Aquarium Management of Haremically Polygynous Cichlids

The chief requirement to be met in any effort to breed haremically polygynous cichlids in captivity is **an aquarium large enough to allow expression of normal territorial behavior by both male and females.**

The crucial consideration here is the tendency of the female's territory to **expand after spawning has occurred.**

If the tank is not large enough to allow for this, the male may find himself in an untenable position once he has performed his essential function. Unless he can move beyond the reach of the newly parental female, he runs a risk of serious injury or even death.

The considerable sexual dimorphism prevalent among these cichlids often deludes novice breeders into believing size alone will protect the male from his erstwhile consort.

This simply is not the case. As the vast majority of these cichlids are dwarf species, housing them properly is hardly an insurmountable obstacle.

Tanks in the 15 gallon to 20 gallon range will comfortably and safely house a trio consisting of a single male and two females of most species.

It is possible to house more than a single male in a tank, but it must afford sufficient space for each to stake out a territory.

Some *Nanochromis* species, as well as the several *Guianacara* and *Gymnogeophagus* species, require considerably larger quarters.

A 40 gallon breeder flat suffices in the first three instances, while *Acarichthys heckeli* should be housed as one would the largest monogamous cichlids.

The dwarf species are relatively retiring cichlids often given to hiding extensively when housed alone.

Addition of six to a dozen **dither fish** goes a long way towards eliminating this shyness. To the extent that they also serve as **target fish,** they often elicit a more reliable manifestation of parental behavior from the female than might otherwise be expected [Figures 198 & 199]. It is not prudent to keep catfish or loaches in the breeding tank.

Such fish pose a real threat to their fry that these cichlids are often at pains to neutralize before spawning.

The prespawning behavior of *Acarichthys* and *Guianacara* may dislodge rooted vegetation.

The remaining species not only tolerate rooted plants, but do best in well planted aquaria. All appreciate the sense of security provided by a screen of floating plants.

Cave spawners appreciate a selection of possible spawning sites.

In nature most Neotropical dwarf species deposit their eggs inside dead leaves that curled up prior to falling into the water [Figure 200]. In captivity, clay flowerpots with enlarged drainage holes [Figure 201], either inverted or placed on their sides, pieces of CPVC pipe or plastic simulacra of hollow pieces of waterlogged wood are all well accepted.

As long as the prospective spawning site has an easily defended entrance, its nature is not usually important.

The only exception to this rule are the Tanganyikan dwarf *Lamprologus* and *Telmatochromis* species that live in intimate association with empty snail shells.

These **ostracophil** cichlids have an uncompromising view of what constitutes a suitable spawning site [Figure 202]. Fortunately, any empty shell of roughly the same size and form as the vacant *Neothauma* shells they occupy in nature satisfies them in captivity.

A mature sponge filter, a thermostatic heater and a tightly fitting cover complete the inventory of necessary tank furnishings.

Because males court females more-or-less continuously, it is not easy to anticipate reproduction. Among cave-spawners, the nature of the spawning site makes it easy to overlook the event until the sudden appearance of mobile fry announces unmistakably that the fish have bred.

Dramatic color changes accompany the onset of parental behavior in the Neotropical genera *Apistogramma, Apistogrammoides, Biotoecus, Crenicara, Taeniacara* and *Nannacara* [Figures 203 & 204].

However, in most cases, changes in female behavior are the best clues to her altered status.

Fig. 198 & 199: Dwarf cichlids such as these *Apistogramma macmasteri* Kullander 1979 are more apt to prove reliable parents when housed with suitable dither/target fish.

Fig. 200:
In nature, *Apistogramma eunotus* Kullander 1981, like many other South American dwarf cichlids, spawns inside curled-up fallen leaves.

Fig. 201: Cave spawning cichlids, such as this pair of oligomelanic orange chromides, *Etroplus maculatus* (Bloch 1785), find small clay flowerpots spawning sites much to their taste.

Fig. 202: The dwarf ostracophil *Lamprologus* such as *L. meeli* Poll 1948 are quite insistent about spawning within an empty snail shell. Such inflexibility is unusual in cave spawning cichlids.

Reluctance to emerge from her shelter combined with extreme intolerance of the male's presence in its vicinity are dependable indications a female is defending a clutch. Females are usually reliable and efficient mothers.

Young fish often devour their first few clutches, then settle down to become model parents.

Aquarists unwilling to exercise patience in this cause or faced with persistent filial cannibalism find the eggs of these species can be artificially incubated following the procedure outlined for those of monogamous cichlids. Parental care usually persists for three to four weeks in captivity.

As she begins to ripen a new batch of eggs, the female looses interest in her older progeny. As spawning approaches she commonly attempts to drive them from her territory.

The male may afford them some protection, but his efforts fall far short of the female's in effectiveness. This is not conducive to fry survival if other fish are present.

It is thus best to remove them prior to this point for rearing elsewhere.

The mobile fry of the smaller *Apistogramma* species, the diminutive *Apistogrammoides pucullpaensis* MEINKEN 1965, *Taeniacara candidae* MYERS 1935 and *Gymnogeophagus balzanii* [Figure 205] require microworms as their initial food.

Those of the remaining species can be started on *Artemis* nauplii.

The microbial fauna in their tank provides an important supplementary food source for these fry.

They grow more rapidly and evince a higher survival rate when spawned in established aquaria furnished with matured sponge filters. All are extremely sensitive to dissolved metabolic wastes.

Not surprisingly, regular partial water changes are an essential adjunct to their successful rearing.

Fry of most of these cichlids grow more slowly than those of their larger relatives even under favorable conditions.

169

Fig. 203 & 204: As can be seen from this comparison of sexually quiescent (above) and parental (below) individuals, female *Apistogramma commbrae* (Regan 1906) undergo an unmistakable color change after spawning. This is the norm among haremically polygynous Neotropical cichlids.

Fig. 204: The involvement of this young male *A. commbrae* in the care of the eggs represents an alternative reproductive strategy he will outgrow when he reaches full adult size.

Fig. 205: Given the size of their parents, it is quite surprising that the fry of this female *Gymnogeophagus balzanii* are too small to take newly hatched brine shrimp for their initial meal.

However, as they mature at a smaller size than do most monogamous cichlids the two factors tend to cancel out.

Sibling cannibalism is less of a problem among these cichlids than it is with most of their larger relatives.

Remember when sorting fry that all these fish are characterized by markedly precocious male growth superiority.

Prespawning Management of Openly Polygamous Cichlids

Openly polygamous cichlids, as already noted, differ in their mating systems.

Fortunately, a single management approach is possible for all under aquarium conditions.

This commonality depends on the simple fact that none of these mating systems is characterized by long-term association of the sexes either before or after spawning.

As a corollary to this, their practitioners lack the behavioral mechanisms that allow male and female of a monogamous pair to occupy the same piece of real estate persistently without intersexual mayhem.

Virtually all failures with these cichlids stem from the mistaken belief they can be maintained as isolated single pairs.

The inevitable consequence of such efforts is a badly battered or dead female.

This unhappy ending can be easily avoided if the fish are housed in an environment that affords the female sufficient space to avoid unwanted male attention, while distracting the male from the incessant pursuit and solicitation of a single female. To satisfy the first requirement, set these fish up in the largest tanks available.

Breeding groups of some of the smaller riverine and Lake Victoria *Haplochromis* [Figure 206] and Malawian **mbuna** [Figure 207] species can be kept successfully in 25 to 30 gallon aquaria.

171

Fig. 206: Most extra-Malawian Haplochromis, such as this *H. (Astatotilapia) callipterus* Gunther 1893 can be successfully kept and bred in tanks of 25 to 35 gallons capacity.

Fig. 207: *Labidochromis chisumulae* Lewis 1982 is one of the few mbuna that can be safely housed in tanks of less than 50 gallons capacity.

Fig. 208: *Pseudotropheus lombardoi* Burgess 1977 is typical of the mbuna in its space requirements. Females of this beautiful cichlid are metallic blue with dark vertical bars.

However, a 50 gallon tank is the smallest that can safely house most of these fish, while tanks in the 75 to 90 gallon range are better suited to their needs [Figures 208 & 209]. For the larger riverine and Victorian haplochromines [Figures 210 & 211], representatives of the haplochromine genera native to Lake Malawi [Figure 212], the Tanganyikan endemics of the genera *Cyphotilapia, Lobochilotes* and *Petrochromis* as well as most *Oreochromis* species, a hundred gallons of water barely suffices. To summarize the situation concisely, the degree of difficulty encountered in efforts to breed these cichlids is inversely related to the volume of their aquarium.

There are two equally effective means of protecting females from male harassment.

The simplest is to maintain the fish as single pairs in a rather crowded community of behaviorally and environmentally compatible cichlids.

Competitive interactions with other males for access to spawning sites keep a male too busy for obsessive pursuit of the female, while limiting extreme manifestations of aggression

to the brief period immediately prior to spawning. These fish are uninhibited about spawning under such conditions, which approximate closely those encountered in the wild. The **mixed species community approach** to housing these cichlids has disadvantages, to which I will return.

However, amateur breeders are partial to it because it allows them to maintain a wider variety of species in the space at their disposal.

The second approach is to maintain each species in single male, multiple female groups usually referred to as harems, though it must be noted the behavior of these cichlids has little in common with that of the harem polygynists already discussed.

The sheer number of potential spawning partners available keeps a male from concentrating on one female long enough to injure or kill her.

Obviously, the more females present, the better this approach will work. A ratio of three females to one male represents the bottom line in this respect.

173

Fig. 209: The smaller endemic haplochromines of Lake Malawi such as the sunshine peacock, *Aulonacara baenschi* Meyer & Riehl 1985, can also be kept and bred successfully in 75 to 90 gallon tanks.

Fig. 210: The large territories defended by males of *Haplochromis (Thoracochromis) bakongo* Thys 1964, a strongly rheophilous cichlid from the Zaire River, dictate that it be housed in sizeable aquaria despite its modest size.

Fig. 211: The large size of *Haplochromis (Harpagochromis) squamulatus* Regan 1922, one of Lake Victoria's few surviving predatory cichlids, makes it imprudent to house breeding groups in tanks of less than 75 gallons capacity.

There may be an upper limit, determined by the number of females a male can adequately service. If so, I have yet to find it.

Commercial breeders are partial to this approach because it maximizes fry output while eliminating all possibility of accidental hybridization, a hazard never entirely precluded when fish are housed in mixed species communities.

The maintenance requirements of these cichlids do not otherwise differ from those of their monogamous counterparts.

The Tanganyikan and Malawian representatives of the group require hard, alkaline water and are much less tolerant of dissolved metabolites than the majority of extralacustrine cichlids.

Correct nitrogen cycle management is thus critically important, for when stressed these cichlids are vulnerable to systemic bacterial infections such as "Malawi bloat".

Providing suitable shelter in their quarters also makes life easier for females. If his object is replication of the fishes' native biotope, their keeper will have to research their natural history, as this assemblage of species is ecologically diverse.

If his approach is strictly pragmatic, he will find that either clay flowerpots or sections of CPVC pipe of appropriate diameter are equally acceptable to these fish.

These cichlids have hearty appetites. Females in particular seem to eat incessantly as spawning approaches. Their need to lay down metabolic reserves is understandable in view of the extended fast that characterizes buccal incubation.

Fortunately, they are not fussy eaters. While all appreciate the addition of live food to their menu, they do well fed a diet based upon prepared foods.

This group includes a number of herbivorous species whose nutritional requirements include regular access to vegetable food. Preliminary research into the feeding pattern of the species he wishes to keep and breed will facilitate the planning of a suitable conditioning program.

175

Fig. 212: Robust Rift Lake cichlids, such as the Malawian *Nimbochromis polystigma* (Regan 1921), require very large tanks for successful maintenance and breeding in captivity.

Postspawning Management of Openly Polygamous Cichlids

As noted, these fish spawn freely either in a mixed species community or when housed in single species, multiple female breeding groups.

A partial water change sometimes triggers an inexplicably reticent female's libido, but overall, only physical separation of the sexes will prevent these cichlids from breeding.

The mechanics of spawning are quite diverse and invariably interesting.

Among most species of this group, the female picks up her eggs immediately after depositing them.

Fertilization subsequently takes place **inside** her buccal cavity.

It is not unusual for the female to leave the nest of the male with whom she has just completed a spawning bout to seek out another consort.

Such overt manifestations of open polygamy appear to underlie field observations that females of several species of the Tanganyikan featherfin genus *Opthalmotilapia* actually approach a displaying male with a mouth already full of unfertilized eggs.

Several mechanisms have evolved to insure fertilization after the eggs have been taken up by the female.

Among Malawian haplochromines, most of their Tanganyikan counterparts, the dwarf mouthbrooders of the genus *Pseudocrenilabrus* and the maternal mouthbrooding tilapias of the genus *Oreochromis*, the female nips directly at the male's vent to elicit ejaculation [Figures 213–218]. His genital papilla is usually contrastingly colored and stands out clearly against a darker abdominal region. It is also likely the female's response is mediated in part by powerful chemical cues.

Among riverine *Haplochromis* and haplochromines endemic to Lakes Victoria, Edward,

George and Kivu, the females instead nip at brightly colored spots conspicuously displayed upon the male's anal fin.

These resemble in shape and color the eggs she has just picked up.

Her response to these "egg dummies" both elicits ejaculation and assures that the sperm reaches its ultimate destination [Figures 219—225].

In several genera of Tanganyikan feather-fins, the swollen, light-colored tips of the male's ventral fins serve the same function [Figure 226].

A few species have even progressed to the point where fertilization occurs with minimal contact between the sexes.

In *Oreochromis macrochir* (BOULENGER 1912) [Figure 227], the male deposits sperm at the spawning site for the ovigerous female to pick up.

His proximity is unnecessary under the circumstances. Indeed, he may be several body lengths distant from the female when fertilization occurs! After spawning, the female seeks out a sheltered spot away from the breeding site.

In lacustrine environments, such "nursery grounds" are typically wave-washed beaches or rocky shallows that combine low visibility with high dissolved oxygen values [Figure 228]. Under aquarium conditions, sudden onset of reclusive behavior combined with refusal to feed are equally valid manifestations of ovigery.

It is usually easy to recognize a laden female. Typically, full flanks are replaced by a distended throat, or when she is seen from above, laterally expanded opercula. Some species have small spawns that do not produce marked distension of the buccopharyngeal

Fig. 213
Fig. 213—218: Spawning sequences of an advanced mouthbrooder, *Oreochromis cf. spilurus* (Gunther 1894). Note how the female mouths the male's contrasting genital papilla after picking up a batch of eggs.

Fig. 214

Fig. 215

Fig. 216

region, but even a small clutch produces evident expansion of the gill covers.

As noted, most ovigerous females do not feed during the incubation sequence.

Such behavior is not universal, but food intake of laden females is obviously reduced even in species that do not fast.

The major decision the breeder faces in postspawning management of these cichlids is whether to move the ovigerous female or to allow her to complete the incubation sequence in the breeding tank.

For some, such as the *Tropheus* of Lake Tanganyika and most, though not all, of the Malawian *mbuna*, a purely naturalistic approach is feasible.

Adults of these essentially herbivorous fishes lack both the motivation and motor skills to prey efficiently upon their newly released fry. If they are maintained as single

Fig. 217

Fig. 218

179

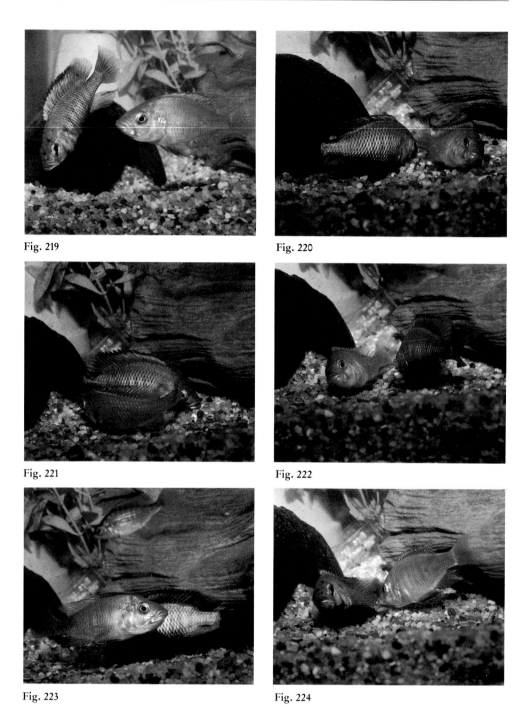

Fig. 219

Fig. 220

Fig. 221

Fig. 222

Fig. 223

Fig. 224

Fig. 219—225: Spawning sequences of the Lake Victoria blue and gold *Haplochromis*, an undescribed species often confused with *H. obliquidens* Hilgendorf 1888. Note how the female nips at the pseudo-ocelli on the male's anal fin after picking up a batch of eggs.

Fig. 225

species breeding groups in well-furnished tanks and fed well, there is no need to isolate ovigerous females.

Their fry run little risk of predation once released into such an environment [Figure 229].

In most cases, however, this approach is impractical.

A parental female comes in for more harassment in a mixed species group than she would encounter either in nature or a single species breeding group.

This can provoke premature termination of the incubation sequence as the persecuted female either spits out or eats her brood, although it should be noted that such an extreme response is more likely from an inexperienced female.

In any event, fry survival in a mixed species community is a very dubious proposition, as relatively few females can effectively defend their mobile progeny in such a setting.

The question is thus not **whether** a female should be moved into a separate nursery tank, but rather **when** the move should be undertaken [Figure 230].

At first glance, it might seem that the obvious answer would be as soon as possible after spawning.

Regrettably, females in the initial stages of incubation are apt to respond to the trauma of capture by ejecting their burden in transit to the nursery tank.

Zygotes in the earliest stages of development are seldom taken up by their mother once expelled from her buccal cavity and are extremely difficult to incubate artificially.

Females that have carried for some time are less apt to eject their progeny when moved and more likely to pick them up again should they do so.

Furthermore, if the female does not resume her maternal duties, it is easier for the aquarist to act *in loco parentis* towards relatively advanced embryos.

Prudence dictates waiting at least **three** and preferably **seven** days before removing an ovigerous female.

In a breeding tank well provided with cover, the female runs minimal risk of harassment in this interval.

Scale the nursery tank to the size of the female. A five gallon tank suffices for females of most riverine haplochromines and the smaller **mbuna** species, a fifteen gallon tank for those of all save the group's largest representatives.

Fig. 226: The light-colored, expanded ventral fin tips of this male *Opthalmotilapia ventralis* (Boulenger 1898) function as "egg dummies" during the spawning act.

Fig. 227: Males of *Oreochromis macrochir* (Boulenger 1912) deposit sperm in their nest pits that the female takes into her buccal cavity to fertilize eggs already held therein.

Fig. 228: Yacht Club Beach near Jinja, Uganda, a typical nursery ground for ovigerous female haplochromines in Lake Victoria.

Fig. 229: If the breeding tank is well furnished with rockwork, ovigerous female *Mbuna* such as this *Pseudotropheus socolofi* Jonson 1974 can be left undisturbed in the reasonable expectation that most of the fry released into such an environment will survive.

The tank should contain freshly drawn water of the same temperature and chemical makeup as that of the breeding tank. Furnish it with a thermostatically controlled heater and a mature sponge filter appropriate to its volume.

Cover the bottom with a thin layer of gravel to eliminate disturbing reflections and provide the female with some sort of shelter.

A clay flowerpot, its mouth facing away from the front glass, serves satisfactorily. A layer of floating plants is appreciated, though not essential. A tight cover is.

Ovigerous females are extremely intolerant of one another's proximity. Thus, one should **never** house more than one per tank, or in the case of a partitioned aquarium, one per compartment. In the latter instance, it may also be necessary to separate the fish with opaque partitions.

If the fish can see one another they may become sufficiently disturbed to expel or eat their broods. As noted, many females maintain a light food intake during incubation.

However, it is not essential to feed them at this time.

Indeed, from the standpoint of proper nitrogen cycle management in the nursery tank, much can said against the practice. Remember that metabolic functions do not cease simply because a fish is not eating.

Over and above the female's contribution, the developing embryos also generate a significant amount of metabolic waste. It is therefore prudent to replace some of the nursery tank's water every three to five days until the young become mobile.

The duration of buccal incubation varies between species and is also influenced by ambient temperature. At 85 °F, ovigerous female Malawian haplochromines carry for twenty-one days. Lowering the temperature 5 °F adds another week to the developmental interval.

Fig. 230: This ovigerous female *Haplochromis (Prognathochromis) perrieri* (Pellegrin 1909) will complete the incubation sequence in a community tank. However, her inability to provide effective protection to free-swimming young in such a setting makes her isolation in a nursery tank essential if any fry are to be saved.

In general, riverine haplochromines and mouthbrooding tilapias carry for two weeks at 85 °F, Tanganyikan and Malawian endemic species for three weeks at the same temperature.

There is sufficient variability among these cichlids to make further generalizations impossible.

Duration of the developmental interval is a reproductive idiosyncracy that must be researched for each species.

The breeder may be faced with the need to artificially incubate embryos of these advanced mouthbrooding cichlids.

There are many workable designs for an "artificial mouth".

All have in common some arrangement for **gently** circulating the water in a small container in a manner that imitates the tumbling the developing young are given in their mother's buccal cavity. Strong currents that dash the young against its walls must be avoided.

The developing embryos are extremely fragile.

Such treatment will either kill them or cause congenital deformities. Addition of a bacteriostatic agent is essential, as the developing embryos are susceptible to microbial attack.

The medications suggested for use when artificially hatching the eggs of substratum-spawning cichlids suffice for the present case, though prudence dictates using them at lower concentrations.

Partially replace the contents of the "artificial mouth" every other day with water of the same temperature and chemical make-up. Remember to replace medication lost in the process.

Check the vessel frequently and remove any dead young **immediately**.

If their decomposition fouls the water, further losses are inevitable.

Be it noted mortalities are inevitable with the best of care.

The percentage depends largely upon the embryos' stage of development at the time of their ejection.

The younger they are, the more fragile, and the higher the probable loss rate.

The same rule applies to the incidence of congenital abnormalities in artificially incubated fry.

Given the less than satisfactory outcome of the process and the time and effort entailed in its implementation, it is incredible that many breeders will strip a female of her young as early as three days postspawning to put the embryos into an "artificial mouth"!

Cichlids have had over 65 million years to refine the techniques of buccal incubation; aquarists have been imitating them for three decades.

There is no better reason for regarding artificial incubation as an emergency measure only and making every possible effort to encourage ovigerous females to complete a normal incubation sequence.

In nature, the female seeks a secluded area to release her fry. Depending upon both her species and the environment in which she finds herself, she either abandons her progeny at this juncture or else continues to guard them as they forage.

Faced with a threat to their safety, she signals their return to the shelter of her mouth [Figure 231]. In captivity, females are often reluctant to release their offspring in the nursery tank's bare surroundings.

Others do release them, but are so ill at ease they pick them up again at the slightest disturbance [Figure 232].

Though such postrelease defense may be essential to fry survival in nature, this behavior seriously interferes with normal feeding in captivity.

There is thus little benefit to prolonging the association of mother and fry once the latter are free-swimming.

It is a simple matter to remove fry from the buccal cavity of females 3"–4" SL and larger. Hold the female within the folds of a net head down over a container filled with water from the nursery tank. Gently pull open her lower jaw and immerse her head in the vessel.

The young usually swim out into the container without further urging, though gentle shaking may be required to dislodge the last few from their refuge.

Smaller species must be handled differently. The easiest way to dislodge their fry is to insert the female head down in an ordinary kitchen baster from which the squeeze bulb has been removed.

Replace the bulb and insert the tip of the baster into a container filled with water from the nursery tank.

Squeeze the bulb gently several times to force water back and forth through the female's buccal cavity.

This flushes the fry into the receiving container.

If several minutes of squeezing have no effect, remove the baster from the water and hold it opening down over the container for a few moments.

Then re-immerse it and repeat the cycle of flushing.

Fry should begin to emerge from the baster's opening after a few squeezes.

Some breeders advocate a reconditioning period for the female prior to reintroducing her to the society of other fishes.

This is not absolutely essential provided the existing peck order in her tank of origin is somewhat disrupted concurrently with her return.

A partial water change coupled with rearrangement of tank furnishings serves this purpose effectively.

The ease with which both flowerpots and sections of CPVC pipe can be reshuffled to accomplish this end is a powerful argument for their use as tank furnishings in preference to natural rockwork.

Fry of these cichlids are robust and well able to take *Artemia* nauplii and finely powdered prepared foods for their initial meal. They should be handled in the same manner as substratum spawner fry.

Overall, their rearing poses few difficulties as long as the aquarist is conscientious in managing the nitrogen cycle in their tank.

185

Fig. 231: The female *Geophagus steindachneri* continues to defend her mobile young for weeks following their initial release. Such behavior is common among advanced mouthbrooders.

Fig. 232: When danger threatens, most female mouthbrooders behave in the same manner as this female *Pseudotropheus cf. macropthalmus* and allow the fry to shelter within their buccal cavities when confronted by a perceived threat.

They grow rapidly even by cichlid standards.

Precocious male growth superiority is particularly evident in these fish.

As with monogamous cichlids, the difficulties aquarists encounter in efforts to breed these fish stem from a misunderstanding of the aquaristic implications of their mating systems.

Cichlids with openly polygamous mating systems do not possess the behavioral adaptations that permit monogamous pairs to coexist in the same territory over the long term. Thus attempts to maintain them as single isolated pairs are doomed to failure.

Maintained either in mixed species communities or in single species, multiple female breeding groups, these cichlids can be counted upon to spawn freely, while their highly evolved parental care makes them among the most easily bred of all aquarium fishes.

CHAPTER 8

CATALOG OF RESIDENTS FOR THE CICHLID AQUARIUM.

OLD WORLD CICHLIDS. PART I.

Introduction

Thus far, I have presented an overview of the natural history of the Family Cichlidae as a whole and elucidated broadly applicable approaches to the maintenance and breeding of cichlids in captivity.

It should by now be evident that the family is as rich in species as it is biologically diverse.

This affords much satisfaction to aquarists, who quickly discover the Cichlidae offer a selection capable of satisfying the most varied tastes in aquarium fishes. However, this embarrassment of riches complicates the task of conveying essential information about individual species.

To do justice to each would require a work of several volumes.

In this chapter and the one following, I address this problem by dividing the family into several operationally defined groups whose shared characteristics dictate similar approaches to their maintenance.

In selecting species to illustrate each of these groups, I have based my choice largely upon their aquaristic desirability and overall commercial availability.

However, it would be disingenuous to deny I have sometimes inserted a few personal favorites into this roster! This chapter and the one following are devoted to Old World cichlids.

Chapter 10 will deal with the Neotropical representatives of the family, while Chapter 11 will be devoted to dwarf cichlids. Thus dividing the family along geographic lines is unlikely to provoke comment, but placing dwarf cichlids in a separate chapter requires some explanation. Dwarf cichlids represent a purely operational category.

It comprises both African and South American species grouped together because of their common husbandry requirements. There are thus sound practical reasons for treating these diminutive species as a single group regardless of their point of origin.

Given the upsurge of interest in these diminutive cichlids, no less than the dramatic increase in the number of species available to aquarists, it seems appropriate to afford them a separate chapter.

The Cichlids of India, Sri Lanka and Madagascar

At first glance, this may seem a most peculiar grouping of cichlids. There is certainly no question that the closest relatives of the Indian genus *Etroplus* CUVIER 1830 are the Malagasy species of the genus *Paretroplus* BLEEKER 1868.

The relationships of the remaining Malagasy cichlids are less immediately obvious.

Fig. 233: A spawning pair of *Etroplus suratensis*. The green chromide is a prolific cichlid with a preference for enclosed spawning sites in captivity.

In the first edition of this work, I suggested grouping all of these fish with the etropline lineage in its narrow sense purely for convenience's sake.

However, in a recent paper, Dr. MELANIE STIASSNY has since suggested that all the Malagasy cichlids plus *Etroplus* represent a natural evolutionary grouping.

Her evidence, based upon detailed studies of the skeletal anatomy of these fishes, is persuasive and dovetails nicely with what is known of the historical biogeography of Madagascar and the Indian subcontinent.

It thus seems both biologically and operationally defensible to group these cichlids under a common heading.

Etroplus comprises three recognized species.

Two of these, the green chromide, *Etroplus suratensis* (BLOCH 1790), and the orange chromide, *Etroplus maculatus* (BLOCH 1795) are native to lowland fresh and brackish water biotopes in the southern third of India and the entire island of Sri Lanka.

The third species, *Etroplus canarensis* DAY 1878, is restricted to coastal rivers in the Indian state of Karnataka.

The green and orange chromides coexist in nature and enjoy an unusual and intimate ecological relationship.

Adult orange chromides prey on the eggs and larvae of green chromides.

However, subadult orange chromides act as "cleaner fish" for subadult and adult green chromides, ridding them of ectoparasites.

Such behavior can be elicited in captivity by housing these two cichlids together.

Etroplus suratensis is a deep-bodied species capable of attaining 10" SL under favorable conditions, though specimens half that size are considered large in nature.

Albeit found in pure fresh water throughout its range, it is most abundant in brackish habitats and displays a marked preference for such conditions in captivity.

Kept at salinities between 10% and 15% those of sea water, the green chromide is a hardy, easily cared for cichlid.

Fig. 234: A sexually active female of the wild color form of the orange chromide, *Etroplus maculatus*. Note the iridescent white spot on the upper and lower distal margins of the caudal fin.

Fig. 235: Like other *damba* species, *Paretroplus damii* Bleeker 1868 lives in close association with water-logged wood in nature.

Fig. 236: This specimen of *Paretroplus petiti* Pellegrin 1929 was collected from Lac Andropongy in north-western Madagascar, one of the few remaining localities where this formerly widespread species can still be found.

Fig. 237: *Paretroplus kieneri* Arnoult 1960 displays a great deal of individual variation in color pattern. Oligomelanic individuals have been collected from Lac Kinkony, but it remains to be determined if this population is truly polymorphic.

However, when maintained in strictly fresh water, however hard and alkaline, it is usually prone to skin parasites and bacterial infections and rarely looks its best.

This species also appreciates warmth.

It can tolerate temperatures up to 92 °F, and it seems unhappy if its water drops below 80 °F.

Its feeding pattern in nature is markedly herbivorous.

This dietary preference carries over in captivity.

Hence, *E. suratensis* is a poor candidate for a planted aquarium whose diet must include a generous amount of vegetable matter.

The green chromide can be safely housed with smaller non-cichlids, as it is at best an inept predator. Adults become intolerant of conspecifics with the onset of breeding.

Though its formidable dentition might suggest the contrary, this is an otherwise unaggressive cichlid.

The green chromide has the reputation of being difficult to spawn in captivity.

This seems in part due to ignorance of its environmental preferences and dietary requirements, to the absence of obvious external sexual distinctions, and to the fact this slow-growing cichlid must be at least 4.5" SL before attaining reproductive competence.

Etroplus suratensis is a biparentally custodial substratum spawning cichlid. In nature it places its eggs upon exposed holdfasts of the aquatic plants in whose vicinity it spends most of its time.

In captivity, it displays a preference for vertical spawning sites [Figure 233]. Spawns number from 500 to 1000 eggs.

Hatching occurs in 72 hours at 82 °F, and the fry become mobile five days later. Young pairs usually eat their first few spawns, then settle down to become model parents.

In nature, several pairs may collaborate in defense of their pooled fry, but such creching behavior has yet to be reported in captivity.

Fry survival and growth are enhanced when the young are raised with their parents, as they rely to a degree upon parental mucus as food.

Fig. 238: The combination of bold markings and a deeply lunate caudal fin make *Paretroplus maculatus* Kiener and Mauge 1966 a truly striking *damba*.

Parental care can persist up to 12 weeks under aquarium conditions.

The fry grow fairly slowly and do not attain sexual maturity until the eighteenth month postspawning.

The orange chromide, *Etroplus maculatus* [Figure 234] is, to the contrary, one of the most easily bred small cichlids known to the hobby.

Its popularity has increased enormously since the introduction of an oligomelanic strain sold under the somewhat misleading trade name of "red chromide", whose base color ranges from bright orange-red to golden yellow depending upon its diet. Like its larger congener, it relishes warmth. Unlike the green chromide, it does not require brackish water to do well in captivity.

As long as extremes of pH and hardness are avoided, it will prosper in whatever water it finds itself.

The orange chromide nibbles at soft leafed plants, but hardly poses the threat to aquatic vegetation of its more robust relative.

It is a more accomplished predator than *E. suratensis,* but as the orange chromide rarely exceeds 3" SL, it poses no danger to any fish larger than a male guppy. The presence of conspecifics is not appreciated at breeding time, but even when spawning, *E. maculatus* is an acceptable community tank resident. It seems to have the knack of successfully defending its fry without attempting the wholesale massacre of its tankmates.

Etroplus maculatus is a biparentally custodial cave spawning species. Spawns number up to 300 elliptical tan to olive-grey eggs. The developmental interval for the zygotes is identical to that of the green chromide. Parental care is intense, comprising elaborate hygienic and custodial elements.

As with its larger congener, young pairs often devour their first few spawns before attaining full reproductive competence. Rearing the young apart from their parents is possible, but fry mortality is substantially greater than when the young have access to parental mucus for their first few weeks.

191

Parental care in nature can persist for four months, but rarely lasts longer than eight weeks in captivity.

The young grow rapidly, attaining sexual maturity between four and six months post-spawning at just under 1.5" SL. Even at this size, females can be recognized easily by the opalescent white distal spots on their caudal fins.

These patches of specialized tissue release a pheromone that plays an important role in courtship.

The Malagasy genus *Paretroplus* comprises five robust species virtually indistinguishable from *E. suratensis* in body shape, but possessed of more or less deeply emarginate caudal fins.

Referred to collectively as *damba* by the Malagasy people, these cichlids were formerly the basis of a significant fishery.

They have been displaced over much of their range by introduced tilapia species, although the mechanism underlying this phenomenon is unclear. Direct competition for available food resources seems unlikely.

The tilapias naturalized on Madagascar are for the most part detritus-feeders.

Preliminary work done on *damba* feeding patterns by French fisheries biologists suggests that as adults, they feed upon the leaves and bulbs of aquatic plants and upon zooplankton.

Their massive pharyngeal dentition certainly affords them the option of supplementing this bill of fare with snails and aquatic arthropods. Perhaps juvenile tilapias and *damba* are direct competitors for food.

Alternatively, the introduced cichlids may interfere with *damba* reproduction by displacing them from suitable spawning sites.

However, the biology of all *Paretroplus* species is poorly known and further research will be required to test the validity of these hypotheses. Suffice it to say that these formerly abundant cichlids have become quite rare and face an increasingly uncertain future in their homeland.

Fig. 239: The pinstripe *damba*, an undescribed *Paretroplus* species now restricted to Lac Sarodrano, a small oxbow lake in the Kamoro River basin, may enjoy the dubious distinction of being Madagascar's most highly endangered freshwater fish.

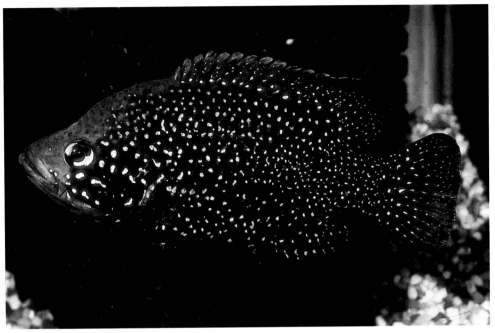

Fig. 240: A parental female *Paratilapia polleni* descended from fish collected on the eastern coastal plain of Madagascar.

Paretroplus damii BLEEKER 1868, type species of the genus [Figure 235], occurs in both fresh and brackish waters along the northwestern coast of Madagascar, while *P. polyactis* BLEEKER 1878 inhabits comparable biotopes along the entire eastern coast of the island. The remaining three species, *Paretroplus petiti* PELLEGRIN 1929 [Figure 236], *P. kieneri* ARNOULT 1960 [Figure 237] and *P. maculatus* KIENER and Mauge 1966 [Figure 238] are restricted to strictly freshwater biotopes in the northwestern region of Madagascar.

All five species were brought back to Europe between 1991 and 1992 by French aquarists, who also collected two additional undescribed species.

One of these, the pinstripe *damba*, is restricted to a single small lake on the western coastal plain [Figure 239].

The second is a strikingly colored rheophile species native to tributaries of the Sofia River basin near the town of Mandritsara in northwestern Madagascar.

Interestingly, this cichlid, whose bright orange-red breeding coloration is accented by two black midlateral bars, was quite familiar to the local people, who refer to it as *lamena* or *damba mena* [= red *damba*].

At first glance, the *lamena* appears to be a modified *Paretroplus* that stands in the same relationship to the deeper-bodied *damba* species as do the rheophilous *Theraps* species to the other representatives of this Mesoamerican genus.

According to Dr. MELANIE STIASSNY, who has examined the anatomy of preserved specimens in some detail, the Malagasy fishermen who aided NOURISSAT and his companions are quite correct to regard the *lamena* as a somewhat modified *Paretroplus*.

The behavior of *damba* under aquarium conditions is reminiscent of *E. suratensis*, but wildcaught individuals seem less tolerant of conspecifics as they grow to maturity than is their Asian relative.

To date, only one of these biparentally custodial substratum spawners, *P. kieneri*, has spawned successfully in outdoor ponds in France and Florida. Behavioral similarities between this *damba* and the green chromide

193

Fig. 241: A young male *fiamanga, Paratilapia bleekeri* Sauvage 1891. Like its congener *P. polleni*, this adaptable small predator was once widespread on both versants of Madagascar.

appear to extend to details of its reproductive biology as well.

The Swiss aquarist PATRICK DE RHAM has successfully bred the *lamena.*

He reports that parental care in this spectacularly colored cichlid is male dominated, but otherwise similar to that of the Asian etroplines.

It remains to be determined if the fry of the Malagasy etroplines share the mucus-feeding proclivities of their Asian cousins.

The *lamena* is clearly the most brightly hued *damba.*

Indeed, its saturated orange-red breeding dress puts in in the top running for the title of most intensely colored cichlid! However, *Paretroplus polyactis,* with its overall orange hue, red-trimmed vertical fins and bright red eye, *P. petiti* and *P. damii* compare favorably with any genus of Paleotropical or Neotropical cichlids in this regard.

Though their coloration is more subtle, even *P. maculatus* and the pinstripe *damba,* with their graceful movements and deeply

emarginate caudal fins reminiscent of the Tanganyikan *Lamprologus brichardi,* also have a fair shot at winning popularity among aquarists.

One can only hope that all of the *damba* win places among the ranks of aquarium residents, for their survival prospects in Madagascar are tenuous in the extreme.

Madagascar is home to an even more highly specialized rheophilous cichlid than the *lamena. Oxylapia polli* KEINER and MAUGE 1966 is native to fast-flowing upland streams in the Mangoro River drainage of Tamatave Province in east-central Madagascar. Details of its skeletal anatomy proclaim the etropline affinities in this monotypic genus.

Superficially similar to the rheophile Central American cichlids of the genus *Theraps,* its dentition and feeding behavior are reminiscent of the Tanganyikan invertebrate-picking genera *Eretmodus, Spathodus* and *Tanganicodus.*

Nothing is known of its reproductive biology, a state of affairs likely to persist into the immediate future, given the remoteness of its habitat and the logistic difficulties that complicate fish collecting in Madagascar.

The genus *Paratilapia* is somewhat reminiscent of the West African genus *Hemichromis* or the smaller *guapotes* of the Neotropical genus *Nandopsis* in overall aspect.

Formerly thought to be monotypic, the genus actually comprises three species. The type species is *Paratilapia polleni* BLEEKER 1868.

The *marakely*, as it is known to the Malagasy people, was described from material collected on Nosy Be, a large island just off the northwest coast of Madagascar.

The present aquarium strain of this species is descended from fish collected on the east coast of Madagascar, a fact which suggests *P. polleni* occurs on both slopes of Madagascar.

The second species of the genus, *Paratilapia bleekeri* SAUVAGE 1891, was described on the basis of material collected from swamps and rice paddies on the central plateau near Antananarivo.

This area constitutes the headwaters of the westward flowing Betsiboka River.

The aquarium strain of the *fiamanga*, as this species is known to the Betsileo people of southeastern Madagascar, is descended from fish collected in the headwaters of the Sofia, another western slope river and from east coast streams near the cities of Diego Saurez and Toamasina.

This suggests that the *P. bleekeri* is also widely distributed in Madagascar.

A third, undescribed species is known only from preserved material collected in Lake Ihotry, in the dry southwestern corner of the island.

The two *Paratilapia* species available to aquarists are easily distinguished.

Paratilapia polleni is variably marked with numerous small metallic blue and gold spangles on the head, body and fins, lacks an unbroken black bar across the forehead when sexually active and has the posterior margin of the lower jaw exposed.

The metallic spangles of *P. bleekeri* are much larger and sport a greenish tint. An unbroken dark bar is present across the forehead in aggressive sexually active individuals of

Fig. 242: The egg mass of *Paratilapia polleni* immediately prior to hatching.

both sexes and the posterior margin of the lower jaw is covered by a fold of skin.

Both species are robust predators capable of reaching 12" SL, although specimens two-thirds that size would be considered large by Malagasy fishermen today.

These distinctive cichlids were effectively ubiquitous in Madagascar, having the widest temperature and salinity tolerances of any endemic cichlid.

On the basis of museum collections, it can be inferred that they existed sympatrically. However, while both species may have occurred in the same river basin, it is unclear whether they occurred in the same habitats.

Their situation is suggestive of that enjoyed by the banded jewelfishes *Hemichromis fasciatus* and *H. elongatus* in West Africa.

However, given the present relictual distribution of both the *marakely* and the *fiamanga*, it is unlikely that a clear picture of their interactions will ever emerge.

Both species have been replaced in the central plateau region by an exotic competitor, the black bass, and face the threat of both competition from and predation by another introduced species, the Asian snakehead, both on the plateau and in the coastal lowlands.

Their ability to tolerate a degree of salinity may afford them a refuge from these two antagonists, but their future in the wild, like that of most other Malagasy cichlids, seems far from secure.

Both the *marakely* [Figure 240] and the *fiamanga* [Figure 241] are attractively colored species.

Like their mainland African and Neotropical look-alikes, *Paratilpia* cannot be described as highly social species.

However, adults are more tolerant of conspecifics than either the larger *Hemichromis* species or *guapotes* of comparable size. The behavior of sexually quiescent individuals towards companions too large to swallow can be described as exemplary.

Neither the *marakely* nor the *fiamanga* eats or gratuitously uproots aquatic plants. However, sexually active individuals are energetic diggers and move substantial volumes of gravel when preparing a spawning site.

Fig. 243: A young male *Ptychochromis oligoacanthus* (Bleeker 1863) of the east coast population.

Fig. 244: A female *Teleogramma brichardi* Poll 1959, the most frequently exported of the Zairean worm cichlids.

Such activity can pose a risk to even well-rooted plants should they occur within the bounds of a pair's territory.

Both *Paratilapia* species are biparentally custodial substratum spawning cichlids.

Males are larger than females, display a more rounded cranial profile and have somewhat longer dorsal and anal fins. Sexual color differences are absent.

These cichlids are prolific, producing spawns of up to 3600 ovoid pinkish brown eggs, whose mode of attachment to the substratum has no parallel within the entire Family Cichlidae [Figure 242].

The first published account of the reproductive behavior of that species by the French biologist RENÉ CATALA stated that the embryos of *P. polleni* were characterized by an extremely lengthy developmental interval.

Time from spawning to hatching was given as ten days, with another nine days to go before the wrigglers become free-swimming.

STIASSNY, NOURISSAT and I have all found that *Paratilapia* eggs hatch in 48 hours at 82 °F with another four days passing before the young are fully mobile. Both parents defend their progeny diligently for up to six weeks thereafter.

The young of both species are large enough to take *Artemia* nauplii and finely powdered dry food for their initial meal. If due attention is given to nitrogen cycle management, they are easily reared.

Despite robust appetites, they grow slowly until they reach a length of c. 2.0 cm TL, at which point their growth rate surges forward quite dramatically.

The *marakely* and the *fiamanga* are less given to sibling cannibalism than their African and Neotropical analogues, but larger individuals are given to battering smaller sibs at feeding time.

This can result in quite a dramatic drop-off in fry numbers by their eighth week unless their keeper intervenes and sorts them by size beforehand.

Sexual maturity is attained 12 to 14 months postspawning at a length of 3.5" SL for males, 2 " SL for females.

Ptychochromis STEINDACHNER 1880 was erected for a genus of superficially *Geophagus*-like Malagasy cichlids.

Ptychochromis oligoacanthus (BLEEKER 1863) is another robust species, growing to 12" SL.

The *saroy*, to give this species the Malagasy name it enjoys along the eastern coast of the island, has a moderately emarginate caudal and rather enlarged lips reminiscent of some of the labiate haplochromine species of the African mainland.

A single recognized species with four distinct geographical races is widely distributed in lowland streams along the northwestern, southwestern and entire eastern coasts of Madagascar.

The *saroy*, the form of *Pt. oligoacanthus* [Figure 243] native to the eastern coast, is characterized by conspicuous lateral spotting and relatively plain fin coloration. Representatives of the northwestern population, known locally as *juba*, are marked with metallic blue highlights on the head and body and possess wine-red vertical fins but lack the distinct lateral spots of the *saroy*.

Fish native to the offshore island of Nosy Be lack both the lateral spots and red vertical fins, instead sporting an attractive overall metallic blue cast. Finally, fish from the southwestern portion of the island, near the city of Toliara, lack both red fin coloration and lateral spots. Such extreme variability is otherwise unknown among Malagasy cichlids.

In view of our incomplete understanding of this fauna, it would be imprudent to dismiss out of hand the possibility that these geographical races actually represent distinct species.

Ptychochromis are generalized invertebrate feeders that include some plant matter in their diet. Though a moderately social fish in nature, adult *saroy* are relatively intolerant of conspecifics in captivity.

Fig. 245: A male *Chromidotilapia guntheri* (Sauvage 1882), the most generally available of these West African eartheater analogs.

Fig. 246: A female of the Nyong River population of *C. batesi.*

Individuals will sometimes assert themselves rather forcefully at feeding time, but heterospecific companions too large to be eaten are otherwise ignored.

This behavior is reminiscent of that of such ecologically analogous Neotropical cichlids as *Amphilophus alfari.* NOURISSAT has bred this biparentally custodial substratum spawning cichlid successfully under both pond and aquarium conditions.

He reports that pairs excavate a large, shallow depression, close to a meter in diameter, within which they dig up to a score of smaller pits. The fry are moved from one pit to another until they become mobile.

This "shell game" strategy of fry protection has been reported for *Tilapia* species in nature and comparable behavior has been observed in several genera of Neotropical cichlid in captivity.

Its occurrence in such disparate cichlid lineages suggests that such behavior is of very ancient origin indeed.

The east coast form of *Ptychochromis oligoacanthus* appears to be holding its own reasonably well in nature, possibly due to its ability to live in slightly brackish water.

The long-term prospects of the other recognized populations of this species are less reassuring.

According to NOURISSAT, as of 1992 the northwestern and Nosy Be races were still extant, though greatly reduced in numbers.

The situation of the closely related *Ptychochromoides betsileanus* (BOULENGER 1899) is much less encouraging.

This striking species, whose Malagasy name *trondro mainty* (= black fish) refers to its adult coloration, differs from all forms of *Pt. oligoacanthus* in details of its dentition and its possession of a prominent nuchal hump as an adult. As its specific name implies, this species was restricted to the Betsileo region, in the central and southern uplands of Madagascar.

It grew to 12" SL and formerly supported a commercial fishery in Itasy, the region's largest lake.

Repeated efforts by STIASSNY and REINTHAL in 1988 and 1990 and by NOURISSAT and his companions in 1991 to find this fish in either Lake Itasy or any of the smaller crater lakes in its vicinity were unsuccessful.

Local fishermen, who still remember the *trondro mainty*, state that they have not encountered it in over a decade.

The Lake Itasy fishery is now dominated by tilapias and black bass.

Regrettably, these populations of this interesting Malagasy cichlid appear to be extinct. It remains to be seen if relict populations persist in clear mountain streams near the city of Fianarantsoa.

The only known extant representative of the genus *Ptychochromoides* KIENER and MAUGE 1966 is an undescribed species discovered by STIASSNY and REINTHAL in a tributary of the Mangoro River near the town of Marilambo in 1990.

While it lacks the spectacular nuchal hump of its highland congener, this riverine species is a strikingly marked black and yellow cichlid likely to be well received by aquarists if it ever becomes available. According to its discoverers, its habitat has not been invaded by exotics

and supports a substantial population of the new *Ptychochromoides*.

If this fortunate state of affairs persists, cichlid enthusiasts may yet have an opportunity to work with this interesting species.

Introduction of the Malagasy species to the hobby is easily the decade's the most exciting development in cichlid keeping.

These interesting, and in many cases, strikingly beautiful cichlids are well worth the attention of serious aquarists on their own merits.

However, given that their long-term survival in nature is questionable in the face of massive human degradation of their environment and competition from exotic species, their availability affords serious aquarists a unique opportunity to contribute to the preservation of aquatic biodiversity.

As any information on their behavior will prove crucial in designing effective conservation programs for Malagasy cichlids, I cannot emphasize how important it is that aquarists working with these fishes publish their observations in a timely manner.

Fig. 247: A young male of the Moliwe population of *Chromidotilapia finleyi* Trewavas 1974.

Fig. 248–251: Spawning behavior of *Chromidotilapia guntheri*. Note that fertilization is extrabuccal and that the male initially picks up the fertilized eggs.

Serious cichlid keepers can also play a critical role in implementing any long-term captive breeding programs established for these species.

However much one might wish it to be otherwise, continued habitat deterioration in the wild makes it essential that aquarium stocks of all Malagasy cichlids be maintained as insurance against their complete disappearance. Reintroduction to their native waters may be a distant hope, but unless captive populations of these cichlids are available to draw upon, this option will be permanently foreclosed to future generations.

West African Riverine Cichlids

Though it can be subdivided into smaller biogeographic provinces, it is convenient when sorting Africa's superabundant cichlids into more manageable groups to treat the area from the Senegal basin to that of the Zaire as a single region.

West Africa in this expanded sense is home to a diverse cichlid fauna comprising eight distinct lineages.

The enigmatic genus *Heterochromis* REGAN 1922 appears to represent the sister group of all other Old World cichlids.

The sole representative of its lineage, *H. multidens* (PELLEGRIN 1904) is restricted to the central Zaire basin.

To date, this most interesting species is known only from a limited number of preserved specimens in museum collections on both sides of the Atlantic.

Two of the remaining seven lineages, the *Haplochromis* group and the *Lamprologus* group, are poorly represented in this region. Haplochromines dominate the cichlid fauna east of the Rift Valley and south of the Zaire basin.

Their center of evolution lies in that region and they appear to be a recent intrusive element in the cichlid fauna of Africa's Atlantic drainage rivers.

The genus *Lamprologus* SCHILTHUIS 1891, on the other hand, seems indigenous to the Zaire drainage.

However, this lineage has expressed its full evolutionary potential only within the long-isolated Lake Tanganyika basin.

In this riverine setting, where *Lamprologus* is represented by a handful of species, the lineage may have given rise to the worm cichlids of the genus *Teleogramma* BOULENGER 1899. These are elongate, morphologically specialized cichlids with vestigial swimbladders whose distribution is restricted to the extensive rapids of the Zaire River. Four species are known.

Teleogramma monogramma (NICHOLS and LA MONTE 1934) lives in the rapids of the Kassai River in south central Zaire. The remaining three species, *T. gracile* BOULENGER 1899, *T. brichardi* POLL 1959 and *T. depressum* ROBERTS and STEWART 1976 are endemic to the rapids of the lower Zaire.

All *Teleogramma* are persistently territorial sexually dimorphic cave-dwellers.

They display such extraordinary antipathy towards conspecifics that it is virtually impossible to house more than a single individual per tank. Other fish are effectively ignored.

These cichlids are invertebrate feeders in nature that accept a wide range of foods in captivity.

They are very intolerant of dissolved waste buildup and demand water movement in their tank.

This apart, they are easily maintained.

Worm cichlids are maternally custodial cave spawners that practice harem polygyny in nature.

Teleogramma brichardi, the only species regularly exported from Zaire, has been bred several times in captivity [Figure 244]. These are interesting fish, but their behavioral peculiarities recommend them to none but the most experienced of cichlid keepers.

The tilapias also seem to have originated in western Africa, but unlike the lamprologines, representatives of this lineage have extended its

Fig. 249

Fig. 250

range well beyond the limits of a single river system or faunal province. Measured by number of species no less than the degree of biological diversity they comprise, the tilapiine cichlids have done well in evolutionary terms. A sufficiently large number are available as aquarium residents to warrant giving these cichlids, along with their distant haplochromine and lamprologine relatives, subsequent separate coverage herein.

Two of the remaining four lineages are unrepresented among the ranks of aquarium fishes. Cichlids of the genus *Tylochromis* REGAN 1920 are large, superficially *Geophagus*-like fishes characteristic of the main channels of large rivers or the open waters of lakes. They are sand-sifting invertebrate feeders and several species possess the specialized pharyngeal apparatus that allows them to exploit aquatic mollusks as food. All are advanced maternal mouthbrooders characterized by marked sexual dimorphism.

Males grow larger than females and are overall more brightly colored, but the females of all species studied to date possess a bright red spot or streak on the snout, the so-called "lipstick mark".

Nothing further is known of their reproductive biology in nature and little can be said of their husbandry in captivity.

Sensitive to low oxygen tension and metabolic waste build-up, they ship poorly; hence, they fail to become established in the hobby.

This is unfortunate, for as a group they appear to be relatively unaggressive cichlids, while mature males of several species are strikingly colored.

The *Pelmatochromis* lineage as strictly defined comprises two genera, *Pelmatochromis* STEINDACHNER 1894 and *Pterochromis* TREWAVAS 1973.

The former comprises three medium-sized species.

Pelmatochromis buettikoferi STEINDACHNER 1895 occurs in coastal rivers from southern Senegal to central Liberia, while *P. ocellifer* BOULENGER 1899 and *P. nigrofasciatus* PELLEGRIN 1900 are indigenous to the central Zaire basin.

Fig. 251

All are generalized invertebrate feeders typically found in small streams flowing under forest cover.

All are biparental custodial substratum spawners.

Isolated specimens of all three species have been imported over the past two decades, but there are no reports of successful breeding in captivity. The genus *Pterochromis* is monotypic, comprising the single species *Pt. congicus* (Boulenger 1897).

It differs from *Pelmatochromis* in details of its jaw structure and gill raker morphology. As its specific name implies, it too is native to the central Zaire basin.

Like its near relatives in the genus *Pelmatochromis*, *Pt. congicus* is a biparentally custodial substratum spawning cichlid that feeds upon a wide selection of aquatic vertebrates.

These cichlids are all attractively colored. What is known of their behavior under aquarium conditions suggests they are relatively unaggressive species that would amply repay a serious effort to assure their importation and subsequent establishment in the hobby.

They appear to be quite hardy, and unlike the many *Tylochromis* species, they appear to travel well.

It is particularly difficult to understand why the group's Zairean representatives are not regularly imported. As they are common inhabitants of small streams flowing into the Malembo Pool near Kinshasa, an active focus of tropical fish exportation, their capture would seem a relatively simple matter to arrange.

Of the two remaining lineages, the cichlids of the *Nanochromis* group comprise five genera. Four are dwarf cichlids and will be discussed under that heading.

The fifth genus, *Chromidotilapia* Boulenger 1898, comprises eight species of medium-sized, substratum-sifting invertebrate feeding cichlids.

Until relatively recently, only one, *C. guntheri* Sauvage (1882) [Figure 245], is routinely available to American aquarists through commercial channels.

The very closely related *C. linkei* Staeck 1980 and a number of distinctive populations referred to respectively as *C. batesi* (BOULENGER 1901) [Figure 246] and *C. finleyi* TREWAVAS 1974 [Figure 247] have been bred successfully by European aquarists. Fry of these species are sometimes to be had on this side of the Atlantic.

Representatives of two additional *Chromidotilapia* species, the Gabonese *C. kingsleyae* BOULENGER 1898 and *Chromidotilapia* sp./Shiloango, an undescribed species native to coastal rivers from southern Gabon to Cabinda, are also known to European cichlid enthusiasts but have yet to make their North American debuts as aquarium residents.

These fish are typical inhabitants of small to medium-sized forest streams. They prosper over a temperature range of 75°–80°F for ordinary maintenance, with a rise to 82°–85°F for breeding.

The Eseka race of *C. batesi* and the Campo race of *C. finleyi* have been bred successfully only in very soft [< 0.5 DH total hardness] water with a pH of 5.0–6.0.

Other representatives of the genus can be expected to do well in neutral to slightly alkaline, moderately hard water.

Like other cichlids from such habitats, *Chromidotilapia* are sensitive to nitrogenous waste build-up and low oxygen tension.

Regular partial water changes and the use of an outside power filter facilitate their successful maintenance. These cichlids are heavy eaters that accept a wide range of live and prepared foods.

They are not herbivorous and do not go out of their way to uproot plants.

However, like other sand-sifting invertebrate feeders, they will sometimes accidentally dislodge rooted plants during the course of normal foraging activity.

Indifferent predators, they can be expected to ignore heterospecific tankmates too large or too fast to make an easy mouthful. Outside periods of sexual activity, they are moderately tolerant of conspecifics.

Chromidotilapia guntheri is a monogamous mouthbrooder that practices long-term

Fig. 252: A male *Hemichromis elongatus* (Guichenot 1861). Unlike the closely related *H. fasciatus*, this species undergoes dramatic color changes with the onset of spawning.

defense of its mobile fry [Figures 248–251]. The range of this widely distributed species extends from the eastern Ivory Coast to extreme western Cameroon inclusive of both the Volta and Niger Rivers. Notwithstanding its mode of parental care, this hardy species has a monogamous mating system and must be managed accordingly. Pairs usually defend a territory c. 2' square and spawns can number up to 100 fry.

Thus if they are to be spawned on a single pair basis, the breeding tank should be of at least 25 gallons capacity.

Males are larger than females. However, the latter are more colorful than their consorts and often initiate the preliminaries to spawning. A prolonged courtship is followed by oviposition in the typical manner of substratum spawning cichlids.

The fertilized eggs are then picked up by one parent, usually the male.

Both sexes typically take turns carrying the developing embryos during the 10 to 14 day incubation period.

The newly released fry are large enough to take brine shrimp nauplii and finely powdered dry food for their initial meal.

They are vigilantly defended by both parents for up to eight weeks postrelease. Faced with serious danger, they return to their parents' buccal cavities, which often prove incapable of accommodating all of the fry after their first few weeks of mobile existence!

Given a regime of frequent partial water changes and plenty of food, they are easily reared and can be expected to grow rapidly.

If they are properly cared for, spawning can begin as early as eight months postspawning, but it usually takes another four months for individuals to attain full reproductive competence.

Chromidotilapia linkei and the three races of *Chromidotilapia finleyi* bred to date in captivity are all advanced mouthbrooders.

During the course of a prolonged and often intense courtship, the male digs a pit at the base of a sloping surface, which is vigorously cleaned by the female. The eggs are deposited

Fig. 253: Known erroneously since its introduction to the hobby as *Hemichromis bimaculatus*, the original jewelfish of the aquarium trade is actually *Hemichromis guttatus* Gunther 1862.

Fig. 254: As can readily be noted, the true *Hemichromis bimaculatus* Gill 1862 is a very different fish from its better-known congener.

Fig. 255: A male *Hemichromis cristatus* from southwestern Nigeria. This small species is often sold under the name forest jewelfish.

Fig. 256: A female *H. cristatus*. The well ocellated median spot is diagnostic of this attractive species.

Fig. 257: A young male *Sarotherodon galilaeus* (Artedi 1757). This monogamous biparental mouthbrooder ranges from West Africa to Palestine.

Fig. 258: The natural distribution of *Oreochromis niloticus* (Linnaeus 1757) extends into the Jordan basin. Its utility as a subject for aquaculture has led to its introduction as a food fish throughout the tropics.

on the precleaned surface, fertilized and picked up by the female.

The male then picks up any eggs which have failed to adhere to the spawning site and fallen into the associated pit.

In the Campo race of *C. finleyi*, the two sexes trade off the task of brooding their zygotes several times during the developmental interval.

In *C. linkei*, the typical population of *C. finleyi* from Mungo in western Cameroon and in the Moliwe race of the latter species, the female broods the developing young with only rare assistance from her consort. The developmental interval and postrelease brood care in all three forms are identical to those reported for *C. guntheri*.

The race of *Chromidotilapia batesi* native to the upper reaches of the Nyong River basin near the Cameroonian town of Eseka is, on the other hand, a delayed mouthbrooder. The eggs are initially deposited on the roof of a cave.

Hygienic care is carried out by the female alone, while the male defends the breeding

territory against intruders. The eggs hatch in just under three days at a temperature of 80 °F.

At this point, the female takes them into her mouth and carries them until they are fully mobile, some four days later.

At this point, both parents care for the mobile fry in the manner described for *C. guntheri*.

The fry of all these Cameroonian *Chromidotilapia* are large enough to take *Artemia* nauplii for their initial meal, and with ample feeding grow fairly rapidly. If properly cared for, they attain sexual maturity 10 months to a year postspawning. These desirable aquarium residents are not as widely available as they deserve to be, but are well worth whatever effort is required to secure them.

The final West African cichlid lineage consists of the jewel fishes of the genus *Hemichromis* and their allies.

It comprises a rough dozen or so species grouped in three genera. Two of these comprise species that can properly be considered dwarf cichlids and will be considered at greater length under that heading.

The representatives of the genus *Hemichromis* PETERS 1857, on the other hand, are small to medium-sized predators with marked piscivorous tendencies. Most species are of West African provenance, but *Hemichromis fasciatus* PETERS 1858 and *H. letourneauxi* SAUVAGE 1880 also occur in the Chad and Nile basin, while *H. elongatus* (GUICHENOT 1861) [Figure 252] has managed to penetrate as far south as the upper Zambezi basin.

These hardy cichlids occur in a wide range of biotopes in nature.

They prefer moderately soft, slightly acid to neutral conditions, but are less particular about water chemistry than most West African cichlids. Nevertheless, their ability to briefly withstand high nitrite levels is not to be taken as a license for sloppy nitrogen cycle management.

A temperature range of 72°—78°F serves for day-to-day maintenance, with an increase to 82°—85°F for breeding.

Given their not entirely unjustified reputation for belligerence, it is wise to remember that all cichlids behave more aggressively at the upper end of their preferred temperature range. *Hemichromis* have large and unselective appetites. They are, in consequence, more concerned with how much than with what kind of food they are offered.

All *Hemichromis* are biparentally custodial substratum spawners.

Males grow somewhat larger than females and tend to have longer soft dorsal and anal fins.

Females of the smaller species, such as *Hemichromis guttatus* GUNTHER 1862 [Figure 253], *H. bimaculatus* GILL 1862 [Figure 254], *H. paynei* LOISELLE 1979 [Figure 130] and *H. cristatus* LOISELLE 1979 [Figures 255 & 256] usually sport more red coloration and fewer metallic blue spangles than do males.

Pair formation is complicated by pronounced intolerance of conspecifics regardless of sex.

Fig. 259: Type species of the genus, *Tilapia sparrmani* A. Smith 1840 is a small species native to southern Africa. The lattice pattern on the flanks of this sexually quiescent male is characteristic of many tilapias.

Fig. 260: Sexually quiescient male *Tilapia rendalli* (Boulenger 1896). Breeding fish develop an intense red ventral flush that extends well upwards onto the flanks. An important aquaculture subject, this species has also been successfully employed to control infestations of soft leafed aquatic weeds.

Furthermore, once formed the pair bond erodes easily under aquarium conditions. The use of target fish and large tanks are particularly advised if one wishes to breed jewelfish on a single pair basis.

The robust *H. fasciatus* and *H. elongatus* defend territories 3' to 5' square, while their smaller congeners make do with a demesne half that size. The dimension of the breeding tank should reflect this fact.

After a brief but often stormy courtship, the pair deposits a compact round plaque of ovoid tan to olive-grey eggs [Figure 179].

A flat, solid surface is the preferred spawning site, though some pairs of *H. cristatus* will spawn by preference on a vertical surface. Custodial and hygienic duties are shared more or less equally by both sexes.

Possibly in consequence, hemichromines are the only African cichlids whose behavior includes an obvious "relief ceremony" when male and female swap off their respective duties. Hatching occurs 36 to 48 hours post-spawning, and the fry become free-swimming c. four days thereafter.

The larger *Hemichromis* can spawn up to 3000 eggs, but the smaller species rarely produce more than 500. Jewelfish are usually superb parents in captivity.

Indeed, the ferocity of their parental care makes it unwise to attempt breeding them in a community setting unless the aquarium in question has a bottom area at least twice that of the pair's territory or its other residents are regarded as expendable target fish.

The crisp black dorsal and midlateral stripes of the newly mobile fry set them apart from all other African cichlids, although such markings are characteristic of several Neotropical cichlid genera. The fry are easily reared and grow rapidly with good care.

Fragmentation of the generically diagnostic juvenile color pattern signals the end of parental care and subsequent fry dispersal out of the breeding territory in nature.

In captivity, it marks the onset of serious intersib aggression and ultimately, of sibling cannibalism.

Parental care is protracted in the wild, but rarely persists more than six weeks in captivity.

Fig. 261: *Tilapia busumana* (Gunther 1902), a largely insectivorous tilapia native to western Ghana and eastern Ivory Coast.

Parents and fry should be separated at the first sign of respawning, for jewelfish do not tolerate a previous brood in their territory at this time.

The larger *Hemichromis* are sexually mature between 10 months and a year post-spawning, while their smaller congeners begin spawning four months earlier.

The larger jewelfish are best left to the attentions of the experienced cichlid keeper with a taste for the family's predatory representatives.

The smaller *Hemichromis* are beautiful, easily maintained and highly desirable aquarium residents well worth the consideration of anyone with interest in substratum spawning cichlids.

Tilapias and Allied Genera

The tilapias comprise three large genera, *Tilapia* A. SMITH 1840, *Sarotherodon* RUPPELL 1854 and *Oreochromis* GUNTHER 1894, and a number of smaller genera derived from a *Tilapia* or *Sarotherodon*-like ancestor.

Tilapia and *Oreochromis* have in turn been divided into a number of more or less well defined subgenera.

The group is the focus of considerable taxonomic research.

It is thus probable that some of these subgenera may eventually be elevated to full generic status.

Notwithstanding their mouthbrooding habits, the genera *Tristamella* TREWAVAS 1942, *Danankilia* THYS 1968 and *Iranocichla* COAD 1982 appear to be morphologically specialized *Tilapia*-derivatives.

The last two of this trio of genera each comprise a single species endemic to relict hot springs in extreme desert habitats.

Iranocichla hormuzensis, as its specific name implies, it is restricted to the region of Hormuz in southeastern Iran, while *Danankilia franchetti* (VINCIGUERRA 1931) is restricted to Lake Afrera, in the Danankil Depression of Ethiopia. The two species appear to be closely related.

Their occurrence on either side of the Arabian Peninsula, an area presently devoid of native cichlids, strongly suggests the family was represented in the ichthyofauna of that region during late Pliocene and early Pleistocene, when the climate was significantly wetter.

Tristamella comprises two species native to the Jordan basin and the Damascus area immediately to the north.

None of these Middle Eastern tilapiines have entered commercial channels and there is no information on their maintenance and behavior under home aquarium conditions.

The contrary is true of two other *Tilapia*-derived riverine genera, *Chilochromis* BOULENGER 1902 and *Steatocranus* BOULENGER 1899.

Representatives of these western African genera are kept with sufficient regularity to warrant coverage herein.

A third rheophile tilapiine genus, *Gobiocichla* KANAZAWA 1951, native to rapids in the Niger and Cross River basins, has yet to be exported and remains an aquaristic cipher.

Sarotherodon has undergone a remarkable evolutionary radiation in Barombi-Mbo, a

phenomenon paralleled by the genus *Tilapia* in Bermin, two small crater lakes in western Cameroon.

Representatives of several of these crater lake tilapiine species have been bred by European researchers and hobbyists, but as yet, none of these interesting species are regularly available to American aquarists.

Those interested in learning more about them are referred to the recommended readings in Chapter 12.

Most tilapias are to be found in Africa south of the Sahara. However, *Tilapia zillii*, *Sarotherodon galilaeus* [Figure 257], *Oreochromis aureus* and *O. niloticus* [Figure 258] are present in the Nile basin and the first three members of this quartet of species have further extended their range north and east into the Jordan River basin. This foursome of tilpias is also to be found in the major rivers of West Africa as well as in the Lake Chad basin, a distribution pattern that reflects a much wetter climate in the Sahel than prevails at present.

Representatives of all three genera are also to be found in the Zaire River, but the *Tilapia*

Fig. 262: A young pair of *Tilapia joka* Thys 1969. The cave spawning habits of this species no less than its distinctive head shape set this West African tilapia apart from its congeners.

and *Sarotherodon* species richness is at its greatest in the region between the Senegal and Ogowe Rivers in West Africa.

Most *Oreochromis* species, on the other hand, occur east of the Great Rift and south of the Zaire basin, a distribution pattern that essentially parallels that of the haplochromine cichlids.

The generality of *Tilapia* are robust cichlids that reach 10" to 15" SL in nature and equal such marks easily in captivity. Only the species of the nominate subgenus *Tilapia*, such as *T. sparrmani* SMITH 1840 [Figure 259], the West African *Tilapia brevimanus* BOULENGER 1911 and several representatives of the subgenus *Coptodon* endemic to Lake Bermin, a crater lake in the Cameroons, stand as notable exceptions to this rule.

Indeed, *Tilapia ruweti* (POLL and THYS 1965) and several of the Cameroonian crater lake endemics qualify in all respects as dwarf cichlids and will be considered more fully in Chapter 11.

All representatives of the genus are sexually precocious, breeding freely at well under their full adult sizes.

However, there is no escaping the fact that most *Tilapia* can be adequately housed only in tanks of 50 gallons capacity or larger when fully grown.

This may account for their lack of popularity, their hardiness and attractive coloration notwithstanding. These cichlids are not fussy about pH and hardness.

They display considerable tolerance of elevated nitrite levels, though it is unreasonable to expect them to look their best or breed in such a polluted environment.

A temperature range of 70°−78°F suffices for day-to-day maintenance, with an increase to the mid-80's for spawning.

Most species of the genus are more-or-less herbivorous. Indeed, several species of the subgenus *Coptodon* are used as aquatic weed control agents with considerable success! [Figure 260]

Fig. 263: A subadult *Chilochromis duponti* Boulenger 1902. Its color pattern is reminiscent of closely related coptodont tilapias such as *T. zillii*.

Fig. 264: A male *Steatocranus gibbiceps* Boulenger 1899. This small, snail-eating species frequently turns up as a "contaminant" in shipments of *S. casuarius* from Zaire.

It is thus hardly surprising that with very rare exceptions, captive tilapias treat planted aquaria as self-serve salad bars.

However, *Tilapia busumana* (GUNTHER 1902) [Figure 261] is one of several West African species that feed chiefly upon aquatic invertebrates in nature, while *Tilapia buttikoferi* is a specialized — and highly proficient — molluscivore.

In captivity, these cichlids are gluttonous and unselective feeders, whose diet should nevertheless contain substantial amounts of plant matter.

All *Tilapia* studied to date are biparentally custodial substratum spawning cichlids. Males grow larger than females, but the genus is not characterized by marked sexual color differences. They are easily bred in captivity and should be handled like any other robust monogamous cichlid.

Large tanks are essential, as the area defended by a pair in nature ranges from 2' to 6' square, and spawns of up to 5000 fry are not unusual!

Courtship may be stormy and pair formation proceeds more smoothly if the fish are kept in a community setting.

The pair bond ruptures easily when fish are held in isolation. Use of target fish minimizes the likelihood of such an outcome.

The ovoid, tan to olive-green eggs are deposited in the open as a loose, roughly circular plaque.

The cave spawning *Tilapia joka* THYS 1969 [Figure 262] provides the most dramatic exception to this pattern.

Most species prefer to place their eggs on a flat, solid surface, but both *T. mariae* and *T. brevimanus* routinely select vertically oriented spawning sites in captivity.

Hygienic care is a predominantly female responsibility, but even in nature, she will swap off with her mate and take a turn at defending the territorial perimeter.

Hatching occurs 60 to 72 hours postspawning and the fry are mobile three to four days later.

Pairs experience little difficulty keeping predators from the developing embryos, but their defense of the large, rather unresponsive swarm of fry is considerably less efficient.

The reproductive patterns of at least two *Tilapia* species are characterized by rudimentary mouthbrooding behavior.

215

There is evidence that parental *Tilapia discolor* (GUNTHER 1902), a *Coptodon* species endemic to Bosumptwi, a crater lake in central Ghana, pick up and hold their wrigglers in their mouths when threatened.

I have observed male *T. ruweti* do likewise to freeswimming fry in response to an attempt to net some of their offspring out of the breeding tank. It would not surprise me were comparable episodes to be reported from other small to medium-sized representatives of the genus.

Parental care can persist for two months in nature, but in captivity, pairs usually are ready to respawn in three to four weeks' time.

It is essential to remove the fry at this point. They are otherwise likely to be killed by their parents.

Fry are easily reared, but it is necessary to thin their numbers drastically to obtain optimum growth. Remember when culling that all tilapias are characterized by precocious male growth superiority. Most species begin breeding at c. 3" SL, between eight months and a year postspawning.

The maintenance requirements and reproductive pattern of *Chilochromis duponti* BOULENGER 1902 [Figure 263], a rock-dwelling algae grazer native to the lower Zaire River do not differ from those outlined for the genus *Tilapia*.

Apart from one nominal species endemic to the Volta River, *Steatocranus irvinei* (TREWAVAS 1943), all known representatives of the genus *Steatocranus* BOULENGER 1899 are native to the Zaire River drainage.

Both *Chilochromis* and *Steatocranus* are fish of strongly flowing waters in nature. They are thus less tolerant of poor nitrogen cycle management in captivity than are most *Tilapia* species.

By way of compensation, they are also less inclined to regard rooted aquatic plants as a self-service salad bar, though *Steatocranus* may uproot plants accidentally when modifying the vicinity of their caves prior to spawning.

Like most highly rheophilous cichlids, *Steatocranus* species have vestigial swim bladders and swim with a rather droll hopping motion.

Fig. 265: *Steatocranus tinanti* (Poll 1939), a distinctive slender-bodied rheophile species from the lower Zaire River.

Fig. 266: A male *Sarotherodon caudomarginatus* (Boulenger 1916), a robust tilapia native to the rapids of coastal rivers from Guinee to Sierra Leone.

This places them under no obvious handicap either at feeding time or when defending fry!

Steatocranus casuarius POLL 1939 is the most commonly available species of the genus.

Aquarists with a sharp eye can often find individuals of such more-or-less syntopically occurring species as *S. gibbiceps* BOULENGER 1899 [Figure 264], *S. mpozoensis* ROBERTS and STEWART 1976 and *S. tinanti* (POLL 1939) [Figure 265] in lots of fish exported from Kinshasa.

Though far from brightly colored, *Steatocranus* enjoy considerable popularity because of their bizarre appearance and interesting behavior.

They are the most easily kept rheophilous cichlids presently available to hobbyists and can be recommended enthusiastically to anyone wishing to keep a cichlid whose lifestyle is out of the ordinary.

The reproductive pattern of *Steatocranus* deviates from the *Tilapia* norm in that they are all cave spawners.

Sexual dimorphism is also more pronounced in these fishes, females rarely attaining half the size of their mates.

Pairs defend an area c. 1.5' square around a central cave.

Pair formation is straightforward in a community setting, and it is safe to allow these cichlids to spawn in such surroundings.

Parental care, while efficient, poses few risks to other fish in a large tank.

These tilapiines produce smaller clutches of larger eggs than do their less specialized relatives.

Spawns of 200 fry are unusual.

The developmental interval in also longer.

Hatching occurs in five to six days at 76°–78°F, and the fry require an additional four to five days to become free-swimming.

In compensation, newly mobile *Steatocranus* are as large as month old *Tilapia* fry.

Parental care persists in captivity until the fry are 1.5 cm SL. There is no rush to separate parents and progeny when the former show signs of respawning.

Fig. 267: A courting pair of *Sarotherodon occidentalis* Daget 1962, a male-mouthbrooding tilapia from West Africa.

Older fry are tolerated within the pair's territory even after a new clutch has been spawned. With proper care, the young are sexually mature six to eight months postspawning.

The genus *Sarotherodon* comprises a baker's dozen medium-sized to large detritus and algae browsing tilapiines.

With the exception of *Sarotherodon melanotheron* RUPPELL 1854, type species of the genus, an inhabitant of coastal lagoons from Senegal, northern Angola, and the widely distributed *Sarotherodon galilaeus*, the genus is restricted to West Africa.

Most species are river dwellers.

Indeed, one, *Sarotherodon caudomarginatus* (BOULENGER 1916) [Figure 266] could legitimately be described as rheophilous.

The genus has also given rise to a minispecies flock of endemic cichlids in Lake Barombi-Mbo.

Although morphological distinctions between *Sarotherodon* and *Oreochromis* are slight, I concur with TREWAVAS' decision to recognize these two groups of species as generically distinct on the basis of their quite different reproductive patterns.

All *Sarotherodon* species practice advanced buccal incubation of their zygotes. However, the genus appears to be unique among African cichlids in that it comprises paternal, biparental and maternal mouthbrooders.

The extralacustrine species to date studied are either paternal mouthbrooders, *e.g., S. melanotheron* or biparental mouthbrooders, *e.g., S. galilaeus*. These tilapiines are characterized by minimal sexual dimorphism, a monogamous mating system and a vestigial pair bond.

Their reproductive behavior resembles that of the several *Chromidotilapia* species in that the female frequently initiates courtship [Figure 267].

These *Sarotherodon* species should be handled in the same manner as the representatives of that genus in captivity, notwithstanding the absence of postrelease brood care in any of these tilapias. Several of the Barombi-Mbo endemics, on the other hand, are maternal mouthbrooders.

These species should be handled in the same manner as haplochromine cichlids.

Although their temperament is mellow and their reproductive behavior interesting, aquarists wishing to keep these cichlids are likely to find acquiring specimens a real challenge.

Tilapias as a group are not greatly appreciated as ornamental fish and the combination of large adult size and plain coloration effectively puts *Sarotherodon* species beyond the pale as an aquarium residents.

The genus *Oreochromis* likewise comprises mostly very large species that can begin breeding at a fraction of their maximum size [Figure 268].

A few species endemic to hot springs in east and south central Africa such as *Oreochromis grahami* (BOULENGER 1912) could be regarded as dwarfs were it not that under the more benign conditions prevalent in captivity, they grow substantially larger than their counterparts in nature.

This suggests their modest dimensions in the wild is influenced as much by the harsh environment they inhabit as by any genetic factors. The genus is unusual in that it is characterized by adaptations that allow *Oreochromis* species to function as microphages, feeding in nature upon organic detritus [Figure 269] or, in the case of the *ngege*, *O. esculentus* (GRAHAM 1928), even suspended phytoplankton.

These dietary specializations make *Oreochromis* ideal candidates for pond culture. Indeed, the suitability of several species as aquaculture subjects has earned them a pantropical distribution. None feeds upon vascular aquatic plants in the wild, but several species will indulge a taste for such fare in captivity.

Like their relatives of the genus *Tilapia*, these cichlids prosper over a wide range of water conditions and can briefly tolerate elevated nitrite levels.

Many can survive temperatures as high as 92 °F, but the temperature range suggested for the various *Tilapia* species is recommended for their maintenance in captivity.

Oreochromis have heroic appetites. Fortunately, they are not choosy feeders and eagerly devour ordinary aquarium fare.

Fig. 268: A male *Oreochromis chilwae* (Trewavas 1966), one of the mouthbrooding tilapias with more than three anal fin spines.

Fig. 269: A courting male *Oreochromis leucostictus* (Trewavas 1933). Native to Lakes Edward and George, this detritus-feeding tilapia has been extensively translocated into both natural and man-made lakes in East Africa.

All *Oreochromis* species are maternal mouthbrooders.

The species to date studied are characterized by marked sexual dimorphism and a lek or arena-type mating system in nature. Males grow up to twice as large as females and are more colorful.

Captive individuals should be managed as suggested in the section of the preceding chapter on breeding openly polygamous cichlids.

Sexually active males excavate spawning pits whose diameter equals twice the standard length of the resident fish, and may defend a zone that extends up to 1' beyond their rim against intrusion by other males and sexually unresponsive females.

Other fish are ignored until the onset of spawning.

In captivity, females are courted with persistent vigor that can result in injury if they prove unreceptive to the male's advances. Spawning follows reciprocal circling at the bottom of the pit.

The female picks up the newly deposited eggs immediately.

In most instances, she then nudges or bites at the male's often greatly elaborated or contrastingly colored genital papilla to elicit ejaculation.

The female of at least one species, *O. macrochir*, picks up a spermatophore previously deposited in the spawning pit by the male. Fertilization is primarily intrabuccal.

Spawns can number 3500 eggs in such robust species as *O. niloticus*, a remarkably high number for a mouthbrooding cichlid. However, the usual clutch numbers closer to several hundred eggs.

Male harassment may cause an ovigerous female to abort the incubation sequence in captivity, but as a rule, females are superb mothers. The developmental interval is 10 to 14 days, depending upon water temperature. In nature, females seek out extremely warm peripheral waters in which to release and subsequently abandon their mobile fry.

Fig. 270: A male *Haplochromis (Astatotilapia) nubilus* (Boulenger 1906), a morphologically unspecialized omnivore widely distributed in northern Uganda including the Lake Victoria basin.

When such thermal refuges are unavailable, females guard their newly released fry as they forage and allow them to shelter in the maternal mouth when threatened for up to 10 days after their initial release. The fry are easily reared and if properly cared for grow with astonishing speed.

Most riverine *Oreochromis* attain sexual maturity between six and eight months postrelease.

Lacustrine endemics are somewhat slower, becoming reproductively competent 10 months to a year postrelease.

Though tilapias are important food fishes, most species are shunned by aquarists despite their hardiness and often spectacular coloration.

The reasons for their unpopularity are not immediately obvious. Size alone cannot explain it, for such Neotropical genera as *Heros*, *Theraps* and *Amphilophus* enjoy great popularity notwithstanding that most of their constituent species grow as large as

or larger than the generality of tilapias, and much more aggressive in the bargain.

I consider tilapias to be very desirable aquarium residents and I venture to predict those aquarists willing to overcome their prejudices long enough to give them a try will come to a similar conclusion.

Haplochromis and Allied Genera

Introduction

The haplochromines, comprising the genus *Haplochromis* HILGENDORF 1888 and the numerous genera with which it shares common ancestry, are the most species-rich lineage of the Family Cichlidae.

While haplochromines dominate the riverine cichlid faunas of eastern and southern Africa, the group owes its commanding position to its great success in colonizing the African Great Lakes.

221

The cichlid dominated ichthyofaunas of the Lake Victoria basin in the broad sense as well as of Lakes Edward/George, Kivu, Fwa and Malawi are preponderantly haplochromine.

These cichlids are also well represented in the more phyletically diverse Tanganyikan fauna.

Not surprisingly, this evolutionarily dynamic group has been the subject of intense scientific scrutiny for over half a century.

This activity has resulted in a substantial body of knowledge about the systematics, natural history and behavior of these fishes that serious aquarists will find worth the effort of exploring.

I refer interested readers to the recommended readings in Chapter 12 for relevant titles.

Such research often leads to proposed changes in the nomenclature of its objects.

This has proven true of the genus *Haplochromis*.

In a recent series of publications, the British ichthyologist P. H. GREENWOOD proposed

limiting the nomen *Haplochromis* to a handful of species endemic to Lakes Victoria, Nabugabo, Edward/George and Kivu, revived a number of nomina previously treated as junior synonyms and published new generic names for the remaining riverine and extra-Malawian lacustrine species formerly referred to that genus. Subsequently ECCLES and TREWAVAS have revised the genera of Malawian haplochromines and proposed a number of new generic names for species endemic to that lake formerly included in *Haplochromis*.

The distinctive nature of Lake Malawi's haplochromine fauna was recognized as early as 1921 by the British ichthyologist C. TATE REGAN, although he did not propose new genera for its many component species.

The schema proposed by ECCLES and TREWAVAS can thus be viewed as the long-awaited follow-up to REGAN's pioneering studies.

In the first edition of this book, I expressed my reluctance to accept without reservation GREENWOOD's scheme because it took neither behavioral nor colorational data into

Fig. 271: A male *Haplochromis (Astatotilapia)* sp. "spot/bar", an undescribed dwarf insectivore endemic to Lake Victoria.

Fig. 272: A male *Haplochromis cronus* Greenwood 1959. The specialized feeding pattern of this paedo-phage is not obvious from its unspecialized morphology.

consideration in the definition of such smaller genera.

I continue to sympathize with Green-wood's view that even with the Malawian haplochromines excluded from consideration, *Haplochromis* as broadly understood should be divided into more biologically meaningful units.

Unfortunately, the problem of defining them has not grown any easier with the passage of time.

Recent genetic studies of these haplochromines have demonstrated both the monophyletic nature of the Lake Victoria species flock and the amazing similarity of its component species at the molecular level.

The decision to retain the nomen *Haplochromis* in its broader sense when discussing these fishes while treating Greenwood's genera as subgenera appears in retrospect to have been a prudent one.

This usage, which will be continued in the present edition, remains consonant with a similarly conservative response to Green-wood's revision by the Dutch scientists of the University of Leiden's *Haplochromis* Ecology Study Team and by the institutional participants in the American Association of Zoological Parks and Aquariums' captive breeding program for these cichlids.

For aquaristic purposes, one may conveniently divide the haplochromines as follows:
1) riverine species and those endemic to the northern Great Lakes such as Victoria, Kyoga, Nabugabo, Edward/George and Kivu as well as to Lake Fwa;
2) species endemic to Lake Malawi formally placed in the genus *Haplochromis* and those genera closely allied to them;
3) Malawian haplochromines of the *mbuna* group; and
4) haplochromines endemic to Lake Tanganyika.

Each of these groups shares biological characteristics relevant to their maintenance and breeding in captivity.

The Malawian and Tanganyikan endemics will be discussed in Chapter 9, while the

Fig. 273: A male *Haplochromis (Labrochromis) ishmaeli* (Boulenger 1906), one of Lake Victoria's many snail-eating cichlids. This species appears to be extinct in nature.

balance of this chapter will be devoted to riverine haplochromines and those species endemic to the remainder of Africa's lakes.

Riverine and Northern Lacustrine Haplochromines

The *Haplochromis* of the northern Great Lakes include species whose extreme morphological specializations reflect an equally specialized feeding pattern.

However, while the representatives of what remains of Lake Victoria's rich and diverse cichlid fauna available to aquarists may differ substantially from their riverine counterparts in morphology, these differences do not extend to behavior or life history characteristics [Figures 270–278]. Though many species can — and regularly do — grow larger in captivity, few usually exceed 4" SL in nature and all begin breeding at about half their adult size.

Such sexual precocity, an adaption to the rigors of an unpredictable and often ephemeral

environment, should come as no surprise in riverine species [Figure 279].

Its persistence in the Victorian and northern Rift Lake haplochromines [Figure 280], whose habitat is both predictable and stable over time, reflects the relative youth — by geological standards — of both these lakes and their endemic haplochromine faunas.

Ability to prosper under such often difficult conditions implies tolerance of a broad range of water conditions [Figures 281 & 282]. These haplochromines do well under all save the most extreme conditions of pH and hardness. With the exception of such species as *H. (Ctenochromis) polli* THYS 1964 [Figure 283] and *H. (Thoracochromis) bakongo* THYS 1964 and the representatives of the genus *Orthochromis*, specialized riffle dwellers from the Zaire River basin, extralacustrine haplochromines and, to a lesser extent, their counterparts from the northern Great Lakes, can withstand elevated nitrite levels for considerable periods of time. However, like all hardy cichlids, they respond positively to proper nitrogen

Fig. 274: A male of an undescribed *Haplochromis* species of the nominate subgenus reminiscent of *H. obliquidens* Hilgendorf 1888. This periphyton-feeder was originally collected in the Tanzanian waters of Lake Victoria.

Fig. 275: A sexually quiescent male *Haplochromis (Neochromis) nigricans* (Boulenger 1906), an *mbuna* analog from Lake Victoria.

225

cycle management in their aquaria. A temperature range of 72°–78°F suffices for ordinary maintenance, with an increase to 82°–85°F for breeding.

Prolonged exposure to temperatures in excess of 82°F appears to compromise the immune systems of haplochromines endemic to Lakes Victoria and Kivu [Figure 284]. Fish stressed in this manner are much more vulnerable to systemic bacterial infections.

Regardless of their diet in nature, captive individuals eagerly take all the usually available live and prepared foods.

The red and orange coloration of many of these haplochromines is extremely sensitive to dietary factors.

To keep their coloration at its full intensity, it is essential to offer captive specimens foods rich in essential pigment precursor substances.

All haplochromine species studied to date are maternal mouthbrooders. In nature, most have lek mating systems.

Characteristically, males are both larger and more brilliantly colored than females.

Persistent defense of what appears to be a feeding territory against both conspecific and heterospecific intruders has been reported in a few algal-grazing species endemic to Lake Victoria, notable among them *H. (Neochromis) nigricans* (BOULENGER 1906).

In the overwhelming majority of species, territoriality is restricted to periods of sexual activity.

Males typically defend a spawning territory from 1' to 4' square often centered on a spawning pit excavated and maintained at a considerable cost in time and effort.

Sexually active males are extremely intolerant of conspecifics of the same sex and vigorously exclude them from their territories. They often extend this intolerance to heterospecifics with a similar color pattern. It may prove feasible to house several males in the same tank as long as it is large enough to allow each to hold a territory.

However, the aquarist should appreciate that in the case of some of the Lake Victoria species, such as *Haplochromis* sp. "rock kribensis" or *H. (Harpagochromis) squamulatus* REGAN 1922, such peaceful coexistence is likely only in an aquarium in excess of 250 gallons capacity!

Fig. 276: A male *Haplochromis (Prognathochromis) perrieri*, a dwarf piscivore that specialized on newly released cichlid fry. This species has followed most of Lake Victoria's predatory cichlids into extinction.

Fig. 277: Pelagic zooplankton feeders like this male *Haplochromis (Yssichromis)* sp. "argens" are critically endangered in Lake Victoria, for their habitat preference renders them vulnerable to predation by the Nile perch.

Fig. 278: A male *Haplochromis nyrerei* Witte-Maas and Witte 1985, a small plankton-feeding species closely associated with rocky coasts in Lake Victoria. Its habitat preference affords it protection from the depredations of the Nile perch.

227

Fig. 279: Many *Haplochromis* species live in swamps and permanent marshes, like this male of an undescribed representative of the *H. bloyetii* complex, which hails from the Malagarazi drainage along the eastern shoreline of Lake Tanganyika.

These cichlids spawn freely in captivity. The methodology outlined for breeding openly polygamous cichlids in the previous chapter is totally applicable to their management in captivity. Spawning follows the same pattern in all lacustrine and the overwhelming majority of riverine *Haplochromis*.

After a period of reciprocal circling and vent nudging, the female lays a few eggs which she immediately picks up. She then mouths the brightly colored pseudo-ocelli present on the male's anal fin or, less commonly, nibbles at the vent itself.

This triggers ejaculation. As the female continues her efforts to pick up these egg-like markings, she gets a mouthful of sperm. This assures fertilization of the eggs previously taken into her buccal cavity.

The possession of anal fin pseudo-ocelli that function as egg dummies is a trait shared by males of most riverine *Haplochromis* species as well as those of their endemic Victorian and northern Rift Lake allies.

The only known exceptions are a small number of rapids-dwelling species restricted to Zaire River basin, of which the best known to American aquarists is *H. (T.) bakongo*.

These species lack male pseudo-ocelli.

It should thus come as no surprise that while fertilization of the eggs occurs within the female's mouth in these species, the mechanics of the process are more reminiscent of the spawning behavior of *Oreochromis* than of the generality of *Haplochromis* species.

In nature, ovigerous females leave the male's territory and move into special nursery areas. In captivity, this option is denied them and males usually continue to actively court females well after they are spent.

Such harassment may provoke abortion of the incubation sequence, hence the importance of providing the female with sufficient cover to escape such unwanted attention. At 82°F, the developmental interval is 10 days for riverine species, 14 days for those endemic to the northern Great Lakes.

Females are excellent mothers. Parental females of many species continue to defend their mobile fry for several days postrelease in nature, allowing them to shelter in the buccal cavity when danger threatens.

Such behavior serves no useful function in captivity.

Hence most breeders separate mother and fry as soon as the latter are mobile.

Fecundity is clearly related to both adult size and a female's nutritional state among haplochromines.

Females of the few surviving representatives of the larger predatory species endemic to Lake Victoria often produce spawns in excess of 100 eggs in captivity.

Among smaller riverine and lacustrine species, broods as a rule range from 25 to 75 fry.

The large, well-developed young are easily reared. With generous feeding and frequent water changes, they grow very rapidly.

Riverine and peripheral lacustrine *Haplochromis* such as *H. (Astatotilapia) burtoni* (GUNTHER 1893) can begin spawning between the sixth and eighth week postrelease, while most northern lacustrine haplochromines [Figures 285 & 286] usually require an additional month or two to attain reproductive competence.

There is nothing unnatural about such reproductive precocity nor anything to be gained by preventing the fish from spawning at this size. Indeed, most problems encountered with these fish arise from efforts to breed overgrown specimens.

The relationship between male size and aggressiveness seems to be exponential rather than linear.

Hence such "supermales" routinely terrorize heterospecifics and are more apt to kill a female than spawn with her under aquarium conditions.

Overgrown specimens make good display subjects and show entries, but young fish are better as breeding stock.

The foregoing observations apply equally to the Victorian *Astatoreochromis allaudi*

Fig. 280: An aggressive male *Haplochromis* cf. *schoutedeni* Poll 1932. The strong antipathy this species displays towards loricariid catfishes is as puzzling as its marked reproductive precocity under aquarium conditions.

Fig. 281: Male *Haplochromis (Ctenochromis) polli,* a small rheophilous species native to the lower Zaire River.

Fig. 282: A male *Haplochromis (Astatotilapia) burtoni,* a hardy species native to the peripheral waters and tributary streams of Lake Tanganyika.

Fig. 283: An isolated lakeside pool near Bujumbura, Burundi, typical *H. burtoni* habitat.

Fig. 284: Prolonged exposure to temperatures in excess of 82°F renders Lake Victoria endemics like this male *Haplochromis (Paralabidochromis) plagiodon* (Regan & Trewavas 1928) susceptible to systemic bacterial infections.

231

PELLEGRIN 1903 [Figure 287] and its Tanganyikan analog, *A. vanderhorsti* (GREENWOOD 1954) and to the several haplochromine species endemic to Lake Fwa in southwestern Zaire [Figures 278—280], with the proviso that these haplochromines grow substantially larger and consequently require roomier quarters than do most of the forgoing species.

Sexual dimorphism is not so pronounced in these genera as it is in *Haplochromis*. This makes sexing young breeders a bit more difficult, but even an inexperienced aquarist can readily distinguish between the sexes when confronted with larger individuals.

A cardinal defining feature of *Astatoreochromis* is a massive pharyngeal mill. This allows these fish to feed upon aquatic mollusks with great efficiency.

If kept hungry, these cichlids do a creditable job of ridding an aquarium of unwanted snails.

Pseudocrenilabrus multicolor (HILGENDORF 1903) [Figure 288] is the doyen of the numerous haplochromines currently available to aquarists, having made its debut in 1903.

For decades it was the only representative of this group kept as an ornamental fish and to this day remains one of the most commercially available African cichlids.

Pseudocrenilabrus species are common inhabitants of small streams and marginal waters throughout their range [Figures 289—291]. These colorful little cichlids are hardy, easily bred and were it not for their distinctly peppery disposition during periods of sexual activity, could be regarded as dwarf cichlids, for few individuals ever attain 3" SL even in captivity.

Though more sensitive to dissolved metabolites than their larger relatives, their maintenance requirements are essentially identical. Notwithstanding their small adult size, *Pseudocrenilabrus* demand spacious tanks.

Males defend territories up to 3' square in nature, behavior that carries over in captivity.

It is difficult to house more than a single territorial male in any aquarium under 35 gallons capacity. The intolerance of resident males towards heterospecific intruders dictates their companions be chosen with care.

Fig. 285: *Haplochromis (Paralabidochromis) paucidens* Regan 1921 is a polymorphic insectivore from Lake Kivu. This is a male of the "normal" morph.

Fig. 286: A female of the black morph of *H. (P.) paucidens*. A "salt and pepper" heteromelanic morph is also known.

Fig. 287: A male *Astatoreochromis allaudi* Pellegrin 1903. This robust snail-eating haplochromine is found throughout the Lake Victoria basin and over much of northern Uganda.

233

Fig. 288: A pair of Egyptian mouthbrooders, *Pseudocrenilabrus multicolor* (Hilgendorf 1903), the first haplochromine cichlid imported as an aquarium fish.

It is not a good idea to house these fish with larger haplochromines.

The larger adult size of most *Haplochromis*, for example, gives them an edge in any contest with a male *Pseudocrenilabrus*, while similar reproductive patterns guarantee a conflict over available space.

Spawning preliminaries follow the pattern described for riverine *Haplochromis*.

Male *Pseudocrenilabrus* court their prospective consorts with great vigor. Prudence thus dictates affording females plenty of cover.

The actual mechanics of spawning differ somewhat from what has been described for *Haplochromis* and its lacustrine allies.

Fertilization has both extra- and intrabuccal components and the spawning female nibbles at the male's vent rather than at any structures on his anal fin.

Ovigerous females should be handled like those of riverine *Haplochromis* species. The incubation period is 10 to 14 days, depending upon water temperature.

The newly released fry are smaller and slenderer than those of other haplochromines thus far discussed. Offer them microworms initially, as their mouths may be too small to allow them to take *Artemia* nauplii. With proper care, the young attain sexual maturity between eight and twelve weeks postrelease.

There is some evidence that the sex ratio in the Zairean *Pseudocrenilabrus nicholsi* (PELLEGRIN 1928) [Figure 284] may be influenced by water chemistry. Males tend to predominate when the fish are bred in hard, alkaline water.

All these haplochromines have been somewhat overshadowed by their larger and more flamboyant Malawian relatives.

Experienced aquarists look upon them strictly as beginner's fish, whose only strong feature is the ease with which they can be induced to spawn in captivity. In fact, they are highly desirable fish in their own right.

Most species do not require the large aquaria that are a prerequisite for success with Malawian haplochromines.

Fig. 289: A male Ugandan mouthbrooder, *Pseudocrenilabrus victoriae* (Trewavas 1933). This small, colorful haplochromine has been confused with the South African *Pseudocrenilabrus philander dispersus* (Trewavas 1936) by European aquarists.

This automatically endears them to cichlid fanciers with limited tank space.

These haplochromines not only tolerate rooted plants, but actually look their best in planted tanks.

Of considerable importance to most aquarists, they are breathtakingly beautiful cichlids whose breeding dress encompasses the entire spectrum of possible color combinations. This stands in sharp and pleasant contrast to the overwhelming reliance upon shades of blue or yellow that characterizes the majority of their Malawian counterparts.

Finally, the conservation status of the Lake Victoria endemics is extremely uncertain.

Several representatives of the pitiful remnant of this species flock presently under culture are extinct in nature and the prospects of short-term survival for many of the remainder in the face of continued predation by the introduced Nile perch are not good.

Institutional captive breeding programs will save some of these cichlids, but limited resources have already forced the managers of

these programs to make some hard choices between potential candidates.

Cichlid enthusiasts can make a significant contribution to the survival of these cichlids. Serious amateurs can make an immediate impact on the problem by devoting tank space and effort to their captive propagation.

The effectiveness of such efforts is greatly multiplied if they can be integrated into existing institutional captive breeding programs.

Readers who desire to involve themselves in such programs are referred to the Chapter 12 for further information.

Over the long term, even hobbyists with a more casual interest in these cichlids can contribute to their preservation.

By creating a market demand for these cichlids, aquarists promote their large-scale production by commercial breeders in Florida and the Far East.

Obviously, not all Victorian cichlids are equally likely to enjoy equal commercial success, while the vagaries of the market make it imprudent to rely solely upon its operation to

Fig. 290: A male of the Zambezi basin population of *Pseudocrenilabrus philander* (Weber 1897).

assure the long-term survival of any endangered species. However, each Victorian cichlid that does win a secure place in the ranks of commercially available ornamental fishes allows institutional programs that much more freedom to focus their limited resources upon those species most clearly in need of them.

The long-term goal of any captive breeding program for endangered organisms is to return them to their natural environment.

For this to happen, conservationists must in the short term work to maximize options while minimizing regrets.

Until the end results of limnological processes triggered by the introduction of the Nile perch are more clearly known, it is impossible to assess the likelihood of successfully reintroducing any endemic cichlids to Lake Victoria.

However, given a reasonable degree of collaboration between institutional conservation programs, serious amateurs and commercial fish breeders, this option can be indefinitely preserved and the survivors of this debacle can be assured of a future regardless of the eventual outcome of the ecological drama being played out in Lake Victoria.

Fig. 291:
A male *Pseudocrenilabrus nicholsi* (Pellegrin 1928), a vividly colored species native to the eastern Zaire River basin.

CHAPTER 9

CATALOG OF RESIDENTS FOR THE CICHLID AQUARIUM.

OLD WORLD CICHLIDS. PART II.

Lake Malawi Cichlids.

Species formerly included in *Haplochromis* and Genera Allied to Them.

With the extirpation of most of Lake Victoria's endemic cichlids, the Lake Malawi species flock constitutes the largest remaining assemblage of haplochromines. It has always been the most morphologically diverse [Figure 292].

As noted above, the British ichthyologist REGAN nonetheless pointed out as early as 1921 a suite of features that distinguished Malawian

from extra-Malawian *Haplochromis*, but forbore to recognize these differences formally by referring the former to other genera. Seventy years after the fact, one can only speculate upon the reasons for such forbearance on the part of so practiced a taxonomist. One good guess is that the sheer magnitude of sorting out over a hundred species, many represented by very incomplete preserved material, may have had a lot to do with his decision!

Be that as it may, unconditional acceptance of GREENWOOD's more recent nomenclatorial proposals automatically would have made

Fig. 292: A female *Nimbochromis polystigma* (Regan 1922), first Malawian *Nimbochromis* species to be bred in captivity. The spotting of this species has earned it the Chitonga name of *nyarumbwe* — the hyaena.

237

Cyrtocara BOULENGER 1902, the group's oldest genus-level junior synonym, the recognized generic name for the Malawian species formerly referred to *Haplochromis*.

Several aquaristic references and scientific works published since GREENWOOD's proposed revision chose to follow this line.

However, I opted to retain the nomen *Haplochromis* for these cichlids in the first edition of this book on the grounds that *Cyrtocara moorii* BOULENGER 1902 [Figure 293], type species of the genus, differs so markedly from all other Malawian haplochromines as to make the genus *Cyrtocara* monotypic.

It was clearly evident that the remarkable range of morphological diversity that characterizes Malawian *Haplochromis* [Figures 294−302] warranted recognition through erection of multiple genera rather than the application of a single generic name to all of its constituent species.

Thus, to replace the nomen *Haplochromis* with *Cyrtocara* would have been to sanction a short-term taxonomic usage as biologically

misleading as the one it was intended to replace.

It seemed a better idea at the time to await the eventual publication of a taxonomic schema that reflected more fully the diversity of Lake Malawi's cichlid assemblage.

In 1989, Mr. DAVID ECCLES and Dr. ETHELWYN TREWAVAS published a major generic revision of the haplochromine cichlids of Lake Malawi.

This monograph accepts as valid the previously described haplochromine genera endemic to the lake, recognizes the artificial nature of *Lethrinops* REGAN 1922 and establishes two new genera, *Taeniolethrinops* and *Tramitichromis,* for those species improperly included therein, rehabilitates three genera formerly considered junior synonyms of *Haplochromis, Cyrtocara, Champsochromis* BOULENGER 1915 and *Otopharynx* REGAN 1920 and erects twenty-one new genera for the balance of the species formerly comprised in that genus. This scheme certainly recognizes the remarkable diversity of the Malawian species flock.

Fig. 293: A male *Cyrtocara moorii* Boulenger 1902, type species of the genus Cyrtocara. Its distinctive color pattern and morphology have earned it the popular name of Malawi blue dolphin cichlid.

As it is clearly destined to define future research into the evolutionary relationships of these cichlids for the foreseeable future, the nomina proposed by Eccles and Trewavas are likely to remain current for some time to come.

Adoption of any new taxonomic usage entails a trade-off between increased biological precision and nomenclatorial stability.

The terms of the exchange in this instance amply justify such a move, which is reflected in the generic nomina employed in this edition.

Assimilating nomenclatorial changes on this scale is neither an easy nor an agreeable process.

In the hopes of facilitating this task, the accompanying table consists of an alphabetized list of the species names of those Malawian haplochromines at least episodically available to American aquarists through commercial channels matched with their current generic designation.

Note that the majority of species familiar to aquarists are now grouped in the genera *Nimbochromis* Eccles and Trewavas 1989 [Figures 6a, 34, 212 & 292], *Copadichromis* Eccles and Trewavas 1989 [Figures 312 & 313] and *Protomelas* Eccles and Trewavas 1989 [Figures 299 & 300]. This should simplify to a degree the task of mastering new names for old favorites.

Lake Malawi's species flock includes haplochromines that differed sufficiently from the most extremely specialized nominal *Haplochromis* species recognized by earlier workers to have warranted generic recognition well prior to the publication of Eccles and Trewavas' monograph.

Of these cichlids, aquarists are most familiar with the ten genera of **mbuna**. By virtue of their ecological and behavioral peculiarities, they warrant separate consideration in any treatment of haplochromine cichlids.

Of the remaining eleven derived genera, representatives of nine have to date been imported as aquarium fish.

However they might differ from *Haplochromis* as formerly defined in details of their anatomy, they are sufficiently similar in details of their aquarium husbandry to warrant inclusion in the present discussion.

Fig. 294: Few Malawian cichlids undergo a more dramatic sexual color change than male *Dimidiochromis compressiceps*.

Fig. 295: A male *Buccochromis atritaeniatus* (Regan 1922), a cruise predator associated with open sandy bottoms in the south of Lake Malawi.

Fig. 296: A male of the aptly named *Tyrannochromis macrostoma* (Regan 1921), an ambush predator that grows large enough to prey on adult *mbuna*.

Fig. 297: A courting male *Fossochromis rostratus* (Boulenger 1899), a large substratum-sifter that also undergoes a dramatic color metamorphosis with the onset of sexual activity.

Fig. 298: A male *Placidochromis electra* (Burgess 1979), a distinctively marked invertebrate feeder known as the deepwater Haplochromis with reference to its preferred habitat in Lake Malawi.

Fig. 299: A magnificent male *Protomelas similis* (Regan 1922), one of several species sold as the red empress *Haplochromis*.

The defining features of the genera *Aulonacara*, *Lethrinops*, *Taeniolethrinops*, *Tramitichromis*, *Hemitilapia* BOULENGER 1902 and *Chilotilapia* BOULENGER 1908 relate in large measure to their specialized feeding patterns.

Chilotilapia rhoadesi BOULENGER 1908 [Figure 303] uses its modified jaw teeth to crush mollusc shells, while the several *Hemitilapia* species are either herbivores or mollusc feeders.

Lethrinops [Figure 305], *Tramitichromis* and *Taeniolethrinops* are substratum-sifters.

The genus *Aulonacara* TREWAVAS 1935 [Figures 306−310] derives its name from enlarged cephalic lateral line pits, which resemble the holes of a flute, *aulos* in Greek.

Available information on their ecology suggests enhanced lateral line sense allows these cichlids to forage effectively for aquatic invertebrates under conditions of low ambient lighting.

The barracuda cichlids of the genus *Ramphochromis* REGAN 1922 are pelagic cruise predators that actively chase down the smaller fish

upon which they prey, while the monotypic *Aristochromis christyi* TREWAVAS 1935 [Figure 311] and *Lichnochromis acuticeps* TREWAVAS 1935 are specialized predators on the fry of *mbuna* and other rock-dwelling cichlids.

Under aquarium conditions, such adaptations are less important to the well-being of their possessors than is the case in nature.

From the aquarist's perspective, their maintenance requirements are identical to those of less ecologically specialized haplochromines, which dictates that they be managed in the same manner. The range of morphological variation within the cichlid assemblage of Lake Malawi raises the question of how many ancestral species were involved in colonizing the newly inundated lake basin.

Recent studies of the DNA of these cichlids reveals the existence of two assemblages of genera and a number of outrider genera that stand well apart from the other representatives of this fauna.

The first − and smaller − of these two groupings comprises all of the highly modified rock-frequenting species collectively known as *mbuna* plus several other genera, most prominent among them *Lethrinops* and *Aulonacara* REGAN 1922.

The second comprises the remainder of the genera formerly comprised in *Haplochromis*.

Standing well apart from both groupings are the highly modified barracuda cichlids of the genus *Ramphochromis* and the deep-water predators of the genus *Diplotaxodon* TREWAVAS 1935.

All of these cichlids require large tanks and **scrupulous** attention to management to the nitrogen cycle in their aquaria. Tanks in the 50–70 gallon range represent acceptable accommodations for the smaller and less aggressive *Aulonacara* and *Copadichromis* [Figures 312 & 313] species.

The majority of these Malawian haplochromines cannot be expected to survive for any length of time in tanks under 75 gallons capacity and neither look nor act their best in aquaria smaller than 90 gallons.

Representatives of such predatory genera as *Champsochromis, Buccochromis* ECCLES and TREWAVAS 1989 [Figure 295], *Nimbochromis* and *Tyrannochromis* ECCLES and TREWAVAS 1989 [Figure 296] or the robust *Fossorochromis rostratus* (BOULENGER 1899) [Figure 297], which can grow to 12" SL, need even larger quarters to prosper in captivity.

Such spacious quarters allow the stocking densities necessary to keep intramural fighting at a minimum, permit males to hold territories without dangerously disturbing the other fish present, minimize the likelihood of accidental hybridization and greatly simplify nitrogen cycle management.

The aquarist who cannot provide these fish with adequate living space should turn his attentions elsewhere.

To disregard this aspect of their biology is guaranteed to prove expensive in the short and highly discouraging in the long run. These cichlids have a low tolerance of dissolved metabolic wastes.

Fig. 300: A male *Protomelas* cf. *fenestratus* (Trewavas 1935). This attractive species is often marketed as the "German *fenestratus*".

Fig. 301: A male *Maravichromis mola* (Trewavas 1935), one of many Malawian cichlids whose enlarged pharyngeal teeth allow it to feed upon snails.

Fig. 302: A female *Placidochromis milomo* (Oliver 1989), one of several Malawian cichlids with greatly enlarged lips.

Fig. 303: A sexually active male of the mollusc-feeding *Chilotilapia rhoadesi* Boulenger 1908, one of the most beautiful large Malawian haplochromines.

Fig. 304: A male *Hemitilapia oxyrhynchus* Boulenger 1902, a common inhabitant of *Vallisneria* beds in Lake Malawi.

Fig. 305: A male *Lethrinops lethrinus* (Gunther 1893), type species of this large genus of substratum-sifting haplochromines.

Given their almost oceanic environment, this is hardly surprising.

A combination of biological and mechanical filtration in conjunction with frequent partial water changes represents the safest and most efficient approach to managing the nitrogen cycle in a tank of these large Malawian haplochromines.

As the males of most species dig to a greater or lesser extent when sexually active, undergravel filters are not recommended in their tanks. I prefer to set up a bioactive bed in a canister filter, run in conjunction with a high capacity outside power filter charged with a reusable medium.

When esthetic considerations need not be taken into consideration, a large sponge filter mated to a rotary impeller driven power head may be substituted for the canister filter. The filter media should be purged as necessary and between 25% and 40% of the tank water replaced every ten to fourteen days.

Feedback from friends who have used trickle filters on Malawi cichlid tanks on an experimental basis suggest that this new technology can also be applied profitably to managing the nitrogen cycle for these fish.

Whether such an innovation represents a cost-effective approach to this problem given the price of such units is another matter altogether.

The maintenance routine outlined above will keep dissolved nitrite well below stressful levels even in a heavily stocked tank.

These fish do well at the temperatures recommended for their riverine cousins. They do require hard, alkaline water to prosper.

Use commercially available Malawi salt mixes to replicate such conditions in areas with naturally soft tap water.

These cichlids are easily fed.

All accept the usual live and prepared foods eagerly.

Trophic specialists like the robust piscivores of the genera *Buccochromis*, *Champsochromis*, *Dimidiochromis*, *Nimbochromis*, *Rampho-chromis*, *Stigmatochromis* and *Tyranno-chromis*, mollusc-eaters such as *Chilotilapia rhoadesi* and *Maravichromis mola* (TREWAVAS 1935) [Figure 301] or zooplankton feeding *utaka* of the genus *Copadichromis* show superior color and breed more frequently if one regularly includes in their diet the foods they would normally encounter in nature.

multi-purpose territory in nature. In captivity they should be managed in the same manner as their riverine counterparts, with due awareness that males defend **much** larger territories.

Sexually active males of robust species, e.g., *Nimbochromis polystigma* REGAN 1921 or

The current generic placement of some commonly available Lake Malawi haplochromines

Species	Current Genus	Species	Current Genus
ahli	*Sciaenochromis*	*livingstoni*	*Nimbochromis*
annectens	*Protomelas*	*macrostoma*	*Tyrannochromis*
atritaeniatus	*Buccochromis*	*milomo*	*Placidochromis*
azureus	*Copadichromis*	*modestus*	*Stigmatochromis*
borleyi	*Copadichromis*	*mola*	*Maravichromis*
caeruleus	*Champsochromis*	*moorii*	*Cyrtocara*
chrysonotus	*Copadichromis*	*nitidus*	*Ctenopharynx*
compressiceps	*Dimidiochromis*	*nkatae*	*Copadichromis*
electra	*Placidochromis*	*ornatus*	*Electochromis*
epichorialis	*Maravichromis*	*pleurospilus*	*Stigmatochromis*
ericotaenia	*Maravichromis*	*pleurostigma*	*Copadichromis*
euchilus	*Cheilochromis*	*pleurostigmoides*	*Copadichromis*
fenestratus	*Protomelas*	*pleurotaenia*	*Protomelas*
fuscotaeniatus	*Nimbochromis*	*polystigma*	*Nimbochromis*
heterodon	*Otopharynx*	*quadrimaculatus*	*Copadichromis*
incola	*Maravichromis*	*rostratus*	*Fossorochromis*
jacksoni	*Copadichromis*	*similis*	*Protomelas*
johnsoni	*Placidochromis*	*spilonotus*	*Protomelas*
kirkii	*Protomelas*	*taeniolatus*	*Protomelas*
kiwinge	*Dimidiochromis*	*tetrastigma*	*Otopharynx*
labridens	*Protomelas*	*triaenodon*	*Protomelas*
lateristriga	*Maravichromis*	*urotaenia*	*Hemitaeniochromis*
lepturus	*Buccochromis*	*venustus*	*Nimbochromis*
leuciscus	*Nyassachromis*	*verduyni*	*Copadichromis*
likomae	*Copadichromis*	*virgatus*	*Protomelas*
linni	*Nimbochromis*	*woodi*	*Stigmatochromis*
lithobates	*Otopharynx*		

Apart from a few specialized herbivores such as *Protomelas similis* (REGAN 1922) [Figure 299] and *Hemitilapia oxyrhynchus* BOULENGER 1902 [Figure 304], these fish will not eat aquatic plants, although they may uproot them during the course of normal foraging activities and are certainly apt to do so in the course of excavating a spawning pit.

All are maternal mouthbrooders with a polygamous mating system.

Some are specialized lek breeders, while males of others practice long-term defense of a

Fossorochromis rostratus, defend an area almost 9' square in nature.

In such cases, it is obviously impossible to house more than one male per tank unless one has access to the facilities of a public aquarium!

At the other end of the scale, *utaka* males and those of the several *Aulonacara* species are usually satisfied with a territory 2' square.

Males of most medium-sized Malawian haplochromines defend territories somewhere between these extremes in area.

Fig. 306: A young male *Aulonacara hueseri* Meyer, Riehl & Zetzsche 1987. This small peacock cichlid was erroneously identified as *Aulonacara auditor* (Trewavas 1935) in the first edition of this book.

Fig. 307: A magnificent male *Aulonacara stuartgranti* Meyer & Riehl 1985.

Fig. 308: A male *Aulonacara sualosi* Meyer, Riehl & Zetzsche 1987. Observations made in Lake Malawi suggest this small peacock cichlid may have an aterritorial mating system.

Fig. 309: A wild-caught male Kande Island orchid peacock, *Aulonacara kandeensis* Tawil & Allgayer 1988.

Hence the necessity of housing these cichlids in spacious tanks.

The mechanics of courtship and spawning are more reminiscent of *Oreochromis* or *Pseudocrenilabrus* than of *Haplochromis* species, in that the female mouths the male's vent rather than any specialized markings on his anal fin to elicit ejaculation. Females are more likely to abort the incubation sequence if disturbed in its early stages than are their riverine or Victorian counterparts. Hence it is prudent to wait at least three and preferably five days before attempting to move them to a nursery tank.

At 82°−85°F, the developmental interval lasts twenty-one days.

Females of most species provide postrelease care for their fry in nature, but there is little point in keeping mother and offspring together past this point in captivity. Brood sizes vary considerably between species.

Some of the more robust can release as many as 300 fry. Broods of 35 to 75 fry are the rule for the group's smaller representatives.

Newly released fry are well developed and can take a wide selection of live and prepared foods for their initial meal.

Given due attention to keeping nitrite levels as low as possible through frequent partial water changes, rearing them poses no particular difficulty.

Malawian haplochromines do not display the extreme reproductive precocity of their riverine and Victorian cousins. The smaller species attain sexual maturity eight months to a year postrelease.

The larger become reproductively competent between twelve and eighteen months postrelease.

These cichlids are unusual in their proclivity to hybridize under aquarium conditions.

Accidental hybridization usually occurs when a sexually aroused heterospecific male involves himself in the activities of a consorting couple or when a male and female of two closely related species are housed together in the absence of conspecifics of the opposite sex.

Such behavior is by no means unique to Malawian haplochromines and has been reported in a wide range of other fishes.

However, Malawian haplochromines differ from **most animals by the tendency of**

Fig. 310: The swallowtail peacock is often sold under the trade name "Aulonocara caroli". It remains to be determined whether this fish is a valid species or a geographical color variant of *Aulonocara jacobfriebergi* (Johnson 1974).

Fig. 311: A sexually quiescent male *Aristochromis christyi* Trewavas 1935, a distinctive piscivore from Lake Malawi.

females to **respond positively to heterospecific male advances even in the presence of a conspecific male.**

Such a situation arises when one male becomes so dominant in a community setting that he can inhibit the normal courtship behavior by heterospecific males. A ripe female cannot respond to nonexistent signals. In the absence of appropriate courtship behavior by a conspecific male, it is thus no wonder that a female should respond to overt heterospecific advances. The greater the similarity in male breeding dress and display between the species in question, the less resistance the female displays to such inappropriate advances.

However, repeated occurrence of crosses between such unlikely partners as *Nimbochromis venustus* (BOULENGER 1908) and *C. moorii* or *Dimidiochromis compressiceps* (BOULENGER 1908) and *Cheilochromis euchilus* (TREWAVAS 1935) suggest it is unwise to rely strongly upon the efficacy of whatever prespawning isolating mechanisms these fish rely on in nature under the less than natural conditions prevailing in captivity.

There are three reasons why this problem arises under aquarium conditions.

First, the basic reproductive biology and associated courtship displays of these closely related cichlids are very similar. Females of any given species thus find much of a heterospecific male's frantic solicitation fully comprehensible.

Second, the inherent space limitations of aquarium living simply do not allow these fish either to disperse as they would in Lake Malawi or to hold normal-sized territories.

This has the effect of putting **all** the males in a given tank in competition for whatever breeding sites are available.

This situation is exacerbated by the fact that generous regular meals allow captive male haplochromines to exist in a state of perpetual rut. As some species are inherently more aggressive than others, a situation in which a single male comes to control the entire aquarium can readily arise.

Third, aquarists regularly house together species that seldom, if ever, come into contact in nature, either because their ranges do not

Fig. 312: A courting male *Copadichromis quadrimaculatus* (Regan 1921), one of the most attractive and generally available of the *utaka* group of zooplankton feeders.

overlap or because they are restricted in occurrence to specific habitats within the lake.

Such species are unlikely to have evolved foolproof isolating mechanisms, because some history of contact, however brief, between two breeding populations is a prerequisite for this process to occur.

Hybridization between Malawian cichlids poses particular dangers.

Not only are the resulting hybrids both viable and fertile, but contrary to the usual case, it may take several generations of incrossing before the inevitable loss of reproductive competence occurs.

If hybrid individuals inadvertently backcross with either parental species, it may take even longer before the genetically contaminated strain thus produced loses viability.

However long the consequences may take to manifest themselves, hybridization ultimately leads to a biological dead end. It thus must be avoided at all cost.

An additional disincentive to the practice arises from the fact that correct identification of Malawian haplochromines is an ongoing problem facing wholesalers and hobbyists alike.

The introduction of hybrid phenotypes into normal distribution channels only muddies these waters further by introducing the uncertainty of whether an unfamiliar fish is a valid biological entity or the consequence of miscegenation.

The importance of housing these cichlids in the largest possible aquaria should thus be obvious. There are additional steps the conscientious aquarist can and should take to prevent hybridization between Malawian haplochromines.

First, avoid housing species that differ greatly in size and temperament together. To ignore this rule is to invite the biggest, most aggressive male to move into a position of hyperdominance.

Second, do not house closely related species together. Such fish are often characterized by extreme similarity in both male breeding dress and courtship behavior.

Fig. 313: A male *Copadichromis pleurostigmoides* (Iles 1960). Though not closely related to *Aulonacara*, this *utaka* species is widely sold as the ivory-headed peacock.

This is apt to enhance already inordinate female receptivity to heterospecific solicitation.

Third, **never** house species with very similar juvenile and female color patterns together. Should a *mesalliance* occur, such similarity makes it impossible to recognize the resulting progeny as hybrids until the males develop their full breeding dress.

By this time, they may have been dispersed so widely that there is no hope of recalling them before they can do further damage.

Finally, watch a Malawian community carefully for any indication of hyperdominance. Be particularly alert for signs that a male is paying serious attention to and eliciting unwanted interest from heterospecific females. If such behavior is noticed, isolate the offending party at once and keep him in isolation until the object of his illicit interest has spawned with her appropriate consort. Even extreme vigilance will not always prevent the occurrence of reproductive errors.

However, it will limit unwanted hybridization between these cichlids.

Needless to say, any hybrid fry should be destroyed as soon as possible.

It would be disingenuous to suggest that these Malawian haplochromines should be attempted by any save experienced cichlid keepers.

Furthermore, their housing requirements place them beyond the ability of many aquarists to maintain.

These disadvantages notwithstanding, the unmatched intensity of their coloration guarantees these cichlids an honored and persistent place in the ranks of ornamental aquarium fishes.

The Mbuna

It is difficult to convey to new cichlid keepers the tremendous impact the importation of the first *mbuna* had upon all aspects of the tropical fish hobby [Figure 314]. These highly modified Malawian haplochromines were so utterly unlike any freshwater aquarium fish then known in their intense coloration and viva-

253

cious behavior that stunned hobbyists could only compare them to coral reef fishes.

The *mbuna* conferred upon all cichlids an aura of desirability that contributed significantly to the popularity the family enjoys today.

It is a measure of the group's success as ornamental fishes that species extremely rare a decade ago are now regarded as rather commonplace by cichlid enthusiasts, who take for granted their ready availability and low prices.

The name *mbuna* itself is a Chitonga word meaning "rockfish".

The name is quite appropriate. Though not all *mbuna* are intimately associated with rocky biotopes [Figures 313–317]; the majority certainly are.

Furthermore, the skeletal, reproductive and behavioral features that define the group appear to have evolved in response to the challenges and opportunities posed by a strongly **petricolous**, or rock-dwelling mode of life.

The *mbuna* are compact, small to medium-sized cichlids characterized by greatly reduced scales in the throat and nape regions, a number of cranial, buccal and dental modifications that facilitate collection of food from solid surfaces, a single functional ovary, a restricted number of distinct whitish yellow to golden orange pseudo-ocelli medially or posterodistally placed on the anal fin of adult males, and a strongly developed tendency towards persistent male territoriality.

Mbuna differ from most haplochromines in that sexual color dimorphism is not universal. Deviations from this pattern are often, though not invariably, associated with defense of an all-purpose territory by both sexes, behavior unusual for the family as a whole and with few parallels among haplochromine cichlids.

The group is also noteworthy for a very high incidence of color polymorphism among its constituent species.

Both **oligomelanic** (black pigment restricted to the eyes alone) [Figures 25, 91, 318 & 319] and **heteromelanic** (black pigment distributed irregularly on the body and fins) [Figures 166, 325 & 333] color forms characterize half a dozen *mbuna* species.

Fig. 314: The spectacular coloration of *mbuna* such as this male of the normal or BB morph of *Pseudotropheus zebra* (Boulenger 1899) accounts for much of the popularity these cichlids currently enjoy.

Fig. 315: Though an *mbuna* in good standing, *Pseudotropheus lanisticola* Burgess 1976 lives over open sandy bottoms in close association with empty shells of the snail *Lanistes*.

A comparable number boast only heteromelanic color morphs.

In a few instances, the same species boasts both types of polymorphism [Figures 320−323].

The group comprises ten genera.

Pseudotropheus REGAN 1921, *Labeotropheus* AHL 1927 [Figures 324 & 325], *Petrotilapia* TREWAVAS 1935 [Figure 326] and *Iodotropheus* OLIVER and LOISELLE 1972 [Figure 327] are adapted to feed mainly upon aufwuchs, the mat of filamentous algae and its associated microscopic life that covers rock surfaces to depths of approximately thirty feet in the lake.

As presently understood, the genus *Pseudotropheus* comprises a wide range of morphologically diverse cichlids [Figures 328−333].

Several subgenera have been proposed for the more obvious species assemblages, and it would not be surprising were the genus to be split into smaller, more biologically meaningful genera at some time in the near future.

Cyathochromis TREWAVAS 1935 and *Gephyrochromis* BOULENGER 1901 [Figure 317] are defined by dental modifications that allow them to feed upon loose algae and organic detritus taken from plant leaves or sandy surfaces.

Cynotilapia REGAN 1924 [Figure 316] lives in association with rocky shores, but feeds chiefly upon zooplankton.

Melanochromis TREWAVAS 1935 comprises a group of short-snouted feeders on aufwuchs and aquatic invertebrates [Figures 334−339] and another of long-snouted predators [Figure 341] that feed largely upon cichlid fry.

One species, *Melanochromis parallelus* BURGESS and AXELROD 1976 [Figure 340] is reported to function as a facultative cleaner fish in nature.

Another as yet undescribed species feeds on the fins and scales of other fish [Figure 342], a trophic specialization shared with the monotypic genus *Genyochromis* TREWAVAS 1935 [Figure 343].

Labidochromis TREWAVAS 1935 comprises numerous species [Figures 344−347] that utilize their tweezer-like anterior teeth to

Fig. 316: Though it never moves very far from rocky outcroppings, *Cynotilapia afra* (Gunther 1893) spends much of its time schooling in midwater, where it feeds upon zooplankton.

selectively pick aquatic invertebrates from the algal mat.

Notwithstanding their various trophic adaptations, all *mbuna* are quite plastic in their feeding behavior and will forage on any locally superabundant food item in nature. This catholicity carries over into captivity.

Mbuna feed enthusiastically on all usually available live and prepared foods.

At the time of their aquaristic debut, the *mbuna* were thought to comprise just over two dozen species.

More recent estimates, based upon careful surveys of the littoral zone of Lake Malawi, raise this number to well over a hundred, and there is no reason to believe the list is complete. To an evolutionary biologist, this comes as no surprise.

The success with which the *mbuna* have adapted to a petricolous lifestyle constrains their ability to disperse across open bottoms.

Because it restricts gene flow between spatially separated populations, the sedentary character of these cichlids facilitates the evolution of species with highly localized ranges.

Only *Labeotropheus fuelleborni* AHL 1927 and *Genyochromis mento* TREWAVAS 1935 occur throughout the Lake. Most species occur only along a few miles of shoreline, or are endemic to a single island group or reef.

With commercial collecting restricted for logistic reasons to only a fraction of the lake's extensive shoreline, it is no wonder hobbyists have come to regard Lake Malawi as an inexhaustible treasure chest crammed with dazzling novelties!

The *mbuna* fall midway between the previous two haplochromine groups with respect to ease of maintenance.

Like all Malawian cichlids, they require hard, alkaline water to prosper and simply cannot tolerate nitrogen cycle mismanagement.

The maintenance approach outlined in the previous section is equally applicable to these cichlids. They also do well over the same temperature range as their distant cousins.

Fig. 317: A sexually quiescent male *Gephyrochromis moorii* Boulenger 1901, an *mbuna* that lives over open sandy bottoms.

Fig. 318: A male cobalt zebra, *Pseudotropheus callainos* Stauffer & Hert 1992. Both sexes of the blue morph of this species are common in nature.

Remember, however, that male aggressiveness in some *mbuna* increases to the point of hyperactivity at its upper end.

As noted, these cichlids are not fussy eaters.

However, it is advisable to include a substantial amount of vegetable food in their diet. This both promotes their general well-being and provides the pigment precursor substances necessary to maintain their coloration at full intensity.

While they should be housed in the largest quarters available, the *mbuna* can make do with smaller aquaria than those required by other Malawian haplochromines.

This is due partly because as smaller fish, *mbuna* defend smaller territories, and partly to the fact that visual isolation greatly reduces intermale aggression.

To a significant degree, out of sight is out of mind in these cichlids!

It is thus possible to house a community of such smaller *mbuna* as the several *Labidochromis* and *Cynotilapia* species in properly furnished 35 to 50 gallon aquaria, while all save a handful of very aggressive or notably robust species can be kept successfully in 75 to 90 gallon community tanks.

However, it is essential that each male have his own territorial focus, usually a cave or partially enclosed area, and that these foci be separated by a visual barrier. The likelihood of serious fighting is further diminished if one never houses more than one male of a given species per tank and avoids putting heterospecific males with similar coloration together.

It is, for example, imprudent to house two *Melanochromis* species together in any save the very largest of aquaria.

Mbuna share the proclivity of Malawian haplochromines to hybridize readily in captivity. The same rules should thus dictate the composition of a *mbuna* community as apply for the other representatives of this species flock kept by aquarists. Most *mbuna* are inept predators that ignore midwater swimming fishes.

The factor that usually disrupts a harmonious *mbuna* tank enters in consequence of their continuous growth in captivity.

Fig. 319: A female of the white morph of *P. callainos*. Males of this color form are extremely rare in nature.

Fig. 320: Perhaps the most complex instance of color polymorphism among the *mbuna* involves the red zebra. This undescribed member of the *P. zebra* complex derives its name from the color pattern of oligomelanic females such as this.

Fig. 321: Though oligomelanic male red zebras such as this one are common in captivity, they are almost nonexistent in nature. A female red zebra will produce all-red fry when bred to such a male.

Fig. 322: The most commonly encountered male color morph of the red zebra in Laka Malawi is this fish, known commercially as a powder blue zebra. When bred to such a male, a female red zebra will produce red female and powder blue male progeny.

Fig. 323: The red zebra is unusual in that not only oligomelanic but heteromelanic, or OB morph individuals such as this male are also found in nature.

Fig. 324 & 325: A male of the commonly available blue morph (above) and the rare yellow OB morph (below) of *Lambeotropheus fuelleborni.*

Fig. 325:

Fig. 326: A male *Petrotilapia tridentiger* Trewavas 1935, one of the largest *mbuna* species. Its extreme adaptions to feeding from solid surfaces are very reminiscent of those seen in the Tanganyikan *Petrochromis* species.

Fig. 327: A male *Pseudotropheus harlowi* McKaye and staufer 1986. This deep-water *mbuna* was originally mantreted in North America under the misleading name of "Gold-fin *Gephyrochromis*".

Fig. 328: A male *Pseudotropheus crabro* (Ribbink & Lewis 1982). This robust *mbuna* is both a predator on smaller fish and a cleaner fish, feeding in part on the ectoparasites of the giant catfish *Bagrus meridionalis*.

Fig. 329: A male *Pseudotropheus lucerna* Trewavas 1935, a beautiful but highly aggressive inhabitant of *Vallisneria* beds in Lake Malawi.

Fig. 330: Courting male of a small undescribed *Pseudotropheus* species often sold under the trade name "Pseudotropheus kingsleyi".

Fig. 331: Though it resembles *P. elongatus* in overall appearance and color pattern, *Pseudotropheus minutus* Fryer 1956 is a smaller, less belligerent species and hence, a more satisfactory aquarium resident.

Fig. 332: This male *Pseudotropheus* cf. *macropthalmus* "yellow" displays the rounded head and slightly inferior mouth typical of the subgenus *Tropheops*.

Predation pressure and limited access to high protein foods constrain the size these cichlids can attain in Lake Malawi.

When these limiting factors are removed, *mbuna* can grow nearly twice as large as they do in the lake.

For example, males of *Pseudotropheus zebra* rarely attain 4" SL in nature, but can grow to 7" SL in captivity. Unfortunately, as a male *mbuna* increases in length, so does the size of the territory he attempts to defend.

Thus as times passes, a tank large enough to satisfy the territorial needs of half a dozen males will no longer suffice to satisfy one.

The first sign of trouble is the persistent harassment of heterospecifics of the same sex by a previously well-behaved male. Housing *mbuna* at the low end of their preferred temperature range and offering them a diet higher in roughage and lower in protein slows this process somewhat, albeit at the expense of reproductive output, but nothing arrests it totally.

The only solutions entail moving the fish to a larger tank as they outgrow their quarters or else replacing them with smaller specimens. These cichlids are easily induced to spawn in captivity.

Mbuna are polygamous maternal mouth-brooders whose mating system is based upon more or less persistent defense and occupancy of a multi-purpose territory by sexually active males.

They should thus be handled as previously recommended for openly polygamous cichlids.

Fertilization of the eggs is intrabuccal.

Notwithstanding the presence of well defined pseudo-ocelli in the anal fins of males, the mechanics of spawning are not usually characterized by their use as egg dummies. Females instead mouth the male genital region to elicit ejaculation.

Males of many species continue to drive the female after she is spent; hence, the importance of providing plenty of hiding places for an ovigerous female in the breeding tank.

265

Fig. 333: A male OB morph *Pseudotropheus* cf. *macropthalmus* "red shoulder".

Young females may botch their initial efforts by aborting the incubation sequence prematurely. Experienced females are superb mothers. The developmental interval is 21 days at 82°–85°F.

Labidochromis do not practice postrelease brood care, instead carefully selecting secure sites into which, one at a time, they release their fry.

The remaining *mbuna* do so to a greater or lesser degree.

Such behavior doubtless enhances fry survival in nature, but the extreme female overprotectiveness typically manifested in captivity interferes with normal foraging by the fry; hence, the desirability of separating the fry from their mother as soon as they are free swimming.

Brood sizes vary considerably within the group.

Labidochromis rarely produce more than two dozen eggs per spawning effort, while the several *Petrotilapia* species and the larger *Pseudotropheus* can spawn over a hundred.

Females of most mid-sized species usually release between 35 and 50 fry. The fry themselves are robust and well developed.

They can immediately take a wide range of live and prepared foods, and share their parents' eclectic approach to feeding.

As with other Malawian haplochromine fry, they are easily reared with proper attention to keeping dissolved metabolite concentrations at subcritical levels.

Save for such precocious species as *Pseudotropheus lanisticola* BURGESS 1976 and *Iodotropheus sprengerae* OLIVER and LOISELLE 1972, which begin breeding as early as 12 weeks postrelease, most *mbuna* attain sexual maturity between six and eight months postrelease in captivity.

Mbuna are superb recruiting agents for the cichlid hobby. I would estimate that whatever their present areas of specialization, at least half the membership of the American Cichlid Association traces a commitment to serious cichlid keeping to an encounter with the *mbuna*.

Fig. 334 & 335: The differences between the coloration of male (above) and female (below) *Melanochromis auratus* (Boulenger 1897) are diagnostic of the genus. The species name recognizes the coloration of juveniles and females.

This is less surprising than it might seem.

A tank stocked with these assertive, lively haplochromines presents a constantly shifting montage of color and action.

Maintenance poses few difficulties and, given the presence of both sexes in the same aquarium, spawning occurs automatically.

Such a combination of brilliant coloration, hardiness, ease of breeding and fascinating behavior has no counterpart among either marine or freshwater ornamental fishes and guarantees the *mbuna* a permanent — and prominent — place in the tropical fish hobby.

Fig. 336 & 337: Male (above) and female (below) of the undescribed *Melanochromis* species sometimes sold as the "dwarf *auratus*".

Fig. 337

Fig. 338 & 339: The coloration of male (above) and female (below) *Melanochromis jojannii* (Eccles 1973) differ so dramatically that observers unfamiliar with the sexual dimorphism prevalent in the genus often assume the two sexes represent two different species!

Fig. 339

269

Fig. 340: A female *Melanochromis parallelus* Burgess & Axelrod 1976. This strikingly marked *mbuna* is a facultative cleaner species in nature.

Fig. 341: Male *Melanochromis chipokae* Johnson 1975, one of the long-snouted predatory representatives of the genus.

Fig. 342: Male of a recently discoverd *Melanochromis* species with a lepidophagous feeding pattern.

Fig. 343: A female of the orange morph of *Genyochromis mento* Trewavas 1935. This lepidophage is one of the few *mbuna* found ubiquitously in Lake Malawi.

271

Fig. 344: A male *Labidochromis vellicans* Trewavas 1935, type species of its genus.

Fig. 345: A male *Labidochromis exasperatus* (Johnson 1975). This species is unusual in that both sexes are attractively colored. The females of most *Labidochromis* species are quite drab.

Fig. 346: A male *Labidochromis freibergi* Johnson 1976, one of the most colorful and generally available representatives of the genus.

Fig. 347: A male *Labidochromis* sp. "Lions' Cove yellow" a spectacular new addition to the ranks of commercially available Malawi cichlids.

The Cichlids
of Lake Tanganyika

Introduction

Lake Tanganyika is unique among the African Great Lakes in the diverse character of its endemic cichlid fauna.

Although the ichthyofaunas of Lakes Victoria, Edward, George, Kivu and Malawi include a few tilapias, some of them endemic, the cichlid assemblages of these lakes are to all intents and purposes **monophyletic,** comprising exclusively haplochromines.

The cichlid fauna of Lake Tanganyika, on the contrary, is markedly **polyphyletic.** In a recent review of this assemblage, the Belgian ichthyologist MAX POLL recognized the presence of twelve distinct lineages, eight of them endemic to the lake.

Recent studies of the evolutionary genetics of these cichlids on the molecular level largely confirm this picture, although these data require a reworking of POLL's original schema.

There appears to be no basis for his recognition of a *Tropheus* lineage distinct from the haplochromines.

On the other hand, the robust predators *Boulengerochromis microlepis* (BOULENGER 1899) and *Cyphotilapia frontosa* (BOULENGER 1906), grouped by POLL with the tilapiines and the tropheine lineages respectively, appear to stand well isolated from other Tanganyikan cichlids, in much the same manner as *Ramphochromis* does to the other endemic cichlids of Lake Malawi.

Admittedly, the representation of these lineages in the Tanganyikan fauna is very uneven.

Of the non-endemic cichlids, the ancient *Tylochromis* lineage is represented by only a single species, *Tylochromis polylepis* (BOULENGER 1900).

The tilapiines number four *Oreochromis* and one *Tilapia* species in the Tanganyika basin, of which only two of these, *Oreochromis tanganyikae* (GUNTHER 1893) and *O. karomo* POLL 1948 regularly inhabit the lake proper.

Fig. 348: A sexually quiescent male *Lobochilotes labiatus* Boulenger 1915. This robust haplochromine uses its stout jaw teeth to crack the shells of freshwater bivalves.

Fig. 349: The red and black race of *Tropheus moorii* Boulenger 1998, native to the Burundi coast of Lake Tanganyika, was the first to be exported as an aquarium fish.

Of the endemic lineages recognized by POLL, the *Eretmodus* and *Cyprichromis* groups each comprise only four species.

Of the remaining recognized lineages, that comprising the genus *Lamprologus* SCHILTHUIS 1891 and its allies dominates the ichthyofauna, while the haplochromines are tied for second place with another group of species allied to the genus *Opthalmotilapia* PELLEGRIN 1904.

Their position within the Tanganyikan fauna stands in dramatic contrast to their dominant place in that of the other African Great Lakes. Though these lineages are not closely related and their constituent taxa differ in many aspects of their natural history, there are sound aquaristic reasons for treating all Lake Tanganyika cichlids as a single unit.

Regardless of their evolutionary relationships, all have, over the course of its nearly ten million year history, become exquisitely adapted to Lake Tanganyika's virtually oceanic environment.

By virtue of its immense size, Lake Tanganyika enjoys remarkable stability with regard to temperature and chemical make-up.

There is, for example, a difference of just under 5 °F between the surface and the bottom of this nearly mile-deep lake, while its superficial waters vary seasonally only 3 °F around a value of 82 °F.

The lake's enormous volume — nearly 8400 cubic miles of water—buffers it against large-scale changes in chemical composition.

Torrential rains may produce localized fluctuations with regard to hardness or nutrient load.

However, these are restricted to the vicinity of inflowing streams and do not affect the balance of a littoral zone that extends along 940 miles of shoreline.

Finally, throughout most of its long history, Lake Tanganyika has been a closed drainage basin. Consequently its waters are very alkaline and highly mineralized.

Reported pH values range from 8.6 to 9.2. Total hardness is c. 24 °DH, carbonate hardness 18 ° DH.

The tremendous buffering capacity inherent in such hard water precludes abrupt changes in pH as effectively as the lake's enor-

Fig. 350: A male of the magnificent kaiser race of *T. moorii,* my personal favorite of the twenty-odd color forms of this Tanganyika *mbuna* analog.

mous volume acts to stabilize water temperatures.

Lake Tanganyika's remarkable environmental stability and the distinctive chemical composition of its waters have profound aquaristic implications.

In contrast to their riverine counterparts, for whom often abrupt fluctuations in water temperature, pH and hardness are a routine occurrence, Tanganyikan cichlids have lost the ability to cope well with short-term environmental changes.

They have become thoroughly adapted to a distinctive biotope and demand it be closely reproduced in captivity if they are to prosper. In this respect, they resemble marine fishes rather than the generality of cichlids.

This resemblance further extends to an extreme sensitivity to dissolved metabolic wastes.

Careful nitrogen cycle management is an absolute prerequisite to their successful maintenance, the more so because the pH range within which they prosper makes Tanganyikan cichlids among the few representatives of the family that run any serious risk of ammonia poisoning in captivity.

Unlike marine fishes, all Tanganyikan cichlids are acutely sensitive to nitrite and there is evidence linking elevated nitrate levels to large-scale asymptomatic mortality of their fry.

However, nitrogen cycle management for these cichlids is complicated by the marked intolerance of many species to water changes in excess of 25 % their tank's volume.

This is not to imply that Tanganyikan cichlids are inordinately difficult to keep in captivity.

In many respects their upkeep poses fewer problems than that of some of their more physiologically plastic relatives. However, their prospective keeper must appreciate from the start of his involvement that a different approach to basic husbandry is essential to their successful maintenance and breeding.

The following suggestions are not difficult to implement.

The aquarist who takes them to heart should experience few difficulties in keeping Tanganyikan cichlids happy and fecund. It is a simple matter to provide these fishes with suitable water conditions.

Note that while these cichlids do not tolerate acidic water conditions, they will live and breed at alkaline pH values lower than those recorded from Lake Tanganyika.

If slowly acclimated, Tanganyikan fishes prosper over a pH range of 7.5 − 8.5 and at carbonate hardness levels as low as 6 °DH. Aquarists living in areas with soft to moderately hard tap water can easily duplicate lacustrine conditions by using any commercially available Tanganyika salt mix according to the manufacturer's direction.

Remember that calcium carbonate, a major ingredient, requires two to four days to dissolve completely at aquarium temperatures. It is therefore prudent to initiate any measures required to modify the chemical make-up of its water **at least a week before** the anticipated introduction of its residents into a Tanganyikan cichlid tank. It is also wise to keep sufficient pretreated water on hand to make two or three 25 % water changes in the event of an emergency requiring prompt replacement of part of its volume.

Aquarists living where the water supply is naturally hard and alkaline are spared the necessity of such treatments.

Many successful breeders of Tanganyikan cichlids believe it prudent to provide reserve buffering capacity in their tanks even where naturally suitable water is readily available. This is easily accomplished by introducing a slightly soluble alkaline material such as crushed oyster shell or Philippine coral gravel into the filtration system.

Suitable approaches are discussed in Chapter 5.

There is evidence that the addition of naturally occurring calcareous materials to an aquarium cannot in itself push the pH above 7.8.

While this is of considerable import to marine aquarists, whose charges tolerate pH values inferior to 8.0 poorly if at all, it has little

Fig. 351: A male *T. moorii* from Mpulungu, a locality in the south of Lake Tanganyika.

Fig. 352: This color form of *T. moorii* hails from Bemba. [*Tropheus moorii* color form to be determined].

bearing on the husbandry of Tanganyikan cichlids.

Putting a "floor" of 7.8 on possible pH drops in an aquarium containing these cichlids, however, makes a great deal of sense, the more so as such precautionary measures are easily implemented.

Tanganyikan cichlids dislike cool water and should never be maintained at temperatures lower than 70 °F for any length of time. A range of 78 °–82 °F is ideal for both normal maintenance and breeding.

They are also more susceptible than the generality of their riverine relatives to abrupt fluctuations in water temperature. It is simple to provide stable temperatures during the cool months of the year.

Little more is required than an efficient and reliable thermostatic heater. The task is more complicated during the warm months, however.

In many regions, summer is characterized by heat waves followed by rapid cooling.

Unless aquaria are kept in an air-conditioned room, the temperature of their water follows that of the surrounding air quite closely.

This can have serious consequences, for a thermostatically controlled heater can only prevent the water temperature from falling **below** a certain minimum value.

Unless that value rises concurrently with rising air temperature, only the thermal inertia of the water mass itself works to delay a drastic temperature plunge when the tank's surroundings suddenly cool off. Contrary to popular belief, an abrupt drop from 85 °F to 75 °F is as stressful to fish as a change from 75 °F to 65 °F over a comparable interval.

Tanganyikan cichlids can successfully cope with temperature changes of 1 °F per hour. It is thus important to raise the thermostat setting as surrounding temperatures increase, then **slowly** adjust it downwards once they have dropped to more normal levels. Tanganyikan cichlids vary in their tolerance of water changes.

These distinctions will be appropriately noted and should enter into the design of a given species' nitrogen cycle management plan.

278

Fig. 353: A male *Tropheus brichardi* Nelissen & Thys 1975, a species once thought to be a color form of *T. moorii*.

As a rule of thumb, changing between ten and twenty five percent of their tank volume every seven to ten days is unlikely to interfere with normal reproductive behavior even in highly sensitive species.

Assuming conservative stocking rates and the operation of an efficient biological filter, such a regime should suffice to maintain water quality at acceptable levels.

Happily, most Tanganyikan cichlids limit their digging to the excavation of spawning pits and although there are exceptions to the rule, such gravel-moving is usually of relatively modest proportions.

Furthermore, to date none of the Lake's many species has manifested a taste for matured sponge cartridges.

The full spectrum of biologically active filtration systems is thus at their keeper's disposal.

The prospective breeder of Tanganyikan cichlids who follows the steps outlined in Chapter 5 for establishing a biological filter should not encounter any difficulty in providing a congenial environment for his fish.

Because it is not always easy to determine a filter bed's carrying capacity ahead of the fact, add fish to the system gradually and monitor its progress for several months with regular testing for ammonia, nitrite and nitrate.

It is inadvisable to allow nitrate levels exceed 30.0 ppm for any length of time in a tank housing Tanganyikan cichlids.

The rapidity with which nitrate concentrations reach this level furnishes a clear notion of how frequently small-scale water changes should be integrated into the management plan or any chemically active media incorporated into the system replaced.

Tanganyikan Haplochromine Cichlids

Haplochromines, as noted, do not play a dominant role in the ichthyofauna of Lake Tanganyika. Five *Haplochromis* species, two *Astatoreochromis* species and one species each of *Orthochromis*, *Pseudocrenilabrus* and *Serranochromis* are present in the Tanganyika basin. However, with the exception of the

Fig. 354: The crescentic tail of *Tropheus polli* Axelrod 1977 sets it apart from all its congeners.

predatory *H. (Ctenochromis) horei* (GUNTHER 1893) and *H. (Ctenochromis) benthicola* MATTHES 1962, their occurrence in the lake proper is episodic at best.

Rather, these cichlids are residents of inflowing streams and peripheral swamps along the lake margin.

Within the lake itself, the most conspicuous haplochromines are the robust mollusc and crab eating *Lobochilotes labiatus* BOULENGER 1915 [Figure 348] and several genera analogous to the *mbuna* of Lake Malawi.

POLL has suggested that the genera *Limnotilapia* REGAN 1920, *Petrochromis* BOULENGER 1898, *Pseudosimochromis* NELISSEN 1977, *Simochromis* BOULENGER 1898 and *Tropheus* BOULENGER 1898 warrant recognition as a separate lineage.

However, certain elements in their color patterns and behavioral repertoires and data on their genetic relationships at the molecular level suggest that like the *mbuna*, these petricolous cichlids are really highly derived haplochromines.

Indeed, the morphological similarities of these Tanganyikan genera to representatives of the Malawian genera *Pseudotropheus* and *Petrotilapia* are so striking that one might be tempted to explain them in terms of recent shared ancestry.

However, both the recent findings of molecular geneticists and what is known of the history of these two lake basins and their respective cichlid faunas suggest otherwise.

Both lines of evidence indicate that these assemblages of petricolous cichlids have evolved independently from a generalized ancestor.

Their similarities have arisen from the constraints imposed by the successful pursuit of essentially identical modes of living and so constitute a striking instance of evolutionary convergence.

These Tanganyikan aufwuchs grazers are among the most eagerly sought-after of all African cichlids. The genus *Tropheus* has proven particularly rich in aquaristically desirable representatives. Over a dozen distinctive color forms of *Tropheus moorii* BOULENGER 1898 [Figures 349—352] have been exported from Lake Tanganyika, and there is no reason to believe this list is exhaustive.

Fig. 355 & 356: Female (above) and male (below) *Petrochromis trewavasae* Poll 1948. This species owes its popularity to a color pattern reminiscent of juvenile *T. duboisi*. Many aquarists are surprised to discover the dominant male shows no trace of lighter spots whatsoever.

Fig. 356.

Most of these so-called color forms, like their ecological analogs in Lake Malawi, enjoy highly localized distributions.

In pleasant contrast to their distant *mbuna* cousins, however, many are notably disinclined to regard any but representatives of their own phenotype as suitable spawning partners.

Recent findings that they also differ markedly from one another in the structure of their DNA will thus come as no surprise to knowledgeable aquarists.

In the light of this body of evidence, it seems safe to predict that several of these putative color forms will ultimately join the roster of other *Tropheus* phenotypes recognized as valid species [Figures 353 & 354].

The genera *Petrochromis* [Figures 355, 358] and *Simochromis* [Figures 359 & 360] are comparably speciose.

Further exploration of the lake's extensive shoreline has likewise turned up several distinctive phenotypes of both genera that bid fair to prove undescribed species.

With a few notable differences, these fish should be managed like *mbuna* of comparable

size. They tolerate large-scale water changes better than the majority of Tanganyikan cichlids, though reproductive activity is depressed as the frequency of water changes increases.

They seem more trophically specialized than their Malawian analogues and require more attention to their diet in captivity. Foods with a high content of animal protein must be avoided.

Tubifex worms and frozen brine shrimp in particular should never be offered them. To disregard such advice courts the onset of dangerous systemic bacterial infections.

Although flake or pelletized foods with a high vegetable content are an acceptable dietary staple for these cichlids, the more fresh vegetable matter included in the diet, the better.

In addition to the usual leafy vegetables, these fish also relish thinly sliced, blanched zucchini or similar marrow squashes and cooked peas.

If the situation of their tank promotes a copious growth of algae on its back, sides and furnishing, so much the better. The several

Fig. 357: A male *Petrochromis famula* Matthes & Trewavas 1960, a robust species once from the Burundi coast of Lake Tanganyika.

Fig. 358: A male *Petrochromis* sp. "Texas", without a doubt the most spectacularly colored species of the genus.

Petrochromis species particularly appreciate the opportunity to express their natural feeding pattern in captivity.

Petrochromis, Pseudosimochromis and *Simochromis* live in much the same way in nature as do the *mbuna*, with males holding persistent territories through which groups of females freely move. Like them, they are rather easily sexed.

Lobochilotes labiatus appears to live a solitary life, while *Limnotilapia* species are quite social. Territorial behavior in nature is restricted to the brief defense of a spawning site in both genera.

Males of these haplochromines are usually more vividly colored, and have larger, more clearly defined and usually more numerous pseudo-ocelli on their anal fins than do females.

Large specimens also have longer ventral fin filaments and more pointed soft dorsal and anal fins [Figures 356 & 357].

It is possible to manage captive populations of *Limnotilapia, Pseudosimochromis* and

Simochromis in the manner recommended for their Malawian counterparts.

This approach does not work well for *Lobochilotes* and *Petrochromis*, however.

Attempts to keep a single male and a group of females together invariably results in the loss of the females.

Many of the difficulties encountered in the husbandry of these related but ecologically quite different cichlids appear to arise from their large adult size.

Several *Petrochromis* grow to 12" SL in nature, while *L. labiatus* 15" SL have been reported from the lake.

These fish, as one might predict, hold territories scaled to their size.

Sufficient space to satisfy their demands might be forthcoming in the display tanks of a public aquarium.

The odds are certainly against it being so in a basement fish room. The most successful approach to breeding these fish entails placing a single pair in a tank packed with rockwork, feeding both heavily and hoping for the best.

283

Fig. 360: A male *Simochromis pleurospilus* Nelissen 1978. Though a moderately social species in nature, it also behaves rather aggressively towards others of its own species in captivity.

If all goes well, their keeper can look forward to one or two successful spawnings before the female's luck runs out.

Tropheus differ from their Malawian counterparts in the virtually total impossibility under home aquarium conditions of maintaining more than a single male in a tank containing both sexes.

Several males will coexist in absolute amity until a female is introduced into their midst. What follows thereafter resembles full-scale warfare rather than the usual manifestations of intraspecific aggression in cichlids.

If males restricted their violence to others of their sex, aquarists could more readily live with its consequences. However, females are as likely to be victims of such unrestrained fighting as rival males.

This is particularly unpalatable in *T. moorii*, for the preponderance of males

among imported fish automatically places females in short supply.

The extreme intolerance of males for one another stems from an aterritorial mating system. Instead of excluding others of their sex from a fixed display site, males instead attempt to sequester receptive females. When the object of aggression is real estate, one can minimize intermale fighting by providing a surplus of territorial foci.

This approach is hardly practical when the resource in contention is a sexually receptive female.

Furthermore, when males contest for access to a ripe female and successful intrusion can result in interruption of the spawning act, the stakes are too high for ritualization of combat to have evolved.

Under such conditions, males fight for keeps.

Thus the only hope losers have is to move as far away from the winners of such brawls as possible. This is seldom possible in captivity. Consequently, their existence tends to be brutish, nasty, and above all, brief.

To avoid such carnage, make absolutely certain one and only one male is maintained with a group of females.

This entails knowing how to distinguish between the sexes, a normally simple task in haplochromines, where dramatic sexual color differences are the rule.

Regrettably, many *Tropheus* are a conspicuous exception to this pattern.

While males of *T. polli* are usually unbanded and have a more deeply lunate caudal fin than do females, the remaining *Tropheus* species cannot be reliably sexed by means of color pattern or fin shape.

When dealing with imported adults, bear in mind that males grow larger than females.

Most also have a protuberance on the snout that gives them a somewhat Roman-nosed appearance.

However, the only absolutely certain means of ascertaining an individual's sex is to examine its genital papilla.

Apart from the fact that spawning does not invariably occur at a fixed location, there is little to set the reproductive act of these cichlids apart from that of their Malawian analogues.

The developmental interval is somewhat longer, 24 to 26 days at 82 °F.

Ovigerous females continue to eat while carrying, though their intake of food is considerably reduced.

Postrelease brood care is reported for all these *mbuna* analogs to date bred in captivity.

These cichlids do not molest newly released fry if well fed.

If they are not housed with predatory tankmates, there is no need to isolate ovigerous females, who can be allowed to carry and release their fry into the breeding tank with every expectation the young will survive and prosper therein. The pyriform eggs are extremely large, measuring c. 0.12″ along their

Fig. 361: A male of the aptly named *Cunningtonia longiventralis* Boulenger 1906.

285

major axis. Brood sizes are, in consequence, modest.

Females of the larger *Petrochromis* and *Simochromis* species may release up to fifty fry in captivity, but spawns are usually smaller in nature. Exceptionally fecund female *Tropheus* will produce up to two dozen progeny per reproductive effort, but the usual output of young is between eight and fifteen per spawn.

By way of compensation, the fry measure nearly ¾" TL at release, and are easily reared.

They are somewhat slower growing than *mbuna*, attaining sexual maturity between ten months and a year postrelease.

The logistic problems of collecting many of these cichlids in the wild, the low densities at which they must be shipped and their reduced fecundity conspire to limit their availability and assure such specimens as can be found will command a handsome price.

These considerations notwithstanding, there is no noticeable decline in the popularity of these Tanganyikan haplochromines. Nor, given their often brilliant coloration and

always interesting behavior, should any diminution of their appeal be anticipated in the foreseeable future.

Tanganyikan Featherfins and Their Allies

The American ichthyologist KAREL LIEM and his British colleague P. H. GREENWOOD have established the existence of a distinctive assemblage of ten genera that stand well isolated not only from other endemic Tanganyikan cichlids but from extralacustrine African lineages as well. The American aquarist THOMAS J. KOZIOL has proposed the common name featherfins for the genera *Cunningtonia* [Figure 361], *Cyathopharynx* [Figure 362] and *Opthalmotilapia* [Figure 363 & 364] for the more spectacular representatives of this "*Opthalmotilapia*-group".

Since the publication of the first edition of this book, this lineage has been given formal status by POLL as the tribe Ectodini.

Fig. 362: A sexually active male *Cyathopharynx furcifer* (Boulenger 1898). Its irridescent blue coloration recalls Neotropical butterflies of the genus *Morpho*.

Fig. 363: A male of the Kipili population of *Opthalmotilapia boops* (Boulenger 1901). The specific epithet, which translates literally as "cow-eye", refers to the very large eyes of this featherfin.

The assemblage comprises the genera *Ectodus* BOULENGER 1898 [Figure 365], *Opthalmotilapia* PELLEGRIN 1904, *Cunningtonia* BOULENGER 1906, *Cyathopharynx* REGAN 1920, *Cardiopharynx* POLL 1942, *Lestradea* POLL 1943, *Asprotilapia* BOULENGER 1901, *Aulocranus* REGAN 1920, [Figure 366], *Callochromis* REGAN 1920 [Figure 367], *Xenotilapia* BOULENGER 1899 [Figure 368], *Grammatoria* BOULENGER 1899, *Enantiopus* BOULENGER 1906 [Figure 369] and *Microdontochromis* POLL 1986.

While the remaining genera lack the filamentous fin processes that inspired this name, it remains a convenient vernacular designation for the group as a whole.

The number of formally recognized species in this assemblage is misleading. Commercial collecting has discovered distinctive color forms of restricted distribution, the majority well documented by the German researcher AD KONIGS.

It is quite likely that more intensive analysis of their status will show many of them to be valid species.

LIEM and GREENWOOD defined this group on the basis of common anatomical features, but its representatives share natural history characteristics of comparable interest and considerably greater aquaristic significance.

These fish are highly social, free-ranging cichlids.

The true featherfins of the genera *Cunningtonia*, *Cyathopharynx*, *Cardiopharynx* and *Opthalmotilapia* live in mid-water over rocky bottoms.

The remaining representatives of the group occur in close association with sandy or rocky bottoms.

These cichlids are either microphagous, feeding upon plankton or aufwuchs, or else substratum-sifting invertebrate feeders. They are extremely fragile fish, subject to lethal postcapture trauma.

They also ship poorly.

These considerations have limited the commercial availability of wild-caught specimens. Fortunately for aquarists, individuals prove reasonably hardy once they have adjusted to captivity.

287

Fig. 364: A male of the Cape Kachese population of *Opthalmotilapia nasuta* (Poll & Matthes 1962). This distinctive featherfin is, for obvious reasons, sometimes known as the "Jimmy Durante cichlid"!

Fig. 365: A male *Ectodus descampsii* Boulenger 1898. The several geographic color variants of this widely distributed sand-dweller may prove to be valid species.

Fig. 366: A male *Aulocranus dewindti* (Boulenger 1899). The enlarged cephalic lateral line pits of this beautiful featherfin are reminiscent of those seen in the *Aulonacara* species of Lake Malawi.

Fig. 367: *Callochromis pleurospilus*

Fig. 368: A courting pair of *Xenotilapia ochrogenys* (Boulenger 1914).

They accept the usual range of live, frozen and prepared foods and given due attention to water quality and sufficiently large quarters, most species will breed successfully under aquarium conditions.

Captive-bred youngsters respond more positively to both handling and shipping than do their imported counterparts.

These considerations notwithstanding, featherfins still remain far from readily available through the usual commercial channels. These fish require the same care as other Tanganyikan cichlids. They should be housed in tanks of at least 50 and preferably 75 to 100 gallons capacity.

Many featherfins are large fish and require considerable room for normal social interactions. All are **extremely** sensitive to dissolved metabolites.

Greater ease of nitrogen cycle management is another good reason for affording them as much living space as possible.

Featherfins dislike large-scale water changes.

If necessary to replace water in their tank, changes should be limited to 10% of its total volume weekly. Indeed, a strong case can be made for the use of chemically active media as a regular adjunct to their maintenance.

Notwithstanding varied feeding patterns in nature, all featherfins are easily fed in captivity, readily accepting generally available live and prepared foods.

All species for which information is available are advanced mouthbrooders.

The extent to which these cichlids display sexual dimorphism is a function of their mating system.

Opthalmotilapia, Cunningtonia, Cyathopharynx, Cardiopharynx, Lestradea, Aulocranus, Callochromis, Enantiopus and some *Xenotilapia* are maternal mouthbrooders with lek-type mating systems. Sexual dimorphism ranges from moderate to spectacular in these species, which should be managed in the manner suggested for openly polygamous cichlids.

Asprotilapia, Grammatoria and a number of *Xenotilapia* species are monogamous biparental mouthbrooders.

Sexual dimorphism in these species is slight to non-existent.

Ectodus and *Microdontochromis* are also female mouthbrooders but the nature of their mating system is unclear.

Given the absence of dramatic sexual dimorphism in either genus, however, it would be a safe bet to predict both to practice some form of monogamy.

These cichlids should be handled in the same way as the West African *Chromidotilapia* species.

Regardless of mating system, the often spectacular breeding dress of these cichlids relies primarily upon structural pigmentation, in marked contrast to that of most haplochromines and tilapiines.

Since the publication of the first edition of this book, considerably more has been learned about the reproductive biology of these cichlids.

According to Konigs, *Ectodus, Cardiopharynx, Lestradea, Asprotilapia, Grammatoria, Enantiopus,* and *Microdontochromis* construct pit nests within which the eggs are deposited and fertilized before being taken into the female's buccal cavity. It is unclear whether

Cyathopharynx also practices extrabuccal fertilization.

Aquarium and field observations have been made that support the operation of both modalities in this species.

In any event, this featherfin differs from the preceding species in its habit of constructing its nests by laying down a circular rim of gravel on a flat rock.

Males of *Opthalmotilapia* dig crater nests in patches of sand among the rocks.

More detailed observations of the mechanics of spawning in these featherfins suggests that females do not approach courting males with eggs already in their mouths as reported by Pierre Brichard and that fertilization is at least in part intrabuccal, the spatulate yellow tips of the male's ventral fins functioning as egg dummies during spawning.

Intrabuccal fertilization of the eggs has also been observed in the genera *Cunningtonia, Aulocranus* and *Callochromis.*

The incubation period is 21 days at 78 °F for the maternal mouthbrooding representatives of this group.

Fig. 369: A sexually active male *Enantiopus melanogenys* (Boulenger 1898).

There is no indication of any postrelease care of the mobile fry in these species.

By way of contrast, in the biparentally mouthbrooding species the female typically broods the eggs for ten days, then transfers her burden to the male.

He in turn carried the developing young for another seven to ten days. Both parents then protect the free-swimming fry for up to a week post-release.

Broods rarely exceed 30 young for the true featherfins.

Spawns of 10 to 40 fry are the norm for *Callochromis* and the lekking *Xenotilapia* species, while the more robust *Enantiopus* can release up to 80 young.

The fry are large enough to take *Artemia* nauplii as their first food. Those of the true featherfins are delicate and rather slow growing.

Great care must be taken to prevent nitrate buildup in their tanks.

Even under favorable conditions, it is unusual for these cichlids to attain reproductive competence sooner than 12 months postrelease.

In contrast, those of *Callochromis, Xenotilapia* and *Enantiopus* are robust and grow rapidly.

If handled as recommended for Malawian haplochromine fry, the young can attaining sexual maturity between six and eight months postrelease.

The Limnochromis Species Group

With the unique exception of *Reganochromis calliurus* (BOULENGER 1901) [Figure 370], the species in this assemblage were formerly included within the large genus *Limnochromis*.

The comprehensive character of this genus was formally recognized in 1974 when POLL and THYS VAN DEN AUDENAERDE erected the genus *Triglachromis* for the highly distinctive *Limnochromis otostigma* REGAN 1920 .

Since that time, POLL has revised the genus and erected five additional genera to accommodate morphologically distinctive species formerly placed within *Limnochromis,* and 1986 afforded this assemblage of genera formal standing as the tribe Limnochromini.

Fig. 370: A male *Reganochromis calliurus* (Boulenger 1901).

Fig. 371: A male *Gnathochromis premaxillaris* (David 1936), Lake Tanganyika's version of a basketmouth cichlid!

As defined by POLL this lineage includes the genera *Limnochromis* REGAN 1920, *Reganochromis* WHITLEY 1921, *Triglachromis* POLL and THYS 1974, *Gnathochromis* POLL 1981, *Tangachromis* POLL 1981, *Greenwoodochromis* POLL 1983, *Baileychromis* POLL 1986 and *Benthochromis* POLL 1986.

The relationships of these genera to one another and to the other cichlids of Lake Tanganyika are by no means clear.

Furthermore, *Gnathochromis* is clearly an artificial grouping of quite unrelated species.

While *Gnathochromis premaxillaris* (DAVID 1936) [Figure 371] appears closely related to other limnochromines, the color pattern and reproductive modality of the type species, *Gnathochromis pfefferi* (BOULENGER 1898) [Figure 372], betray its haplochromine affinities. This group of species invites analysis at the molecular level and it would not surprise me were such research to result in the synonymization of some of these genera.

The limnochromines live for the most part over muddy bottoms, often at considerable depths.

Such habitats facilitate neither observations nor the collection of live specimens.

This goes far to explain why the natural history of three of these genera is effectively a cipher.

It doubtless also accounts for the fact that attractive coloration notwithstanding, it took some time for many of these distinctive cichlids to be exported from the lake.

Limnochromis auritus BOULENGER 1901 [Figure 373] and *Triglachromis otostigma* REGAN 1920 [Figure 158] are conspicuous exceptions to this pattern.

Because both species can be collected in quantity from the outflow of the Ruzizi River in Burundi, they were among the first Tanganyikan cichlids to be exported *en masse* by the BRICHARD team in the early 1970s.

Although these benthic omnivores are relatively unaggressive and easily maintained in captivity, few spawnings of either have been reported.

The recently published observations on the behavior of these fish in nature by KONIGS provide a partial solution to the mystery.

293

Fig. 372: A male *Gnathochromis pfefferi* (Boulenger 1898). The color pattern of this species suggests haplochromine affinities.

Fig. 373: *Limnochromis auritus* (Boulenger 1901), a common inhabitant of Lake Tanganyika's deeper waters.

Both of these cichlids are monogamous biparental mouthbrooders that deposit their eggs within caves they excavate in nature.

The absence of an enclosed spawning chamber of suitable dimensions effectively inhibits pair formation and spawning in captivity.

The scale of their tunnel-digging activity in the lake renders impractical any attempt to allow the fish to express the full gamut of such behavior in a home aquarium.

An acceptable compromise would be to offer them a partially buried network of CPVC pipe. Excavating this prefabricated tunnel system facilitates pair formation and ultimately affords the fish the privacy they require to spawn.

This caveat aside, they should be managed in the manner suggested for other monogamous cichlids.

Fertilization occurs outside of the female's mouth. The two sexes alternate as spawn carriers over the course of the developmental interval.

At 80 °F, this lasts ten days in *L. auritus* and two weeks in *T. otostigma*.

Both sexes vigilantly protect the mobile young, which can number in excess of 100 fry for both species.

The newly released fry are large enough to take *Artemia* nauplii and grow quite rapidly for those of a Tanganyikan cichlid.

Sexual maturity comes between six and eight months postrelease for *T. otostigma*, roughly four months later for *L. auritus*.

Greenwoodochromis christyi (TREWAVAS 1953) [Figure 374] and *Reganochromis calliurus* are also monogamous biparental mouthbrooders that practice the long-term postrelease defense of their mobile fry. Both species are prodigious diggers and should be managed as suggested for the previous two genera.

The developmental interval is just over two weeks at 80 °F and broods of 60 to 100 fry appear to be the norm in captivity.

The fry can take *Artemia* nauplii for their initial food. They appear to be somewhat more sensitive to dissolved metabolites than those of

Fig. 374: A male *Greenwoodochromis christyi* (Boulenger 1901), a relatively recent addition to the roster of Tanganyikan cichlids available to aquarists.

either *T. otostigma* or *L. auritus*, but as long as due attention is paid to nitrogen cycle management in their tanks, they are easily reared.

Gnathochromis pfefferi is a polygamous maternal mouthbrooder.

Data on the behavior of wild fish leave no doubt that this species is not an arena breeder, suggesting instead a consort-type mating system.

Captive specimens should be managed like any other openly polygamous cichlid.

The mechanics of spawning no less than the presence of pseudo-ocelli on the male's anal fin betray the haplochromine affinities of this species.

Fertilization is intrabuccal and the female carries the developing young for 21 days at 80 °F. It is not known if this species practices postrelease care of its fry in nature.

Careful observations of parental female *G. pfefferi* under aquarium conditions could yield valuable information on this aspect of its reproductive behavior.

The fry respond well to the management regime suggested for the other species of this group.

Under favorable conditions, they attain sexual maturity eight to ten months postrelease.

Gnathochromis premaxillaris is a sexually isomorphic species with a monogamous mating system.

According to the American aquarist DON WALZ, the female is the initially ovigerous parent. The developmental interval is c. 14 days at 78 °F.

The possibility that this species is a biparental mouthbrooder cannot be excluded, as human intervention has characterized the few successful spawnings to date reported.

The spectacularly colored *Benthochromis tricoti* (POLL 1948) [Figure 375] is a lek breeding maternal mouthbrooder.

Although aquarium spawnings have been reported in both Europe and North America, information is lacking on the normal developmental interval, as the females in question have yet to carry a brood to full term.

Nothing is known of the mating systems or modality of parental care practiced by *Benthochromis melanoides* POLL 1984, *Baileychromis centropomoides* (BAILEY and STEWART

Fig. 375: A male *Benthochromis tricoti* (Poll 1948), one of the most beautiful of all cichlid species.

Fig. 376: The specialized feeding behavior of *Plecodus paradoxus* Boulenger 1898 limits its appeal as an aquarium resident.

1977), *Greenwoodochromis bellcrossi* (POLL 1971) or *Tangachromis dhanisi* (POLL 1949).

However, given the ongoing exportation of cichlids from several different points on its extensive shoreline, it seems only a matter of time before the efforts of Tanganyikan cichlid enthusiasts unlock the reproductive secrets of these distinctive species.

Scale-Eating, Pelagic and Benthic Cichlids of Lake Tanganyika

The cichlid radiations of all three of Africa's Great Lakes can count among their number species that feed upon the scales and fin tissue of other fishes.

The most morphologically specialized of these **lepidophagous** cichlids are the seven species grouped by POLL in the Tribe Perissodini. *Perissodus microlepis* BOULENGER 1898, type species of its genus, and *P. eccentricus* LIEM and STEWART 1976 are the most structurally generalized representatives of this lineage.

Increasing dental, skeletal and behavioral specialization is demonstrated by the four species of the genus *Plecodus* BOULENGER 1898 [Figure 376] and the monotypic *Xenochromis hecqui* BOULENGER 1899.

Though it does not share their lifestyle, shared skeletal specializations link the pelagic predator *Haplotaxodon microlepis* BOULENGER 1906 [Figure 377] to these extreme dietary specialists.

Several *Plecodus* species, *Perissodus microlepis* and *Haplotaxodon microlepis* have been exported episodically from Lake Tanganyika.

Unlike their ecological counterparts from Lake Malawi, Tanganyikan scale-eaters tend to persist in their peculiar feeding behavior when kept under aquarium conditions.

The delights of flake and freeze-dried foods notwithstanding, these cichlids will descale tankmates with remarkable alacrity.

This debars them from a community tank and doubtless explains why, though very attractively colored, these cichlids have not managed to gain a significant following on either side of the Atlantic.

Although it is not burdened by such a disagreeable feeding pattern, *H. microlepis* has likewise failed to establish itself as an aquarium resident.

In this instance, large adult size — males can attain 10" SL — appears to have counted more in the judgment of hobbyists than the bright colors that usually guarantee a degree of popularity as an aquarium resident. Most representatives of this lineage live in proximity to rocky biotopes and in consequence are easily observed in nature.

Thus while none of these species appears to have been bred in captivity, a good deal is known about their reproductive biology.

All are monogamous mouthbrooders that practice the long-term defense of their mobile progeny.

The scale-eating species are all biparental mouthbrooders.

Haplotaxodon microlepis appears to be a strictly maternal brooder with biparental care of the mobile fry.

Spawns range from 100 to 300 fry and parental care has been observed to persist for three to four weeks.

Fertilization is known to be extrabuccal in the best-studied member of the tribe, *P. microlepis,* whose developmental interval appears to be seven days long in the lake. Such details remain to be ascertained for the other representatives of the Tribe Perissodini.

The open waters of Lake Tanganyika are home to a distinctive assemblage of pelagic fishes dominated by *Stolothrissa* and *Limnothrissa,* two genera of freshwater herrings referred to collectively by native fishermen as *ndangala.*

These clupeids are accompanied by the highly specialized cichlids of the genera *Cyprichromis* SCHEUERMANN 1977 and *Paracyprichromis* POLL 1986.

This community of zooplankton feeders is in turn preyed upon by an assemblage of open-water predators that includes the meter-long *Boulengerochromis microlepis* (BOULENGER 1899) [Figure 20], the seven

Fig. 377: *Haplotaxodon microlepis* Boulenger 1906 differs from its relatives in its piscivorous feeding pattern.

species of the genus *Bathybates* BOULENGER 1898 and the monotypic genus *Hemibates* REGAN 1920.

The last two of these three genera have been grouped by POLL in the Tribe Bathybatini.

These strikingly marked cruise predators play essentially the same role in Lake Tanganyika as the barracuda cichlids of the genus *Ramphochromis* do in Lake Malawi.

As is the case with their Malawian analogs, little is known of their natural history, as their pelagic lifestyle makes them extremely difficult to observe in nature.

Considerable numbers of these medium-sized to large predators are caught by commercial vessels fishing for *ndangala*. From examination of such material ichthyologists have determined their diets and learned that they are maternal mouthbrooders.

Nothing is known of their spawning sites, mating systems or of the actual mechanics of the spawning act.

As fish that have spent time in the cod end of a purse seine are poor candidates for a life insurance policy, it is likely to be some time before these gaps in our knowledge can be filled through observation of captive specimens.

The bathybatine cichlid most likely to be exported in the foreseeable future is *Hemibates stenosoma* (BOULENGER 1901).

According to KONIGS, juveniles of this spectacularly colored 11" SL predator school in shallow waters inshore. Such behavior renders them much more accessible to collectors than their more pelagic relatives in the genus *Bathybates*.

A great deal more is known about the natural history of *Boulengerochromis microlepis*, a cruise predator that vies with the Neotropical *Cichla* species for the distinction of the world's largest cichlid.

Its importance as a food fish has attracted the attention of fisheries biologists, while its tendency to move into shallow water to spawn makes in accessible to students of cichlid behavior.

In the first edition of this book, I included this species with the lamprologine cichlids.

Fig. 378: A male of the Kamilani Island population of *Cyprichromis leptosoma*. It is likely that some of the geographic color forms of this sardine cichlid will be recognized eventually as valid species.

Fig. 379: A male *Paracyprichromis brieni* (Poll 1981). This lyretailed beauty is one of the most sought-after of Lake Tanganyika's sardine cichlids.

POLL subsequently placed it in his Tribe Tilapiini, but more recent molecular data indicate that *B. microlepis* has no close relatives within or without the Lake Tanganyika cichlid fauna. For aquaristic purposes it remains useful to treat it as a giant open-water *Lamprologus*. Juveniles 4"-6" SL are sometimes imported.

Sheer novelty value usually assures them a ready market. Their owners enthusiasm for his new pets is usually dimmed by the twin discoveries that while this species requires frequent offerings of live fish to remain healthy, linear growth in size is linked to exponential increase in appetite!

Even half-grown specimens require tanks of 100 gallons capacity and larger to prosper, and it is unlikely a fully grown individual would feel comfortable anywhere outside the display tanks of a public aquarium.

Young specimens tolerate conspecifics quite well and essentially ignore tankmates too large to swallow.

Captive specimens are prone to jump when startled.

While a firmly placed cover will keep such fugitives off the floor, it poses its own risk to their well-being, for even juveniles can strike a tank lid with sufficient force to do themselves serious injury.

Boulengerochromis microlepis is a biparentally custodial substratum spawning cichlid that ferociously defends its mobile young. Reproductively active individuals 18" SL have been recorded from the lake.

Thus there is a fair possibility that *B. microlepis* could be induced to spawn successfully in the aquarium. However, the mind boggles at the number of feeder goldfish necessary to fuel such a project!

According to KONIGS, pairs move into the shallows and search out the abandoned pit nests of such species as *Oreochromis tanganyikae* or *Cyathopharynx furcifer* and spawn therein.

Spawns can number as many as 10,000 eggs, which makes this species the unchallenged champion in any cichlid fecundity competition.

Pairs defend their progeny so aggressively that there are reports of attacks on SCUBA divers who approached a school of fry too closely.

Such behavior is common enough on the part of small cichlids, but quite unusual in the larger members of the family.

Most have to contend with formidable predators about the same size as a diver and hence tend — quite understandably — to find discretion the better part of valor in such encounters.

As the fry become more mobile, parental pairs move into deeper water where observation of their behavior becomes more difficult. Hence, nothing is known of the duration of parental care in nature.

Based upon changes in the morphology of the intestinal tract observed in reproductively active individuals, KONIGS has suggested that like Pacific salmon, *B. microlepis* spawns only once and then dies. Such a **semelparous** reproductive strategy would explain both the amazing fecundity of this species and the intensity of its spawn defense.

If this species can be induced to breed successfully in captivity, it will be possible to test this hypothesis by observing if parental pairs resume normal feeding after they have concluded their parental duties.

Beyond question, the most popular of Lake Tanganyika's pelagic cichlids are the four taxa placed respectively in the genera *Cyprichromis* and *Paracyprichromis*.

These fish, at one time thought to be highly derived *Limnochromis* species, are now placed by POLL in a Tribe of their own, the Cyprichromini.

It is uncertain exactly how many species of these sardine cichlids actually occur in the lake.

Both *Cyprichromis leptosoma* (BOULENGER 1898) [Figure 378], type species of its genus, and *C. microlepidotus* (POLL 1956) display male color polymorphism at their type localities.

This complicates the task of determining the status of populations from other localities that differ somewhat in morphology and even more obviously in coloration.

Fig. 380: An adult male *Cyphotilapia frontosa* (Boulenger 1906) is one of the most impressive representatives of the Family Cichlidae.

Paracyprichromis nigripinnis (BOULENGER 1901) and *P. brieni* (POLL 1981) [Figure 379] are also characterized by what seems to be geographic variation in color pattern, but neither species has to date manifested the sort of intrapopulational variation in male color pattern characteristic of the two *Cyprichromis* species.

Until ichthyologists sort things out, cichlid keepers would do well to manage each geographic color variant as if it were a distinct species.

As prior experience with the *mbuna* of Lake Malawi has clearly shown, it is better to be safe than sorry in this regard!

These cichlids are small, rarely attaining 4" SL, tolerant of rooted plants as well as of heterospecific tankmates and vividly colored in the bargain.

Highly social, they are best kept in groups of six to eight individuals in relatively deep aquaria.

Their preference for the upper half of the water column makes them ideal companions for such committed bottom dwellers as the eretmodine and smaller lamprologine cichlids.

Indeed, they are among the very few cichlids that can be put effectively to use as dither fish!

Given their slender build and inoffensive nature, their tankmates must be chosen with care.

If too large and predatory, they are apt to treat the sardine cichlids as live food!

If too aggressive, even smaller tankmates may effectively inhibit cyprichromine reproductive activity.

As sardine cichlids respond to both novel stimuli and sustained harassment by demonstrating their well-developed leaping abilities, a tight-fitting cover glass is an essential adjunct to their successful maintenance.

All *Cyprichromis* are midwater spawners with lek mating systems divorced from the usual male defense of a substratum-linked spawning territory.

Males hold position about a foot apart from one another in the water column and display to passing females. In nature, such arrays of displaying males may number several thousand individuals.

Fig. 381: A young male *Lamprologus congoensis* Schilthuis 1891, a riverine species native to the lower Zaire River.

Fig. 382: A female *Lamprologus nkambae* Staeck 1978, a representative of Lake Tanganyika's large assemblage of piscivorous *Lamprologus* species.

Sexually receptive females enter a displaying male's "spatial bubble", assume a head-down position and deposit a few eggs, which the female snaps up as they fall past her mouth.

Fertilization is intrabuccal, the displaying males' brilliantly colored ventrals apparently serving as egg-dummies.

Male *Paracyprichromis*, in contrast, leave their school to establish a temporary territory. In nature, this is typically on a vertical rock face. In captivity, the aquarium wall will often suffice.

A territorial male will attempt to sequester a ripe female and lead her to his territory.

A receptive female will assume a head down position in close proximity to the substratum, with the male above and slightly to her rear.

As she releases a few eggs, the male discharges a cloud of sperm, which he fans towards them as they fall downwards.

The female snaps up the fertilized eggs as they pass her mouth.

Relatively few eggs are produced per spawn — a brood of two dozen fry would be considered exceptional.

Brooding females will also continue to take food, albeit gingerly, for the duration of the three week developmental interval. Thus unless the keeper has had the good fortune to witness the exercise, he often finds it difficult to know if a spawning has taken place.

A female's laterally expanded opercula as seen from above are the surest indication of her condition.

Unless the breeding group is housed in a very large aquarium, it is prudent to isolate parental females, who may be the victims of post-spawning harassment by both their erstwhile consort(s) and other females.

Ovigerous females of both genera have a reputation for skittishness during the initial stages of the developmental interval.

It is thus unwise to try moving them from the breeding tank for at least a week post-spawning.

303

Fig. 383: When in full color. an adult *Lamprologus moorii* Boulenger 1898 is the closest approximation known to a naturally all-black cichlid. The so-called yellow color form is merely the juvenile color pattern of this species.

Young females may abort the first few incubation sequences before attaining full maternal competence.

In nature, ovigerous females form large schools and practice the synchronous release of their fully developed young. There is no post-release brood care. Spawns rarely exceed two dozen young.

Newly released fry require the smallest of *Artemia* nauplii as their first food.

They are extremely sensitive to inadvertent pollution of their environment.

Hence, great care must be taken to avoid accidental overfeeding.

This caveat aside, their rearing poses no extraordinary difficulties.

Both *Cyprichromis* and *Paracyprichromis* are somewhat slow-growing, attaining reproductive competence just under a year postrelease.

The eight species of the genus *Trematocara* BOULENGER 1898 are benthic invertebrate feeders whose massively enlarged cephalic lateral line pits allow them to detect the movement of their prey under conditions of greatly reduced illumination.

Though they share this adaptation with a number of other Tanganyikan cichlids, not to mention the Malawian genus *Aulonacara*, their only close relative is the monotypic *Telotrematocara macrostoma* (POLL 1952).

POLL has grouped the two genera together in his Tribe Trematocarini.

During the day, these small cichlids have been trawled from a depth of 650 feet, which affords them the distinction of being the deepest-living cichlids in Lake Tanganyika, and by extension, the world. At night, they migrate into shallow waters to feed.

Given the problems collectors encounter bringing cichlids captured at a depth of less than 200 feet to the surface, the ability of trematocarine cichlids to manage a diel vertical migration of this scope without suffering the effects of uncontrolled decompression is most impressive.

It is assumed that their swimbladders are modified to permit them to make such relatively rapid ascents with impunity, but the nature of the compensatory mechanism remains a mystery.

Trematocara species are maternal mouthbrooders with a markedly seasonal reproductive pattern.

Contrary to the usual case in cichlids, males are smaller than females.

KONIGS has suggested that this might signify aberrant reproductive behavior.

Nothing is known of either their mating system or their spawning grounds in nature and given the exigencies of their lifestyle, this state of affairs is unlikely to change anytime soon.

Surprisingly, one representative of the genus, *Trematocara nigrifrons* BOULENGER 1906, has not only been exported but has even bred successfully in captivity.

The Dutch aquarist RENE KRUTER found this species to be highly social and somewhat delicate.

His fish bred after being in his care for a year.

He was unable to observe the actual spawning, but reported that the female carried 40 large yellow eggs for three weeks.

The newly released fry measured c. 8.0 mm TL at release and were able to take *Artemia* nauplii for their initial food.

Initial growth proved fairly rapid, the fry measuring just under 2" SL three months post-release.

With tank-bred fish now available in fair numbers, information on both the mating system and the actual spawning behavior of this species hopefully will be soon forthcoming.

The final species to be considered under this heading is the popular *Cyphotilapia frontosa* (BOULENGER 1906). Both generic and specific names refer to the remarkably developed frontal gibbosity of this cichlid [Figure 380]. This is one of the few species in which even females develop a conspicuous nuchal hump, albeit one considerably smaller than that sported by adult males.

Several geographic color forms of this species, differing in the number of vertical

Fig. 384: The specific name of *Lamprologus mustax* Poll 1978 refers to its mustachelike black facial markings.

bands and in small details of their fin coloration, have been exported from Lake Tanganyika.

The appearance of seven-banded young in broods produced by six-banded parents and *vice versa,* as well as the existence of individuals with six bands on one flank and seven on the other suggest that these color pattern distinctions are of no taxonomic significance. The relationships of this distinctive deep-water piscivore are unclear. POLL placed it in his Tribe Tropheini, for no immediately obvious reasons.

Recent molecular data suggest that like *Boulengerochromis microlepis,* this species stands well apart from the other cichlids of Lake Tanganyika and has no close extralacustrine relatives either.

Robust but lethargic, this strikingly colored species can for maintenance purposes be regarded as a giant maternal mouthbrooding *Lamprologus.*

Large enough to be the target of a trotline fishery in the lake, male *Cyphotilapia frontosa* can easily grow to 14" SL in captivity. Females do not grow as large, but 8"−10" SL females are not unheard of.

As might be expected, dimly lit tanks in the 75−100 gallon range are essential to its well-being.

Otherwise easily maintained, this species should not be housed with faster-moving, more aggressive tankmates.

Even if substantially smaller than the *Cyphotilapia frontosa,* such companions are likely to outcompete them at feeding time and may very well inhibit spawning in the bargain.

For a large predator, *C. frontosa* displays remarkable tolerance of the close presence of conspecifics.

It is even possible to keep more than a single male per tank provided the aquarium is large enough and they differ substantially in size.

Such an exercise would not turn out so well if it were attempted with the larger Malawian haplochromines or most predatory Neotropical cichlids.

If afforded quiet surroundings, *C. frontosa* spawns readily in captivity.

Fig. 385: Superficial similarity to the highly social *L. brichardi, Lamprologus savoryi* Poll 1949 is a solitary and rather aggressive species.

It is best managed in the same manner as the larger Malawian haplochromines, as it has much the same sort of mating system.

Spawning usually takes place in an enclosed space and fertilization of the eggs is extrabuccal.

Ovigerous females have a reputation for maternal unreliability and do not appreciate being moved early in the incubation sequence. It is therefore extremely important that the breeding tank be both large and well furnished with refuges from male postspawning harassment.

The developmental interval lasts for 26 days at 77 °F.

Spawns of as many as 75 fry have been reported, but broods of half that number are closer to the norm.

The fry measure c. 0.30—0.35" TL and are perfect miniatures of their parents.

They can easily take *Artemia* nauplii and chopped frozen bloodworms for their initial meal.

If due attention is paid to water quality in the rearing tank, the fry are easily raised.

By virtue of their beautiful coloration, considerably more pleasing than that of their parents, young *C. frontosa* find a ready market, to such an extent that a breeding group of these cichlids can make a considerable contribution to defraying the costs of their owner's hobby.

Like the generality of Lake Tanganyika cichlids, this is a slow-growing species.

Sexual maturity is attained 10 to 12 months postspawning.

The Genus Lamprologus and Its Allies

The genus *Lamprologus*, while represented in the fauna of the Zaire basin, has exploited its full evolutionary potential only in Lake Tanganyika. Here it numbers in excess of fifty species, making it the most speciose genus in the lake, and has given rise to several endemic genera as well. Overall, the **lamprologines** comprise just over 50% of Lake Tanganyika's endemic cichlids. The evolutionarily formidable haplochromines, on the other hand,

Fig. 386: A young male *Lamprologus lemairei* Boulenger 1899, the Lake Tanganyika analog of marine scorpionfishes.

make up just under 20%. This contrasts sharply with the haplochromine dominated cichlid faunas of other African Great Lakes. Given as well the modest role of the genus *Lamprologus* in the Zairian ichthyofauna, it is difficult to avoid concluding that absence of any morphologically generalized *Haplochromis* from the nascent lake's pool of colonizers was probably a necessary precondition for the Tanganyikan lamprologine radiation.

It would be interesting to know what attributes gave those ancestral *Lamprologus* the competitive edge that led ultimately to the present lamprologine dominance.

Though much has been learned of the behavioral ecology of Tanganyikan cichlids since the first edition of this book was published, ichthyologists still know too little even to speculate intelligently upon this fascinating question.

The Zairian *Lamprologus* are elongate cichlids, round-bodied in cross-section, with elevated dorsal and anal fin spine counts, rounded tails, and large heads whose most conspicuous feature is a wide mouth equipped with a most formidable dentition [Figure 381]. As might be expected in essentially rheophilous cichlids, riverine *Lamprologus* are characterized by a tendency towards swim bladder reduction.

Its most extreme manifestation occurs in the blind *L. lethops* ROBERTS and STEWART 1976, whose swim bladder is totally non-functional.

The Tanganyikan species display a much greater morphological diversity.

The basic torpedo-like body form characterizes all of the open-bottom living species as well as a substantial number of their petricolous congeners [Figures 382].

However, there is a tendency towards lateral compression among lacustrine *Lamprologus* clearly evident in such species as *L. moorii* BOULENGER 1898 [Figure 383], *L. mustax* POLL 1978 [Figure 384], *L. savoryi* POLL 1949 [Figure 385] and *L. brichardi* POLL 1974 [Figure 187].

It reaches its most extreme development in *L. lemairei* BOULENGER 1899 [Figure 386], *L. compressiceps* BOULENGER 1898 [Figure 387] and *L. calvus* POLL 1978 [Figure 388], whose overall appearance is more reminiscent of leaf-fishes (Family Nandidae) than of the generality of cichlids!

Such a wide range of phenotypes suggests that the genus *Lamprologus* as presently understood represents an unnatural lumping of several evolutionarily distinctive lineages.

A comparable level of morphological diversity within the haplochromine cichlids has invited major revisionary efforts, whose consequences have already been discussed herein.

Since the first edition of this book was published, The French workers J. COLOMBE and R. ALLGAYER have attempted to split *Lamprologus* into a number of smaller, and presumably, more evolutionarily meaningful genera.

In their revision, COLOMBE and ALLGAYER restricted *Lamprologus* to the species found in the Zaire River, rehabilitated the genus *Lepidolamprologus* PELLEGRIN 1904 and erected three new genera of Tanganyikan endemics, *Variabilichromis*, *Paleolamprologus* and *Neolamprologus*.

In his final overview of the Tanganyikan cichlids, POLL rejected both the restriction of *Lamprologus* to the riverine representatives of the lineage and the genera *Variabilichromis* and *Paleolamprologus*, accepted the validity of both a resuscitated *Lepidolamprologus* and *Neolamprologus* and erected a new genus, *Altolamprologus* for *L. compressiceps* and *L. calvus*.

Regrettably, the shared focus of both studies on superficially accessible characteristics and lack of a true comparative perspective constitute such serious methodological deficiencies as to cast considerable doubt on their conclusions.

Their end result is the replacement of one large, probably comprehensive genus, *Lamprologus*, with a number of smaller genera, each a collection of more or less morphologically similar species and one large genus, *Neolamprologus*, that remains a grab-bag for any lamprologine that cannot plausibly be placed anywhere else.

Both studies have the effect of destabilizing the nomenclature of these cichlids on both the species and genus levels without casting a great deal of light on lamprologine evolutionary relationships.

Fig. 387: A young male *Lamprologus compressiceps* Boulenger 1898. Several geographic color forms of this widely distributed species have been exported to date.

It seems likely that in its broad sense, the genus *Lamprologus* may well represent an unnatural grouping of species.

However, until such time as their conclusions are tested using the full spectrum of modern methods, I see little advantage in adopting the nomenclatorial innovations proposed by either COLOMBE and ALLGAYER or POLL.

Riverine *Lamprologus* are cichlids of modest size and moderate sexual dimorphism. Males rarely exceed 5" SL; females usually grow to 3" SL.

Their Tanganyikan congeners range in size from dwarf shell-dwellers that barely attain 2" SL to robust, actively predatory species such as *L. cunningtoni* BOULENGER 1906 [Figure 389] and *L. profundicola* POLL 1949, which can grow to 12" SL.

The majority fall midway between these extremes.

Sexual dimorphism is often pronounced in the ostracophil species, considered at greater length in the dwarf cichlid section.

In the remainder, males are characteristically larger than females, have slightly longer fins and usually some sort of nuchal hump.

Sexually related color differences range from slight to non-existent.

All *Lamprologus* to date studied are carnivorous.

Riverine species take a wide range of invertebrates and feed upon smaller fishes when opportunity allows.

Most petricolous lake dwellers share this feeding pattern, whereas the larger **arenicolous**, or sandy-bottom associated, species are strongly piscivorous.

The enlarged, molar-like lower pharyngeal teeth of *L. tretocephalus* BOULENGER 1899 [Figure 6b] are indicative of a specialized mollusc feeder, while *L. cunningtoni* is known to feed upon freshwater crabs.

These instances apart, the only dramatic examples of dietary specialization in the genus are such zooplankton feeders as the *L. brichardi* species group and the numerous dwarf shell-dwellers.

Regardless of their dietary preferences, all lacustrine *Lamprologus* possess formidable jaw teeth.

The dwarf species in particular sport enlarged anterior, or pseudocanine teeth scaled to a cichlid thrice their size! Such dental equipment makes sense in a piscivore, but seems a bit excessive in fish that feed on planktonic crustaceans.

I suggest this exaggerated dentition has evolved as a weapon, to be used in the defense of shelter in the case of petricolous and ostracophil species and of eggs and fry by all representatives of this nonmouthbrooding genus.

Though the combination of powerful jaws and predatory tendencies makes it unwise to attempt housing them with smaller non-cichlid tank-mates, most *Lamprologus* are well suited to life in a cichlid community.

Outside periods of sexual activity, they tend to ignore its other residents, who quickly learn it does not pay to play dominance games with such well-armed tankmates. Breeding pairs will not tolerate any intrusions into their territory.

However, the defended area is not large, ranging from 1' to 2' square.

Thus it is by no means impossible for a pair — or for that matter, several heterospecific pairs — to coexist with a wide range of companions if they share a sufficiently large aquarium. However, with rare exceptions, the rule for these cichlids is one — and only one — pair of any given species per aquarium.

Juveniles live amicably together until the onset of sexual maturity. The first pair to form will then drive all conspecifics from their territory.

If, as is usually the case, the tank is not large enough to afford the option of escape, they will instead systematically eradicate these potential competitors.

This end is accomplished either by outright assassination or by such persistent harassment of their victims that only prompt human intervention keeps them from jumping out of the tank to escape their persecutors.

Hence experienced breeders of these fish often refer to the group approach to pairing as the "rejection/ejection method"!

Fig. 388: *Lamprologus calvus* Poll 1978 and the closely *L. compressiceps* represent the most extreme instances of a trend towards lateral compression characteristic of the Tanganyikan representatives of the genus.

A single male and female will usually pair readily in a community situation.

This approach to pair formation is often less apt to result in fatalities, for heterospecific tankmates are typically ignored until after spawning.

Fortunately, most Tanganyikan *Lamprologus* are monogamous, and even haremically polygynous species seem to possess remarkably strong intersexual bonds. They and their near relatives are the only monogamous cichlids that can be housed safely in isolation once they have paired.

A 20 to 25 gallon tank suffices for pairs of most mid-sized lamprologines, while aquaria in the 30 to 40 gallon range comfortably house those of the more robust lacustrine species.

These strong pair bonds are all the more unusual in that monogamy appears to be a derived condition in the Tanganyikan *Lamprologus*.

Their riverine congeners, who presumably represent the ancestral lamprologine condition with regard to both morphology and behavior, are harem polygynists. A possible explanation of this situation is that monogamy re-evolved as a response to the greater intensity of spawn predation under lacustrine conditions [Figure 390]. Such a view gains credence from both the distribution of the two mating systems within the lake and the behavior of a number of monogamous species in captivity.

All of the arenicolous species, which breed in an environment devoid of shelter for their eggs and fry, are strictly monogamous [Figure 391]. Harem polygyny and its associated maternal brood care is restricted to a few cave spawning and dwarf ostracophil *Lamprologus* species.

Their choice of spawning site facilitates single-parent defense of the eggs and young.

Furthermore, there is a documented tendency for petricolous species that breed monogamously in nature, such as *L. brichardi* or *L. leleupi* POLL 1956 [Figure 392], to shift easily to polygyny in an aquarium environment devoid of spawn predators. These are easily bred cichlids.

Notwithstanding the strength of the pair bond, courtship is peremptory.

Fig. 389: A male *Lamprologus cunningtoni* Boulenger 1909, one of Lake Tanganyika's "torpedos with teeth".

311

Fig. 390: The biparental brood care practiced by this pair of *Lamprologus tetracanthus* Boulenger 1899 may have evolved in response to more intense fry predation in the densely populated littoral of Lake Tanganyika.

It often happens that joint defense of a territory is the first indication that something is afoot.

The arenicolous species typically spawn at the bottom of a substantial pit, whose excavation affords their keeper an unmistakable warning of an impending reproductive effort.

Petricolous *Lamprologus* are less obvious in their preparations.

Indeed, the sudden appearance of mobile fry is often the first indication a spawning has occurred! Brood sizes vary substantially within the genus.

Arenicolous species may lay several thousand eggs, while petricolous species are much less prolific, spawning from two dozen to 200 eggs at a time.

The opaque eggs vary in color from dead white to chrome green. More than one novice breeder has removed a spawn-covered rock from the breeding tank in disgust, believing the eggs to be fungused.

Despite their decidedly unwholesome appearance, such eggs are perfectly viable, producing fry three to four days postspawning at 80 °F. The fry become mobile a week thereafter.

Parental care in *Lamprologus* appears hygienically deficient compared with that of many other cichlids and seems to be primarily custodial in character.

More to the point, the pair seems chiefly concerned with defense of their territory rather than of fry.

As long as the young remain within the limits of their parents' demesne, they are effectively protected.

If they move beyond its boundaries, they are on their own, nor will their parents make any attempt to retrieve straying fry.

Parental care may persist for several months in nature, but rarely lasts longer than four weeks in captivity.

It is prudent to separate parents and offspring three weeks after the latter become mobile.

The response of adults to older fry with the onset of respawning is unpredictable.

Fig. 391: A male *Lamprologus elongatus* Boulenger 1898. Pairs of this strictly monogamous. free-ranging species have been observed sheltering mobile fry within their buccal cavities when threatened.

Fig. 392: Males of many strongly petricolous *Lamprologus* species, such as this *L. leleupi* Poll 1956 will shift from monogamy to polygyny in captivity.

313

Fig. 393: A male *Lamprologus caudopunctatus* Poll 1978. Juveniles of this small plankton-feeding species remain on the parental territory and assist in the rearing of subsequent broods of fry.

At one extreme, pairs of *L. brichardi*, the closely related *L. pulcher* TREWAVAS and POLL 1952 and *L. caudopunctatus* POLL 1978 [Figure 393] allow older young to remain in the parental territory until they have attained sexual maturity.

These subadults not only refrain from molesting their younger sibs, but actually participate in their defense.

At the other, the larger arenicolous species systematically drive older fry from their territory, destroying any that remain within its limits.

The fry share the sensitivity of all Tanganyikan endemics to dissolved metabolites. Take great care, therefore, to avoid overfeeding and concomitant water fouling. Frequent small water changes represent the safest means of keeping nitrates in their tanks at acceptably low levels. Fry of the more predatory species must not be crowded.

Otherwise, the growing young will adjust population density downwards through sibling cannibalism.

The rearing of *Lamprologus* fry otherwise poses few difficulties, though their relatively slow growth may tax their keeper's patience. The larger arenicolous species and *L. brichardi* can begin breeding between the sixth and eighth month postspawning, though it usually takes them another six months to get into full reproductive stride.

Most petricolous species are slower growing, attaining sexual maturity a year to 18 months postspawning.

The genera *Julidochromis* BOULENGER 1898, *Telmatochromis* BOULENGER 1898 and *Chalinochromis* POLL 1974 [Figure 394] differ from *Lamprologus* as broadly understood in details of their cranial and dental morphology. These four genera constitute POLL's Tribe Lamprologini.

Both *Julidochromis* and *Telmatochromis* include diminutive species that will be considered in the dwarf cichlid section.

The remaining species of these two genera are identical in their maintenance requirements and reproductive patterns to the mid-sized

Fig. 394: Known to aquarists by the trade name of two-striped *Chalinochromis*, this undescribed species is the least aggressive and most generally available representative of the genus.

Fig. 395: *Julidochromis marlieri* Poll 1956 was the first large representative of the genus imported as an aquarium fish.

Fig. 396: A male *Telmatochromis temporalis* Boulenger 1898, a hardy and easily bred but very aggressive lamprologine.

petricolous *Lamprologus* species and should be managed accordingly [Figure 396].

The large *Julidochromis* species [Figures 153 & 395] are unusual in that they can allocate their reproductive output in two different ways.

Sometimes, a pair will spawn in the same manner as one of the mid-sized petricolous *Lamprologus* species, producing as many as 200 eggs, then protecting the resulting fry for up to two months before respawning. In the majority of cases, however, pairs produce batches of up to two dozen eggs every seven to ten days for up to six weeks. The successive cohorts of fry are allowed to remain within the pair's territory, where they continue to enjoy parental protection. The end result can be as many as half a dozen different size classes of fry coexisting amiably under parental surveillance.

A given pair can switch abruptly from one spawning modality to another, for reasons that remain to be determined. The fry of these species share the slow growth rate of most *Lamprologus* and require the same sort of care. The lamprologines are without doubt the hardiest and most easily maintained of all the endemic Tanganyikan cichlids.

Their attractive coloration places them among the most sought-after of all African cichlids.

Finally, the ease with which most can be induced to live and spawn in relatively small aquaria endears them to numerous aquarists who lack the tank space demanded by their haplochromine counterparts.

With so many desirable qualities, the group's present popularity is easily understandable, and its place in the hobby seems assured.

CHAPTER 10

CATALOG OF RESIDENTS FOR THE CICHLID AQUARIUM

NEW WORLD CICHLIDS

Introduction

Current ichthyological opinion groups New World cichlids into five lineages.

Three, the *Geophagus* group, the *Cichlasoma-Aequidens* group and the *Heros* group, are characterized by considerable morphological diversity. Each comprises numerous genera, some extremely rich in species.

All have given the hobby a multitude of desirable cichlids and in consequence each merits the detailed treatment it will subsequently receive.

The remaining two lineages are less well represented in both the Neotropical cichlid fauna and the ranks of aquarium fish.

The first of these lineages groups the genera *Cichla*, *Crenicichla* and *Teleocichla*.

The *Chaetobranchus* lineage comprises three genera, none of which comprises more than a handful of species. Neither of these minor lineages enjoys notable aquaristic importance, although representatives of each are more or less regularly available to cichlid enthusiasts. Hence, each merits treatment before consideration is given to the three principal Neotropical cichlid groups.

Peacock Bass and Pike Cichlids — The Genera Cichla, Crenicichla and Teleocichla.

Cichla is the genus upon which the Family *Cichlidae* was originally based. This has frequently proved troublesome to ichthyologists, for these giant predators are in many respects very atypical cichlids.

Until recently, the genus had no known sister-group and was thought to be the only surviving representative of an extremely ancient lineage.

More detailed examination of the anatomy of South American cichlids by STIASSNY has led her to conclude that the pike cichlids of the genera *Crenicichla* and *Teleocichla* represent the sister group of *Cichla*.

Recent revisionary work by the Swedish ichthyologist SVEN O. KULLANDER has revealed the genus *Cichla* to be substantially more species-rich than was believed to be the case when the first edition of this book was published. KULLANDER recognizes five described species.

Cichla ocellaris BLOCH and SCHNEIDER 1801, type species of the genus, is endemic to coastal rivers in Guyana and Suriname.

The species most familiar to aquarists under that name is actually *Cichla monoculus* SPIX 1831 [Figure 397], a widely distributed Amazonian species.

The other representative of the genus sometimes exported as an aquarium fish is *Cichla temensis* HUMBOLDT 1833 [Figure 146]. This robust species is native to both the Orinoco and Amazon basins and appears to have been introduced into Guyana as an aquaculture subject.

Two further species are recognized from the Orinoco basin, *Cichla orinocoensis* HUMBOLDT 1833 and *C. intermedia* MACHADO-ALLISON 1971.

The status of a sixth nominal species ostensibly native to the Rio Parana basin, *C. chacoensis* HOLMBERG 1891 is uncertain, but KULLANDER has suggested that as many as eleven distinctive local *Cichla* populations warrant recognition as valid species.

These giant predators, known as *pavon* in Spanish-speaking South America, *tucunare* in Brazil and *lukunani* or peacock bass in

Fig. 397: *Cichla monoculus* Spix 1831 is one of the largest representatives of the Family Cichlidae.

Guyana, are contenders for the title of the world's largest cichlid. The official size record for *C. monoculus* is 28" SL, for *C. temensis* 30" SL, but both local fishermen and knowledgeable ichthyologists maintain large males can grow to just over 3' SL.

As might be expected, peacock basses are important food fish in their native waters. They are also avidly pursued by sport fishermen and have been introduced successfully to Panama, Puerto Rico and Hawaii to create recreational fisheries.

In the absence of a native freshwater fish fauna, the Puerto Rican and Hawaiian exercises have had minimal environmental consequences.

The same cannot be said of the impact of introduced *C. monoculus* in the Chagres basin of Panama, where these giant predators have had much the same effect upon the fish fauna of the Gatun Lakes as the Nile perch has had on that of Lake Victoria.

Though these cichlids are not difficult to maintain, large adult size and a predatory feeding pattern severely limit their popularity.

First, these cichlids require live food in the form of smaller fish for their continued well-being.

Juveniles are less accommodating in this respect than large adults.

Specimens between 3" and 8" SL require their own weight in smaller fish daily to maintain condition and a normal growth rate.

Subadult and adult individuals can make do with frozen fish or pellets supplemented by a weekly offering of a few dozen feeder goldfish.

Second, peacock bass are **extremely** sensitive to dissolved metabolites.

Erosion of the cephalic lateral line system, resulting in the typical manifestations of "hole in the head disease" is their usual response to poor water quality. This challenge of keeping dissolved metabolite concentrations as low as possible, as much as their large size, dictates that *Cichla* be housed in the largest available aquaria.

Finally, their companions must be chosen with care. While they ignore tankmates too small to be easily swallowed, it is easy to underestimate their abilities in this regard.

A further complication is introduced by the extreme fragility of their jaws. This puts them at a severe disadvantage in aggressive interactions with cichlids having more robust jaw bones.

For example, *Cichla* rarely prosper when housed with more aggressive Central American cichlid species, notwithstanding their larger size.

On the positive side of the ledger, peacock bass are, unlike the generality of predatory cichlids, remarkably tolerant of conspecifics, do not dig outside periods of reproductive activity and are at all times indifferent to rooted plants.

Cichla monoculus and *C. temensis* have been bred under pond conditions, but there are no published accounts of an aquarium spawning of any peacock bass.

Male peacock bass grow larger than females and develop a distinct nuchal hump when sexually active.

Other sexual distinctions are lacking, so the only reliable way of ascertaining an individual's sex is to examine its genital papilla. All *Cichla* are monogamous biparentally custodial substratum spawners.

The eggs are either placed on a flat horizontal surface such as a rock or log, or at the bottom of a massive pit dug in shallow water.

Hatching occurs in two days at 85°F, and the fry are mobile three days later. Spawns number up to 4000 eggs.

Defense of the free-swimming fry persists up to two months. Parental care is intense.

The aggressiveness parental *Cichla* display towards all potential fry predators, however well armed they might be, has earned them the nickname *matapiranha* [= piranha killer] in the Peruvian Amazon.

MACHADO-ALLISON reports that the parents take the young into their mouths when danger threatens.

The fry grow rapidly, attaining sexual maturity just under a year postspawning, at a length of c. 1″ SL. The true pike cichlids are so known because of their elongate bodies, pointed heads and capacious jaws.

Like their namesakes, the real pikes of the genus *Esox*, pike cichlids are specialized ambush hunters that feed upon smaller fishes and large aquatic invertebrates.

This species-rich assemblage of predators was formerly split into two genera on the basis of differences in their dentition.

Pike cichlids whose inner series of jaw teeth are depressible were placed in *Crenicichla* HECKEL 1840, while those in which they are fixed were placed in *Batrachops* HECKEL 1840 [Figure 398].

Since the first edition of this book was published, KULLANDER has shown that some nominal *Batrachops* species are actually more closely related to species presently placed in *Crenicichla* than they are to any of their putative congeners.

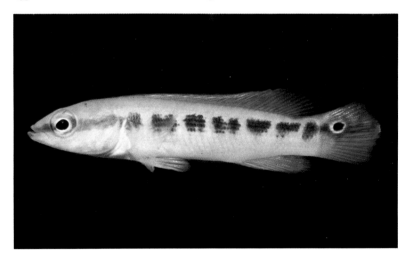

Fig. 398: A sub-adult *Crenicichla semifasciata* (Heckel 1840). This robust pike cichlid was formerly placed in a different genus, *Batrachops*.

Fig. 399 & 400: Male (above) and female (below) *Crenicichla notopthalmus* Regan 1913, one of the so-called "dwarf" pike cichlids.

Fig. 400.

This has led him to place *Batrachops* in the synonymy of *Crenicichla*.

Over three dozen species of pike cichlid are known from the literature. These range from giant piscivores capable of exceeding 15" SL to "dwarf" species that barely grow a third as large [Figures 399—400] and include such aberrant forms as the rheophilous bottom-hopping *Crenicichla sedentaria* KULLANDER 1986 [Figure 401].

The species-level taxonomy of pike cichlids is hopelessly confused. This makes applying the correct name to the eighteen-odd species that have been imported a major challenge even for professionals familiar with the South American fauna. The names given to species illustrated herein should thus be considered tentative.

The maintenance requirements of all pike cichlids are identical.

Like many specialized predators, they are violently intolerant of conspecifics and not a great deal more willing to share quarters with other pike cichlid species.

Conspecifics of the opposite sex represent an obvious exception to this rule.

However, pairs will seek out and destroy other pike cichlids with the same single-mindedness that characterizes the behavior of lamprologines towards unpaired conspecifics.

This quirk aside, pike cichlids ignore any fish that cannot be swallowed easily and actually make satisfactory residents in a large species community tank.

When not preparing to spawn, they neither dig nor bother rooted plants.

They do well under a broad range of pH and hardness conditions, and most species tolerate indifferent nitrogen cycle management better than many other Neotropical genera [Figure 402].

They prefer small live fish to other offerings, but will accept and do well on a diet of strips of frozen fish or other seafood, freeze-dried krill and pellets.

Pike cichlids display sexual dimorphism, often of a very dramatic sort. Males are a third to half again as large as their mates.

Fig. 401: A female *Crenicichla sedentaria* Kullander 1986. Like the African *Steatocranus* species, this rapids-dwelling pike cichlid has only a rudimentary swim bladder and moves by "hopping" over the bottom.

Fig. 402: Rheophilous species such as *Crenicichla compressiceps* Ploeg 1986 are more susceptible to the effects of nitrogen cycle mismanagement than are the generality of pike cichlids.

Females are frequently more colorful, however.

Many sport a red to rosy violet flush over their ventral regions [Figure 403], which become tremendously distended as they ripen eggs.

Such sexual color differences are reminiscent of African cichlids of the *Nanochromis* lineage, as is the female's tendency to take the initiative in courtship.

The two groups, however, have little else in common.

Pairing is difficult to accomplish due to the previously noted intolerance for the close presence of conspecifics.

Success is most likely in a community situation, and it is prudent to provide suitable target fish if the pair is moved into a separate breeding tank.

All pike cichlids are monogamous biparentally custodial cave spawners.

These are prolific cichlids, not uncommonly producing spawns of several thousand eggs.

Hatching occurs in three days at 82 °F. The fry are free-swimming six days to a week thereafter.

Their parents usually attempt to keep the fry near the cave mouth for two or three days after they become mobile. They subsequently allow them to move more or less freely about the pair's territory. Parental care is efficient and may persist several months in nature.

Under aquarium conditions, it is best to separate parents and fry between four and six weeks posthatching.

By this time the female has begun to ripen a new batch of eggs.

This poses the risk that the pair will eliminate their older progeny as a prelude to respawning.

The fry grow rapidly and are much given to sibling cannibalism if crowded to excess.

Sexual maturity is attained eight to ten months postspawning for the smaller *Crenicichla* species, ten months to a year postspawning for the larger representatives of the genus.

Teleocichla KULLANDER 1988 are small, rapids-dwelling species characterized by a vestigial swim bladder, highly modified ventral fins, reduced squamation and a tendency towards fusion of the usual two incomplete lateral lines into a single structure.

The choice of generic name is felicitous, as these fish do resemble a cross between a pike cichlid and one of the Zairian worm cichlids of the genus *Teleogramma!*

The genus comprises six described species, all described by KULLANDER from northward flowing tributaries of the Amazon.

Teleocichla centrarchus, T. gephyrogramma and *T. monogramma* are found living together in the Von Martius rapids of the Rio Xingu.

Of the remaining trio of species, *T. prionogenys* and *T. proselytus* are native to the Rio Tapajos near the town of Itaituba while *T. cinderella* appears restricted to the Rio Tocantins at Tucurui.

As the Guianan and Brazilian highlands support extensive rapids systems that have yet to be thoroughly collected, the discovery of additional *Teleocichla* species can be confidently anticipated.

Several species of these attractively colored small pike cichlids have been exported, most shipments going to European importers. Like their African rheophile counterparts, they require clean, well-oxygenated water to prosper in captivity.

While they tend to be intolerant of conspecifics, they do not carry such behavior to the extreme lengths observed in *Teleogramma.*

Midwater-dwelling tankmates too large to make a convenient mouthful are ignored.

Like their more robust relatives the pike cichlids, *Teleocichla* species are cave spawners that practice biparental care of their mobile offspring.

They can be expected to respond favorably to the management approaches outlined for *Steatocranus.* These rheophile mini-pikes would doubtless enjoy a greater following were they more generally available.

As spectacularly colored loricariid catfishes tend to predominate in shipments of Rio

Fig. 403: Pike cichlids are easily sexed. The bulging abdomen and rosy red ventral coloration of this female *Crenicichla lepidota* are characteristic of the genus.

Xingu fishes exported to North America, wild-caught *Teleocichla* are rarely available on this side of the Atlantic.

Several species have been induced to breed by German aquarists; fry are sometimes available through commercial channels, but never in large numbers and always at prices that tend to discourage all but the most fanatic cichlidophile from purchasing them.

This state of affairs parallels that of many newly introduced Tanganyikan cichlids, which offers the hope that these interesting and attractive cichids will become more generally available once they have been bred domestically.

The Genus Chaetobranchus and Its Allies

This lineage is represented by three genera widely distributed in South America east of the Andes mountains.

STIASSNY has shown that *Chaetobranchus* and *Chaetobranchopsis* are related and makes a plausible case for considering *Astronotus* the sister group of these two genera.

The lineage does not appear to have any close relatives among either the Neotropical or Old World cichlids.

This suggests that like the representatives of the *Cichla* lineage, these genera may be real evolutionary relics. These fish occupy very different niches in nature.

Chaetobranchus and *Chaetobranchopsis* are deep bodied, large-mouthed cichlids with feeble dentition and numerous long, bristle-like gill rakers.

These adaptations suggest, quite correctly, that these cichlids are specialized plankton feeders.

Astronotus species, on the other hand, are robust predators with strong piscivorous tendencies.

There are two recognized *Chaetobranchus* species.

Chaetobranchus flavescens HECKEL 1840, type species of the genus, is found throughout the Amazon basin and in the coastal basins of the Guianas.

The closely related *C. semifasciatus* STEINDACHNER 1875 occurs in both the central Amazon and Orinoco drainages.

Fig. 404: A male *Chaetobranchus australis* (Eigenmann & Ward 1907).

324

These are robust cichlids, with a maximum recorded length of just under 12" SL.

Sexually quiescent specimens of these cichlids are superficially *Oreochromis*-like in overall appearance, but no tilapia sports so impressive a mouth!

Their long, pointed snouts have earned representatives both genera the vernacular name of *bujurqui embujo* [= funnel cichlid] in the Peruvian Amazon.

Chaetobranchus flavescens displays a reticulated pattern in the soft dorsal and anal fins and a conspicuous midlateral spot but lacks an ocellus at the base of the caudal fin.

Chaetobranchus semifasciatus sports reddish brown vertical markings in the soft dorsal, soft anal and caudal fins and an ocellus on the caudal peduncle, but lacks the midlateral spot.

Despite their superficial similarity, *Chaetobranchopsis* can be easily distinguished from *Chaetobranchus* by virtue of having more than three anal fin spines.

Chaetobranchopsis orbicularis STEINDACHNER 1875, type species of the genus, and *C. bitaeniatus* (AHL 1936) are both restricted to the Amazon basin.

Best known to North American aquarists of this trio of species, *C. australis* (EIGENMANN and WARD 1907) [Figure 404], is native to the Rio Parana system.

Though all three *Chaetobranchopsis* are similar in overall color pattern to *Chaetobranchus*, they lack a caudal peduncle ocellus and often display two parallel lateral stripes. They are also much smaller cichlids, with a maximum recorded length of just over 6" SL.

These cichlids are infrequently exported, usually as "contaminants" in shipments of eartheaters. They are essentially solitary in nature.

Neither species of *Chaetobranchus* appreciates the proximity of conspecifics in captivity.

Chaetobranchopsis are somewhat more social under aquarium conditions.

Representatives of both genera are unaggressive towards other cichlids.

At best opportunistic piscivores, they can be counted on to ignore tankmates too agile to be easily captured or too large to be easily swallowed. They neither dig nor molest rooted plants.

Fig. 405: An albino oscar, the latest catatechnic color form of *Astronotus ocellatus*.

Like the eartheaters with which they are often confused, these cichlids are sensitive to dissolved metabolites and do best in fairly soft, neutral to slightly acid water.

While obviously partial to live *Daphnia* and adult *Artemia,* they will take a wide range of frozen and prepared foods quite eagerly. *Chaetobranchopsis australis* owes its regular availability to its willingness to breed under pond conditions in Florida. However, there are no published accounts of its breeding under aquarium conditions, nor are there any reports of spawning in captivity by any other *Chaetobranchopsis* or by any species of *Chaetobranchus.*

As nothing is known of their reproductive biology in nature, the first aquarist to breed any of these species can make a valuable contribution to science by publishing his observations.

The genus *Astronotus* comprises two described species.

The extremely popular oscar, *Astronotus ocellatus* (AGASSIZ 1831) [Figure 150], the best known representative of the genus, is native to the coastal rivers of the Guianas, the Orinoco basin and the northern and western drainages of the Amazon basin.

The rarely exported *Astronotus crassipinnis* HECKEL 1840 replaces *A. ocellatus* in the southern drainages of the Amazon basin such as the Rio Madre de Dios system of Bolivia and Peru or the Rio Guapore of Brazil and in the Rio Parana basin.

KULLANDER has suggested the possibility that additional species remain to be described.

I regard this as a likely contingency, having examined material from the Ecuadorian tributaries of the Amazon that differs sufficiently from either *A. ocellatus* or *A. crassipinnis* to warrant recognition as a distinct species.

The oscar exists in a number of catatechnic forms.

Most familiar to aquarists is the tiger oscar, which retains the species-typical black markings over a much more extensive background of metallic orange-red.

In the red oscar, the dark marbling is completely absent, resulting in an almost solid orange-red fish.

Fig. 406: A male *Biotodoma cupido* Heckel 1840. The generic name derives from the putative brooding of the zygotes within the gill chambers. It is now known that this species is a substratum spawner. The egg-like structures on the gills of the type material have proven to be parasitic cysts.

Fig. 407: A male *Biotodoma* sp. "Santarem".

True albino forms of all three of these phenotypes have recently been marketed by commercial breeders in the Far East [Figure 405].

Upon viewing adult specimens of these fish, one is left with the overwhelming impression of a superfluity of pink. However, given the popularity enjoyed by albino strains of other ornamental fishes, it seems safe to predict a mass market for the several flavors of albino oscar.

The final — and mercifully least commercially successful — of these variants is a long-finned mutant.

Wild form, tiger and red long-finned oscars are available. At present, albino long-finned oscars are not, but given the obsessive desire of Chinese breeders to make as many tropical fish as possible over in the image of fancy goldfish, their eventual appearance seems only a matter of time.

Astronotus are unquestionably the largest representatives of their lineage.

Under favorable circumstances, the oscar can attain 15" SL, although 12" SL represents a more realistic figure under home aquarium conditions.

Unabashed predators with strong piscivorous tendencies in nature, they devour with gusto any fish small enough to fit into their capacious maws.

Despite such a feeding pattern they are surprisingly unaggressive for cichlids of their size.

Oscars live in amity with companions too large to make a convenient meal, but are frequently victimized by smaller yet more aggressive cichlids with which they are mistakenly housed.

While not herbivorous, both *Astronotus* will disrupt rooted plants and do dig extensively during periods of sexual activity. These fish are very sensitive to dissolved metabolites.

Oscars typically respond to poor nitrogen cycle management by developing the environmentally induced degeneration of the cephalic lateral line system referred to as "hole in the head disease".

Maintaining nitrate concentrations at an acceptable level in an oscar tank is complicated by a combination of prodigious appetite and messy feeding habits.

The only effective approach combines efficient mechanical filtration with frequent replacement of up to 75% of their tank's volume with fresh water of the same temperature and chemical composition.

Fortunately *Astronotus* are not fussy about the chemical make-up of their water.

They do quite do well over a broad range of pH and hardness values, although like the generality of Amazonian cichlids, they prefer soft, neutral to slightly acid water.

They are less tolerant of cool water. A temperature range of 75°−80°F is fine for ordinary maintenance, with an increase to 82°−85°F for breeding.

Oscars are voracious feeders.

They rapidly learn to associate their keeper with the appearance of food.

Indeed, their reputation for intelligence rests largely upon their ability to learn which behavior patterns are most likely to elicit a snack.

Oscars relish such live foods as feeder goldfish, earthworms or small crayfish, and are amazingly adroit at persuading their keepers that in the absence of such fare they will perish of starvation.

In point of fact, they do just as well on more plebeian — and affordable — fare.

Pelletized foods, freeze-dried krill and frozen seafood strips constitute a sound and practical staple diet, although it may take an enforced fast of several days to persuade an oscar of this!

Neither species of *Astronotus* can be reliably sexed on the basis of color difference.

In some strains of the wild phenotype of *A. ocellatus,* males have several dark spots at the base of the soft dorsal.

This is not a fully reliable indicator of sex, for in others, neither sex sports such markings.

Males are larger than females of the same age, and have a more rounded cranial profile. However, the only certain means of ascertaining an individual's sex is to catch it and examine its genital papilla.

Fig. 408: A male *Geophagus brasiliensis,* a cold-hardy and very beautiful eartheater from southern Brazil and Uruguay.

Fig. 409: A young male *Geophagus crassilabris* Steindachner 1877, the northernmost representative of the eartheater lineage.

While the preliminary stages of this operation are often trying for all parties concerned, the sheer size of this structure precludes any possibility of an erroneous determination!

Pair formation is complicated by large adult size.

If it is impractical to attempt pairing in a community setting, both *Astronotus* species are excellent candidates for the incomplete divider approach to breeding.

Astronotus are biparentally custodial, substratum spawning cichlids.

The preferred spawning site is a flat, solid surface either parallel with or perpendicular to the tank bottom.

These are **extremely** prolific species, depositing up to 3000 eggs in a compact plaque.

Quite apart from their large adult size, the number of fry in an average spawn dictates that these cichlids be bred in the largest available aquaria.

Even a small pair should never be housed in a tank of less than 50 gallons capacity. A 75 gallon tank is closer to the optimum.

Both sexes share hygienic and custodial duties.

Hatching occurs 36 to 40 hours postspawning at 82 °F, and the fry become fully mobile six days to a week later.

With heavy feeding and frequent partial water changes, the young grow quickly. If crowded, they rapidly and efficiently adjust the stocking rate downwards through sibling cannibalism.

The need to sort the growing fry by size is a potent factor predisposing commercial breeders to an essentially interventionist approach to oscar rearing.

Those breeders that allow pairs to rear their own fry separate parents and offspring no later than the fourth week to avoid the complications that arise when a pair wishes to respawn in the presence of older fry.

Sexual maturity is attained a year to 14 months postspawning under aquarium conditions.

Young pairs of oscars often devour their first few clutches. This behavior underlies its reputation for parental unreliability.

Fig. 410: A young male *Geophagus pellegrini* Regan 1912. This distinctive species has been confused with the more commonly encountered *G. steindachneri*, the redhump eartheater.

Given time, such pairs usually become excellent parents. Regrettably, few commercial breeders have the patience to allow nature to take its course.

Hence most oscar clutches spawned in captivity are artificially incubated.

For this reason, there are surprisingly few detailed accounts of how oscars care for their young in captivity.

There is also very little information on the nature and duration of parental care in the wild for either *Astronotus* species.

The American aquarist TONY SILVA reports that a pair of *A. crassipinnis* seined from a tributary of the Rio Parana in northern Argentina and placed in a holding container were subsequently found surrounded by a swarm of youngsters.

This observation suggests that like *Cichla*, parental individuals of at least one species of *Astronotus* allow their mobile fry to take refuge in their mouths in the face of a major threat.

Breeders willing to permit pairs to spawn in a naturalistic setting in captivity might very well find that such behavior is also characteristic of *A. ocellatus*.

For many years the oscar, as the only really large cichlid generally available to aquarists, monopolized the "pet fish" market.

Numerous competitors notwithstanding, the oscar continues to enjoy enormous popularity, as evinced by the number of juveniles sold annually.

Regrettably, many oscars are purchased on impulse by aquarists with little appreciation for either how large they will become or how much they will eat in the process.

Confronted with the problem of disposing of a fish that has, more often than not, quite literally outgrown its welcome, these aquarists soon discover that finding a new home for an adult oscar falls midway in difficulty between placing a litter of kittens and locating a site for a toxic waste incinerator.

Many desperate oscar owners thus opt to release their unwanted pets into the nearest accessible body of water.

Such actions are neither environmentally responsible nor humane, given the fate of any tropical fish introduced into temperate waters as winter approaches. However difficult it may be to contemplate, euthanasia of unwanted large aquarium fish is in all respects a superior alternative to their release into natural waters.

This disagreeable contingency is best avoided by researching all fish purchases ahead of the fact and making a commitment to buy only those species whose needs one can satisfy over the long haul.

Eartheaters and Demonfish

The *Geophagus* lineage as here understood comprises fifteen genera.

Apistogramma, Apistogrammoides, Taeniacara, Biotoecus, Papiliochromis and the checkerboard cichlids of the genera *Crenicara, Mazarunia* and *Dicrossus* are dwarfs and will be considered under that heading.

The remaining genera are referred to collectively as eartheaters in several vernaculars because of their habit of sifting through the substratum in search of food.

All representatives of this lineage are characterized by the presence of a more-or-less well developed modification of the first gill arch known as the epibranchial lobe.

This structure is best developed in those species that forage most actively through the substratum, an observation that lends credence to hypothesis that this structure plays a significant role in the feeding mechanics of these cichlids.

The least anatomically and behaviorally specialized of these is the genus *Biotodoma* EIGENMANN and KENNEDY 1903.

Two species have been formally described, *Biotodoma cupido* (HECKEL 1840), [Figure 406], native to the coastal rivers of the Guianas and the northern and western portion of the Amazon basin, and *B. wavrini* (GOSSE 1963), from the Orinoco River and the Colombian and Brazilian tributaries of the Rio Negro. Both are sporadically exported under the former name.

A third undescribed species from the Rio Tapajos, a major northward-flowing tributary than enters the Amazon near its mouth in eastern Brazil, has been imported under the name *Biotodoma* sp. "Santarem" [Figure 407].

Biotodoma are medium-sized cichlids of relatively unagressive temperament.

Fig. 411: A male of the true demonfish, *Satanoperca jurupari* Heckel 1840.

Males will often quarrel among themselves, particularly if housed in cramped quarters, but on the whole these are social fish, tolerant of both conspecifics and other fish too large to make an easy mouthful. Their attractive adult coloration and elegant finnage make them a desirable addition to any large species community tank.

These eartheaters can usually hold their own in disagreements, but it is unwise to house them with bellicose companions, such as many Central American cichlids. They will not look their best and certainly will not breed under these conditions.

Their day-to-day activities pose little risk to rooted plants, but these eartheaters do dig extensively in conjunction with spawning.

Like the generality of Amazonian species, these are warm-water cichlids. Temperatures from 74° to 80°F suffice for ordinary maintenance with an increase to 85° to 88°F for breeding.

All three species of *Biotodoma* will live happily in slightly acid to slightly alkaline, moderately hard water.

However, none will breed successfully at pH values in excess of 5.5 or in water with a total hardness in excess of 1°DH.

Like all eartheaters, *Biotodoma* are extremely sensitive to dissolved metabolites.

As the usual recourse to frequent partial water changes is complicated by their preference for very acid, extremely soft water, recourse to chemically active filter media to manage the nitrogen cycle in their tanks may prove a cost-effective alternative in areas where hard, alkaline water is the norm.

These eartheaters are monogamous, biparentally custodial substratum spawners. Sex differences are subtle.

Males are slightly larger and tend to have longer ventral and caudal fin streamers.

However, these differences are evident only in adult specimens and may not be visible in newly imported fish, whose finnage is often in less than perfect condition.

However, males of all three species are marked with conspicuous metallic blue streaks on their cheeks and preopercula, whereas those of females are marked with a more modest pattern of small spots.

The paucity of recorded spawnings in captivity is due in no small part to the preponderance of one sex or the other in shipments of wild fish.

The compact, circular plaque of eggs is deposited on a precleaned flat surface.

Hygienic behavior is largely the female's task, while her mate defends the perimeter of the pair's territory.

The eggs hatch in 72 hours at 85°F and the fry are mobile three days later.

They are large enough to take newly hatched brine shrimp for their initial meal.

With due attention to nitrogen cycle management, they are easily reared, attaining sexual maturity eight to ten months postspawning.

The remaining four geophagine genera are more highly — and obviously — modified substratum-sifting cichlids.

Two of these eartheater genera comprise relatively short-snouted species with terminal to slightly inferior mouths.

With ten described and half as many undescribed species, *Geophagus* HECKEL 1840 is the largest genus of South American eartheaters.

It also enjoys the most extensive range.

While the majority of species live in the coastal rivers of the Guianas and the Orinoco and Amazon basins, one nominal species, *Geophagus brasiliensis* (QUOY and GAIMARD 1824) [Figure 408] is native to the coastal rivers of southeastern Brazil and Uruguay.

Three relatively long-snouted species are to be found in Pacific and Caribbean slope rivers west of the Andes Mountains [Figure 409] while a fourth, *Geophagus crassilabris* STEINDACHNER 1877 [Figure 410] ranges as far north as the Rio Chagres in central Panama.

The naked eartheaters of the genus *Gymnogeophagus*, so named with reference to the absence of scales on the nape, enjoy an essentially complementary distribution.

This genus comprises seven species, all native to the coastal rivers of southern Brazil and Uruguay or to the Rio Paraguay-Rio Parana drainage. With their long, pointed snouts and markedly inferior mouths, representatives of the last two geophagine genera are quintessential exemplars of the eartheater feeding guild.

Their distinctive appearance has earned the Peruvian representatives of the genus *Satanoperca* HECKEL 1840 the same vernacular designation of *bujurqui embujo* that is afforded to the superficially similar but quite unrelated *Chaetobranchus flavescens*.

The rather alarming generic name of these eartheaters has led many American aquarists to refer to them as demonfish.

The genus comprises seven described and a number of undescribed species, of which *Satanoperca leucostictus* (MULLER and TROESCHEL 1849) [Figure 35] and *S. jurupari* HECKEL 1840 [Figure 411] are most familiar to aquarists.

With the exception of *S. pappaterra* HECKEL 1840, whose range includes the Rio Paraguay, all hail from the coastal rivers of the Guianas or the Orinoco and Amazon basins.

The genus *Retroculus* comprises three species of rapids dwelling cichlids.

Retroculus lapidifer (CASTELNAU 1855) is native to the Rio Tocantins. Rio Araguaia and Rio Guama, *R. xinguensis* GOSSE 1971 [Figure 412] to the Rio Xingu and *R. septentrionalis* GOSSE 1971 to the coastal rivers of French Guiana.

Like many other rheophile cichlids, *Retroculus* have only a vestigial swim bladder.

Their droll hopping movements, taken with the presence of a conspicuous dark spot in the soft dorsal fin has led several American aquarists to describe these fish as "eartheaters trying to be bumpheads"!

Whatever their generic placement, the maintenance requirements of eartheaters are similar enough to dictate a common approach to their aquarium husbandry.

Most eartheaters are river dwellers. Like all cichlids native to running waters, they are **very** intolerant of dissolved metabolic wastes in captivity.

If the nitrogen cycle in their aquaria is mismanaged, they develop "hole in the head" disease at the very least and may well contract stress-induced systemic bacterial infections such as "Malawi bloat".

Most aquarists employ the approach recommended for oscars to keep nitrite/nitrate concentrations at acceptable levels.

Their tendency to root in the substratum makes undergravel filters of questionable value in an eartheater tank.

Fig. 412: Note the "tilapia-spot" in the soft dorsal fin of this female *Retroculus xinguensis* Gosse 1971.

However, as these cichlids do not molest sponge filters, there is no reason why this alternative approach to biological filtration cannot be employed as an adjunct to the traditional combination of mechanical filtration and water changes.

Eartheaters native to the Amazon-Orinoco system and the Guianas prefer soft, slightly acidic to neutral water. All tolerate somewhat alkaline, moderately hard water well enough for ordinary maintenance and some will even spawn successfully under such conditions.

Extra-Amazonian species [Figure 413] are essentially indifferent to the chemical make-up of their water as long as extremes of pH and hardness are avoided.

Gymnogeophagus species can withstand prolonged exposure to temperatures as low 60 °F [Figure 414].

Like North American sunfish, they seem to do best if their temperature is allowed to vary on a seasonal basis. Indeed, they seem much more susceptible to systemic bacterial infections if kept in water warmer than 70 °F year around.

Representatives of the remaining three genera of eartheaters are warmth-loving cichlids that should not be kept cooler than 72 °F [Figure 415]. Temperatures between 75 °−80 °F suffice for ordinary maintenance, with an increase to 85 °−88 °F for breeding.

Eartheaters are easily fed in captivity.

Pelletized foods, freeze-dried krill and any of the usually available frozen foods are readily accepted.

The larger species have robust appetites and seem particularly fond of earthworms.

The demonic allusions that abound in the scientific names of eartheaters are particularly ironic, for these are among the least aggressive of all cichlids.

Males of such polygynously spawning species as *G. steindachneri*, *Gg. balzanii* and *Gg. gymnogenys* (HENSEL 1870) [Figure 416] are extremely intolerant of others of their sex.

The remaining species are moderately to highly social fish that appreciate the company of conspecifics outside periods of sexual activity. Their behavior towards heterospecifics makes them excellent community residents.

Fig. 413: Male *Gymnogeophagus rhabdotus* (Hensel 1870), a substratum-spawning species with a tendendy to harem polygyny when the operative sexratio favors females. Like other extra-Amazonian species, it does well in hard, alkaline water.

Fig. 414: A young male *Gymnogeophagus meridionalis* (Reis and Malabarba 1988), an eartheater that does best in cool water.

Fig. 415: Like other eartheaters from the Amazon and Orinoco Rivers, the Venezuelan species *Geophagus taeniopareius* Kullander, Royero and Taphorn 1992 prefers warm water.

Fig. 416: As might be expected in a cichlid with a polygynous mating system, this male *Gymnogeophagus gymnogenys* Hensel 1870 is apt to prove intolerant of conspecifics of the same sex.

Though they will eat smaller fish when the opportunity to do so presents itself, the predatory abilities of eartheaters are poorly developed.

Any fish the size of a platy or larger need not fear their attentions. Indeed, notwithstanding their size, many species of eartheaters are often quite shy under aquarium conditions and benefit greatly from the presence of appropriate dither fish.

When choosing tankmates for eartheaters, take particular care to exclude more aggressive cichlids from their aquarium.

Satanoperca species in particular cannot hold their own in such company, even if their tormentors are only a fraction of their size. In the face of such persecution, they neither look nor do their best and certainly cannot be expected to spawn.

The substratum-sifting behavior of these cichlids poses some risk to shallowly rooted aquatic plants.

It rarely disturbs species with extensive root systems, such as Amazon sword-plants.

However, all eartheaters engage in serious pit digging as a preliminary to spawning. Such systematic earthmoving can dislodge even the most firmly rooted plants. This digging tends to be highly localized, but the surest way to protect rooted plants under these circumstances is to pot them separately.

The eartheaters display a diversity of mating systems and reproductive modalities without equal in the Family Cichlidae.

A succinct description of eartheater reproductive biology is therefore impossible.

Pertinent information on individual species may be found in the accompanying table.

Both substratum spawners and polygamous advanced mouthbrooders are easily bred under aquarium conditions when handled as recommended in Chapter 7.

Primitive mouthbrooders, regardless of their mating system, pose a greater challenge, as do monogamous advanced mouthbrooders that practice prolonged biparental care of their mobile young, such as *Geophagus megasema* Heckel 1840 [Figure 417].

With the exception of the several *Gymnogeophagus* species, these eartheaters are also difficult to sex.

The usual external characteristics are unreliable. Hence, the only way to ascertain an unfamiliar individual's sex is to examine its genital papilla.

As previously noted, these fish are, for the most part, quite timid.

More aggressive tankmates effectively inhibit both pair and formation and territorial defense; hence, privacy is a prerequisite to breeding success.

Fortunately, the monogamous representatives of this reproductive guild enjoy strong pair bonds.

They can thus safely be moved to a separate breeding tank once they have paired. A thirty-five gallon tank represents the bare minimum for breeding eartheaters. A fifty gallon aquarium would serve even better.

Many of these cichlids grow quite large and are in addition prolific.

Substratum spawners routinely produce clutches of up to 500 eggs, while the primitive mouthbrooders can release as many as 300 fry.

The preferred spawning site is a smooth flat or slightly inclined surface.

Species that live over open, sandy bottoms, such as *Retroculus lapidifer* are often hard put to find suitable places to deposit their eggs in nature. This species resolves the problem by carrying flat pebbles to its territory and constructing a platform thereupon as a spawning site; hence, the derivation of its species name, *lapidifer* [= stone carrier].

Some primitive mouthbrooders cover the zygotes with gravel immediately before chewing them free of their egg shells.

Among monogamous species, the division of labor between the sexes follows the usual pattern for biparentally custodial cichlids.

Hatching occurs between 60 and 70 hours postspawning at 82°F and the fry become mobile five to six days thereafter regardless of whether they are taken into their parents' buccal cavities or moved to predug pits.

Advanced mouthbrooding eartheaters regardless of their mating system release their

Fig. 417: A male *Geophagus megasema* Heckel 1840, an Amazonian species formerly regarded as a junior synonym of *G. surinamensis*, from which it differs in its advanced mouthbrooding behavior.

mobile fry eight to ten days postspawning depending on water temperature.

Newly free-swimming eartheater fry are large enough to take *Artemia* nauplii and finely divided prepared food for their initial meal.

They even more sensitive to dissolved metabolites than their elders. They cannot be crowded and must be maintained under a regime of frequent partial water changes to avoid serious losses. This apart, rearing them poses few problems.

The primitive mouthbrooding species rarely attain sexual maturity earlier than 10 months postrelease. The remaining eartheaters tend to sexual precocity under aquarium conditions, breeding as early as five months postspawning.

Acarichthys EIGENMANN 1912 and *Guinacara* KULLANDER and NIJSSEN 1989 are both superficially *Geophagus*-like cichlids that lack an epibranchial lobe.

The two genera share a number of skeletal and color pattern characteristics and exhibit the same reproductive pattern and mating system. Both have a number of skeletal and superficial anatomical features with the geophagines.

However, as KULLANDER and NIJSSEN point out, these are all primitive characteristics and thus of limited value in ascertaining the evolutionary relationships of the animals possessing them.

The presence of a black spot on the first two rays of the spiny dorsal and several other features of the adult color pattern of both genera as well as their practice of cave spawning and harem polygyny also suggest that these are essentially aberrant geophagine cichlids. However, a comparative electrophoretic study of South American cichlid genera by the American biologist WAYNE S. LEIBEL suggests that the picture may be more complicated than this.

Enzyme data clearly suggest geophagine affinities for *Acarichthys* but not for *Guinacara*.

This raises the possibility that the features these two genera of cichlids represent convergent evolution rather than a shared common ancestry.

Fig. 418: A female *Guianacara oroewefi* Kullander and Nijssen 1989. This and related *Guianacara* species were formerly placed in the genus *Aequidens*, but their anatomy and reproductive pattern dictated they be recognized as generically distinct.

The only described species of *Acarichthys*, *A. heckeli* (MULLER and TROSCHEL 1840) [Figure 169].

Native to the Essequibo River of Guyana and the basins of the Orinoco and Amazon Rivers, this robust eartheater is noteworthy for both scintillating coloration and the spectacular filamentous extensions of the soft dorsal fin present in both sexes.

Guinacara comprises four described and a number of undescribed species native to the coastal rivers of the Guianas and such northerly tributaries of the Amazon as the Rio Branco and the Rio Trombetas.

The widely available species known to aquarists under the name *Guinacara geayi* (PELLEGRIN 1904) appears in reality to be *Guinacara oroewefi* KULLANDER and NIJSSEN 1989, a species widely distributed in the Marowijne River basin of Suriname whose range appears to extend into the adjacent Essequibo River basin in Guyana [Figure 418].

Restricted to the Oyapock and Approuage Rivers in French Guiana, the true *G. geayi* has not to date been imported.

Guinacara sphenozona KULLANDER and NIJSSEN 1989, a species native to the Corantin River drainage of Suriname and the Essequibo River drainage of neighboring Guyana has been imported at least episodically into Europe. It can be distinguished from the more familiar pseudo-*geayi* by the absence of a dark spot on the first two dorsal spines of adult specimens.

At least two other *Guinacara* species, neither referable to any described *Guinacara*, have been illustrated in European aquarium references since the publication of the first edition of this book. The aquarium husbandry of both genera is uncomplicated.

These cichlids have the same maintenance requirements as the Amazonian *Geophagus* species.

They are, however, notably more aggressive than the generality of true eartheaters, both towards other fishes and towards conspecifics.

Adult males are notably intolerant of one another. This may arise from the fact that both *Acarichthys* and *Guinacara* are cave spawning harem polygynists.

Reproductive Modalities and Mating Systems in Eartheaters			
Mating System	Substratum spawners	Primitive mouthbrooders	Advanced mouthbrooders
Monogamy	G. argyrostictus G. brasiliensis S. daemon Gg. australis[1] Gg. meridionalis[1] Gg. rhabdotus[1] Gg. setequedas[1]	G. brachybranchus S. jurupari R. lapidifer S. leucostictus S. pappaterra	G. altifrons G. megasema G. proximus
Harem Polygyny		Gg. balzanii Gg. gymnogenys	
Open Polygyny			G. crassilabris G. pellegrini G. steindachneri

[1] The mating system of these species in captivity is plastic. Older, large males will spawn polygynously when the operative sex ratio favors females.

These fish excavate extensive burrow systems in nature and their attempts to do likewise in captivity make it virtually impossible to grow rooted plants in their quarters.

Most of the burden of preparing a spawning site falls upon the female.

Care of the zygotes is also exclusively maternal, though the male may assist in defense of the mobile young.

Hatching occurs between 60 to 72 hours postspawning at 82°—85°F and the fry become mobile five to six days thereafter.

They are large enough to take *Artemia* nauplii and finely powdered prepared food for their initial meal. Under a regime of frequent water changes, the fry are easily reared.

Guinacara species grow fairly quickly, attaining reproductive competence between eight and ten months postspawning. *Acarichthys heckeli* is slower growing, seldom reaching sexual maturity at less than a year of age.

Acaras

The *Cichlasoma-Aequidens* lineage represents the dominant group of South American cichlids. It embraces a broad spectrum of morphological diversity and beyond doubt boasts the largest number of genera and species. It is convenient to call these cichlids by their Tupi-Guarani name of **acara**, a usage well established in the aquaristic literature.

Apart from the genus *Acaronia* MYERS 1940, whose two species are specialized piscivores, all acaras are morphologically generalized invertebrate feeding cichlids.

Five of the group's remaining eight genera are midsized to moderately large cichlids.

Of the remaining three genera of acaras, one, *Laetacara* KULLANDER 1986, includes a number of species small enough to be considered dwarfs, as indeed are all known species of *Nannacara* REGAN 1905. More information on these diminutive acaras can be found in Chapter 10.

Acaronia may felicitously be described as blue acaras trying to be leaffish.

These cichlids were first considered by REGAN to be specialized *Aequidens* derivatives, a judgment which subsequent researchers still accept.

Fig. 419: A ripe female basketmouth acara, *Acaronia nassa.*

Fig. 420: The port acara, *Cichlasoma portalegrense,* an old stand-by that virtually disappeared from the hobby during the Second World War. Its recent reintroduction should see it promptly reestablished as a favorite of Neotropical cichlid fanciers.

Known as **bocca de juquia** [= giant mouth] in Brazil and as basketmouth cichlids to Anglophone aquarists, their Portuguese and English vernacular names highlight the most immediately obvious feature of these acaras.

The genus *Acaronia* comprises two species. *Acaronia nassa* (HECKEL 1840), the basketmouth acara, native to the Amazon basin and the coastal rivers of the Guianas [Figure 419] and *Acaronia vultuosa* KULLANDER 1989, the masked basketmouth acara, which is found in the entire Orinoco drainage but has colonized only the Rio Negro of the Amazon basin. Both species are solitary ambush predators in nature.

Not surprisingly, they display little liking for the proximity of conspecifics in captivity.

Heterospecific tankmates too large to make a convenient mouthful are typically ignored.

However, as these cichlids can grow to 8" SL, the prudent aquarist will err on the side of caution when assessing their capacity in this respect! Basketmouths neither dig nor molest aquatic plants.

Indeed, they appear to be most at home in a well planted aquarium.

Basketmouths are quite sensitive to dissolved metabolites, resembling in this respect eartheaters rather than the generality of acaras.

Notwithstanding an understandable preference for live fish, both *Acaronia* species will take a wide range of frozen and prepared foods in captivity.

Frozen mysid shrimp and freeze-dried krill are particularly appreciated.

The reproductive patterns of basketmouths correspond well to those of the better known substratum spawning acaras and they can be expected to respond favorably to the same management in captivity.

The acaras proper comprise eight genera.

Of these, *Cichlasoma* SWAINSON 1839, as recently redefined by KULLANDER, comprises two familiar aquarium residents, the black acara, *Cichlasoma bimaculatum* (LINNAEUS 1754) [Figure 66] and the port acara, *C. portalegrense* (HENSEL 1870) [Figure 420].

341

Fig. 421: *Aequidens diadema* (Heckel 1840) is a colorful mid-sized acara from the Peruvian Amazon.

Eleven additional species are known from the coastal rivers of southern Brazil and Uruguay, as well as the Orinoco, Amazon and Parana basins, but these are rarely imported as aquarium fish. All are biparentally custodial substratum spawning cichlids.

The remaining cichlids formerly included in *Cichlasoma* have, since the publication of KULLANDER's revision of the genus, been reassigned to other genera.

In the first edition of this book, I noted that the genus *Aequidens* EIGENMANN and BRAY 1894 was badly in need of revision and predicted that the outcome of such a project would be the erection of a number of smaller, more biologically meaningful genera.

Since its publication, KULLANDER has turned his attention to the genus *Aequidens* as broadly understood.

The outcome of his revisionary efforts has been the dramatic restriction of the nomen *Aequidens* and the publication of five new genera of acaras.

The effects of KULLANDER's work on the nomenclature of those species familiar to

aquarists are summarized in tabular form below.

As narrowly defined, *Aequidens* comprises roughly a dozen species of medium-sized to quite large cichlids that differ most obviously from *Cichlasoma* in having only a few scattered scales or no scales at all along the bases of the dorsal and caudal fins.

Apart from a few outlier species native to the coastal rivers of the Guianas and one species from the Rio Parana drainage, *Aequidens* are conspicuous residents of the Orinoco and Amazon basins.

Aquarists usually encounter juvenile specimens of *Aequidens tetramerus* (HECKEL 1840) [Figure 21] and *Ae. diadema* (HECKEL 1840) [Figure 421] in shipments from Iquitos, while *Ae. metae* EIGENMANN 1922 [Figure 422] is exported on a fairly regular basis from Colombia.

Although many *Aequidens* species are intensely colored as adults, the genus has never enjoyed wide popularity.

It seems likely that neither their large adult size nor the length of time it takes many species to develop their full coloration has endeared them to most cichlid fanciers.

To complicate matters further, most species are not easily induced to spawn in captivity.

KULLANDER reports that *Ae. diadema* is a biparentally custodial primitive mouth-brooder.

I have taken a female *Ae. tetramerus* from the Rio Nanay in Peru with fry in her buccal cavity, which suggests a similar reproductive modality for this species.

The other *Aequidens* species for which reproductive data are available are substratum spawners.

KULLANDER has suggested, in my opinion correctly, that the representatives of the blue acara green terror species complex do not belong in *Aequidens*, but he has not to date proposed a new genus for them.

The blue acara, *Ae. pulcher* (GILL 1858) [Figure 92], was described from the island of Trinidad.

Similar fish of uncertain biological standing have been reported from the lower Orinoco basin and the rivers of the Caribbean coast of Venezuela.

The blue acara is replaced in the Rio Magdalena and Caribbean drainages of Colombia by *Ae. latifrons* (STEINDACHNER 1879) [Figure 423].

The northernmost representative of the acaras is *Ae. coeruleopunctatus* (KNER and STEINDACHNER 1863) [Figure 58], a common inhabitant of rivers on both the Atlantic and Pacific slopes of Panama that barely squeaks across the border into southwestern Costa Rica.

The Pacific slope rivers of Colombia are home to a complex of undescribed "green acaras".

Aequidens sapayensis (REGAN 1903) [Figure 424] is native to the Rio Esmereldas and other coastal streams of southwestern Ecuador.

The Currently Recognized Generic Placement of the Species Formerly Included in *Aequidens*

Former Name	Current Name
Aequidens biseriatus	*Ae. biseriatus*
Aequidens coeruleopunctatus	*Ae. coeruleopunctatus*
Aequidens curviceps	*Laetacara curviceps*
Aequidens diadema	*Ae. diadema*
Aequidens dorsigerus	*Laetacara dorsiger*
Aequidens flavilabris	*Laetacara flavilabris*
Aequidens geayi	*Guianacara oroewefi*
Aequidens guianensis	*Krobia guianensis*
Aequidens itanyi	*Krobia itanyi*
Aequidens latifrons	*Ae. latifrons*
Aequidens mariae	*Bujurquina mariae*
Aequidens metae	*Ae. metae*
Aequidens paraguayensis	*Bujurquina vittata*
Aequidens patricki	*Ae. patricki*
Aequidens plagiozonatus	*Ae. plagiozonatus*
Aequidens portalegrensis	*Cichlasoma portalegrense*
Aequidens pulcher	*Ae. pulcher*
Aequidens rivulatus	*Ae. rivulatus*
Aequidens sapayensis	*Ae. sapayensis*
Aequidens syspilus	*Bujurquina syspilus*
Aequidens tetramerus	*Ae. tetramerus*
Aequidens thayeri	*Laetacara thayeri*
Aequidens zamorensis	*Bujurquina zamorensis*

Fig. 422: A male *Aequidens metae* Eigenmann 1922, a large and frequently imported acara native to the Colombian Amazon.

Fig. 423: Though currently included in the genus *Aequidens*, *Ae. latifrons* (Steindachner 1879) will probably soon join other relatives of the blue acara in a new genus.

Fig. 424: The intense coloration of *Aequidens sapayensis* Regan 1903 has earned it the common name of emerald acara.

Of the four fish currently ascribed to the *Aequidens rivulatus* species complex, one, the so-called dwarf green terror, appears to hail from the Rio Magdalena drainage in Colombia.

The remaining three species are native to the Pacific slope rivers of southern Colombia, Ecuador and northern Peru [Figure 425]. The distribution of these attractive acaras is thus essentially complementary to that of *Aequidens* as narrowly defined.

All the representatives of this group studied to date are substratum spawners that practice long-term biparental defense of their mobile fry.

The smiling acaras of the genus *Laetacara* KULLANDER 1986 are small to mid-sized, superficially *Cichlasoma*-like fishes [Figure 426].

They differ from the larger acaras with regard to numerous skeletal features, but their most immediately obvious diagnostic characteristics are the presence of preopercular scales, of three rows of scales on the nape immediately anterior to the origin of the dorsal fin,

unscaled vertical fin bases and a pattern of light and dark streaks about the mouth which have inspired both their English vernacular and generic names [Figure 427].

The smiling acaras are restricted to the Orinoco, Amazon and Parana drainages.

As already noted, the most popular species of the genus are small enough to be considered dwarf cichlids and will be discussed at greater length under that heading.

The closest relative of the smiling acaras appears to be the monotypic genus *Cleithracara* KULLANDER and NIJSSEN 1989.

Its only known species, the popular keyhole cichlid, *Cleithracara maronii* (STEINDACHNER 1882) [Figure 428], replaces the smiling acaras in the coastal rivers of the Guianas.

The two genera differ with respect to several skeletal characteristics, but the diagnostic feature most evident to the aquarist is the keyhole cichlid's unique color pattern.

The keyhole cichlid and all species of smiling acara bred to date are biparentally custodial substratum spawners.

345

Fig. 425: This male orange-finned acara, a representative of the *Aequidens rivulatus* species complex, is one of the few acaras sufficiently bellicose to hold its own in the company of the more aggressive *Heros* species.

Fig. 426: The superficial resemblance of this female *Laetacara thayeri* (Steindachner 1875) to an acara of the genus *Cichlasoma* is plainly evident.

Fig. 427: This male *Laetacara flavilabris* (Cope 1870) clearly shows the facial markings upon which both its generic and vernacular names are based.

Fig. 428: The keyhole acara, *Cleithracara maronii* Steindachner 1882 is one of the least aggressive Neotropical cichlids. Like most of the less assertive acaras, it does best in a well-planted tank containing suitable dither fish.

Bujurquina KULLANDER 1986, *Tahuatin-suyoa* KULLANDER 1986 and *Krobia* KULLANDER and NIJSSEN 1989 complete the roster of true acaras. These three genera share a number of arcane skeletal characteristics but to the observant aquarist their most obvious common features are the presence of an oblique lateral band that runs from the rear margin of the eye to the posterior base of the soft dorsal fin and the retention in some form of a suborbital stripe by adult individuals.

Krobia have scaled vertical fin bases and a rounded truncate to weakly emarginate caudal fin.

These mid-sized acaras display a reticulate pattern of lighter spots on the caudal and soft dorsal fins but lack discrete metallic spangling on the head and flanks.

The species studied to date are all biparentally custodial substratum spawners.

The genus comprises two described species.

Krobia guianensis (REGAN 1905) [Figure 429], native to the coastal rivers of

Guyana and Suriname, has a long history in the aquarium hobby under the name *Aequidens itanyi.*

The true *Krobia itanyi* (PUYO 1943) is a valid but to date unimported species endemic to the Marowijne River basin in Suriname and French Guiana. KULLANDER and NIJSSEN acknowledge the existence of additional undescribed Guianan species and imply that *Krobia* is also present in the Rio Xingu in the south central Amazon basin.

Bujurquina have unscaled vertical fin bases. Like *Krobia,* their lower lateral line extends onto the caudal fin between the third and fourth rays of its upper lobe.

Unlike *Krobia,* they have weakly to strongly emarginate tail fins and variably developed patterns of metallic spangling on their heads and flanks [Figure 168]. The genus comprises sixteen described and at least half that number of undescribed species.

A few species, such as *Bujurquina peregrinabunda* KULLANDER 1986, are widely distributed in lowland Amazonia.

Fig. 429: A male *Krobia guianensis* (Regan 1905), a species sometimes marketed under the name dolphin acara.

Most, however, are to be found in the upper reaches of the Orinoco, Amazon and Parana drainages.

All *Bujurquina* species to date studied in nature or bred in aquaria are biparentally custodial primitive mouthbrooders [Figures 180 & 181].

The monotypic genus *Tahuatinsuyoa* KULLANDER 1986, described from the Rio Aguaytia drainage in Peru, differs most obviously from the previous two genera in having somewhat enlarged lips, a distinct midlateral spot, an elongate caudal peduncle, and a rounded caudal fin.

The prolongation of the lower lateral line onto the caudal fin between the second and third branched rays of its upper lobe set the genus apart from all other acaras.

Tahuatinsuyoa macantzatza KULLANDER 1986 looks rather like the outcome of a blind date between *Bujurquina vittata* (HECKEL 1840) and some representative of the *Ae. rivulatus* species complex.

The remoteness of its habitat notwithstanding, this attractive acara has been exported to Europe and bred by German aquarists.

It is also a biparentally custodial primitive mouthbrooder.

Most acaras are cichlids of relatively unaggressive temperament.

Though most representatives of the *Ae. rivulatus* complex represent a notable exception, acaras are rather social fish, tolerant of both conspecifics and other fish too large to make a convenient meal.

By virtue of their pleasing coloration, most make a desirable addition to any large species community tank.

While they generally hold their own in disagreements, it is best not to house them with bellicose companions such as the West African jewelfishes and majority of Central American cichlid species.

Acaras seldom look their best and rarely breed under these conditions. A few species dig with sufficient energy at spawning time to pose some risk to rooted plants, but most are indifferent to their presence.

A number of the shyer species, such as the keyhole and smiling acaras, actually prefer well planted aquaria and rarely breed successfully if otherwise housed.

Although species native to the coastal rivers of southeastern Brazil and the Rio Parana basin, such as *Cichlasoma portalegrense* and its near relatives tolerate plunges into the low 60's, most acaras are warm-water cichlids. Temperatures from 72° to 78°F suffice for ordinary maintenance.

Most spawn freely between 78° to 82°F, but a few Amazonian species prefer warmer water, between 85° to 88°F, in the breeding tank.

Acaras native to the Amazon-Orinoco region and the Guianas prefer acid to neutral, moderately soft water, but will tolerate harder, alkaline conditions if bacterial counts are kept down through regular partial water changes.

Extra-Amazonian species are essentially indifferent to the chemical make-up of their water as long as extremes of pH and hardness are avoided.

They are also somewhat more forgiving of short-term dissolved metabolite build-up than are their Amazonian counterparts, though this is no excuse to slack off on proper nitrogen cycle management in their aquaria.

Acaras are easily fed, taking eagerly all usually available live and prepared foods.

Though most *Aequidens* species pose a challenge even to an experienced cichlid keeper, the great majority of acaras spawn freely under aquarium conditions.

Males grow larger than females, have a more rounded cranial profile and longer, more flowing soft dorsal and anal fins.

Sexually related color differences range from slight to non-existent.

With the exception of the Panamanian *Aequidens coeruleopunctatus*, which breeds polygynously when the opportunity arises, acaras are monogamous. They respond well to techniques for encouraging pair formation presented in Chapter 7.

Although the group comprises both classical substratum spawners and primitive mouthbrooders, this distinction is irrelevant to their management in captivity. Representatives of both groups deposit a compact plaque of eggs upon a previously cleaned solid surface.

Fig. 430: A pair of *Cichlasoma paranense* Kullander 1983 demonstrating one of the advantages of a mobile spawning platform!

Many acaras deposit their eggs upon large fallen leaves in nature [Figure 430]. They carry this preference for a mobile spawning platform over into captivity and will freely make use of such substrata if given the opportunity to do so.

Male and female share hygienic duties, the degree of male involvement depending upon the density of potential spawn predators present in their aquarium.

Hatching occurs in 60 to 70 hours at 82 °F. Regardless of whether the zygotes are taken into their parents' buccal cavities or moved to predug pits, they become mobile five to six days thereafter.

The tendency of most pairs to begin another reproductive episode four to six weeks postspawning usually terminates parental care in captivity. However, under exceptional circumstances it can persist up to ten weeks.

The fry are easily reared and with frequent water changes grow quickly.

Some of the smaller acaras attain reproductive competence as early as six months postspawning.

In most cases, sexual activity begins ten months to a year postspawning.

Acaras and eartheaters belie the popular notion that medium-sized to large cichlids are invariably aggressive predators unfit for residence in a community aquarium. They are ideal fish for the aquarist who lacks the tank space or desire to manage the family's more aggressive representatives. They are beautiful fish in the bargain and offer the prospective breeder an opportunity to witness an amazing spectrum of reproductive patterns.

It is thus hardly surprising this group continues to appeal equally to both novice and experienced cichlid keepers.

The Genus Heros and Its Allies

The genus *Heros* and its allies comprise the most morphologically diverse New World cichlid lineage.

Superficially, the only features these cichlids seem to share are possession of more than three anal fin spines, a tendency towards enlargement of the anterior jaw teeth, and a monogamous mating system coupled with a biparentally custodial substratum or cave spawning reproductive pattern.

Morphological specializations abound in this group, as exemplified by *Geophagus* analogs such as the firemouth cichlid and laterally compressed genera like *Mesonauta, Pterophyllum* and *Symphysodon* whose body shape allows them to live among waterlogged brush in the flooded forests of Amazonia.

This state of affairs has come about because these cichlids have exploited a remarkably full spectrum of food resources.

This lineage consequently boasts robust piscivores, an impressive assortment of plant and fruit eaters, rheophilous algae scrappers, substratum-sifting invertebrate feeders, molluscivores, and even generalists with no obvious trophic specializations whatsoever!

While the *Heros* group is well represented in South America, its morphological diversity is due chiefly to historical accident.

This is the only cichlid lineage to successfully colonize Mesoamerica.

In the absence of competitors, it underwent an impressive adaptive radiation, filling niches occupied to the south by representatives of other cichlid lineages or even by fishes of other families.

In the older aquaristic literature, most of these cichlids are referred to the genus *Cichlasoma*. As noted above, the type species of that genus, *C. bimaculatum,* has been shown to be more closely related to certain *Aequidens* species than to the majority of its nominal congeners.

Hence KULLANDER's decision to redefine *Cichlasoma* in a more restrictive sense. As presently understood, the genus now includes only *C. bimaculatum* and those acaras to which it is closely related.

As is the rule in such cases, the provisions of the International Code of Zoological Nomenclature dictated that the oldest available synonym would automatically become the

Fig. 431: A male *Nandopsis umbriferus* (Meek & Hildebrand 1913), one of the largest representatives of the specialized piscivorous genus *Nandopsis*.

recognized generic name for the substantial residue of species formerly included in *Cichlasoma*. When the first edition of this book was written, the generic nomen *Heros* HECKEL 1840, originally applied to the majority of these cichlids, satisfied this criterion.

In the intervening decade, KULLANDER has shown that *Heros* should be restricted to a handful of distinctive South American species, of which *Heros severus* HECKEL 1840 is most familiar to aquarists.

KULLANDER has addressed the nomenclatorial vacuum this action has left among the South American species formerly included within *Heros* as broadly understood by erecting the genus *Hypselacara* for the chocolate cichlid and its relatives and rehabilitating the genera *Mesonauta* Gunther 1862, *Hoplarchus* KAUP 1860 and *Caquetaia* FOWLER 1945.

Although he recognized its biological validity, KULLANDER forbore to propose a generic name for *"Heros" facetus* (JENYNS 1842) and the other representatives of this species group.

The effects of KULLANDER's work on the nomenclature of the South American species of the *Heros* lineage familiar to aquarists are summarized in tabular form below.

Herichthys BAIRD and GIRARD 1854 is the oldest available generic name for the Mesoamerican representatives of the *Heros* lineage. However, the diversity encompassed within its Central American representatives is so great that shoehorning them into a single genus seems a singularly pointless exercise.

As noted in the first edition of this book, a persuasive case could have been made even then for recognizing as valid genera such taxa as *Thorichthys* MEEK 1904. While further research may refine his definitions and alter the generic placement of some species, the time has come to recognize that the views expressed by the British ichthyologist C. TATE REGAN on the genus-level classification of Middle American cichlids in the first decade of the century are broadly correct.

Hence, the decision herein to raise all of REGAN's subgenera to full generic rank should

Fig. 432: An adult female *Nandopsis motaguensis* (Gunther 1866).

not come as a complete surprise. This said, I do not intend to depart significantly from the approach to grouping representatives of this lineage utilized in the first edition.

While systematists are mainly concerned with a system of classifying animals that reflects their evolutionary relationships, aquarists are more concerned with similarities in maintenance requirements.

These are determined by adult size and behavioral characteristics, in turn largely a function of a given species' feeding guild. Because morphology reflects both ecology and evolutionary history, there is a certain amount of overlap in these systems of classification.

However, further reading will dispel any notion of absolute congruence.

A given subgenus will often be represented in several of the subgroups employed herein.

Guapotes and Mojarras — Robust Piscivores and Invertebrate Feeders

On both phylogenetic and ecological grounds, this is a highly artificial assemblage.

In the wild there are real differences between the modes of living of specialized fish eaters like *Petenia splendida* GUNTHER 1862 [Figure 30] and the numerous species of the genera *Nandopsis* GILL 1862 [Figure 431 & 432] and *Caquetaia* [Figure 433] on the one hand and invertebrate Caquetaia [Figure 413] on the one hand and the large feeders of the genera *Hypselacara* KULLANDER 1986 [Figure 147], *Amphilophus* AGASSIZ 1858 [Figures 85, 171, 174, 434] and *Herichthys* [Figures 14 & 177] on the other.

The Currently Recognized Scientific Names of the South American Representatives of the *Heros* Lineage

Former Name	Current Name
Heros appendiculatus	*Heros appendiculatus*
Heros arnoldi	*Hypselacara coryphaenoides*
Heros autochthon	*"Heros" autochthon*
Heros coryphaenoides	*Hypselacara coryphaenoides*
Heros facetus	*"Heros" facetus*
Heros festae	*Amphilophus festae*
Heros gephyrus	*Amphilophus gephyrus*
Heros hellabrunni	*Hypselacara temporalis*
Heros kraussi	*Caquetaia kraussi*
Heros myersi	*Caquetaia myersi*
Heros oblongus	*"Heros" oblongus*
Heros ornatus	*Amphilophus ornatus*
Heros psittacus	*Hoplarchus psittacus*
Heros severus	*Heros severus*
Heros spectabilis	*Caquetaia spectabilis*
Heros umbriferus	*Nandopsis umbriferus*

Fig. 433: A female *Caquetaia spectabilis* (Steindachner 1875), a beautiful cichlid native to Amazonia and the Guianas. Unlike their Mesoamerican analogs of the genus *Nandopsis*, *Caquetaia* species are not characterized by pronounced sexual color differences.

However, these differences tend to disappear under the constraints of aquarium living.

Without exception, the behavior of these species in captivity corresponds to the negative stereotype of the Family Cichlidae prevalent among aquarists.

Though not all are piscivores in nature, all enthusiastically devour smaller fish in captivity, their depredations limited only by the size of their capacious mouths.

Though they vary in their tolerance of heterospecific tankmates, none appreciates the proximity of conspecifics outside periods of sexual activity. This intolerance can be so acute that without active human intervention, efforts to induce pair bonding in captivity are more likely to lead to a funeral than a honeymoon.

These cichlids have elevated demolition of their immediate surroundings to a high art, and by virtue of their large size and prodigious appetites, pose a major challenge to effective nitrogen cycle management in their quarters.

The key to maintaining these fish successfully is room — lots of room!

Most of the aggressive behavior they display in captivity stems from need to defend a territory or maintain a certain critical distance from other fishes.

The less living space available, the more intolerable the behavior of these cichlids will be.

Single specimens can be kept as "pet fish" in a 40 to 50 gallon tank, while a community of single specimens will live in reasonable amity if housed in tanks of 75 gallons capacity or larger.

If pairs are maintained in a community situation, the inevitable onset of reproductive activity and its associated territorial defense dictates these very large cichlids be housed in tanks of at least 100 gallons capacity.

Because of the fragility of its highly protrusible jaws, the constraints in selecting companions for *Cichla* species apply to *Petenia splendida*. The remainder of these robust cichlids do best in the company of tankmates comparable in size and temperament or those sufficiently well armored to shrug off their attacks, such as the larger loricariid catfishes.

Like the tilapias, both *guapotes* and *mojarras* have voracious but mercifully unselective appetites. Smaller live fish and earthworms are eagerly taken, but economic considerations usually limit the frequency of their appearance on the menu.

Pelletized foods, whole frozen topsmelt and strips of frozen fish or lean meat are the most practical staple diet for these cichlids.

By virtue of their heroic appetites, they generate a waste load beyond the capacity of any biological filtration system available to the amateur aquarist to manage.

The only workable approach to nitrogen cycle management in their aquaria is the combination of efficient mechanical filtration and frequent partial water changes.

This rarely poses problems, for these cichlids prosper over a wide range of pH and hardness values.

Water changes of 30%—40% of the tank volume every seven to ten days are by no means out of line for these robust cichlids.

A final warning: Of all cichlids, these are most likely to respond aggressively to such impedimenta as filter siphons and heaters.

It is thus prudent to protect vulnerable equipment with a permeable plastic barrier as suggested in Chapter 3.

Sexual dimorphism in both size and finnage is well developed in all these genera.

Females rarely exceed two thirds the size of males the same age, and have shorter, more rounded soft dorsal and anal fins.

Males of many species develop a pronounced nuchal hump with the onset of sexual activity.

Sexually related differences in color pattern range from substantial, in the case of the true *guapotes* of the genus *Nandopsis* [Figures 435 & 436] to slight in the South American genera *Hypselacara* and *Caquetaia;* hence, they are not universally useful as indicators of sex as one might wish.

The American biologist IRVING KORNFIELD and his coworkers have unequivocally demonstrated that the Cuatro Cienegas cichlid, *Nandopsis minckleyi* (KORNFIELD and TAYLOR 1983) [Figure 437] is an openly polygynous species with exclusively maternal brood care.

There is some evidence that the Hispaniolan *guapote Nandopsis haitiensis* (TEE-VAN

Fig. 434: The brilliant coloration of this female *Amphilophus festae* is matched only by her aggressiveness.

Fig. 435 & 436: Male (above) and female (below) of the typical, or Nicaraguan, population of *Nandopsis dovii* (Gunther 1864). Such sexual color pattern differences are characteristic of the genus *Nandopsis*.

1935) [Figure 70] is a harem polygynist in nature and its close relative, the Cuban guapote, *Nandopsis tetracanthus* (VALENCIENNES 1831) [Figure 62] will certainly adopt such a mating system if offered the opportunity in captivity.

The remaining representatives of this assemblage of species are monogamous and engage in prolonged biparental defense of their mobile young.

Pair formation is complicated by large adult size and the marked aggressiveness of these cichlids towards conspecifics.

The natural approach is best attempted only if one can raise a group of future breeders to maturity in a community setting.

If only large adults are available, prudence dictates employing one of the alternative methods suggested for handling monogamous cichlids in Chapter 7.

The aquarist who wishes to spawn these cichlids in a naturalistic setting should be aware that in nature, pairs defend territories 3' to 12' square and rarely seem satisfied with less than the minimum value under aquarium conditions.

The prospective breeder who opts for either the separate bedroom or incomplete divider approach should plan on providing these cichlids with a tank of **at least** 50 and **preferably** 75 gallons capacity.

These are extremely prolific cichlids, often producing spawns of several thousand eggs. The resulting fry require plenty of growing room during their first four to six weeks of life. These cichlids are not choosy about where they spawn.

Virtually any solid surface may be chosen to receive the eggs, although the Central American species seem to have a preference for enclosed spawning sites.

The parental behavior of these cichlids is characterized by well-marked role division between the sexes. The male concentrates upon perimeter defense, while the female carries out appropriate hygienic behaviors.

The adults chew the zygotes free of their eggshells 72 hours postspawning at 82 °F, and

Fig. 437: A young male *Nandopsis minckleyi* (Kornfield & Taylor 1983), a polygynous cichlid endemic to the Cuatro Cienegas basin of northern Mexico.

the fry become free-swimming three to four days thereafter.

If not crowded and maintained under a regime of frequent partial water changes, they grow rapidly.

Crowding leads to intense sibling cannibalism in *Nandopsis, Caquetaia* and the more aggressive *Amphilophus* species. This is best avoided, as it may result in a preponderance of males among the survivors.

In the wild, custodial care can persist for up to ten weeks postspawning.

However, in captivity it is prudent to separate parents and fry four to six weeks postspawning to prevent their destruction by their erstwhile protectors as the opening act of a new spawning cycle.

Full reproductive competence by the smaller *Herichthys* and *Amphilophus* species is attained between ten months and a year postspawning.

Petenia splendida, the larger *Amphilophus* species, *Hypselacara, Caquetaia* and *Nandopsis*

may require an additional two to four months to reach the same stage of development.

Despite an impressive inventory of undesirable traits, these robust cichlids enjoy a dedicated — some would even say fanatic! — and steadily growing coterie of partisans.

Guapotes and *mojarras* are certainly not the most easily kept representatives of the family.

They require very large quarters and a substantial input of highly skilled labor simply for ordinary maintenance. They are not easily bred, nor, once they have done so, are their embarrassingly numerous progeny easily disposed of.

Thus they hardly appeal to all cichlid keepers and certainly cannot be recommended to the neophyte.

Yet to their many admirers, the often brilliant coloration and invariably sophisticated behavior of these capital ships of the cichlid fleet more than repay the considerable effort their husbandry entails.

Fig. 438: A male *Amphilophus calobrensis* (Meek & Hildebrand 1913), a substratum-sifting cichlid from Panama.

Central American Eartheaters — Xixies and Xibales

Unlike the previous assemblage, which includes cichlids native to both South and Central America, all the substratum-sifting representatives of the *Heros* lineage occur north of the Isthmus of Panama.

This feeding guild comprises the genus *Thorichthys*, eight *Amphilophus* species and three anomalous *Theraps*.

The larger representatives are referred to by the Mayan speaking peoples of Mexico and Guatemala as *xibales* (singular: *xibal*) [pronounced shi-BAHL-ess], the smaller as *xixies* (singular: *xixi*) [pronounced shi-SHI-ess].

Species of the first two genera provide eloquent witness to extensive adaptive radiation this lineage has undergone during its isolation in Middle America.

The degree of superficial convergence between such of the substratum-sifting *Amphilophus* species as *A. calobrensis* (MEEK

and HILDEBRAND 1913) [Figure 438], *A. altifrons* (KNER and STEINDACHNER 1863) and *A. rostratus* (GILL and BRANSFORD 1877) [Figure 439] and their ecological analogs of the genera *Geophagus* and *Satanoperca* is truly astounding. The only outward characteristic that sets the true eartheaters apart from their Mesoamerican look-alikes is the presence of more than three anal fin spines in the latter [Figure 440].

Closer examination of their branchial anatomy reveals the degree of similarity is less pronounced than it seems.

Despite identical feeding habits, the substratum-sifting *Amphilophus* lack the modified gill rakers and pharyngeal apparatus of their South American counterparts.

Such similarities in gross morphology as snout length and eye placement obviously represent evolutionary convergence driven by the exigencies of a shared feeding pattern.

What many find more extraordinary is that similarities between these distantly related

Fig. 439: Convergent evolution driven by the demands of a common lifestyle account for the similarities between this male *Amphilophus rostratus* (Gill & Bransford 1877) and the eartheaters of the genus *Satanoperca*.

Fig. 440: A young male *Amphilophus robertsoni* (Regan 1905), a species originally imported under the name "Honduras Geophagus". This designation reflects superficial similarities between the true eartheaters and their Mesoamerican *Heros* analogs.

species extend even to details of their coloration.

This incredulity is based upon a failure to appreciate how effectively such iridescent spangling camouflages these cichlids against the brightly-lit, open bottoms over which they forage in nature.

Convergence again explains remarkable superficial similarity, but in this instance the common selection pressure appears to have been avian predation rather than the mechanics of food gathering. The similarities between these Mesoamerican substratum-sifters and the true eartheaters extends to their intolerance of nitrogen cycle by-products.

Much more sensitive to dissolved nitrite and ammonia than the generality of Central American cichlids, they should be managed in the same manner as their South American analogs.

Happily, these fish prosper over a wide range of pH and hardness values.

This considerably simplifies implementing the regime of regular, substantial water changes that is the cornerstone of their successful husbandry.

This is fortunate, for these cichlids have heartier appetites than do the true eartheaters and are messier eaters in the bargain.

Consequently, any approach to managing the nitrogen cycle in their aquaria must cope with the proportionately greater waste load they generate.

Like their ecological counterparts from South America, *Thorichthys* are moderately social animals that appear even as adults to appreciate the company of conspecifics outside periods of sexual activity.

The *xibales* of the genus *Amphilophus* are moderately social as juveniles, but with the exception of *A. longimanus* (GUNTHER 1966) [Figure 441], they grow very intolerant of conspecifics as they mature.

All are more predaceous than the true eartheaters, but are reasonably good neighbors towards non-cichlid tankmates too large to make an easy mouthful. Notwithstanding a tendency to bluster, both *xibales* and *xixies*

360

are easily intimidated by more bellicose cichlids.

The several *Thorichthys* species [Figures 442—445] in particular rely heavily upon threat displays to hold their own in confrontations with other fishes over some limiting resource.

Their effectiveness is enhanced by a remarkable gular crest, produced by the flaring of greatly elaborated, often brilliantly colored branchiostegal membranes. This has the effect of increasing significantly the apparent size of the displaying fish.

As long as their opponents are intimidated by such displays, the efficacy of this approach cannot be faulted. However, if an opponent calls their bluff, the results can prove disastrous, for *Thorichthys* are poorly equipped for serious fighting. It is thus necessary to select their companions with care.

Guapotes and *mojarras,* for example, constitute a poor choice of tankmates for these *Geophagus* analogues.

The mid-sized acaras, on the other hand, get along quite well with them, as do the larger herbivorous representatives of the *Heros* lineage.

Though *Theraps nicaraguensis* (GUNTHER 1864) [Figure 149] is characterized by pronounced sexual color differences, most of these cichlids can be reliably sexed only on the basis of the sort of differences in finnage and adult size noted for the preceding group of species.

All are monogamous, biparentally custodial substratum spawning cichlids. Their modality of parental care also distinguishes them from the true eartheaters, which number many mouthbrooders in their ranks.

These Mesoamerican substratum-sifting species should be treated as recommended for monogamous cichlids in Chapter 7.

The intolerance adult *xibales* display towards conspecifics, even those of the opposite sex, complicates pair formation and makes these cichlids prime candidates for either the separate bedroom or incomplete divider approaches to breeding.

The larger members of this group typically defend a breeding site 3' square, while the

Fig. 441: A male of the Rio San Juan basin population of the rose-breasted cichlid, *Amphilophus longimanus* (Gunther 1869).

Fig. 442: The most popular and widely available Mesoamerican substratum-sifting cichlid, the Yucatecan, or common aquarium strain of the firemouth cichlid, *Thorichthys meeki* (Brind 1918).

Fig. 443: *Thorichthys pasionis* (Rivas 1962) is the largest known representative of its genus.

Fig. 444: A male *Thorichthys aureus* (Gunther 1862). Its specific name notwithstanding, this spectacular cichlid is more pink and blue than gold in coloration.

Fig. 445: Male *Thorichthys ellioti* Meek 1904. Native to southeastern Mexico and northern Guatemala, this species has been widely confused with *T. aureus*, a quite different species from southeastern Belize and Guatemala.

smaller can make do with a domain a third that size.

Theraps nicaraguensis and the several *Thorichthys* species prefer to spawn in caves. The remaining species place their eggs on a solid substratum in the open. Division of parental responsibilities and the developmental interval of the zygotes are the same as for their predatory relatives.

However, the substratum-sifters are less fecund, seldom producing more than 500 eggs per spawning.

Their fry are less given to sibling cannibalism than are those of either *guapotes* or *mojarras*, but respond to crowding with decreased growth and elevated mortality.

With generous feeding and frequent, regular partial water changes, they typically attain sexual maturity between the eighth and tenth month postspawning.

Xibales and *xixies* make excellent additions to a community of medium-sized cichlids. They are colorful and their behavior is every bit as complex and interesting as that of their larger and more notorious relatives.

While admittedly more demanding with respect to maintenance than most Central American cichlids, their considerably mellower dispositions and the ease with which most can be induced to spawn certainly outweigh any inconveniences associated with frequent water changes.

Large Herbivores — Tubas and Correinteras

In contrast to the exclusively Middle American distribution of the substratum-sifting guild, more or less specialized herbivorous species of the *Heros* lineage are to be found in the cichlid faunas of both South and Central America.

Indeed, the genus *Heros* itself is a representative of this trophic guild.

Three genera of herbivorous cichlids are native to South America: *Heros* HECKEL 1840, with two described species, *H. severus* [Figure 446] and *H. appendiculatus* (CASTELNAU 1855) [Figure 447], *Hoplarchus*, with a single species, *H. psittacus* (HECKEL 1840)

Fig. 446: A male of the golden variety of *Heros serverus* Heckel 1840, a catatechnic color strain more widely kept as an ornamental fish than the wild, or green phenotype.

Fig. 447: A wild-caught male *Heros appendiculatus* (Castelnau 1855). This colorful cichlid replaces *H. severus* in the western Amazon basin.

[Figure 141] and *Uaru* HECKEL 1840, with a single described species, *U. amphiacanthoides* HECKEL 1840 [Figure 448] and at least one undescribed species. Middle America offers a more hospitable environment to cichlids with such a feeding pattern, due in all likelihood to the absence of better adapted characoid and loricariid competitors from this region.

The guild's three Central American genera not only boast a greater number of species than their South American analogs but comprise a wider range of morphological diversity in the bargain.

Most of the twenty-four described and half dozen undescribed species of the genus *Theraps* GUNTHER 1862, are robust cichlids with deep, almost spade-shaped bodies, short caudal peduncles, rounded tail fins and relatively small, terminally placed mouths [Figures 23 & 170]. These cichlids are known by their Mosquito Indian name of *tuba* in much of Central America.

Several *Theraps* have adopted a rheophilous life style and feed in larger measure upon algae nipped from rocky surfaces.

Known as *corrienteras* in Mexico and parts of Guatemala, these species sport an elongate body shape, more or less emarginate caudal fins and wide, subterminal mouths strongly reminiscent of the African genera *Labeotropheus* and *Petrochromis* [Figures 43 and 449].

It is presumably from such an ancestral *Theraps* species than the several species of *Paraneetroplus* REGAN 1905 evolved.

Likewise known as *correinteras,* these slender-bodied algal feeders are even more highly adapted for life in fast-flowing water.

Equally at home in large rivers and the Great Lakes of Nicaragua, the monotypic genus *Neetroplus* GUNTHER 1869 is best described as a specialized rock-dweller.

Neetroplus nematopus GUNTHER 1869 [Figure 57] differs from the remaining Mesoamerican cichlids in its incisor-like jaw teeth, strongly reminiscent of the dentition of several algae-scraping genera endemic to Lakes Malawi and Tanganyika.

All the South American and most of the Central American representatives of this guild are large cichlids [Figure 450]. Though

Fig. 448: An adult male *Uaru amphiacanthoides*, sometimes known as the triangle cichlid. This species undergoes dramatic color changes as it grows to maturity.

Fig. 449: The elongated body of this male *Theraps lentigenosum* (Steindachner 1864) is typical of the many rheophilous representatives of this genus.

Fig. 450: A male *Theraps panamensis* (Meek and Hildebrand 1913), one of the smallest and most beautiful representatives of the genus. This species is less markedly herbivorous than most representatives of the group.

considerably less aggressive than most like-sized representatives of the *Heros* lineage, these herbivorous species still require aquaria in the 75 to 125 gallon range to prosper and attain their full potential.

Juvenile and subadult fish are moderately social, but adults are less tolerant of conspecifics.

Pairs are particularly apt to mount a concerted campaign aimed at excluding others of their own species from their territory. They will not extend their harassment of conspecifics beyond its limits.

However, as the group's larger representatives can hold a territory 3' square, a **very** large tank is a prerequisite for long-term coexistence of a group of adults.

These fish are inept predators and make good tankmates for a wide range of other fish species.

Neetroplus are somewhat given to compulsive digging, but most other representatives of this group restrict earthmoving to periods of sexual activity. The representatives of this guild demand the same approach to day-to-day maintenance as their large piscivorous cousins.

While not such messy feeders, they still have healthy appetites and generate a substantial waste load.

As a group, they are warmth-loving and do not relish temperatures lower than 72 °F.

A range of 74 °−80 °F serves well for ordinary maintenance, with an increase to 85 °−88 °F. for breeding.

Their well-being requires a diet containing generous amounts of fresh vegetable matter. Happily, these cichlids are easily satisfied in this respect.

They take a wide range of leafy vegetables and are partial to thinly sliced, blanched zucchini.

Several species are known to be frugivorous in nature.

Theraps synspilus (HUBBS 1935) [Figure 451] and *T. tuba* (MEEK 1912) [Figure 452] have been observed clustered under the overhanging branches of a laden tree in anticipation of falling fruit.

Fig. 451: A male *Theraps synspilus* (Hubbs 1935), one of the most chromatically variable representatives of the subgenus *Theraps*. No two individuals are colored quite alike.

Large captive specimens relish offerings of fresh or dried fruit.

However, the high sugar content of such foods does poses a serious risk of water fouling.

This does not recommend their use in closed aquarium systems.

All representatives of this guild are monogamous, biparentally custodial substratum spawners.

Heros and a few *Theraps* species display notable sexual color differences.

The usual cichlid differences in adult size, cranial profile and fin development are reasonably useful secondary sexual characteristics, but examination of the genital papillae remains the surest means of reliably distinguishing between the sexes in the majority of cases.

Hoplarchus psittacus and both species of *Heros* and *Uaru* prefer to spawn on vertical surfaces.

Theraps, Paraneetroplus and *Neetroplus* are cave or pit spawners.

Youngsters raised to maturity together pair quite easily. Pairing randomly chosen adults with no prior history of cohabitation is a riskier exercise.

If forced to work with two strange adults, it is best to carry out the attempt in a community situation.

The presence of target fish does not always guarantee success.

However, if matters do go badly for the female, she is likely survive long enough under these circumstances to be rescued by her keeper.

If natural pairing proves impossible to bring about, resort to the incomplete divider approach outlined in Chapter 7.

Once formed, pair bonds are quite firm in these cichlids. Large adult size notwithstanding, many of these fish are not particularly fecund.

Spawns in excess of 1000 eggs are rare, the mode falling closer to 500.

Young pairs are more apt to eat their first few spawns than is usual among species of the *Heros* lineage, but with the exercise of a bit of patience, one can count upon them becoming excellent parents.

Fig. 452: *Theraps tuba* (Meek 1912), a robust fruit-eating cichlid native to the Atlantic slope of Costa Rica.

Developmental interval and mode of parental care are as for other representatives of the lineage.

The likelihood that respawning will be followed by the destruction of the older fry is less than usual for substratum spawning cichlids, but it is still prudent to separate parents and fry between four and six weeks postspawning.

The fry should be treated like those of the preceding species assemblages.

These cichlids mature rather slowly. Females may produce their first clutch by the eighth month postspawning, but as a rule, sexual maturity is attained between ten months and a year thereafter.

Nor is it unusual for a pair to require another four to six months before settling down to competent performance of their parental duties.

The spectacular adult coloration of many *Theraps* species develops more slowly than does the ability to spawn, in some cases taking three years to attain its full intensity.

Taken with their large adult size, this is their chief drawback as aquarium residents.

However, aquarists willing to take a chance on a group of nondescript juveniles and exercise sufficient patience to rear them to adulthood invariably find themselves richly repaid for their efforts.

Trophic Generalists — Chanchitos

The representatives of this guild are trophic generalists.

Though they can be described as detritivores with more-or-less well developed herbivorous tendencies, none of these cichlids are averse to including aquatic invertebrates or even smaller fish in their diet.

The *chanchitos* include three South American species.

"Heros" facetus (JENYNS 1842) [Figure 72] is native to the Rio Parana drainage and the coastal rivers of Uruguay and extreme southeastern Brazil.

It is replaced in the coastal rivers of Brazil from Rio de Janeiro northward by *"Heros" autochthon* GUNTHER 1862 [Figure 453] and

369

Fig. 453: A parental male *"Heros" autochthon* Gunther 1862. This robust *chanchito* has been confused with *"H". facetus* in the aquarium literature.

in the Rio Tocantins-Rio Araguaia basin by *"Heros" oblongus* (CASTELNAU 1855) [Figure 454].

North of the Isthmus of Panama the guild is represented by the seven described and two undescribed *chanchitos* of the genus *Archocentrus* REGAN 1905 [Figure 455] and by *Herotilapia* PELLEGRIN 1904, which differs from all other New World cichlids in having tricuspid jaw teeth.

Herotilapia multispinossa (GUNTHER 1866) [Figure 456] feeds heavily upon filamentous algae.

The other members of this group display a marked tendency to root about the bottom as they feed.

This behavior is reflected in their *vernacular* name, *chanchito,* the Spanish word for "piglet"!

The southern distributional boundary of these two Central American genera coincides exactly with the northern range limits of the ecologically analogous *Aequidens coeruleopunctatus.*

This suggests strongly that representatives of this guild, like their substratum-sifting congeners, have evolved to fill a niche occupied to the south by representatives of another cichlid lineage.

In overall appearance, the South American *chanchitos* resemble a scaled-down *Hypselacara,* while *Archocentrus* and *Herotilapia* look very much like one of the deep-bodied *Theraps* seen through the wrong end of a powerful telescope! [Figure 457]

Most *Archocentrus* species show strong sexual dimorphism. Male rarely exceed 4" SL in nature, although they may do so under more benign captive conditions.

Females larger than 2.75" SL are virtually unheard of in nature or in captivity. Indeed, based upon my field observations of breeding pairs, modal length for males is 3" SL, just under 2" SL for females.

These are the smallest known representatives of the *Heros* lineage and the closest Central America has come to producing a dwarf cichlid.

Fig. 454: A sexually quiescent male *"Heros" oblongus* (Castelnau 1855), smallest and most colorful of the South American *chanchitos.*

Fig. 455: A male *Archocentrus centrarchus* (Gill & Bransford 1877), largest and least aggressive of all *Archocentrus* species. Its slight sexual dimorphism is unusual in this subgenus.

Size apart, the most immediately evident distinction between the two genera is the markedly spinier aspect of *Archocentrus.*

Theraps species can have from 15 to 18 dorsal and from 4 to 7 anal in spines, while the range for *Archocentrus* is 17 to 20 spines in the dorsal and 8 to 12 spines in the anal fin.

Indeed, the species of this subgenus and the derivative *Herotilapia multispinossa* have the highest dorsal and anal spine counts of any Neotropical cichlids [Figure 458].

As their size renders them vulnerable to a broad spectrum of predators, ranging from larger cichlids and water snakes through fish-eating birds, their spininess has probably evolved as an anti-predator adaptation.

Chanchitos tend to be feisty towards conspecifics.

However, as *Archocentrus* breeding pairs defend territories only one to two feet square in nature, it is not difficult to satisfy the space requirements of these Central American compact cichlids in captivity.

As males of the South American *chanchitos* can grow to 8" and females to 6" SL, their space requirements are proportionately greater than those of their Mesoamerican counterparts.

Representatives of this trio of species are best handled in the manner suggested for *guapotes* and *mojarras.* All will energetically pursue and eat smaller fish, but the modest adult size of most species makes them safe neighbors for a wide range of non-cichlid tankmates.

Chanchitos are too aggressive to make good companions for such relatively placid cichlids as the smaller acaras, the true eartheaters or even the majority of substratum-sifting *Amphilophus* species.

However, they have no trouble holding their own with the larger herbivorous representatives of the *Heros* lineage and even manage to earn the respect of their robust piscivorous or invertebrate feeding cousins. As their common name implies, these cichlids are bad news for rooted aquatic plants.

Fig. 456: A ripe female of the Norton black-trim variety of *Herotilapia multispinossa,* named after Dr. Joanne Norton, who first recognized and line-bred the original mutant individuals.

Fig. 457: A male *Archocentrus sajica* (Bussing 1974), a morphologically typical representative of the genus native to the Pacific slope of Costa Rica.

All *chanchitos* are hardy, easily fed aquarium residents.

Only *Herotilapia multispinossa* is markedly herbivorous, but in nature all these small cichlids consume a great deal of vegetable matter and should be offered vegetable foods regularly if they are to retain the full intensity of their coloration under aquarium conditions.

Their modest dimensions makes biological filtration a practical approach to keeping dissolved metabolite concentrations at safe levels. However, a penchant for all-season earth-moving renders undergravel filters of marginal utility in their quarters.

That they are more forgiving of brief exposures to high nitrite levels than most cichlids is no excuse for neglecting regular water changes.

Save for *A. nigrofasciatus* [Figure 459], which has colonized upland volcanic lakes in Guatemala and El Salvador, and *"Heros" facetus*, whose range extends southward into the austral temperate zone, these cichlids are inhabitants of lowland tropical biotopes and thus do not appreciate prolonged exposure to temperatures lower than 70 °F. A range of 72 °—78 °F suffices for day-to-day maintenance, with an increase to 82 °—85 °F for breeding.

As noted, male *Archocentrus* grow considerably larger than females. They also tend to develop a nuchal hump with increasing age as well as much longer soft dorsal and anal fins.

Where sexual color differences are present, the **female** is the more colorful sex [Figures 460 & 461].

In the South American *chanchitos* and *Herotilapia*, marked sexual color distinctions are nonexistent and sexual dimorphism is in other respects much less pronounced.

These are without exception easily bred cichlids.

Indeed, given the presence of both sexes in the same tank, it is virtually impossible to prevent them from spawning!

Pairing occurs freely in a community situation, with the interesting wrinkle that the female often initiates and bears most of the burden of courtship!

373

Fig. 458: A spawning pair of *Archocentrus spinossisimus* (Vaillant & Pellegrin 1902). This diminutive *chanchito* comes honestly by its specific name of "spiniest"!

Fig. 459: A ripe female of the Guanacastecan population of *Archocentrus nigrofasciatus*. The convict cichlid's tolerance of cooler water temperatures accounts for its ability to prosper in streams and lakes as high as 1500 meters above sea level.

Fig. 460: This male topaz cichlid, an undescribed *Archocentrus* species from the Atlantic slope rivers of southern Costa Rica and northern Panama grows larger and sports longer dorsal and anal fin extensions than does his mate.

Herotilapia and the South American *chanchitos* prefer vertical spawning sites and display a tendency to hang their wrigglers from the stems and roots of plants just below the water surface. *Archocentrus* prefer to spawn in caves.

Mating system and developmental interval of the zygotes are as for other representatives of the *Heros* lineage.

Archocentrus display the most pronounced parental role differentiation recorded for the lineage during early stages of brood care.

Taken with the pronounced sexual dimorphism of some species, this might suggest a tendency towards a polygynous mating system.

It is not unusual to encounter solitary parental female *Archocentrus* in nature, but there is no way to determine whether they have been widowed or simply abandoned by their mates.

There appears little doubt that survivorship is much higher in broods where both parents actively engage in the protection of the mobile fry.

For its size, *Herotilapia* is a remarkably prolific fish, producing up to 1000 eggs per spawning. The fecundity of the various *Archocentrus* species is more in keeping with their size.

Spawns of 500 eggs have been reported, but 200 is closer to the norm.

Despite their larger adult size, the South American *chanchitos* also produce relatively modest spawns.

The easily raised fry require the same care as those of their larger herbivorous congeners. They are less given to sibling cannibalism than their larger relatives.

Growth is rapid, sexual precocity defining this assemblage of species as effectively as any morphological features.

In the extreme case, the onset of breeding in *A. nigrofasciatus* can occur between 14 and 16 weeks postspawning. Sexual maturity is more typically attained between six and eight months of age.

I must confess a pronounced partiality for all the representatives of this group.

375

Fig. 461: Though smaller than the male, this female topaz cichlid is both more colorful and more aggressive than her consort.

The several *Archocentrus* species and *H. multispinossa* combine the strong points of the larger representatives of the *Heros* lineage with a minimum of their aquaristic drawbacks. All are attractively colored, hardy and easily housed cichlids.

Their behavior is every bit as complex and fascinating as that of their larger relatives.

If not the most easily bred substratum spawning cichlids, they are certainly strong contenders for the title.

I unhesitatingly recommend them to any aquarist, be he neophyte or expert, who wishes the pleasure of witnessing cichlid parental behavior at its most complex and interesting.

The Genera Mesonauta, Pterophyllum and Symphysodon

Representatives of this group are the antithesis of the popular conception of the Family Cichlidae.

They are unaggressive, highly social species that far from molesting aquatic vegetation do best in planted tanks.

No wonder many aquarists refuse to believe the most popular of these laterally compressed species, the angelfish, is a cichlid!

Notwithstanding their unusual body shape and praiseworthy aquarium manners, these are indeed cichlids in good standing.

While their adult morphology does not suggest affinities with the *Heros* lineage, any aquarist who has reared a brood of fry can attest that all three genera pass through developmental stages that unfailingly betray their true relationships.

These cichlids are characteristic inhabitants of still waters, where they school in close proximity to waterlogged brushwood or stands of aquatic plants. Their distinctive morphology allows them to exploit such shelter when threatened by the numerous predators that share their watery home.

All three genera possess attributes that dictate a common maintenance approach.

376

By virtue of their body shape, these are the only cichlids that require extra-tall tanks to look and do their best.

As might be expected of fishes that hail from the greater Amazonian region, they prefer soft, slightly acid to neutral water. It is the higher ambient bacterial counts of hard, alkaline water as much as its chemical properties that these fish find objectionable.

Provided alternative approaches to inhibiting bacterial growth, such as frequent large-scale water changes, are implemented, even discus can live and even breed in moderately hard, somewhat alkaline water. All are **exceedingly** sensitive to dissolved metabolites.

Fortunately, the full potential of biological filtration can be realized in their aquaria, as none is a compulsive digger.

Even the most efficient bioactive filter bed does not obviate the need for frequent partial water changes, however.

Anyone unwilling or unable to practice such a regime should avoid these cichlids, as his experience of these fish is unlikely to be very satisfying.

These fish are inept predators, whose efforts pose minimal risk to fish larger than a female guppy.

They are **extremely** vulnerable to bullying by more aggressive companions; hence, one must exercise great care in the choice of their tankmates.

Dwarf cichlids with the same water chemistry preferences, the less aggressive acaras and the demonfish of the genus *Satanoperca* will coexist amiably with these laterally compressed cichlids.

However, to best prevent harassment, house them exclusively with non-cichlid companions.

The trailing fins of *Pterophyllum* and *Mesonauta* are an irresistible temptation to fin nippers. Companions with such tendencies must obviously be avoided.

These are shy cichlids that require ample cover in their tanks.

Fig. 462: A young male of the aquarium strain of the undescribed Guyanan *Mesonauta* species sold under the erroneous designation of *M. festivus*. Their elongate finnage and distinctive color pattern have earned these cichlids the name *acara bandeira* — flag acara — in Brazil.

Aquascaping their quarters with water-logged wood is both an environmentally appropriate and aesthetically pleasing means of satisfying this requirement.

A layer of floating plants will greatly ease their apprehensions while serving as a useful adjunct to nitrogen cycle management by acting as a nutrient sink. It is not essential to furnish their quarters with live rooted plants, but such aquascaping unquestionably shows these cichlids off to the fullest extent.

Mesonauta GUNTHER 1862 [Figure 462] is the morphologically least specialized member of this trio of genera.

Since the publication of the first edition of this book, KULLANDER and his colleague ANDERS SILFVERGRIP have shown that *Mesonauta,* long believed to be a very widely distributed monotypic genus, actually comprises a number of biologically distinct species, each restricted to a specific region of Amazonia as broadly understood.

Mesonauta insignis (HECKEL 1840), type species of the genus, is restricted to the Rio Negro and the Rio Orinoco drainages.

It is replaced in the Rio Meta drainage of Colombia by *M. egregius* KULLANDER and SILFVERGRIP 1991; in the Peruvian Amazon by *M. mirificus* KULLANDER and SILFVERGRIP 1991 [Figure 463]; in the Rio Madre de Dios in Peru, in the Bolivian tributaries of the Amazon and in the Rio Parana drainage by the true *M. festivus* (HECKEL 1840); and in the Rio Xingu and Rio Toncantins drainages of Brazil by *M. acora* (CASTELNAU 1855). The status of the populations reported from the Essequibo River in Guyana and the Oyapock River in French Guiana has yet to be determined, but given the level of cichlid endemism in the Guianan region, it would not be surprising if they proved to represent undescribed species.

Given prevailing patterns of tropical fish exportation, it is quite likely that the true *M. festivus* has never been in the hobby.

Fig. 463: A wild-caught female *Mesonauta mirificus* Kullander and Silfvergrip 1991 from the Rio Nanay in Peru.

Fig. 464: *Pterophyllum leopoldi* Gosse 1963 is a rarely seen member of the genus. Little is known of its behavior either in nature or under aquarium conditions.

However, this leaves the status of the aquarium populations of *Mesonauta* far from clear.

Specimens exported from Manaus can only be *M. insignis,* while those shipped from Iquitos are obviously referable to *M. mirificus.* However, the range of *M. mirificus* extends as far east as Leticia and Rio Meta cichlids are episodically included in shipments of ornamental fish from Colombia.

This raises the possibility that both *M. mirificus* and *M. egregius* might have been exported from that country as "festivums".

To further complicate the picture, the preeminence enjoyed by Georgetown as a locus of ornamental fish exportation during the 1950's and early 1960's argues that the founder stock of the "domestic festivum" is very likely of Guyanan provenance.

Until this situation is sorted out, aquarists should take pains to ascertain the origin of any "wild festivums" offered for sale and avoid attempting to pair wild fish of different origin or to attempt breeding any wild-caught fish with the established "domestic festivum".

Fortunately for the aquarist, all *Mesonauta* have essentially identical habitat preferences in nature and thus share the same maintenance requirements. These cichlids are found in a wide range of still water habitats, always in close association with either extensive stands of waterlogged brush or mats of floating vegetation.

While often found in the company of angelfish, *Mesonauta* species are considerably more tolerant of stagnant conditions than either *Pterophyllum* or *Symphysodon.*

They can thus colonize habitats whose low dissolved oxygen levels exclude those two genera. These cichlids are thus more forgiving of brief lapses from good management than are either angelfish or discus. They share the group's preference for warmth.

A temperature range of 74°−80°F suffices for ordinary maintenance, with an increase to 82°−85°F for breeding.

These cichlids feed upon aquatic invertebrates and **aufwuchs** browsed from waterlogged wood in nature.

Fig. 465: The silver and black or wild phenotype of the common angelfish, *Pterophyllum scalare*, is without a doubt the most widely kept of all cichlids.

In captivity, the usual live and prepared foods are readily accepted.

Frozen bloodworms and glassworms are a special treat.

Large adult *Mesonauta* are easily sexed. Males of the "domestic festivum", *M. insignis* and *M. mirificus* grow to 7" SL, while females rarely exceed 4" SL.

Their attempt to develop a nuchal hump also gives males a distinctly Roman-nosed appearance.

Young adults are not as readily sexed. The only reliable means is to examine the shape of the genital papilla.

The simplest way to obtain a compatible pair is to raise a group of youngsters to maturity together, an approach facilitated by the marked sociality of this species.

Pairs defend a territory c. 2' square against all intruders. So long as their tank is large enough to allow each its own demesne, one can safely house more than a single breeding pair per aquarium.

The preferred spawning site is a vertical or slightly sloping surface. Failing the availability of a suitable piece of driftwood or a large plant leaf, pairs will deposit eggs on the side of their tank or the tube of its heater. Spawns run from 200 to 700 eggs.

Most hygienic behavior is carried out by the female. Hatching occurs c. 72 hours postspawning at 82 °F.

Their parents move the fry either to another precleaned vertical surface or to a pit previously excavated by the male.

In oxygen-poor environments, the fry are typically placed close to the surface of the water in a manner reminiscent of *Herotilapia multispinosa*.

They become mobile four days later and are cared for like those of other substratum spawning cichlids.

"Domestic festivum" pairs are usually reliable and effective parents.

Rearing the fry poses few problems if their keeper is conscientious about making regular partial water changes.

Adults have been observed defending fry almost 1 " SL in nature, but pairs usually respawn before the fry attain this size in captivity.

"Domestic festivum" pairs tolerate older fry better at this point than other substratum spawners, but there is little point in imposing on their benevolence.

Separating parents and fry about a month postspawning precludes the possibility of a *contretemps*.

The young begin breeding between the tenth and twelfth month postspawning.

The genus *Pterophyllum* HECKEL 1840 comprises three species.

The spectacular *Pterophyllum paltum* PELLEGRIN 1903 [Figure 100], which can measure 13" from the tip of the dorsal fin to that of the anal, is native to the upper Orinoco River basin.

Given the link between the headwaters of the Orinoco and those of the Rio Negro, its occurrence in the latter would not be surprising.

The two remaining species, *Pt. leopoldi* (GOSSE 1963) [Figure 464] occurs in the

Fig. 466: A lovely specimen of the marbled variety of *Pterophyllum scalare*.

eastern Amazon basin, while *Pt. scalare* (LICH-TENSTEIN 1823) is found throughout the Amazon basin and in the coastal rivers of the Guianas.

Both *Pt. altum* and *Pt. leopoldi* are aquaristic rarities.

They are seldom exported, a state of affairs greatly to be regretted in the case of *Pt. altum*. Like other blackwater fishes, the altum angel is very particular about the chemical make-up of its aquarium water.

By contrast, *Pt. scalare* inhabits both whitewater and blackwater habitats and in consequence tolerates a wider range of pH and hardness values in captivity.

All angelfish demand proper nitrogen cycle management to prosper, but *Pt. altum* and *Pt. leopoldi* are somewhat touchier in this regard than their more widely available congener.

The altum angelfish and *Pt. leopoldi* have both infrequently but successfully bred under aquarium conditions.

Pterophyllum scalare, in contrast, is without question the most popular and generally available member of the entire Family Cichlidae.

Both the silver and black banded wild phenotype [Figure 465] and numerous catatechnic, or artificially selected color and finnage varieties [Figures 466—469] are commercially produced and sold by the millions throughout the world.

Unfortunately, most angelfish are purchased by neophyte hobbyists whose ignorance of proper aquarium husbandry dooms the overwhelming majority to a short and not particularly pleasant life.

The usual mistake entails introducing juvenile angelfish to a newly set-up aquarium. As noted, all these laterally compressed cichlids are extremely sensitive to dissolved nitrogenous wastes. They simply cannot cope with the ammonia and nitrite "spikes" that are inevitable during the first few weeks of an aquarium's life.

If novice fishkeepers would only wait a month or so before buying their angelfish, their experiences with this otherwise undemanding cichlid would be less traumatic.

Angels are also very sensitive to dissolved copper.

Fig. 467: A parental female of the smoky color form of *Pterophyllum scalare.*

Naturally soft water attacks new copper piping until a protective layer of copper oxide forms over its surface.

This results in tapwater carrying significant concentrations of Cu^{++}.

Aquarists living in areas where the water supply is extremely soft should, when confronted with otherwise inexplicable angelfish mortality, check for dissolved copper before initiating any course of medication. Workable techniques for removing Cu^{++} from solution are discussed in Chapter 6.

A dedicated angelfish enthusiast can make a strong case for housing these fish with no companions beyond a handful of *Corydoras* catfish.

These cichlids certainly make a magnificent solo display, but there is no practical reason for excluding other fish from their aquarium. Obviously, neither highly aggressive tankmates nor habitual fin-nippers belong in the company of any *Pterophyllum* species.

I would also exclude otherwise harmless fish of a somewhat hyperactive disposition, such as giant danios.

Their constant high speed swimming tends to make angelfish nervous.

Fig. 468: One of the newer color variants of *Pterophyllum scalare*, the German blue.

They are also likely to outcompete their more sedate tankmates at feeding time. This leaves a tremendous selection of compatible angelfish companions. Gouramis of the genera *Colisa* and *Trichogaster* are particularly well suited for this role.

Looking at this question from the opposite perspective, it is imprudent to house angelfish and the smaller characins and cyprinids together unless the latter are intended as live food. As many a novice fish keeper has discovered, angelfish can — and quite regularly do — eat fish as large as an adult neon tetra.

The only cichlids that can be safely housed with angelfish are festivums, discus, keyhole acaras, and most of the South American and West African dwarf species.

Like other representatives of the *Heros* lineage, the several *Pterophyllum* are monogamous biparentally custodial substratum spawners. Only *Pt. scalare* spawns freely under aquarium conditions.

The prospective angelfish breeder's chief problem is obtaining a true pair. Angelfish are not easily sexed.

Large males typically have a more rounded cranial profile than do females.

Apart from this less than convincing effort to produce a nuchal hump, they are somewhat larger than their consorts, and their ventral profile from the origin of the ventrals rearward slopes sharply downwards. In contrast, the female's is almost flat.

These distinctions are virtually useless when dealing with young adults.

Unfortunately, the extreme lateral compression of their bodies obscures the genital papillae sufficiently to render this otherwise reliable indicator of sex quite valueless.

The easiest means of securing a pair is to raise a group of youngsters together and allow nature to take its course. The newly formed pair can then be treated in the manner recommended for substratum spawning cichlids in Chapter 7.

Angelfish territories measure c. 2' square, so in a large tank more than a single pair can successfully set up housekeeping.

Commercial breeders typically house pairs in a 20 gallon high tank. However, remember that to promote rapid respawning, they routinely pull clutches and incubate them artificially.

If one intends to allow the pair to rear their progeny undisturbed, a tank of at least 30 gallons capacity is in order to afford the fry sufficient living space, as spawns numbering 500 eggs are not unusual.

In nature, angelfish select a stout plant leaf as a spawning site.

Not surprisingly, swordplants of the genus *Echinodorus* are often chosen.

Wild-caught angelfish regardless of species have *extremely* specific notions of what constitutes a suitable place for their eggs. They often refuse to spawn on such frequently employed alternatives sites as slate strips or plastic plants.

The aquarium strain of *Pt. scalare* has no such inhibitions.

Pairs will place their eggs on any vertical surface that can be nipped clean.

At 82 °F the pair chews the zygotes out of their eggshells 36 hours postspawning. The wrigglers are initially shifted from one vertical resting place to another, but as they grow more active, their parents often move them to shallow predug pits in the substratum.

Fig. 469: A lovely black lace veil angelfish, one of the long-finned varities of *Pterophyllum scalare*.

The fry first attempt swimming four to five days later, but usually require an additional day and a half to two days to become fully proficient.

Young pairs are apt to eat their first few spawns, but given time, most settle satisfactorily into parenthood.

It is unfortunate so many hobbyists have imbibed the prevalent commercial attitude that angelfish eggs must be incubated artificially if the object is production of young.

In refusing to take a chance on a pairs's reliability, they deprive themselves of an opportunity to witness a truly marvelous demonstration of cichlid parental behavior.

Custodial care can persist up to eight weeks in captivity, but it is prudent to remove the fry from the breeding tank no later than the fourth week postspawning. By this time most pairs show signs of wishing to respawn.

Angelfish fry are not difficult to raise provided every effort is made to keep metabolite concentrations as low as possible. If their fin-nage is to develop to its fullest degree, they must not be crowded during their first months of life. This is particularly true of the so-called veil strain.

With heavy feeding, regular sorting and frequent partial water changes, the young grow quickly.

Under exceptional circumstances, females begin spawning by the eighth month postspawning. In most instances, sexual maturity is attained ten months to a year postspawning.

Note that the numerous catatechnic color forms of *Pt. scalare* do not differ in their management requirements from the ancestral phenotype, and with two exceptions are no more difficult to rear.

The exceptions in question are the albino strain, whose individuals eventually all become blind, and the solid black strain, characterized by higher than normal juvenile mortality between the second and fourth month postspawning and general lack of hardiness as an adult.

Dr. ROBERT J. GOLDSTEIN has suggested this may be due to a diet deficient in the amino acid **phenylalanine**, an essential raw material of both protein and black pigment synthesis.

While this is a plausible hypothesis, I am unaware of any attempts to test it experimentally. The genetics of body color in angelfish are complex and many commercially attractive phenotypes arise from the interaction of both genetic and environmental factors.

A detailed discussion of this subject is beyond the scope of this book. Interested readers are invited to consult relevant works cited in the list of references.

The unquestioned aristocrats of this trio of laterally compressed genera, and to their partisans, of the entire Family Cichlidae, are the two discus fishes of the genus *Symphysodon* HECKEL 1840.

Symphysodon discus [Figure 470], the so-called Heckel or true discus, is native to the Rio Negro, a major tributary of the Amazon in northwestern Brazil.

The second species, *S. aequifasciata* PELLEGRIN 1903 [Figure 5], the banded discus, is more widely distributed in the west central portion of the Amazon basin in Peru, Colombia and Brazil.

Several subspecies of *S. aequifasciata* based upon differences in body color, particularly the amount of metallic blue or green overlay on the head and flanks, have been proposed. These color forms do not have disjunct distributions, a usual attribute of subspecies.

They appear to represent ecophenotypes rather than geographic races, which renders questionable the utility of these subspecific names.

This variability has been exploited by breeders to produce numerous spectacularly colored aquarium strains of *S. aequifasciata* [Figures 471], including a vigorous and attractive albino form.

Apart from the albino strain, these varieties do not breed fully true.

Only a percentage of the fry produced by a given pair eventually develops the intense green, blue or rusty red base coloration of their parents.

This suggests coloration in discus is determined by many independent genes, a factor that greatly complicate efforts by breeders to "fix" a particular color variant.

One sometimes encounters highly colored juvenile banded discus sold as a distinct color form under a variety of often imaginative trade names [Figure 472]. This brilliant reddish brown and blue coloration is brought about through treatment with methyl testosterone. It fades rapidly unless the hormone dosage is continued.

Discus have a well deserved reputation for being difficult to keep.

The secrets of success are **scrupulous** attention to nitrogen cycle management in their aquarium and warmth.

Discus fish should never be kept cooler than 80 °F. A temperature range of 82 °−85 °F is suitable for day to day maintenance, with an increase to 88 °−90 °F for breeding.

Specimens maintained at suboptimum temperatures respond to such stress by becoming dark in color and refusing to eat. Prolonged exposure to these conditions can result in irreversible deterioration of several organ systems and ultimately in death due to one or more stress-induced systemic bacterial infections.

All *Symphysodon* **species are extremely sensitive to dissolved metabolites.**

"Hole-in-the-head" disease is simply a grossly evident response to a polluted environment.

Efficient biological filtration in conjunction with regular, frequent partial water changes is the most effective means of keeping nitrite and nitrate at subcritical levels. Discus also have the reputation of being picky feeders.

Fig. 470:
One need only glance at a mature *Symphysodon discus* to understand the enormous popularity of these Amazonian *Heros* offshoots.

In fact, an individual that will not eat is patently suffering from environmental stress or disease.

When kept under favorable conditions, these cichlids are voracious feeders that greedily take the usually available live and prepared foods.

Before purchasing any discus, insist the seller offer the specimen in question food. If it refuses to eat, it is a poor insurance risk.

Discus are best kept by themselves. It is not that they are too aggressive or predatory to be housed with smaller fish.

To the contrary, they are markedly less predatory than their distant relatives of the genus *Pterophyllum.*

Rather, the temperatures discus find balmy are simply too warm for most ornamental fishes to endure over a lengthy period of time. When kept under such conditions, their lives are appreciably shortened.

The only exceptions that come to mind are the butterfly dwarf cichlid, *Papiliochromis ramirezi,* and the clown loach, *Botia macracantha.*

Discus are almost as social as angelfish and do well when kept in groups.

As a fully grown male can measure 8" SL, discus clearly require large tanks. A 35 gallon extra-tall tank represents the bare minimum for maintaining a single breeding pair, and it would be unrealistic to expect a small group of half a dozen to make do with less than 75 gallons of water. Rooted plants are appreciated but not essential as long as a layer of floating vegetation is present.

Discus are more easily sexed than are angelfish. Males are easily recognized by their more obviously rounded cranial profile, longer ventrals and more pointed soft dorsal and anal fins. These cichlids have the reputation of being difficult to breed in captivity.

In fact, as long as they are maintained in a favorable environment, adults pair up and spawn readily, both in a community setting or when housed by themselves. However, it is quite another matter to obtain fry from such an effort.

Mating system and choice of spawning site are reminiscent of the angelfishes, but spawns are smaller, seldom exceeding 100 eggs.

Hatching occurs 60 hours postspawning at 88' F, and the fry are mobile four and a half to five days thereafter. At this point, modality of parental care deviates sharply from the cichlid norm.

The newly mobile fry ride about on their parents' flanks, where they feed upon a secretion from specialized skin cells.

Grazing upon parental mucus has been documented for other cichlids, among them *Pt. scalare,* but this feeding pattern is obligate in young *Symphysodon* for at least the first week of their mobile existence [Figure 183].

Although the fry begin to take other foods at this point, parental mucus continues to play a significant role in their nutrition for another ten to fourteen days. Indeed, the young will attempt to graze in this manner as long as they are under parental supervision, an interval that can last eight weeks in captivity.

The male, interestingly enough, is the preferred parent at feeding time.

As the fry grow larger, their grazing becomes progressively more irritating to their parents, who respond with efforts to shake their progeny off.

Alternatively, the recipient of their attentions attempt to pass the fry off onto the flanks of its mate.

This sophisticated trophic care represents a major investment of the breeder's available energy reserves, which may well account for the relatively small spawns produced by discus.

Their reproductive strategy, based upon a substantial investment of energy and effort in each of a relatively small number of young precludes production of massive spawns such as those produced by many *Heros*-lineage species of comparable size, whose per capita investment in their progeny is substantially less.

Once the fry have begun to take other foodstuffs, they are no more difficult to rear than angelfish fry.

Again, careful attention to keeping dissolved metabolite concentrations as low as possible is an essential element in their care.

Like angelfish fry, growing discus must not be crowded if they are to achieve optimal body and fin development. Discus are relatively slow to mature. Under ideal conditions, a female may begin spawning between ten and twelve

Fig. 471: A fine specimen of the Wattley blue discus, one of the many catatechnic color forms of *Symphysodon aequifasciata* Pellegrin 1903.

months postspawning. However, it seems to require up to a year longer before such young adults attain sufficient reproductive competence to bring off a successful spawn.

A further year is usually required for adults to attain their full color potential and reach their peak output of eggs.

Regrettably, it may take a dozen tries before a pair manages to integrate all the elements involved in a successful breeding episode and bring fry to the free-swimming stage. The usual response to parental unreliability is to pull the spawn and incubate it artificially.

Matters are not this simple with discus, as one must also furnish the fry with an accept-

able substitute for parental mucus. Several such approaches have been developed by commercial breeders.

All entail rearing the fry in shallow containers and offering them access to a paste of baker's powdered egg yolk for an hour and a half to two hours a minimum of four and preferably five times daily. After each feeding, the fry must be transferred to another container filled with clean water of the same temperature and chemical make-up. This routine is repeated for a week. It is a tedious and time consuming procedure, calculated to inspire a desire to see nature take its course in the most fanatic advocate of artificial fry rearing!

Commercial breeders with several spawning pairs have discovered some pairs compensate for the unreliability of others by developing the piscine equivalent of "broodiness". Just as some hens will attempt to hatch any object placed under them, so these super-parental individuals (usually males) will unhesitatingly tend and nourish other pairs' spawns. I have even seen a "broody" male simultaneously caring for his own progeny and a batch of younger alien fry while fanning yet another spawn taken from an unreliable pair!

Presumably such behavior stems from an imbalance of the hormone regulating both parental response and skin secretion. Given its importance in mediating a wide range of parental behaviors, prolactin is the likely causative agent. This hypothesis could be easily tested.

Should it prove possible to induce appropriate parental behavior by direct administration of this or any other hormone, the implications for commercial production of discus can readily be imagined.

A final difficulty confronting the discus breeder is the refusal of certain males to exercise their essential function after having spawned several times with a given female. In such cases, the male remains a detached observer while the female methodically deposits a clutch of eggs in his absence.

A return to full participation in the spawning sequence usually follows replacement of his former consort with another female.

Many commercial breeders regularly rotate spawning partners to circumvent this behavior.

The underlying cause of this most peculiar abstinence, also reported in *Uaru amphiacanthoides, Heros severus* and *Heros appendiculatus* is unknown.

The alacrity with which males resume their normal function no less than the efficiency of its discharge suggests nothing is amiss with their gonads.

Students of animal behavior have long been aware that male sexual performance in many birds and mammals is enhanced by contextual factors such as the identity of his sexual partner. It would seem that the scope of this so-called "Coolidge effect" must also be extended to include certain cichlid fishes as well!

Their unusual shape, brilliant coloration and intricate parental behavior have invested the members of the genus *Symphysodon* with a mystique quite without parallel in the Family Cichlidae.

The successful discus breeder is regarded with much the same deference by his fellow aquarists as is the pilgrim to Mecca by other Muslims!

Such aquarists are not significantly more knowledgeable than their fellows. They are simply more disciplined in the application of their knowledge to the simple but extremely specific maintenance requirements of these magnificent cichlids.

Discus are certainly not a satisfactory beginner's fish. They are insufficiently forgiving of even slight lapses from good management to qualify for such a role. But given a modicum of experience with other cichlids, anyone with the patience to meet their demands has an excellent chance of success with the undisputed king of aquarium fishes.

Fig. 472: The red coloration of this catatechnic form *S. aequifasciata* owes both its intensity and its precocious appearance to the creative use of methyl testosterone by commercial breeders in the Far East.

CHAPTER 11

CATALOG OF RESIDENTS FOR THE CICHLID AQUARIUM.

DWARF CICHLIDS

Introduction

The cichlids thus far discussed are medium-sized to large fish. However much their requirements may otherwise differ, large tanks are a prerequisite to their successful maintenance. This consideration automatically places them beyond the pale for hobbyists prevented by space limitations from setting up such aquaria in their homes.

With progressively more aquarists living in apartments or condominia where floor space is at a premium, one might fear for the future of cichlids as aquarium residents.

Fortunately, there exist numerous cichlids whose physical proportions and overall behavior predispose them for life in relatively small aquaria. These are the **dwarf cichlids**, a diverse assemblage of species that can be regarded as the family's gift to the modern apartment dweller [Figure 473]. Thus far, I have grouped cichlids either by geographic region or on the basis of their putative evolutionary relationships. The category of dwarf cichlid corresponds to neither criterion.

This assemblage is geographically disparate, combining both African and Neotropical species, and phylogenetically heterogenous,

Fig. 473: A pair of *Apistogramma agassizi* (Steindachner 1874), the first species to which the name "dwarf cichlid" was applied. Such pronounced sexual dimorphism as this is characteristic of the genus.

Fig. 474 & 475: Male (above) and female (below) *Thysochromis ansorgii* (Boulenger 1901). Though males of this West African cichlid can grow to 5" SL, even such large specimens pose a minimal risk to smaller fish.

Fig. 475.

comprising representatives of half a dozen different lineages. It is a strictly operational grouping of species based upon four defining characteristics.

— First, these are small cichlids, not exceeding 3.5" SL. In the case of sexually dimorphic species, I bend the size requirement a bit and accept those in which the smaller sex does not exceed this maximum provided it meets the remaining criteria for inclusion in the group [Figures 474 & 475].

— Second, a single breeding group must be able to complete its life cycle in a 15 to 20 gallon aquarium [Figure 476].

— Third, the behavior of a given species must be such that sexually inactive individuals pose no danger to smaller non-cichlid tankmates [Figure 476].

— Last, the activity of non-reproductive individuals should pose minimal risk to rooted plants.

Note that these behavioral criteria exclude from consideration a number cichlids that might otherwise be considered dwarf cichlids on purely morphological grounds, such as the dwarf mouthbrooders of the genus *Pseudocrenilabrus* [Figure 281], a number of small *Crenicichla* species [Figure 478] and the Central American *chanchitos* of the genus *Archocentrus* [Figures 11, 85 & 458].

It is also worth noting at this point that not all of these diminutive species are inherently less aggressive than their larger relatives.

There is almost as much variability with respect to such behavior within the group as there is within the family as a whole.

It is merely that both aggression and predatory tendencies are infinitely easier to manage when encapsulated in a package no more than 3" SL. The question of adequate living space for dwarf cichlids deserves further elaboration. The minimum space requirement applies to a single pair, or in the case of a polygynous species, a single male and two females.

That these fish will live and breed under such spatial constraints does **not** mean they do

Fig. 476: A male *Julidochromis dickfeldi* Staeck 1975, most recently described of the dwarf *Julidochromis* species. A pair of these diminutive cichlids will prosper in a 15 gallon tank.

Fig. 477: A sexually quiescent male *Laetacara curviceps* (Ahl 1924), collected near Belem, not far from the mouth of the Amazon. The dwarf smiling acaras are among the most innocuous of cichlids.

Fig. 478: Although small enough to be considered a dwarf cichlid on morphological grounds, this male *Crenicichla regani* Ploeg 1989 fails to make the grade behaviorally.

not appreciate or cannot be displayed to advantage in larger quarters. Most dwarf cichlids clearly show themselves to fuller advantage if afforded more living space and not infrequently display a wider range of behaviors when housed in tanks in the 20 to 35 gallon range.

Single pairs of a harem polygynist like *Apistogramma cacatuoides* HOEDEMANN 1951 [Figures 190 & 191] will certainly breed successfully in an appropriately furnished 15 gallon tank.

However, the behavior of both sexes is far more varied and interesting when the fish are maintained as a multi-male group in a 35 gallon tank.

In more spacious surroundings, their keeper will witness the highly ritualized and quite spectacular boundary fighting of territorial males.

He will discover that females defend their individual territories just as fiercely against others of their sex and compete vigorously for

the attention of the male to whose harem they have attached themselves.

With luck, he may even be able to observe "sneaker males" in action and have the opportunity to compare the relative success of these different male reproductive strategies.

The most astute student of fish behavior could not guess at the existence of such complexity on the basis of observations made on an isolated pair or trio.

Basic Husbandry Requirements

As will shortly become evident, dwarf cichlids are, despite the group's stringent definition, a remarkably heterogenous assemblage of species.

Surprisingly, they do share a number of common husbandry requirements. These can be aptly characterized as non-negotiable demands made by these cichlids on their keeper.

Fig. 479: The preferred pH range of dwarf cichlids endemic to Lake Tanganyika, such as this male *Lamprologus wauthioni* (Poll 1949) puts them at risk of ammonia poisoning if the nitrogen cycle is mismanaged in their tank.

The prospective dwarf cichlid breeder should take them very much to heart before setting out to acquire any of these fish.

If any are beyond his ability to meet, I advise him to turn his attention elsewhere. Dwarf cichlids do **not** tolerate indifferent maintenance and the aquarist who ignores this caveat will find his experience of the group to be both brief and unsatisfactory.

The first requirement of successful dwarf cichlid husbandry is **careful attention to the management of the nitrogen cycle** in their tanks.

Chronic exposure even to low dissolved nitrite levels is extremely stressful to dwarf cichlids.

Brief exposure to elevated levels can quickly prove fatal.

To further complicate matters, the water conditions Tanganyikan dwarfs require to prosper are sufficiently alkaline to make ammonia poisoning a real threat to their well-being [Figure 479]. This being the case, dwarf cichlids should **never** be introduced to a tank that lacks a fully run-in biological filter. Dwarf cichlids are also significantly less tolerant of high nitrate levels than are many other ornamental fish.

Long-term exposure to levels in excess of 100.0 ppm often results in a pattern of asymptomatic mortalities, particularly among fry and subadult individuals. Lower concentrations can inhibit both reproductive activity and fry growth.

Because they generate a very modest waste load in comparison with their larger relatives, it is a relatively simple matter to establish a fully functional biological filter in a dwarf cichlid tank. Any of the filter options discussed in Chapter 3 can be expected to keep ammonia and nitrite concentrations at satisfactory levels.

The problem of nitrate buildup may prove a bit more difficult to manage. The easiest solution is a program of regular, small-scale water changes — replacing c. 10% of the volume of a lightly stocked dwarf cichlid tank weekly will keep most species healthy and stimulate breeding.

However, this option may not be practical if water from the tap has a chemical make-up harmful to the intended beneficiaries of the water change.

The varied origins of these fish are reflected in their quite different pH and hardness requirements. West African and Neotropical dwarf cichlids require neutral to somewhat

Fig. 480:
The butterfly dwarf cichlid, *Papiliochromis ramirezi*, one of the few dwarf cichlids that appreciates extremely warm water.

Fig. 481 & 482: Male (below) and parental female (above) *Laetacara dorsiger* (Heckel 1840). Like other cichlids from the Rio Parana basin, this species can tolerate brief exposure to temperatures as low as 60° F.

Fig. 482

acidic, moderately to very soft water to prosper.

Tanganyikan dwarfs must be treated in the same manner as any other representative of that lacustrine fauna.

If the disparity between the chemical make-up of the local water supply and that demanded by a given species is great enough, it may very well be worth the effort to stretch out the interval between water changes through the use of other techniques. The most immediately obvious of these is the use of chemically active filter media.

Either a sponge filter mated to an outside power filter or a canister filter can provide efficient biological filtration while accommodating such media.

Bear in mind that chemically active media have a finite capacity to remove dissolved wastes. It is therefore necessary to monitor dissolved metabolite levels closely to determine how well they are performing in a given system.

One can also use growing plants as a nutrient sink.

Fast-growing floating plants such as water sprite serve this purpose admirably, but the toleration dwarf cichlids show towards rooted plants opens the door to a very broad range of possible candidates for such a role.

Given the replacement costs of chemically active filter media, the green alternative may seem the most economical approach to keeping nitrate levels down. However, only growing plants take up nutrients, and plant growth is driven by light.

The output of fluorescent tubes degrades quite rapidly.

Such changes are not usually directly obvious to the human eye, but their effects on plant health are very easily spotted indeed.

It is thus prudent to compare the cost of replacing fluorescent tubes at six month intervals with that of replacing chemically active filter media on a comparable schedule before taking any decision in this regard.

Next, dwarf cichlids do not appreciate abrupt temperature changes. A reliable thermostatically controlled heater is an essential element of their tank furnishings.

Fig. 483: Male *Anomalochromis thomasi,* the only dwarf representative of its genus. Most jewelfish are highly predatory, but this species will not molest even newly dropped livebearer fry.

Fig. 484: Like their look-alike relatives in the genus *Julidochromis*, these *Telmatochromis bifrenatus* Myers 1936 appreciate a tank that offers them a multitude of small caves. These serve as both hiding places and spawning sites.

This said, the temperature preferences of individual species reflect the group's diversity.

Neotropical dwarf cichlids, with the unique exception of *Papiliochromis ramirezi*, (MYERS and HARRY 1948) [Figure 480] and the several *Dicrossus* species do best over a temperature range of 72°–75°F for normal maintenance, with an increase to 78°- 82°F for breeding.

The ram is a warm water species that does not appreciate temperatures lower than 78°F and spawns most freely at 85°–88°F.

At the other end of the scale, dwarf cichlids native to the Rio Parana basin, such as *Apistogramma borellii* (REGAN 1906) [Figure 18] and *Laetacara dorsiger* (HECKEL 1840) [Figures 481 & 482] are quite cold resistant and can withstand temperatures as low as 60°F for brief periods of time.

West African dwarf cichlids prefer somewhat warmer temperatures, 74°–80°F for daily living, 82°-85°F for spawning [Figures 157, 483]. The Tanganyikan dwarf species have the same thermal preferences as their larger lacustrine compatriots, whose extreme aversion to abrupt temperature drops they fully share.

The third requirement shared by all dwarf cichlids is a tank well furnished with cover. These small fish simply do not feel secure in the absence of potential shelter.

This is hardly surprising given the levels of predation by larger fish, water snakes and birds to which they are exposed in nature.

A layer of floating plants should be an essential adjunct to the furnishings of any dwarf cichlid aquarium. Rooted plants are less critical in this regard.

However, most West African and Neotropical species appreciate their presence and they contribute significantly to the aesthetic impact of their quarters.

Furthermore, their utility in nitrogen cycle management can also be considerable. There is thus much to be said for their use in aquascaping a dwarf cichlid aquarium.

Fast-growing bunch plants such as the various *Hygrophila* and warm-water *Cabomba*

Fig. 485: A pair of *Lamprologus calliurus* Boulenger 1906. Like most ostracophil *Lamprologus*, it equates "shelter" with "shell"!

species are easy to culture and make the best nutrient sinks.

However, they require intense light to prosper and may not do well under a substantial layer of floating plants. Furthermore, if they find conditions to their liking, they grow so rapidly as to require constant pruning and replanting.

The several *Anubias* species and Java fern will prosper in the partial shade afforded by floating plants, as their lighting requirements are less exacting than those of most aquatic plants.

However, they grow quite slowly, a fact which limits their ability to soak up nutrients. Nevertheless, if low maintenance requirements are an important consideration, they are probably the rooted plants of choice for a dwarf cichlid tank.

Most dwarfs employ caves or similarly enclosed spaces, such as provided by rolled-up fallen leaves, both as shelters and as spawning sites [Figure 484].

Apart from the dwarf **ostracophil**, or shell-dwelling *Lamprologus* species from Lake

Tanganyika, whose idea of what constitutes an acceptable dwelling are quite inflexible [Figure 485], these cichlids accept a wide range of potential shelters in captivity.

Even the ostracophil species will move into any empty shell that reasonably approximates the proportions of the empty *Neothauma* shells with which they are invariably associated in nature.

A few minutes' worth of sorting through the empty sea shells most retail pet stores stock as "hermit crab houses" suffices to turn up an abundance of acceptable shelters for these Tanganyikan dwarfs.

Small clay flowerpots provide a convenient, readily accepted and economical option for most other species. They can either be placed on their sides or turned upside down. In the latter case, it may prove necessary to enlarge the drainage hole sufficiently to afford the fish ready access to the interior.

Many aquarists find empty coconut shells furnished with appropriate entry holes an aesthetically superior alternative to clay flowerpots.

Their intended beneficiaries seem equally comfortable with both types of shelter.

These fish appreciate a choice of hiding places or spawning sites.

It is therefore prudent to always add a few more shelters to a tank than the total number of dwarfs present.

To conclude this discussion of their maintenance requirements, be it noted that contrary to widely-held belief, dwarf cichlids can — and in most instances quite readily do — take other than live foods at mealtime.

Flake and pelletized foods of appropriate size, as well as a wide selection of fresh frozen items are eagerly taken.

However, these diminutive cichlids spawn both more readily and frequently and produce larger clutches when at least half of their diet consists of live food.

Daphnia, mosquito larvae and glassworms are particularly relished, but all of the generally available live foods save *Tubifex* are satisfactory additions to the dwarf cichlid menu.

Artemia nauplii are easily hatched in quantity and much appreciated by adult dwarf cichlids as well as their fry. Like all small fish, these cichlids do best given three or four light feedings daily.

Companions for Dwarf Cichlids

A defining feature of dwarf cichlids is their ability to live peacefully with a wide range of non-cichlid companions.

Indeed, one could make the case that most species actually do better in a community setting than when kept by themselves, for small, midwater-dwelling tankmates effectively function as dither fish for the dwarfs.

As all will spawn readily in their absence, dither fish are clearly not essential to the well-being of dwarf cichlids in captivity. However, their keeper will see a great deal more of his prized pets if they are present.

Fig. 486 & 487: Male (above) and female (next page) *Apistogramma nijsseni*, one of the more assertive Neotropical dwarf cichlid species.

Fig. 487

Dwarf cichlids use the behavior of schooling fish as an indicator of the security of their immediate surroundings. Thus a school of small tetras or danios is just the ticket to bring shy dwarfs out of hiding.

Suitable dither fish must share the pH and hardness preferences of their cichlid tankmates. Characoid fishes are the obvious dither fish of choice for Neotropical and West African dwarf cichlids, as with a bit of effort one can house in the same tank species that live together in nature.

However, considerations of biogeographic authenticity aside, there is no reason why such Asian cyprinids as *Brachydanio, Rasbora* and the smaller, less boisterous *Barbus* species cannot be employed in this capacity.

Although there are a number of livebearer species that will also prosper in the company of these riverine species, the preference shown by most poeciliids for hard water makes them a better choice of dither for Tanganyikan dwarf cichlids.

Many of the smaller Australasian rainbowfishes will also prosper in the company of these hard water dwarfs.

Behavioral considerations are of equal importance in the selection of appropriate dither fish. Large, fast-moving species such as the Buenos Aires tetra, *Hemigrammus caudovittatus,* the giant danio, *Danio aequipinnatus,* or the red New Guinea rainbowfish, *Glossolepis incissus,* are unlikely to pose a direct threat to the well-being of any dwarf cichlids with which they are housed.

However, they are both fast and assertive enough to outcompete many species at feeding time and may pose an unmanageable threat to their free-swimming fry in the bargain.

Indeed, they may well intimidate the cichlids sufficiently to function as anti-dither! The unchecked fecundity of poeciliids can also lead to problems.

Many dwarf cichlids are inept predators, whose activities are unlikely to arrest the livebearers' rapid rate of natural increase [Figures 157, 480, 483].

Failing human intervention, the cichlids in such a situation run a serious risk of being crowded out by the dither fish.

With few exceptions, such as angelfish and some of the mellower acaras, larger cichlids do not make good companions for their dwarf relatives.

Their greater size simply gives them too great an advantage in any conflicts over living space or food that might develop. A permissible exception to this rule are the ostracophil *Lamprologus* species.

Equipped with teeth that would not seem out of place in a fish thrice their size, they are quite capable of teaching manners to much larger cichlids.

It is also unwise to house dwarf cichlids with other bottom-living fishes that are extremely protective of a shelter, such as loaches of the genus *Botia* or upsidedown catfishes of the genus *Synodontis*.

Conflict over the tenancy of a given refuge can easily escalate into serious fighting, whose outcome may not always favor the cichlids.

Neither, in my experience, should one automatically assume that all dwarf cichlids can be safely housed together. The diversity of this group extends to differences in aggressiveness.

At one extreme are such totally inoffensive species as *Dicrossus filamentosus* (LADIGES 1959) [Figure 94], whose lack of aggressiveness leads one to wonder how they survive in nature.

At the other are more assertive species, such as *Apistogramma nijsseni* KULLANDER 1979 [Figures 486 & 487], whose temperament leaves an observer with no doubts whatsoever about their ability to cope with the challenges of life in the wild!

Even species of the same genus can differ markedly in aggressiveness. When two such species are housed together, their similar requirements for living space and spawning sites make continual conflict inevitable, to the detriment of the less assertive of the two contestants.

If one wishes to try putting together a dwarf cichlid community, likelihood of conflict diminishes considerably if species with dissimilar spawning site preferences, such as *Anomalochromis thomasi* (BOULENGER 1916) [Figure 488] and *Pelvicachromis kribensis*

Fig. 488: As the behavior of this spawning female clearly demonstrates, *Anomalochromis thomasi* is not a cave spawner!

(BOULENGER 1901) [Figure 489] share the same tank.

Finally, it is essential to choose the scavengers for a dwarf cichlid tank carefully.

As already noted, the territorial behavior of some catfish and loach species is an invitation to conflict when they are expected to share the same tank with cichlids of comparable size.

Of equal importance is the intolerance some dwarf cichlids display towards catfish either prior to spawning or when defending their eggs or fry.

The golden-eye dwarf cichlid, *Nannacara anomala* (REGAN 1905) [Figure 490], is perhaps unique in adopting the preemptive strike as a response to the threat of catfish predation on its eggs or fry, but extreme intolerance towards scavengers is not that unusual among parental dwarf cichlids.

Possibly because depositing their clutch in the open complicates its defense, those monogamous dwarf cichlids that choose such spawning sites seem most inclined to make life difficult for bottom-feeding tankmates at this time.

Even otherwise mellow species such as *Laetacara curviceps* (AHL 1924) seem to undergo a real Jekyll to Hyde personality

Fig. 489: Cave spawners like this pair of *Pelvicachromis kribensis* (Boulenger 1901) do not compete for spawning sites with species that deposit their eggs in the open. This Cameroonian species is quite different from the Nigerian *Pv. pulcher*, with which it has been long confused.

Fig. 490: A male *Nannacara anomala*, perhaps the most easily bred Neotropical dwarf cichlid. Pairs behave very aggressively towards catfish prior to spawning.

switch when confronted with a perceived threat to their young.

It must be said in their defense that in nature, such behavior, which seeks to drive catfish as far away as possible from the pair's breeding site, is highly adaptive.

Cichlids are visually oriented animals and as such, are almost totally helpless at night. This renders them particularly vulnerable to the depredations of nocturnal predators such as catfishes, which rely upon chemical rather than visual clues to locate their prey.

It is the inability of the harassed catfish to move beyond the reach of its attacker(s) that leads to fatalities under aquarium conditions.

Small callichthyid catfish such as *Corydoras* and *Aspidoras* are particularly vulnerable to the attacks of irate dwarf cichlids.

While most species lack the size to pose a lethal threat to the family's more robust representatives, they can still make their lives thoroughly miserable. Very lightly armored loricariid catfishes, such as *Otocinclus, Paroto-*

cinclus and some of the smaller *Rhineloricaria* species are comparably vulnerable to such persecution.

These catfishes do not have any place in a dwarf cichlid breeding tank.

Neither, albeit for different reasons, do the more robust loricariid catfishes such as *Hypostomus, Pterygoplichthys* or *Panaque*. These fish are so large and heavily armored that they can simply ignore any efforts the cichlids might make to protect their progeny.

Its small size, nocturnal pattern of activity and burrowing habits make the Malaysian livebearing snail close to ideal as a scavenger in a dwarf cichlid aquarium.

Aquarists partial to catfish in this role will find two genera of small to mid-sized loricariid catfishes particularly appropriate choices.

Both the bristlenosed catfishes of the genus *Ancistrus* and the clown plecos of the genus *Peckoltia* are sufficiently robust to be able to shrug off casual harassment but not so large as to be immune to strongly motivated coercion.

403

Reproductive Modalities and Mating Systems of Selected Dwarf Cichlids		
	Mating System	
Reproductive Modality	Monogamy	Harem Polygyny
Substratum Spawners	*Anomalochromis thomasi* *Tilapia* spp. *Laetacara* spp. *Papiliochromis* spp.	*Dicrossus* spp.
Switch Spawners	*Thysochromis ansorgii*	*Nannacara* spp.
Cave Spawners	*Lamprologus* — ostracophil spp.[1] *Telmatochromis* spp. *Julidochromis* spp. *Pelvicachromis* spp. *Nanochromis* spp.[1] *Parananochromis* spp.	*Limbochromis* spp. *Crenicara* spp. *Apistogramma* spp.
	Apistogrammoides *pucallapaensis*[1]	*Taeniacara* *candidae* *Biotoecus* *opercularis*
Advanced Mouthbrooders	*Eretmodus cyanostictus* *Spathodus erythrodon* *Tanganicodus irsacae*	

[1] The mating system of these species is plastic. Older, large males spawn polygynously when the operative sex ratio favors females.

Breeding Dwarf Cichlids

Dwarf cichlid diversity precludes any attempt to set out a general model of their reproductive biology, though apart from the Tanganyikan goby cichlids [Figure 491], none of the species considered herein are mouthbrooders.

Refer to the accompanying table for relevant information on the species treated herein.

The tabular arrangement employed herein groups these fish by mating system.

Once the aquarist knows to which group a given dwarf cichlids belongs, he can apply the apposite suggestions given in Chapter 7 to the problem of encouraging a successful spawning.

Haremically polygynous species are numerically dominant among Neotropical dwarf cichlids, due in large measure to the speciose nature of the genus *Apistogramma*.

However, the group also includes a number of monogamous representatives.

Among African dwarf cichlids, to the contrary, monogamy appears to be the norm, harem polygyny the exceptional condition.

It should be again emphasized that the distinction between monogamy and polygamy is not always as hard and fast as it might seem.

Monogamous pairing seems to be a developmental stage through which young males of several otherwise markedly polygynous *Apistogramma* species pass prior to attaining their full growth.

In the case of such *Nanochromis* species as *N. parilius* ROBERTS and STEWART 1976, mating system seems largely determined by the operative sex ratio.

Where females outnumber males, harem polygyny is the rule, but when the sex ratio is unity, males are capable of functioning effectively as monogamous consorts.

This behavioral plasticity accounts for the relative ease with which polygynous dwarf cichlids can be maintained and bred as pairs in captivity.

Regardless of their mating system, dwarf cichlids have a reputation for parental unreliability. Parental fish do often require several tries before they integrate all of the elements entailed in pulling off a successful spawning [Figures 492 & 493]. This may be due to the fact that like most cichlids, these species begin maturing gametes at a much earlier age in captivity than in nature. As a rule, nothing more is required than the exercise of a little patience to set matters right.

The presence of dither/target fish often seems to elicit parental behavior from previously indifferent or incompetent pairs or females [Figures 494 & 495]. However, take care not to choose species too large or active to be deterred from their attacks on the fry by the parental fish or fishes.

Leaving the tank lights on 24 hours a day until the fry have been free-swimming for a week also often works to inhibit parental cannibalism.

The most consistent problem the prospective dwarf cichlid breeder is likely to encounter stems from the female tendency to ripen a new batch of eggs well before her previous brood has attained independence.

The fate of the older fry at this juncture varies dramatically between species.

At one extreme, parental pairs of *Anomalochromis thomasi* (BOULENGER 1916) and *Tilapia ruweti* POLL and THYS 1965 [Figure 496] simply cannibalize their previous brood. At the other, one encounters the complete tolerance of the dwarf *Julidochromis* and many ostracophil *Lamprologus* species for older young, which can lead to half a dozen cohorts of fry coexisting amiably within the parental territory [Figure 497]. Somewhere in between is the female tendency to involve herself with the new spawn while her consort continues to protect the older fry.

Such behavior is best developed in the several *Pelvicachromis* species but can be seen to a lesser extent in *Nannacara anomala* and many *Apistogramma* and ostracophil *Lamprologus* species.

Regardless of the behavioral idiosyncracies of their parent(s), the only way to guarantee a given breeding effort will yield fry is to separate them from their guardian or guardians two or three weeks after they have become free-swimming.

Dwarf cichlid fry are exceedingly sensitive to dissolved metabolites.

Great care must be taken to avoid fouling their water through accidental overfeeding. A program of regular, frequent partial water changes is **absolutely essential** to their successful rearing.

Fig. 491: *Tanganicodus irsacae* Poll 1950, a goby cichlid from Lake Tanganyika. These droll dwarf cichlids are the group's only mouthbrooding representatives.

405

Fig. 492 & 493: Male (above) and female (below) *Apistogramma steindachneri* (Regan 1908). Females of even this easily bred dwarf cichlid may devour their first few clutches before settling down to competent parenthood.

Fig. 494 & 495: Parental male (above) and ripe female (below) *Pelvicachromis taeniatus* (Boulenger 1901). Pairs of this species often prove more reliable parents when housed with appropriate dither/target fish.

Fig. 496: Courting male *Tilapia ruweti*. Like many cichlids, this species will not tolerate the presence of older fry in their territory after they have respawned.

Fig. 497: Male *Julidochromis transcriptus* Matthes 1959. These Tanganyikan dwarf cichlids are remarkable for their tolerance of older fry in the vicinity of younger offspring.

Fig. 498: Displaying male *Apistogramma bitaeniata* Pellegrin 1936. Males of this species attain reproductive maturity long before the full elaboration of their distinctive secondary sexual characteristics.

This aside, they are no more difficult to raise than other cichlid fry.

With the exceptions of the Tanganyikan *Julidochromis* and *Telmatochromis* species, these are fairly fast growing cichlids, attaining sexual maturity between six and eight months postspawning.

Males of strongly sexually dimorphic dwarf cichlids, such as the many *Apistogramma* species, often do not attain the fullest elaboration of their finnage or coloration until well after the onset of reproductive activity [Figure 498].

The Major Groups of Dwarf Cichlids

Lake Tanganyika Dwarf Cichlids

Dwarf representatives can be found in two of Lake Tanganyika's numerous cichlid lineages. Three lamprologine genera, *Lamprologus*, *Telmatochromis* and *Julidochromis*, have species that fit the operational definition of the group presented in the **Introduction.**

By far the most familiar of these are the three dwarf *Julidochromis* species.

This familiarity arises in part from a rather long history in the hobby — *Julidochromis ornatus* BOULENGER 1898 [Figure 101] was one of the cichlids exported from Lake Tanganyika when the late PIERRE BRICHARD made his first effort to establish a collecting station on its shores in the early 1960s.

However, the equal popularity enjoyed by the much more recently imported *J. transcriptus* MATTHES 1959 and *J. dickfeldi* STAECK 1975 suggest that the bold coloration of these diminutive petricolous cichlids is the real basis of their continuing popularity and general availability. Their vulnerability to predation when away from cover severely limits the mobility of these cichlids in nature.

Each of these three species thus exists as a series of more or less isolated local populations that can differ significantly in coloration, a state of affairs as agreeable to the aquarist as it is instructive to the student of evolutionary processes.

409

The three dwarf julies differ only in size from their more robust congeners and should be managed in the same manner. Notwithstanding their small adult size, pairs share the intolerance of other monogamous lamprologines for the proximity of conspecifics. Failure to appreciate this fact can lead to unnecessary mortalities if pair formation is allowed to occur in a group setting.

The genus *Telmatochromis* boasts three described and a number of undescribed dwarf species. Although they are colorful, easily bred dwarf cichlids, none of the dwarf *Telmatochromis* has to date succeeded in gaining either the degree of popularity or the commercial success enjoyed by the dwarf julies.

Telmatochromis vittatus BOULENGER 1898 and *T. bifrentatus* MYERS 1936 are diminutive laterally banded rock-dwelling cichlids that enjoy a wide distribution within the lake.

Unlike the dwarf julies, these cichlids are notably uniform in appearance throughout the lake.

This suggests a greater degree of gene flow between populations, a possible consequence of the tendency of both *T. vittatus* and *T. bifrentatus* to opportunistically exploit the shelter offered by empty snail shells. This makes it much easier for individuals to cross open, sandy bottoms.

The third described member of this trio, *T. burgeoni* POLL 1942, is an obligate associate of empty snail shells, as are two undescribed species.

Like the numerous ostracophil *Lamprologus* species, these shell-dwelling *Telmatochromis* live over open, sandy bottoms. Although most species are monogamous, the dwarf *Telmatochromis* are more strongly social than their counterparts of the genus *Julidochromis* and can be maintained in small groups under aquarium conditions with minimal risk of serious fighting.

Although close to two dozen *Lamprologus* species are known to use empty snail shells as spawning sites in nature, far fewer are obligate ostracophils.

These small, zooplankton feeding cichlids are found over open sandy bottoms.

Given the intensity of predation pressure in Lake Tanganyika, their survival is absolutely contingent upon continual access to such shelter.

Nine described and a number of undescribed representatives of this guild can be characterized accurately as dwarf cichlids.

All must be provided with empty snail shells if they are to prosper in captivity, but happily, any shell of roughly the same size and shape as those available to them in nature will suffice in captivity.

The assorted sea shells sold as "land hermit crab houses" in many pet shops are perfectly acceptable substitutes for those of Tanganyikan *Neothauma*.

Ostracophil *Lamprologus* differ with regard to both the manner in which they make use of empty shells and their mating system.

The species to date imported are classified with regard to behavioral characteristics in the accompanying table.

The species that bury their shells and dig a "patio" in front of its entrance, such as *L. brevis* [Figure 161], *L. ocellatus* [Figure 97], and *L. ornatipinnis* [Figure 499] should be kept over fine sand bottoms.

Coarser substrata may represent a major obstacle to the expression of this extremely interesting behavior.

The degree of sociality displayed by these dwarf *Lamprologus* varies markedly between species.

Fig. 499: A female *Lamprologus ornatipinnis* Poll 1949. In nature, this dwarf ostracophil cichlid carefully buries the shell it has selected as a shelter.

Fig. 500: As the behavior of these two male *Lamprologus* cf. *signatus* clearly demonstrates, this shell-dwelling species is clearly very intolerant of the close presence of conspecifics of the same sex.

The females of most polygynous species are quite tolerant of one another's presence and will often push their shells together to form a sort of lamprologine condominium, lorded over by the resident male.

The monogamous species, such as *L. signatus* POLL 1952 [Figure 500], are markedly territorial and very intolerant of conspecifics.

However, some of the smaller representatives of the group, such as *L. multifasciatus* BOULENGER 1906 [Figure 517] are highly social.

Pairs will clump their shells together almost as tightly as do the females of a polygynous species such as *L. calliurus* BOULENGER 1906 [Figure 485].

Prospective buyers are thus strongly advised to do their homework **before** introducing any of these diminutive but well-armed cichlids into his tanks.

On balance, these are easily bred dwarf cichlids. The problem is often knowing when they have spawned. By comparison with that of most of the other dwarf cichlids, the courtship behavior of these three genera of lamprologines is much less overt and can be easily misinterpreted or even overlooked by an inexperienced aquarist.

Nor do parental adults undergo a dramatic change in coloration.

The sudden appearance of fry darting across their parent's territory is often a novice breeder's first indication that spawning has occurred.

A female's reluctance to come into the open for more than a quick bite of food should alert her keeper to watch for fry four to seven days later.

Spawnings are easier to detect in those ostracophil *Lamprologus* species in which the female protects her clutch by closing the entrance of the shell employed as a spawning site with her body.

Apart from their eyes, the fry of these species are almost totally devoid of pigment for the first two weeks of their lives.

Mating System and Pattern of Shelter Construction in the Dwarf Ostracophil *Lamprologus*		
	Mating System	
Mode of Shelter Construction	**Monogamy**	**Harem Polygyny**
Buries shell	*L. brevis* BOULENGER 1899 *L. boulengeri* STEINDACHNER 1909 *L. multifasciatus* BOULENGER 1906 *L. signatus* POLL 1952 *Lamprologus* sp. "orange cap"	*L. ocellatus* STEINDACHNER 1901 *L. cf. ornatipinnis*
Shell exposed		*L. calliurus* BOULENGER 1906 *L. hecqui* BOULENGER 1899 *L. wauthioni* POLL 1949

This makes spotting them something of a challenge even when their presence has been advertised by their mother's behavior. As long as the adult fish are offered newly hatched brine shrimp on a regular basis, this should not pose any serious problem.

If *Artemia* nauplii are not regularly featured on their menu, it is prudent to begin feeding them as soon as a female evinces a reluctance to spend more than a few moments away from her shelter.

With good feeding and proper attention to water quality, the fry are easily reared.

Ostracophil *Lamprologus* can usually be sexed on the basis of difference in size between four and six months postspawning, but as a rule, it takes another four or five months for them to attain sexual maturity.

The dwarf julies and *Telmatochromis* species are less easily sexed and slower to mature. Male *Telmatochromis* are usually larger than females of the same age and may have slightly longer soft dorsal and anal fins, while the most reliable external indicator of sex in *Julidochromis* species is the male's conspicuous, somewhat penile genital papilla.

Dwarf *Telmatochromis* may begin breeding as early as ten months postspawning, but julies usually wait until they are a year old before starting a reproductive career that can last over a decade.

With the marginal exception of the robust *Spathodus marlieri* POLL 1950, which can grow to 4" SL in captivity, the Tanganyikan goby cichlids can be considered dwarf species. These fish stand as one of the most remarkable examples of cichlid evolutionary plasticity.

Eretmodus cyanostictus BOULENGER 1898 [Figure 47] uses its spatula-shaped teeth to graze algae from rocky surfaces.

Tanganicodus irsacae POLL 1950 [Figure 491] uses its tweezer-like anterior jaw teeth to pick invertebrates selectively from the bottom.

The two species of the genus *Spathodus* BOULENGER 1900 fall midway between these two dietary extremes.

Numerous Tanganyikan cichlids are characterized by anatomical and behavioral modifications that allow them to make a living in ways unknown to the family's riverine representatives.

Nevertheless, however aberrant their life styles may be, these fish are, at least superficially, clearly recognizable cichlids. However, neither the overall appearance nor the behavior of the four species grouped by POLL in the Tribe Eretmodini are in the least cichlid-like.

Indeed, an unbiased observer of any of these goby cichlids could be forgiven the conclusion that Lake Tanganyika was home to freshwater hawkfishes or blennies.

Although they feed on much the same food items as do *Julidochromis* species, the features that set these cichlids so dramatically apart from other representatives of the family have less to do with what they eat than with where they choose to eat it.

Like their riverine analogues of the genus *Steatocranus*, the Tanganyikan goby cichlids have successfully colonized a habitat characterized by violent water movement, the wave-churned shallows of Lake Tanganyika. Survival in this habitat is synonymous with maintaining close contact with the bottom.

Under such circumstances, the neutral buoyancy conferred by a functional swimbladder represents less an advantage than an active threat.

The vestigial character of this organ in the Tanganyikan goby cichlids and the bottom-hopping style of locomotion it imposes on them, no less than their feeding patterns and associated dental specializations, thus represents another dramatic example of evolutionary convergence.

Markedly inferior mouths, laterally compressed bodies, ventrally placed, muscular pectoral fins and outsized ventral fins that give the eretmodines such a distinctive appearance constitute further adaptations to life in a this productive but rigorous environment. The surge zone of Lake Tanganyika is characterized by high concentrations of dissolved oxygen. These values never fall below saturation and may under some circumstances exceed it.

Goby cichlids are thus much more sensitive to low dissolved oxygen values in captivity than are other lake-dwelling species.

Eretmodines can thus be expected to benefit from the high dissolved oxygen concentrations that accompany the use of trickle filters.

However, as long as their aquaria are well aerated and enjoy thorough water circulation, they can be expected to prosper under the same regime suggested for other Tanganyikan cichlids.

Fortunately for their keeper, goby cichlids resemble *Tropheus* and allied genera in their tolerance for large-scale water changes.

All of the eretmodines are monogamous, biparental mouthbrooders characterized by a strong pair bond.

Juveniles are mildly social towards conspecifics.

Adult pairs are very intolerant of their proximity and will extend this antipathy to other genera of goby cichlids as well.

The aquarist who fails to take this into account when setting up quarters for these fish is in for a rude awakening.

Droll appearance notwithstanding, eretmodines are highly competent practitioners of intramural *thuggee*.

The usual rule seems to be one pair of these fish per tank in all save the largest aquaria.

A twenty gallon tank can thus accommodate a single pair quite comfortably. Similar feeding behavior and habitat preferences suggest it might be imprudent to try housing goby cichlids and *Julidochromis* in the same aquarium.

I have also observed individual *E. cyanostictus* and *T. irsacae* wage protracted, if not always successful, guerilla campaigns against male mouthbrooding cichlids so rash as to try excavating a spawning pit too close to the goby cichlid's personal rockpile.

These caveats aside, eretmodines can be described as good community residents with little interest in midwater-dwelling tankmates. These cichlids produce disk-like eggs more reminiscent of a hockey puck than any other familiar object.

Fertilization is intrabuccal, the female picking up the eggs as soon as she had expressed them, then mouthing the male's vent. Ten to twelve days later, she transfers her burden to the male, who carries the by now well developed larvae for the remainder of the twenty-one day incubation period. None of these species practices postrelease brood care. Once out of their father's mouth, the robust fry are entirely on their own.

About half of the newly released fry are very dark in color, while the remainder of their sibs are much paler in hue.

Konigs reports that this color difference is a premature indicator of sex, the darker fry invariably proving to be males.

If due attention is paid to managing the nitrogen cycle in their tank, the fry are easily reared.

Sexual maturity is usually attained between ten and twelve months postrelease.

The goby cichlids enjoy a solid following among Tanganyikan cichlid enthusiasts.

Though tankbred fry are often marketed through commercial channels, there seems to be a steady supply of wild-caught fish available as well.

Distinctive, geographically delimited color forms of *Eretmodus cyanostictus* and *Spathodus erythrodon* have been exported regularly over the past decade.

As their biological status remains to be determined, it is quite possible that this distinctive lineage will prove more species-rich than originally thought.

West African Dwarf Cichlids

Three distinct cichlid lineages have produced dwarf representatives in West Africa as broadly understood.

The hemichromines are represented by the genera *Anomalochromis* GREENWOOD 1985 and *Thysochromis* DAGET 1988, each with a single recognized species.

When the first edition of this book was written, *Tilapia ruweti* and *T. bemini* THYS 1970, a species endemic to Lake Bermin, a crater lake in the Cameroons, were thought to

be the only dwarf representatives ·of their lineage.

In 1992, however, Drs. MELANIE STIASSNY, ULRICH SCHLIEWEN and WALLACE DOMINEY published a paper describing a diverse and remarkable *Tilapia* species flock from Lake Bermin.

Of its nine recognized species, *T. flava*, *T. bakossiorum*, *T. snyderae*, *T. thysi* and *T. gutturosa*, in addition to the previously cited *T. bemini*, qualify as dwarf cichlids. Indeed, *T. snyderae*, whose females barely exceed 1" SL, is the smallest known tilapiine cichlid.

The *Chromidotilapia* lineage boasts four dwarf genera, *Nanochromis* PELLEGRIN 1904, *Parananochromis* GREENWOOD 1987, *Limbochromis* GREENWOOD 1987 and *Pelvicachromis* THYS 1968.

This is the largest and certainly the most morphologically and behaviorally diverse group of West African dwarf cichlids.

The dwarf jewelfish, *Anomalochromis thomasi*, is native to the coastal rivers of Guinea and Sierra Leone.

Fig. 501 & 502: Male (above) and female (next page on top) *Nanochromis parilius*. This moderately rheophile Zairean species is the most regularly available representative of the genus.

Fig. 502

Individuals of Liberian provenance differ in color pattern from those of the current aquarium strain of *A. thomasi*, descended from fish collected in Sierra Leone. According to the American aquarist GINNY ECKSTEIN, the representatives of these two populations will not interbreed even in a no-choice situation. This suggests the existence of two geographically disjunct but biologically distinct *Anomalochromis* species.

The nomen *Thysochromis* was proposed by DAGET as a replacement name for *Thysia* LOISELLE and WELCOMME 1972, a generic name previously published for an African beetle and therefore unavailable under the provisions of the International Code of Zoological Nomenclature.

Only a single species, *Thysochromis ansorgii* (BOULENGER 1901), is currently recognized, although LOISELLE and WELCOMME left open the possibility that further research might validate the nominal species *T. annectans* (BOULENGER 1913).

The range of *T. ansorgii* is disjunct. Its eastern portion extends from the Cameroons westward to central Benin, the western from central Ivory Coast into the extreme southwestern corner of Ghana.

Tilapia ruweti is native to swampy areas in the watershed of the Zaire and Zambezi Rivers in Zambia and Zaire's Shaba Province.

Mention has already been made of *T. snyderae* and the other dwarf tilapias of Lake Bermin in the Cameroons.

According to the German aquarist Heiko BLEHER, two equally diminutive undescribed tilapias have been imported into Europe from Ejagham, another crater lake in the western Cameroons.

As this volcanic region boasts over a dozen such lakes, the majority of which have never been visited by an ichthyologist, it would not be too surprising were the number of dwarf lacustrine tilapias to increase dramatically in the years to come.

Unlike the generality of *Tilapia* species, these dwarfs feed primarily upon organic detritus and aquatic insects.

Their tolerance of growing aquatic plants no less than their small size and intense coloration recommend them highly as aquarium residents.

Although they are native to a part of the world characterized by soft, neutral to slightly acidic water, representatives of these three genera do well under a wide range of pH and hardness values in captivity.

All of these dwarf cichlids are easily fed and as long as due attention is paid to proper nitrogen cycle management in their quarters, their husbandry is a straightforward matter.

If managed in the manner suggest for other members of the guild, these monogamous substratum spawning cichlids breed freely in captivity.

Three of the Lake Bermin tilapias, *T. flava, T. snyderae* and *T. gutturosa* are colonial breeders in nature.

Several pairs of *Tilapia flava* have been observed collaborating in the joint defense of their pooled fry.

The remaining representatives of these three genera are unexceptional in their practice of long-term biparental defense of their mobile progeny, all of whom are sufficiently large to take *Artemia* nauplii or finely powdered prepared food as their initial meal.

Under a program of frequent partial water changes, the fry grow rapidly.

Tilapia ruweti can begin breeding as early as 14 weeks postspawning.

It would come as no surprise to find the Cameroonian crater lake endemics manifesting a comparable degree of reproductive precocity.

Anomalochromis and *Thysochromis* attain sexual maturity between eight and ten months postspawning.

The *Chromidotilapia* lineage has proven particularly productive of dwarf species in West Africa. The dwarf chromidotilapiines were formerly assigned to two genera, *Nanochromis* and *Pelvicachromis*.

Since the publication of the first edition of this book, GREENWOOD has revised *Nanochromis*, dividing a heterogenous assemblage of species with little in common save the presence of fourteen or fewer scale rows around the caudal peduncle into three smaller genera.

Nanochromis as narrowly defined is restricted to seven described and at least as many undescribed species native to the Zaire River basin.

Fig. 503 & 504: Male (above) and female (next page on top) *Nanochromis transvestitus*, a strikingly marked dwarf cichlid from Lake Maji Ndombe in Zaire.

Fig. 504

This assemblage of short-snouted cichlids includes a number of more or less well adapted rheophile species.

The most familiar of these rapids-dwelling dwarfs is *Nanochromis parilius* ROBERTS and STEWART 1976 [Figures 501 & 502], a species frequently exported from Kinshasa under the name *Nanochromis nudiceps* (BOULENGER 1899).

The true *N. nudiceps* is a valid species from much farther east in the Zaire drainage not to date established as an aquarium fish.

Of the three remaining species reported from the lower Zaire rapids, only *N. minor* ROBERTS and STEWART 1976 [Figure 143] is infrequently exported.

Nanochromis dimidiatus (PELLEGRIN 1900) inhabits small forest streams in the central portion of the Zaire basin.

Recent collecting efforts by the German aquarist HEIKO BLEHER have turned up several populations that differ significantly from one another in coloration but cannot be distinguished morphologically either from one another or from the description of *N. dimidiatus*. Several of these are established in Europe

and their progeny episodically find their way across the Atlantic.

The final representative of the genus available to aquarists is *N. transvestitus* ROBERTS and STEWART 1976 [Figures 503 & 504], a diminutive species endemic to Lac Maji Ndombe in central Zaïre, easily recognized by the striking pattern of black and white vertical bars on the caudal, soft dorsal and soft anal fins.

The nominal *Nanochromis* native to coastal rivers of the Congo Republic, Gabon, Rio Muni and the southern Cameroons are now placed in a separate genus, *Parananochromis*.

The genus comprises four long-snouted, slender bodied cichlids, strongly reminiscent of *Chromidotilapia* in overall appearance and lack of pronounced sexual dimorphism with regard to size or caudal fin shape.

The Cameroonian *Parananochromis caudifasciatus* (BOULENGER 1913) and the Gabonese *P. longirostris* (BOULENGER 1913) are the only representatives of the genus to date bred in captivity. The westernmost outriders of the this group are now placed in the genus *Limbochromis*.

Two species are recognized: *Limbochromis robertsi* (THYS and LOISELLE (1971) is native to the Birim River system in central Ghana, while *L. cavalliensis* (THYS and LOISELLE 1971), as its specific name implies, is restricted to the upper reaches of the Cavally River in western Côte d'Ivoire.

Superficially similar to *Parananochromis,* these cichlids are characterized by marked sexual dimorphism, males growing larger than females and sporting lyrate caudal fins.

No representative of the genus has been bred in captivity, due in no small measure to the fact that only isolated specimens of either species have to date been exported.

Pelvicachromis species have slightly inferior mouths, sixteen scale rows around the caudal peduncle and tend to be deeper bodied than representatives of the *Nanochromis* group. However, their most obvious diagnostic characteristic is the sexual dimorphism in the shape of the ventral fins from which the genus derives its name.

In males the ventrals are pointed in shape, due to the fact that the first soft ray supporting the fin is the longest. In females, the second or third soft ray is the longest, giving the ventrals a rounded shape [Figure 489].

While aquarists are well acquainted with the popular *Pelvicachromis pulcher* (BOULENGER 1901) [Figure 505], it comes as a surprise to many that the genus comprises eight described and three undescribed species.

Pelvicachromis has a disjunct distribution. Seven species are distributed in coastal rivers from the Angolan enclave of Cabinda and the Republic of the Congo northward to eastern Benin. The remaining three species occur in Liberia, Sierra Leone and Guinea.

Pelvicachromis pulcher lends itself well to large-scale culture in the Far East, a fact which goes far to explain both its commercial availability and the existence of a catatechnic albino form. All of the species to date imported have been induced to spawn in captivity, but none has lent itself to mass production to the same degree as *Pv. pulcher.*

This may reflect a failure to appreciate the influence of pH on the sex ratio of captive-bred fish.

The availability of such highly desirable species as *Pv. subocellatus* (GUNTHER 1871) [Figures 506 & 507] is thus more or less dependent upon the continuing importation of wild-caught fish.

The vigorous export business centered on Lagos probably explains why the four species native to Nigeria, *Pv. pulcher, Pv. sacrimontis* LINKE and STAECK 1981 [Figure 157], *Pv. taeniatus* (BOULENGER 1901) [Figures. 494 &

Fig. 505: Male (right) and female *Pelvicacromis pulcher* (Boulenger 1901) one of the few dwarf cichlids bred commercially, a fact which goes far towards explaining its wide availability.

Fig. 506 & 507: Male (above) and female (below) *Pelvicachromis subocellatus* (Gunther 1871), first representative of the genus imported as an aquarium fish. Ignorance of the relationship between spawning environment pH and the sex ratio of the resulting young may explain its initial failure to become established in the hobby.

Fig. 507

419

495] and *Pv. cf. subocellatus* [Figure 84] are more generally available than Cameroonian or Congolese congeners such as *Pv. kribensis* (BOULENGER 1901) [Figure 489] or such western outriders as *Pv. humilis* (BOULENGER 1916) [Figures 508 & 509]. *Pelvicachromis* and *Parananochromis* species are monogamous and practice vigilant biparental custodial care of their free-swimming young.

Nanochromis males will behave as either monogamists or harem polygynists depending upon the operational sex ratio.

In general, the more rheophile species have the strongest polygynous tendencies and are best housed on a harem basis.

However, even the males of markedly polygynous species such as *N. parilius* will participate in the defense of their mobile progeny.

Limbochromis robertsi lives in single male, multiple female groups in nature, an arrangement that suggests a haremically polygynous mating system.

It remains to be seen whether males of this species participate in the defense of their mobile fry.

Most of these dwarf cichlids hail from soft, acidic waters, but sufficient exceptions to this rule can be found to render general pronouncements about optimum water chemistry a pointless exercise.

It clearly pays to research the preferences of a given species before bringing it home, the more so as sex ratio is strongly influenced by pH in most *Pelvicachromis* and at least one *Nanochromis* species, *N. transvestitus*.

All are **extremely** sensitive to dissolved metabolic wastes. However, if due attention is given to keeping nitrate levels in their quarters below 10.0 ppm, their culture poses no particular difficulty.

All of these chromidotilapiines are characterized by a lengthy courtship and a tendency to go through false spawnings.

Both of these behavioral idiosyncracies tend to strain the forebearance of prospective

Fig. 508 & 509: Male (above) and female (next page on top) of the Kenema population of *Pelvicachromis humilis* (Boulenger 1916). The overall appearance of this dwarf cichlid is strongly reminiscent of a *Parananochromis* or *Limbochromis* species.

Fig. 509

breeders to the breaking point, but the aquarist who persists in his efforts is usually well rewarded for his patience.

All dwarf chromidotilapiines are cave spawners characterized by sharply defined sex roles. Hygienic care of the developing clutch and wrigglers is the exclusive responsibility of the female, territorial defense that of the male.

The eggs hatch in two days at 78°–82°F and the fry are mobile five to six days later.

The robust fry are large enough to take newly hatched brine shrimp nauplii for their initial meal. As long as due attention is paid to nitrogen cycle management in their tank, rearing them poses no particular difficulty.

Pelvicachromis can be sexed on the basis of ventral fin shape at five to six months of age; they begin spawning when six to eight months old. It usually takes several months more for young pairs to attain full reproductive competence.

Developmental rates for *Nanochromis* and *Parananochromis* species are comparable.

The West African riverine dwarf cichlids are among the group's most colorful and engaging representatives. It is therefore all the more regrettable that so few of them are readily available to aquarists.

Many of these species are forest-associated fishes whose ability to survive the degradation of their habitat consequent upon deforestation is questionable.

While none is officially recognized as threatened, demographic trends in West Africa do not encourage optimism about the long-term prospects of most species.

The vicissitudes of operating an ornamental fish export business in a part of the world where political instability is endemic would in any event make reliance upon the continued availability of wild-caught fish highly imprudent.

It is hoped that dedicated amateur breeders will discover the key to producing these highly desirable dwarf cichlids in commercial quantities.

In so doing, they will not only ensure the future availability of these fishes to aquarists but contribute materially to their survival as well.

Neotropical Dwarf Cichlids

Two of the five Neotropical lineages discussed in Chapter 10 have given rise to genera whose representatives satisfy my definition of a dwarf cichlid.

The genera *Nannacara* REGAN 1905 and *Laetacara* KULLANDER 1986 are offshoots of the *Aequidens-Cichlasoma* lineage, while *Apistogramma* REGAN 1913, *Apistogrammoides* MEINKEN 1965, *Biotoecus* EIGENMANN and KENNEDY 1903, *Crenicara* STEINDACHNER 1894, *Dicrossus* STEINDACHNER 1875, *Mazarunia* KULLANDER 1990, *Papiliochromis* KULLANDER 1977 and *Taeniacara* MYERS 1935 are geophagines.

The Neotropical dwarf cichlids are a remarkably diverse assemblage of species. As they differ from one another dramatically with regard to morphology, behavior and general husbandry requirements, the most useful way of classifying them is with regard to their mating system.

Only two Neotropical dwarf cichlid genera, *Laetacara* and *Papiliochromis*, are characterized by obligatory monogamy. This stands in sharp contrast to the case among the African representatives of this group.

Like their larger congeners, the smiling acaras of the genus *Laetacara* are monogamous, biparentally custodial substratum spawning cichlids.

The dwarf representatives of the genus include two described species, *L. curviceps* and *L. dorsiger.*

At least three additional species that fit the group's profile are episodically imported. These diminutive acaras differ from their larger relatives only in their more modest space requirements and should be managed in the same manner. Individual species vary markedly in their water quality preferences.

Several of the undescribed species will not spawn successfully unless housed in very soft, acid water [Figure 510], while *L. dorsiger* does best under moderately hard, somewhat alkaline conditions. All deposit their compact, circular egg plaques in the open. After a few false starts, a pair will usually settle down to model parenthood.

Fig. 510: A male of the undescribed *Laetacara* species known to aquarists by its German designation of "Buckelkopf (= hump head) acara".

Fig. 511: A pair of Bolivian rams, *Papiliochromis altispinossa.* The male is the larger of the two fish.

The eggs hatch in 72 hours at 78—82 °F and the young are free-swimming three to four days thereafter.

They are large enough to take *Artemia* nauplii for their initial meal.

With frequent partial water changes and ample food, they grow fairly rapidly, attaining sexual maturity, if not necessarily reproductive competence, between 8 and 12 months post-spawning.

The genus *Papiliochromis* comprises two species, *P. ramirezi,* native to Colombia and Venezuela, and its somewhat larger congener, *P. altispinossa* (HASEMAN 1911) [Figure 511], native to the Bolivian Amazon.

Unlike the generality of Neotropical dwarf cichlids, these species are savannah-associated rather than forest stream dwellers. This may explain the preference the *P. ramirezi* shows for warm water.

This species does not appreciate temperatures below 78 °F and shows itself to best advantage between 82° and 85 °F, with an increase to 88° recommended for breeding.

Its Bolivian congener is less demanding of warmth.

Temperatures of 72° to 80 °F suffice for day-to-day maintenance, with a rise to 82°—85 °F for breeding. The habitats of both species are characterized by very soft water, no more than 1° DH, whose pH can drop as low as 5.0.

As successful captive breeding has been reported in water as hard as 5°DH with a pH of 6.5, it would appear that these diminutive geophagines are more flexible with regard to water chemistry requirements than are some of their distant cousins of the genus *Apistogramma.* They are, however, even less tolerant of nitrogen cycle mismanagement.

Even relatively brief exposure to elevated nitrate levels suffices to provoke systemic bacterial infections that quickly prove lethal to their victims.

Both *Papiliochromis* species are inoffensive, rather social fish that appear to appreciate the company of conspecifics.

As the territories defended by sexually active individuals are compact and intraspecific aggression highly ritualized, it is quite possible to accommodate several breeding pairs of *P. ramirezi* in a 20 gallon aquarium.

Neither the true nor the Bolivian ram fares well in the company of more assertive dwarf cichlids, such as *Nannacara anomala* or some of the larger *Apistogramma* species. Nor do they prosper when housed with overly active dither fish.

Such companions should be smaller than the rams and of a comparably placid temperament.

Neon and cardinal tetras are an excellent choice of dither for these dwarf cichlids, as are most pencilfishes.

Like the dwarf smiling acaras, *Papiliochromis* are monogamous, biparentally custodial substratum spawning cichlids that display moderate sexual dimorphism.

Females of both species are smaller than their consorts and have shorter fins. Those of *P. ramirezi* have a magenta lateral blotch whose color intensifies dramatically as spawning approaches.

Both species place their eggs upon a pre-cleaned surface in the open.

Flattened river pebbles are particularly favored spawning sites in captivity, but some pairs of *P. ramirezi* will place their eggs directly upon the aquarium gravel.

Prudence favors offering prospective breeders as wide a selection of possible spawning sites as possible in the hope of forestalling such an eventuality. It is virtually impossible to remove a spawn so placed for artificial incubation, an option well worth preparing for, given this species' well-deserved reputation for parental unreliability. Rams spawn quite freely, male and female dividing hygienic and custodial duties in a manner reminiscent of the numerous acara species.

Papiliochromis ramirezi eggs hatch 48 hours postspawning at 88 °F, those of *P. altispinossa* 72 hours postspawning at 82 °—85 °F.

The parents commonly devour their progeny before they become fully mobile, a stage attained roughly three days posthatching.

It had been suggested that such filial cannibalism is less likely to occur if dither fish are present and the breeding tank is afforded 24 hour illumination.

For whatever reason, *P. altispinossa* is much less given to the practice of retroactive birth control than its northern relative.

Papiliochromis fry are too small to manage *Artemia* nauplii for their initial meal.

They should instead be offered micro-worms for their first three or four days of mobile existence. Pairs that have brought a brood to this point usually prove exemplary parents thereafter.

If the object is to keep the adults and fry together until the latter have reached a reasonable size, it is prudent to **gradually** lower the temperature in the breeding tank to 78 °F once the fry begin eating brine shrimp nauplii.

At higher temperatures, the female will rapidly mature another batch of eggs. This will prematurely terminate the pair's parental involvement with their first brood and may well result in its destruction as they prepare to respawn. With good feeding and frequent partial water changes, the fry grow very rapidly.

They can be sexed reliably at six months of age and can begin spawning two months later.

Rams can produce clutches of up to 300 eggs and will respawn 10 to 14 days following the loss of their eggs to predation or their keeper's intervention.

This marked fecundity doubtless explains why this is one of the few dwarf cichlids that has lent itself to mass production and in consequence, enjoys widespread availability.

The several mutant varieties of *P. ramirezi* commercially available are by-products of this process.

The robust form sold in Europe under the trade name of "Asian ram" and in North America as the "German ram" is easily the most attractive of these catatechnic forms.

A long-finned mutant analogous to the veiltailed form of the angelfish represents a less successful effort at "improving" an already very desirable aquarium resident.

An oligomelanic variety, the gold ram, is available in both short and long-finned forms.

The dwarf cichlids of the genus *Nannacara* are native to the lower reaches of the Orinoco and Amazon rivers and the coastal drainages of the Guianas.

In the most recent discussion of the genus, KULLANDER and NIJSSEN recognize three described and suggest the existence of at least two additional undescribed species.

Nannacara anomala, the species most familiar to aquarists, is a common inhabitant of small streams in the lowlands of Guyana and Suriname.

A second species often listed in older aquarium references, *N. taenia* REGAN 1912, appears to be a junior synonym of *N. anomala* based upon a parental female.

The recently described *N. aureocephala* ALLEGAYER 1983 appears to replace *N. anomala* in the coastal rivers of French Guiana.

KULLANDER and his Dutch colleague HAN NIJSSEN recognize a third species, *N. bimaculata* EIGENMANN 1912, which appears to be restricted to the Rio Essequibo in Guyana. Preserved specimens of this nominal *Nannacara* are strongly reminiscent of one of the dwarf smiling acaras of the genus *Laetacara.*

This suggests that KULLANDER and NIJSSEN's expressed reservations about this species' generic placement are probably justified.

Specimens unambiguously referable to the genus *Nannacara* have been collected from the lower Orinoco River near the city of Caripito in Venezuela and from the vicinity of the Brazilian city of Belem near the mouth of the Amazon.

These populations differ trenchantly from both *N. anomala* and *N. aureocephala.*

Their formal description awaits the collection of additional preserved material and the acquisition of life color data.

The golden-eyed dwarf cichlid, as *N. anomala* is commonly known, is the dominant constituent in shipments of "mixed dwarf cichlids" exported from Guyana and Suriname.

Widely available and remarkably undemanding, this attractive little fish is the ideal beginner's dwarf. It prefers soft, slightly acidic to neutral water, but will breed freely — and successfully — in water with a pH of 7.5 and a hardness of 12°DH.

Nannacara aureocephala is somewhat more demanding of soft, acid water for both ordinary maintenance and breeding. Otherwise, it differs very little from its more widely available Guyanese congener.

Fig. 512 & 513: Male (above) and female (next page on top) of the common aquarium strain of *Crenicara punctulatum* from the Peruvian Amazon.

425

Fig. 513

Temperatures of 72° to 78°F suffice for routine maintenance, with a rise to 82°–85°F for breeding.

The golden-eyed dwarf cichlid is more predatory than the generality of dwarfs and will prey on fish up to the size of a newborn molly. This argues against the use of small, gracile tetras as dither fish in its tank.

However, as *N. anomala* is also a rather assertive species, it has no trouble coping with deeper-bodied, generally "nippier" characins such as the serpae tetra, *Hyphessobrycon serpae* or the silvertip tetra, *Hemigrammus marginatus* and will even take hyperactive "exotic" tankmates like the Asian *Brachydanio* and *Barbus* species in stride.

As already noted, the golden-eyed dwarf cichlid is quite hard on *Corydoras* and other small catfishes and can even make life thoroughly unpleasant for such medium-sized loricariid catfishes as the bristlenose plecos of the genus *Ancistrus*. This is probably the least picky eater of all the Neotropical dwarf cichlids.

All of the usual live and frozen foods are readily taken and even wild-caught specimens have no trouble recognizing the edibility of flakes.

As might be inferred from their marked sexual dimorphism, harem polygyny is the normative mating system of both *Nannacara* species.

As males can be quite hard on prospective consorts, setting these dwarf cichlids up in multiple female groups in at least a 29 gallon aquarium is strongly recommended.

It is particularly important that the female enjoy a good selection of potential spawning sites and that the tank be large enough to afford the male a secure refuge beyond the limits of the females' territories.

Parental female *Nannacara* turn into veritable Furies, well able to repay a male's prespawning harassment with compound interest despite their smaller size.

Offered a choice of spawning sites, most females will deposit their eggs inside an enclosed space, but it is not that uncommon for some individuals to emulate *Laetacara* species in their choice of spawning site. The eggs hatch in 48 hours at 82°F and the fry become freeswimming three days thereafter.

426

Females are ferociously efficient guardians of their progeny, who can easily take newly hatched brine shrimp and finely powdered prepared food for their initial meal. The female will continue to care for the fry for about a month.

In a community setting, it is not unusual for the male to associate himself with the family unit as the young grow larger, usually two to three weeks post-hatching.

The female seems most likely to accept his custodial involvement if the tank's other residents are large or fast enough to pose a credible threat to the fry.

With good feeding and frequent partial water changes, the young can be reliably sexed four months postspawning and begin their own reproductive careers two months thereafter.

When the first edition of this book went to press, the genus *Crenicara* comprised a heterogenous assortment of species united only in the presence of a serrated preopercular margin and a shared color pattern based upon large, serially repeated black lateral spots.

KULLANDER has since restricted *Crenicara* to *C. punctulatum* (GUNTHER 1863) [Figures 512 & 513] and several presently undescribed deep-bodied, large-eyed species characterized by slight sexual dimorphism with regard to size and fin shape.

The slender-bodied, strongly sexually dimorphic species formerly assigned to the genus he referred to the rehabilitated genus *Dicrossus*, which now comprises two recognized species, *D. maculatus* STEINDACHNER 1875 and *D. filamentosus* [Figure 94].

KULLANDER considers these two genera of checkerboard cichlids and the Guianan endemic *Mazarunia mazaruni* KULLANDER 1992 to represent a natural grouping whose relationships to the major Neotropical cichlid lineages remain obscure.

STIASSNY has suggested that the affinities of another enigmatic Neotropical dwarf species, *Biotoecus opercularis* (STEINDACHNER 1875) [Figures 514 & 515] also lie with this assemblage of genera.

Her suggestion that these cichlids are highly derived geophagines is consistent with what is known of the morphology and,

according to LEIBEL, the molecular genetics of this major lineage.

The type locality of *Crenicara punctulatum* is Gluck Island in the Rio Essequibo, a coastal river in Guyana.

This species also appears to be widely distributed in the Amazon basin.

Other South American cichlids with similarly broad distributions, such as *Cichla ocellaris, Mesonauta festivus* and *Geophagus surinamensis* have proven upon closer study to consist of complexes of allopatric sibling species.

I have collected two quite differently marked populations of nominal *C. punctulatum* from Peru and seen preserved examples of yet a third from the Rio Napo, a major Ecuadorian tributary of the Amazon.

It would therefore come as no surprise were future research to reveal the existence of numerous valid but allopatrically distributed *Crenicara* species.

Crenicara inhabit slow-flowing blackwater streams and are nowhere abundant. Collecting reasonable series of specimens from any given spot is thus a major challenge, a fact which complicates the task of working out the precise relationships of these distinctive populations.

Dicrossus maculatus is native to the lower Amazon, while *D. filamentosus* has been collected from the Rio Negro and the Rio Orinoco drainages.

Both are blackwater species that occur in slow-moving, often heavily vegetated waters.

Biotoecus opercularis can be found in similar situations over a large portion of the central Amazon basin in Brazil.

These are not dwarf cichlids for the beginner.

Native to absolutely soft waters whose pH can drop below 5.0, they can survive harder, less acidic conditions in captivity.

However, they will not reproduce successfully unless these conditions are recreated, as eggs spawned in harder water simply fail to develop.

In their sensitivity to dissolved metabolic wastes they closely resemble *Papiliochromis* and should be managed in the same manner.

A well-planted aquarium simplifies nitrogen-cycle management while affording

Fig. 514 & 515: Male (above) and female (next page) *Biotoecus opercularis* from the Rio Negro in Brazil.

these retiring dwarf cichlids an essential sense of security.

The regular use of chemically active filter media will also help to stretch the interval between water changes.

Suitable dither fish are equally important to their well-being. Any of the species recommended as dither for *Papiliochromis* will serve equally well for both *Biotoecus* and *Dicrossus*. Selecting suitable dither for *Crenicara* is a simpler proposition.

By virtue of a more robust build and assertive temperament, these dwarf cichlids can cope successfully with a much wider range of companions.

Temperatures of 75° to 80°F suffice for routine maintenance, with a rise to 85°F for breeding.

Imported fish are usually unenthusiastic about prepared foods, but with a bit of patience, they can be taught the error of their ways. Fortunately, they have no such reservations about either *Artemia* nauplii or the generality of frozen foods.

Crenicara and *Dicrossus* differ from the generality of polygynous dwarf cichlids in being open rather than cave spawners.

It is likely that both genera of checkerboard cichlids utilize plant leaves as spawning sites in nature.

In captivity, *C. punctulatum* will spawn on flat rocks, while *D. filamentosus* will place its eggs on a variety of vertical surfaces.

Both species have a poor record of parental reliability.

As they will spawn under water conditions that preclude either the successful fertilization of the eggs or normal embryonic development, it seems likely that much egg-eating simply represents a female's response to an egg plaque that is no longer emitting the necessary chemical cues to elicit parental behavior.

If attempts to hatch spawns artificially are likewise unproductive, excessive water hardness is almost certainly to blame. Lowering the mineral content of the water in the breeding tank still further should significantly enhance spawn viability and may well result in a

Fig. 515

dramatic shift in the parental female's behavior towards her clutch.

The fry hatch in 48 hours at 85 °F. As the female is likely to move them several times over the next four days, their abrupt disappearance from the spawning site is not necessarily cause for alarm.

The fry are fully mobile by the seventh day postspawning.

They are large enough to manage *Artemia* nauplii for their initial meal.

Females are attentive but often ineffectual guardians.

Parental care can persist for nearly a month in captivity, but most breeders prefer to separate mother and fry after a few days to minimize the risk of losses.

Biotoecus opercularis is a cave spawner. According to Dr. DAVID SCHLESER, who appears to have been the first person to observe the normal brood care sequence of this species, the behavior of both the parental female and fry do not differ in any meaningful way from that of other cave spawning dwarf cichlids up to the point at which the fry become free-swimming. Once they leave the cave, however, they immediately disperse outward from the female's territory, seeking shelter among the roots and leaves of floating vegetation.

While the female makes no attempt to retrieve the fry once they have left the cave, she does attempt to protect them. Under aquarium conditions, her presence at this point is otiose and she is best removed.

The fry are large enough to manage newly hatched brine shrimp. Given their degree of dispersion, assuring them reasonable access to food for their first few days of mobile life poses something of a challenge.

Until they learn to associate the arrival of their keeper with food, it is advisable to introduce small quantities of nauplii into the tank at several different points with a baster. This increases the likelihood that searching fry will encounter suitable prey.

The fry of all three genera are exceedingly sensitive to dissolved metabolites.

Frequent partial water changes are absolutely indispensable to their well-being.

Prudence further dictates keeping chemically active media in an appropriate filter and maintaining a population of snails in the rearing tank to consume uneaten food before it begins to decompose.

With good feeding and careful attention to water quality, *D. filamentosus* fry can measure c. 1.75" TL four months postspawning. They can be sexed at this point, although it will be two to four months longer before they reach full reproductive maturity.

Crenicara punctulatum displays a comparable growth rate.

The fry of *Biotoecus opercularis* can be sexed c. four months postspawning and begin breeding shortly thereafter.

Apistogramma, *Apistogrammoides* and *Taeniacara* are characterized by marked sexual dimorphism, the practice of harem polygyny and a clear beige to bright yellow female breeding dress with contrasting markings on the head, body and fins.

With fifty-six described and half that number of undescribed species, *Apistogramma* is the most speciose dwarf cichlid genus. Species range in size from the diminutive *A. borellii*, whose males attain a bare 2" SL to the robust *A. steindachneri*, whose males can easily grow to twice that size. *Apistogramma* species have been described from the Amazon, Orinoco and Parana basins as well as from the coastal rivers of the Guianas.

With the sole exception of *A. piauiensis* KULLANDER 1980, described from the Rio Parnaiba, the genus is absent from the coastal rivers that flow into the Atlantic between the mouth of the Amazon and that of the Rio de la Plata.

The remaining two genera of the group are, by way of contrast, monotypic.

Widely distributed in the Peruvian and Colombian Amazon, the diminutive *Apistogrammoides pucallapensis* MEINKEN 1965 differs most obviously from *Apistogramma* in having seven to nine spines in the anal fin rather than three to five.

Fig. 516: A young pair of *Taeniacara candidae* (male above). Males of this slender dwarf cichlid play an active role in the defense of their mobile fry.

Taeniacara candidae MYERS 1935 [Figure 516] is another "dwarf" dwarf cichlid, males barely reaching 2" overall length.

This species has been collected from the Rio Negro and appears to be widely distributed in the central portion of the Amazon basin.

This slender species differs most obviously from *Apistogramma* in its lack of gill rakers and incomplete lateral line.

From the aquarist's perspective, the maintenance requirements of these three closely related dwarf representatives of the geophagine lineage genera are sufficiently similar to mandate a common approach to their husbandry.

These dwarf cichlids can be found in both still and flowing waters, typically over bottoms with a dense overlay of leaf litter.

Apistogrammoides pucallapensis is often found in association with "floating meadows", but the remaining species of this assemblage are typical inhabitants of shallow brooks or the marginal waters of larger rivers and oxbow lakes. Most live in forested habitats.

It should come as no surprise that these dwarf cichlids live longer and are less susceptible to bacterial infections if maintained at relatively low temperatures.

A range of 70°—75°F suffices for routine maintenance, with an increase to 78°—82°F for breeding. It is, however, worth emphasizing that even the handful of *Apistogramma* described from savannah habitats in the *llanos* of Colombia and Venezuela or the *chaco* of Paraguay do best when kept in cooler water.

These *Apistogramma* are found in waters shaded by riverine gallery forest, where the cover afforded by overarching trees can mean a difference of as much as 10°F between the shaded and unshaded portions of the same stream.

As might be expected given the extensive range of the genus, individual species vary markedly in their ability to adapt to differing water conditions.

At one extreme are specialized blackwater residents, such as *T. candidae*, *A. bitaeniata* PELLEGRIN *1936 and A. nijsseni* KULLANDER 1979.

Like the species of the *Crenicara* group, these fish require soft, acid water to prosper.

Fortunately, such blackwater specialists are outnumbered by less demanding congeners. Whitewater associated species such as *A. pucallapensis* and *A. cacatuoides* HOEDEMAN 1951 and ecological generalists such as *A. eunotus* KULLANDER 1981, which can be found in all three types of habitats in nature, make far fewer demands on their keeper with regard to water chemistry.

Novice *Apistogramma* fanciers are advised to concentrate on these relatively hardy dwarf cichlids and leave blackwater species to the attentions of more experienced breeder.

As there is reason to suspect that sex ratio in some species is influenced by the pH of the water in the spawning tank, it is advisable to research pH preferences carefully before attempting to breed it.

These dwarf geophagines share the group's sensitivity to dissolved metabolites and cannot be expected to prosper unless due attention is given to managing the nitrogen cycle in their aquaria. Given the awesome array of predators with which they share their habitat, their retiring nature is quite understandable.

Suitable tankmates go a long way towards overcoming their shyness in captivity, as does a layer of floating plants on the surface of their aquarium.

The more robust *Apistogramma* species can cope with any of the dither fish recommended for use with *Nannacara* species.

Companions recommended as dither for their distant relatives of the genus *Papiliochromis* will prove equally appropriate for their smaller congeners.

All three genera are cave spawners. Harem polygyny, with exclusively maternal brood care, is their normative reproductive pattern.

However, young males of such round-tailed species as *A. trifasciata* (EIGENMANN and KENNEDY 1903) and *A. commbrae* REGAN 1906 may share both hygienic and custodial duties with their consorts.

Their inability to defend a territory large enough to accommodate several females debars these males from maximizing their reproductive output by spawning polygynously.

It is thus selectively advantageous for them to pursue an alternative reproductive strategy

431

by investing in the defense of their single consort's progeny. Young males of several species characterized by dramatic sexual differences in fin development will pursue yet another strategy by attempting to "cuckold" a harem master whenever the opportunity presents itself.

As they grow older and larger, practitioners of this alternative mating systems typically shift over to a haremic social organization.

As females seem to be quite particular in their selection of a spawning site, it is prudent to afford them a selection of alternatives.

A ratio of three potential spawning sites per female is a useful rule of thumb to follow when setting up the breeding tank.

Females assume their species-specific black on yellow parental coloration immediately after spawning. Such a color change, linked with extreme reluctance to leave a cave, is a certain indication that the female is tending eggs.

Females of most of the blackwater species have a reputation for parental unreliability.

The eggs of these species often will not develop unless the pH of the breeding tank is strongly acidic, between 4.8 and 5.0.

As these fish will spawn under more alkaline conditions, it is possible that repeated egg-eating represents a perfectly normal response to an inviable clutch.

Repeated occurrence of such behavior should certainly trigger a careful investigation of water quality in the breeding tank.

The eggs hatch in three days at 78°−80°F. It is not unusual for the female to move the wrigglers several times during the seven day period before they become free-swimming.

As not all the fry can manage *Artemia* for their initial meal, it is recommended to offer them a mixture of nauplii and microworms for their first five to seven days of mobile existence.

A mature sponge filter in the breeding tank will also afford newly mobile fry a rich supplementary food source.

According to SCHLESER, male *T. candidae* aggressively take over the care of the fry as soon as the female brings them out of the spawning cave. Males of even the strongly dimorphic species will often take a desultory

interest in their progeny a week or so after they are fully mobile. The female's response to such a belated show of paternal solicitude is more likely to be positive if fish, which are perceived as potential threats to her fry, are present in the breeding tank.

Females begin ripening a new batch of eggs three to four weeks after their earlier clutch has hatched.

It is thus unusual for parental care to persist much longer than this in captivity. With ample feeding and frequent partial water changes, the fry grow quite rapidly.

They can usually be reliably sexed on the basis of body size and finnage differences 16 to 18 weeks posthatching.

While not unusual for females to spawn their first clutch three months thereafter, it usually takes several months more before they bring off a successful spawn.

From the aquarist's point of view, dwarf cichlids have all of the positive qualities of the Family Cichlidae but very few of its negative attributes.

Perhaps the group's major shortcoming is the general unavailability of its constituent species through commercial channels. *Pelvicachromis pulcher*, *P. ramirezi* and the dwarf *Julidochromis* species are produced en masse by commercial fish culturists, while semi-professional breeders have done a very creditable job with several ostracophil *Lamprologus* species [Figure 517].

Regrettably, aquarists remain dependent upon the vagaries of exportation for access to the remaining species.

The economics of commercial breeding and the low fecundity of the majority of these fishes conspire to perpetuate this state of affairs.

It is thus incumbent upon the hobbyist fortunate enough to secure these less frequently encountered dwarf cichlids to do his best to propagate them and distribute their fry. However, while it is undeniable that tracking these diminutive species down can develop into a major project, it is equally true that no other group of cichlids will so richly repay such efforts.

Fig. 517: Thanks to the efforts of dedicated amateur breeders, ostracophil *Lamprologus* like this pair of *Lamprologus multifasciatus* Boulenger 1906 are among the more readily available dwarf cichlids.

CHAPTER 12

LEARNING MORE ABOUT CICHLIDS

Introduction

This book is intended as a primer of cichlid natural history and husbandry.

These are broad subjects indeed, and an introductory work can barely touch upon many of their aspects.

It is thus the author's responsibility to assist his readers in the further pursuit of such knowledge. A list of related titles is usually regarded as sufficient means to this end.

This approach assumes familiarity with both primary scientific literature and means of obtaining access to it. However, few aquarists have ever had contact with such publications, and most possess only rudimentary notions of how to obtain them. In such circumstances, a comprehensive list of recommended titles better tantalizes than satisfies the desire for further information.

An additional shortcoming inherent in any bibliography arises from its nature as a roster of **past** publications dealing with a given topic.

It thus affords the user no aid in keeping abreast of current developments in a given field.

This reflects the background of the customary audience of such works. In most scientific disciplines the total number of professional researchers is small enough for interested parties to keep track of colleagues' activities through personal contact. Familiarity with modern library procedures allows them to effectively employ available resources to follow progress in their area of interest when this is impossible. The interested hobbyist can rarely exercise the former option and usually lacks sufficient knowledge to avail himself of the latter.

Last, and perhaps most significantly, most ichthyologists are either unaware of specialist hobby groups or indifferent to their potential as allies in the quest for knowledge.

Although this state of affairs has improved somewhat over the past decade, they still lag behind their ornithological colleagues in their appreciation of the contributions that interested amateurs and their organizations can make to their discipline.

Thus, while both avicultural and amateur ornithological journals are routinely reviewed by abstracting services, the aquaristic literature is less apt to work itself into the mainstream of scientific/technical information flow.

Hence an author with a genuine concern for the further education of his readers must also direct their attention to this valuable information source.

In this concluding chapter, my aim is to show readers (1) how to use the modern library system to locate and obtain relevant scientific literature and (2) how to keep abreast of ongoing research on cichlid biology. I will then discuss the benefits of membership in a specialty organization devoted to disseminating information on cichlid natural history and husbandry. Finally, I will conclude with an annotated list of recommended works dealing with the major cichlid groups discussed previously herein.

Cichlids and Libraries: How to Find and Obtain Access to Relevant Scientific Literature

Ardent cichlid enthusiasts often attempt to satisfy their curiosity about their pets' natural history or behavior with a visit to the local library.

The typical outcome of such an effort is the disappointing discovery that apart from a few general aquaristic references, its holdings are devoid of material dealing with cichlids.

After such an experience, most hobbyists abandon such efforts to become better informed.

This is unfortunate, as their difficulties are not entirely due to the library's deficiencies.

They rather reflect the user's ignorance of its role in a widespread information retrieval system.

This makes it difficult for him to phrase requests for information in a manner likely to elicit a useful answer.

Specialized technical literature is regarded by both researchers and librarians as an essential instrument in the pursuit of specific scientific goals.

For example, researchers in a field such as fish systematics require access to literature dealing with the evolutionary relationships and classification of fishes. However, the number of such researchers is small.

They further tend to be concentrated in a few locations.

Hence the overall demand for such material is small. Librarians must operate within tight budgetary and space constraints.

They are thus disinclined to allocate scarce funds and limited shelf space for books or journals with such a restricted readership.

Hence, such materials are absent from the holdings of public libraries and even from those of universities whose faculties do not include persons whose professional activities would justify their possession. To further complicate matters, while most persons are sufficiently familiar with the workings of a library to chase down a particular book, little material dealing with cichlid biology is or ever has been published in such a format.

Most such information has appeared as articles in scientific journals. Even monographs are usually issued serially by the publishing institution.

Library catalogs tell a user whether a particular journal or monograph series is part of its holdings, but they do not list the contents of serial publications. Searching a municipal or even a university card catalog under the heading "Cichlid" is thus unlikely to yield useful results.

To track down cichlid-related material, recourse to specialized serial bibliographies that provide a continuing listing of published books and articles in a given field of knowledge is essential. The two most useful such serials are the **Zoological Record** and **Biological Abstracts.**

Both list their entries by taxonomic group as well as by scientific discipline, geographical region and author.

The aquarist with access to these very useful publications will find it a simple matter to locate titles dealing with cichlids.

The **Zoological Record** is a hand-compiled effort published under the auspices of the British Museum. It is the only such English-language publication that provides an uninterrupted record of the scientific literature from the beginning of the nineteenth century to the present. The nature of the compilation process, together with staff limitations, result in it always being a few years behind in its coverage of current literature.

Nor has its database kept pace with the multiplication of specialized journals over the last fifteen years.

However, it has the virtue of covering much of the commercial aquaristic literature published both in English and other languages.

Municipal libraries are less likely to carry the **Zoological Record** than they are **Biological Abstracts,** but it is ubiquitous in institutional libraries.

Biological Abstracts is a commercially published serial bibliography just over a decade old. It is a computerized list of current material, published every two weeks.

In addition to the usual article citation, it also includes the author's or authors' abstract.

This is of enormous help in deciding whether a given paper is worth the trouble of running down. It is somewhat less convenient to use than the **Zoological Record.**

Entries are listed numerically.

While it is a simple matter to look up a particular group such as the Cichlidae in the taxonomic listing section, the fruit of one's labors is a string of reference numbers, each of which must be checked out in turn. However, its coverage is more thorough than that of the **Zoological Record.**

Add to this the availability of an abstract and the utility of this publication becomes incontestable. The concluding virtue of **Biological Abstracts** is wide availability in both municipal and institutional libraries.

Cichlid enthusiasts with access to a modem-equipped computer will find that electronic bulletin boards such as Compu-Serve© represent an alternative approach to accessing **Biological Abstracts** and other more specialized bibliographies likely to list articles of interest to them.

If one takes the time to learn the protocols necessary to initiate such an electronic literature search, such services as CompuServe©'s **I-Quest** can prove a highly cost-effective means of keeping abreast of currently published material dealing with cichlid biology.

The chief shortcoming of such online databases is that their listings of titles published prior to 1970 are far from complete. Hence, access to even the most up-to-date information technology does not emancipate its users totally from the more traditional approaches to data retrieval!

Having found a title or titles of interest, the next step is to secure the actual material. Remember, the likelihood of finding publications dealing with any aspect of cichlid biology in a given library's holdings is directly related to the professional interests of its readership. Knowing an institution's professional orientation is thus the first step in chasing down a particular reference.

Libraries of museums actively supporting research in fish systematics are most likely to have extensive material dealing with this aspect of cichlid biology on their shelves. The library of a university whose zoology or biology department includes faculty members pursuing research in animal behavior will subscribe to journals that regularly publish articles on the behavior of cichlid fishes.

State or Federal fisheries research facilities often include material on cichlid ecology in their reference holdings.

Thus, as a first step in any literature search, determine whether any such institutions are within convenient distance.

Their libraries are usually accessible to the public, though it may be necessary to arrange a visit in advance, and their librarians are quite willing to assist visitors in their search for specific materials.

Borrowing privileges are usually restricted to staff members, but facilities for copying desired material at reasonable rates are often available.

However, a negative outcome to such preliminaries need not spell a search's failure.

Virtually all libraries participate in one or more regional interlibrary loan programs.

Obtaining a given publication in this manner can be time-consuming, but the option has the advantage of widespread availability.

It is first necessary to learn if the desired publication is held by any of the participants in the exchange arrangements to which the local library is party.

Simply request this information from the library's reference desk.

If the work is a book, the librarian needs to know the author and title.

If a specific edition is sought, that information must also be provided.

In the case of a journal or other serial publication, the title, volume sought and the year of its appearance are required.

This information in hand, a reference librarian can swiftly determine if an interlibrary loan is possible.

If not, the librarian may be able to suggest another local institution through which a loan can be arranged.

While the resources of a large municipal library should not be underestimated in this regard, a positive outcome is almost assured if one works through a local college or university library. These institutions must offer their students and faculty wide access to specialized literature.

This is most economically managed through participation in exchange agreements.

State supported institutions handle requests from non-student residents routinely as part of their overall public service mission.

Private universities are under no such obligation, but their library staffs often prove sympathetic to requests for assistance if their purpose is explained.

If an interlibrary loan can be arranged, it is necessary to fill out a request form, then await notification of the publication's receipt by the requesting institution.

Loan requests can take up to six weeks to bear fruit, depending upon the distances involved, the demand for requested material at its home institution and the manpower available thereat to expedite interlibrary transfers.

Such loans are of brief duration, generally for a period of seven days. Loans arranged through a university library are strictly interinstitutional.

As non-student users do not generally enjoy borrowing privileges, only in-library use of the borrowed material will be possible, though no constraints upon copying need be anticipated.

Quest offers users the option of ordering desired titles from a service that specializes in supplying xerocopies of hard-to-find papers to interested researchers.

Orders are typically filled promptly, but the cost per page for such material is substantial.

Hence most users find it cost-effective to avail themselves of this option only if the paper in question is both short and unavailable via more ordinary channels.

Local Aquarium Societies and National Specialty Organizations: A Complementary Approach to Learning More About Cichlids

Familiarity with the primary scientific literature is a powerful instrument for broadening one's knowledge of cichlid biology.

However, the aquarist who seeks information on the husbandry of a given cichlid species is unlikely to find it in such publications. The aquaristic literature and the personal experience of other enthusiasts are twin sources of such specialized technical information.

The successful cichlid keeper has no reservations about availing himself of either. Access to commercial publications is easily managed.

One need only subscribe to a particular magazine or purchase issues from the nearest retail shop that handles it.

Since the appearance of the first edition of this book, two specialized serial publications aimed at satisfying the demand of cichlid enthusiasts for more detailed information have been launched.

Both are abundantly illustrated in color and tend to devote much space to articles on unusual or newly available cichlid species.

Cichlid News is a magazine published six times yearly by Aquatic Promotions, Inc.

It is sold both over the counter in many large retail establishments or can be obtained on a subscription basis at a cost of U.S.$ 16.00 per annum.

For further information, interested readers should contact:

Cichlid News
P.O. Box 522842
Miami, FL 33152

The Cichlids Yearbook is a hardcover annual edited by the German aquarist and author Ad Konings.

Though published by Cichlid Press in St. Leon Rot, Germany, the language of this collection of articles is English.

The contents are arranged by faunal region and usually include articles on general husbandry techniques and well-written reviews of recent scientific publications likely to be of interest to cichlid hobbyists.

The American distributor of this excellent series is:

Old World Exotic Fish, Inc.
P. O. Box 970583
Miami, FL 33197

Back issues of this most useful reference series are available from the distributor.

Though most of the so-called "slick" aquarium magazines now feature regular columns devoted to cichlid keeping in addition to the usual feature articles, such publications still represent only the tip of the iceberg insofar as such literature is concerned.

Most of what is written about the maintenance and breeding of all tropical fish in captivity is published in the bulletins of local aquarium societies and the journals of national specialty organizations.

Membership in such groups is the only means of access to this substantial body of information.

Joining a local aquarium society also affords opportunities to meet other hobbyists and to participate in the informal information exchanges that inevitably occur whenever two or more aquarists come together.

However, not everyone is able to join a local aquarium society. For myriad reasons, in many parts of North America, both rural and urban, the development of the tropical fish hobby has never favored the formation of such groups.

Furthermore, while I do not want to discourage anyone from joining a local society if that option is available, membership in an organization dedicated to promoting all aspects of the aquarium hobby seldom satisfies fully a cichlid specialist's desire for either information or fellowship.

The ideal would be to join a locally based group of fellow cichlid specialists.

Such organizations do exist, but examination of the accompanying list reveals that they are even thinner on the ground than are general interest aquarium societies.

The antidote to both physical and intellectual isolation is simple: membership in a national specialty group such as the American Cichlid Association.

The accompanying table lists several such organizations, together with a contact address. Regardless of their language of expression, such groups have many common features.

Because of my familiarity with its workings, I will thus use the A.C.A. as a general paradigm in this discussion. The A.C.A. was founded over fifteen years ago to gather, organize and disseminate knowledge of cichlids, further conservation of these fishes and their natural habitats and promote fellowship among its members. It currently numbers over 1500 members.

Most are hobbyists, but retailers, fish farmers and other professionals may also join.

Dues can be paid yearly, or membership can be arranged on a multi-year basis for up to three years.

The organization is governed by a an eight member Board of Trustees, of which four are elected annually for two years terms.

Business is carried out via monthly rounds of correspondence and at the board meeting held at the A.C.A.'s annual convention.

Membership carries with it the right to vote and to run for elective office.

Members may also serve in appointed positions, such as committee chairs.

The A.C.A. offers its members three publications. The organization's official journal, **Buntbarsche Bulletin**, is published six times

yearly. It contains articles, often illustrated in color, dealing with both the natural history of cichlids and their aquarium husbandry.

All submissions are technically edited to assure scientific accuracy.

Among its special features are the *"Keeping up . . ."* series, which introduces newly available cichlids to members and the *"Cichlidists' Library"*, which endeavors keep readers abreast of developments in the primary scientific literature by reviewing or presenting the abstracts of papers deemed to be of particular interest.

The A.C.A.'s second publication, **Trading Post**, affords members an opportunity to list fish for sale or trade and also serves as the organization's newsletter.

Each member is allowed to list gratis five "wants" and five "haves" per issue.

A modest charge must be paid for each additional entry in either category.

TP is an efficient means of locating hard-to-find fish or advertising the results of a successful breeding effort.

TP is printed on odd-numbered months, so its appearance alternates with that of **Buntbarsche Bulletin**.

The third A.C.A. publication is the **Cichlid Index**.

Every volume of this serial publication comprises a number of separate one-page entries.

Each entry is a concise summary of information on the natural history, aquarium maintenance and reproductive pattern of a single cichlid species.

All are illustrated in color in order to facilitate the identification of the species discussed therein.

Members receive two entries bound into each issue of **Buntbarsche Bulletin** until all the entries are distributed.

Its publication schedule depends on the number of submissions received by the Special Publications Committee in the distribution interval of the previous volume.

The ideal is to produce one volume of twelve entries each year.

Members receive all three publications as part of their membership package. They also receive a Membership Guide explaining the operation of the A.C.A.'s several Committees upon receipt of their dues.

A current Roster is available to all members upon request.

It is particularly useful to new members, as it allows them to locate like-minded individuals in their immediate vicinity.

The A.C.A. encourages the formation of specialized Study Groups made up of persons with a strong interest in a particular cichlid group. At present, *Apistogramma* and *"Cichlasoma"* Study Groups are in operation.

The organization also has a program for sanctioning the cichlid classes of fish shows put on by local aquarium societies that allows members to compete each year for a perpetual trophy, awarded the winner at the annual Convention.

This get-together, sponsored jointly by the A.C.A. and a different local aquarium society each year, features lectures on cichlid biology and aquaristics by authorities in the field, photo, art and fish competitions, a mammoth auction and a great deal of good fellowship.

Membership in both a local aquarium society and a national specialty club thus affords the cichlid enthusiast access to a substantial body of useful information unavailable to him elsewhere. In the process, it offers him an opportunity to meet and socialize with others who share his interests. Membership dues thus represent one of the soundest investments an aquarist can make in the longevity of his interest in cichlid keeping.

Aquarists and Cichlid Conservation

Aquarists concerned about the serious threats facing cichlids in many parts of the world often express frustration to me over their inability to halt or at least slow down what seems like their inexorable slide into extinction.

Given the scope of environmental degradation, such feelings of impotence are perfectly understandable.

However, there are productive ways in which concerned aquarists can express their outrage over this state of affairs.

The first is to actively support those orgaizations engaged in efforts to protect the environment. The ultimate goal of any conservation effort is the long-term survival of viable populations of threatened organisms under natural conditions.

This is impossible unless the security of their environments is assured.

Membership in such organizations as the Society for Wildlife Conservation, the World Wildlife Fund or the Nature Conservancy is a tangible means of expressing support for such efforts while offering an effective means of keeping abreast of developments in those areas of the world where they are actively engaged.

Aquarists with the inclination and wherewithal to become more actively involved in conservation issues will find that these organizations afford their members numerous opportunities to engage in environmental advocacy.

The second is to work actively to raise the environmental awareness of their fellow aquarists. This is most readily accomplished through membership in a local aquarium society, whose meetings and publications offer a forum for the discussion of such issues and whose activities can contribute materially to the conservation of endangered fish.

The Breeders' Award Programs sponsored by most local societies, to cite one example, can effectively raise club members' awareness of conservation issues by affording participants particular recognition for both the successful breeding **and** long-term maintenance of threatened species, such as the cichlids of Lake Victoria as well as of those species whose habitats are at particular risk of degradation, such as the generality of West African dwarf cichlids.

Local aquarium societies can — and should — also make meaningful financial contributions to ongoing conservation programs.

In its simplest form, this may entail no more than suppporting the conservation activities of the local zoo or public aquarium with an annual donation.

Many national organizations also solicit support for field programs likely to engage the interest of concerned aquarists. The modest resources at the command of most aquarium societies do not preclude the ability to make a significant contribution to such efforts.

The circumstances under which most conservation projects are carried virtually guarantee that even small sums of money can contribute disproportionately to their success.

Finally, all aquarists interested in saving endangered fish and their habitats should join the Aquatic Conservation Network.

This Canadian-based non-profit orgnization is working to develop opportunities for private individuals world-wide to participate in such conservation efforts.

The ACN's quarterly bulletin, **Aquatic Survival,** has become a leading information resource for both amateur and professional conservation aquarists.

The organization's primary focus is on freshwater fish, with its first project focused on involving serious amateur aquarists in a program to preserve the endemic fishes of Madagascar.

For further information, contact:
Mr. Rob Huntley
Aquatic Conservation Network
540 Roosevelt Ave.
Ottawa, Ontario K2A 1Z8
CANADA
FAX: (613) 729-5613

Recommended Readings in the Natural History of Cichlids

Cichlid enthusiasts are interested in learning more about how cichlids live in nature, in the reasonable expectation that such knowledge will yield further understanding of why they behave as they do.

This in turn often suggests better ways to manage them under aquarium conditions. They also wish to identify their fish correctly and to remain abreast of changes in their taxonomic placement.

In compiling this list, I have been guided by these two considerations. Most of the older taxonomic literature is of marginal value to aquarists; hence, I have restricted coverage of such material to recent monographs whose contents have an immediate impact on the

nomenclature of the cichlid taxa covered therein.

Exceptions have been made for older works that also contain natural history information on the fish described by their authors. Readers with an interest in particular taxonomic issues or wishing to obtain a feel for the historical evolution of cichlid systematics will find a complete listing of such publications in the several specialized bibliographies cited herein.

For historical reasons, much material dealing with certain regional fish faunas has been published in French, Spanish or German.

Reasonable coverage of the cichlids native to these areas therefore requires inclusion of such titles. However, I have tried to keep foreign language titles at a minimum.

Annotations follow each citation wherever additional comment on that work would be helpful to the reader.

SELECTED REFERENCES

Andrews, C., A. Exell, and N. Carrington. 1988. **The Manual of Fish Health.** Salamander Books Ltd., London and New York.
[This clearly written and well-illustrated book is both comprehensive and hobbyist-friendly in its approach to a complex subject. A must for any serious cichlid keeper's library.]

Axelrod, H. R., and W. E. Burgess. 1988. **African Cichlids of Lakes Malawi and Tanganyika.** (12th Edition). T. F. H. Publications, Neptune City.
[Provides a useful checklist of Lake Malawi cichlids as well as color photographs of species not illustrated elsewhere.]

Brichard, P. 1978. **Fishes of Lake Tanganyika.** T. F. H. Publications, Neptune City. 1989. **Pierre Brichard's Book of Cichlids and Other Fishes of Lake Tanganyika.** T. F. H. Publications, Neptune City.
[Unmatched treatment of the cichlids of Lake Tanganyika based on many years of field studies including extensive underwater observations.]

Burchard, J. 1967. The Family Cichlidae. *In*: W. Reed (Ed.). **Fish and Fisheries of Northern Nigeria.**
[Ministry of Agriculture (Northern Nigeria), Zaria. There is an extensive French language literature dealing with the natural history of the fishes of West Africa in the strict biogeographic sense, but this excellent paper is the only such English title dealing with the area's riverine cichlids.]

Bussing, W. A. 1987. **Peces de los aguas continentales de Costa Rica.** Editorial de la Universidad de Costa Rica, San Jose.
[Includes an accurate, well-illustrated and thorough treatment of Costa Rica's native cichlids.]

Conkel, D. 1993. **Cichlids of North and Central America.** T. F. H. Publications, Neptune City.
[A lavishly illustrated treatment of the natural history and husbandry of the cichlids of Middle America.]

Eccles, D. H., and E. Trewavas. 1989. **Malawian Cichlid Fishes. The classification of some Haplochromine genera.** Lake Fish Movies, Herten.
[This comprehensive revision represents current thinking on the genus-level classification of Lake Malawi's haplochromine cichlids. Illustrated with Myrtel Fasken's superb halftone drawings.]

Eigenmann, C. H.
1912. The freshwater fishes of Guiana, including a study of the ecological groupings of species and the relation of the of the fauna of the plateau to that of the lowlands. **Mem. Carnegie Mus.**, 5(67): 1–578.
1924. Fishes of western South America. Pt. 1. The freshwater fishes of northwestern South America including Colombia, Panama and the Pacific slopes of Ecuador and Peru, together with an Appendix upon the fishes of the Rio Meta in Colombia. **Mem. Carnegie Mus.**, 9(1): 1–346.
[Both monographs are unusual for their time in that they contain much interesting cichlid habitat information. They are also well illustrated with black and white photographs and halftones of many of the species discussed in the text.]

Fryer, G. 1959. The trophic interrelationships and ecology of some littoral communities of Lake Nyasa with especial reference to the fishes and a discussion of the evolution of a group of rock-frequenting Cichlidae. **Proc. Zool. Soc. Lond.**, 132: 153–281.
[The first detailed investigation of the natural history of the *mbuna*.]

Fryer, G., and T. D. Iles. 1972. **The Cichlid Fishes of the Great Lakes of Africa.** Oliver and Boyd, Edinburgh.
[A thorough compilation of information on all aspects of the natural history of these fishes as of the date of its publication and an absolute must for anyone with an interest in African cichlids. Though it treats of all the lacustrine faunas, the authors' personal experiences on Lake Malawi make it a particularly valuable reference for keepers of the cichlids native to that lake.]

Giovanetti, T. A. 1991. **Discus Fish — A Complete Pet Owner's Manual.** Barron's Educational Series, Hauppauge.
[A comprehensive yet highly user-friendly treatment of a complex subject, this book should be required reading for all aspiring discus keepers.]

Goldstein, R. J.
1971. **Diseases of Aquarium Fishes.** T. F. H. Publications, Neptune City.
[A useful introductory treatment of this subject.]

1973. **Cichlids of the World.** T. F. H. Publications, Neptune City.
An excellent introduction to the Family Cichlidae.
[The sections dealing with food, fry rearing and parasites and diseases are particularly useful. Well documented with many color illustrations.]

Gosse, J. P. 1975. Revision du genre *Geophagus* (Pisces: Cichlidae). **Mem. Acad. Roy. Sci Outre-Mer** (Bruxelles) 19(3): 1–172.

[A useful revision of this cichlid group. Well illustrated with halftone drawings.]

Greenwood, P. H.
1974. The cichlid fishes of Lake Victoria, East Africa: the biology and evolution of a species flock. **Bull. Br. Mus. nat. Hist. (Zool.)** (Suppl. 6): 1—134.
[An excellent overview, unfortunately now of essentially historic interest, of this now largely extinct assemblage of cichlids, based on two decades of detailed research.]

1979. Towards a phyletic classification of the 'genus' *Haplochromis* (Pisces: Cichlidae) and related taxa. Part I. **Bull. Br. Mus. nat. Hist. (Zool.)**, 35 (4): 265—322.

1980. Towards a phyletic classification of the 'genus' *Haplochromis* (Pisces: Cichlidae) and related taxa. Part II: the species from Lake Victoria, Nabugabo, Edward, George and Kivu. **Bull. Br. Mus. nat. Hist. (Zool.)**, 39 (1): 1—101.
[These papers present the author's latest views on haplochromine classification.]

1980. The *Opthalmotilapia* assemblage of cichlid fishes reconsidered. **Bull. Br. Mus. nat. Hist. (Zool.)**, 44 (4): 249—290.

1981. The genera of pelmatochromine cichlids (Teleostei: Cichlidae). A phylogenetic review. **Bull. Br. Mus. nat. Hist. (Zool.)**, 53 (3): 139—203.

Hildebrand, S. F. 1926. Fishes of the Republic of El Salvador, Central America. **Bull. U.S. Bur. Fisheries**, 41: 237—282.
[Contains valuable information on the natural history of many cichlids native to the Pacific slope of Central America.]

Hubbs, C. L. 1936. Fishes of the Yucatan Peninsula. **Publ. Carnegie Inst. Wash.**, (457): 157—287.
[Contains useful habitat descriptions and some information on the natural history of Yucatecan cichlids.]

Jackson, P. B. N., and A. J. G. Ribbink. 1975. **Mbuna. Rockdwelling Cichlids of Lake Malawi, Africa.** T. F. H. Publications, Neptune City.
[Provides perspective on the history of *mbuna* research, insights into the group's natural history and useful information on the aquarium husbandry of these popular cichlids.]

Keenleyside, M. H. A. (Ed.) 1991. **Cichlid Fishes — Behaviour, Ecology and Evolution.** Chapman and Hall, London.
[This major compendium of review papers by leading experts in the field represents the latest thinking on these subjects.]

Keiner, A. 1963. **Peche, poissons et pisciculture a Madagascar.** Centre Technique Forestier Tropical, Nogent-sur-Marne.
[A well-illustrated work containing habitat descriptions and much information on the natural history of Malagasy cichlids.]

Keiner, A., and M. Mauge. 1966. Contributions a l'etude systematique et ecologique des poissons Cichlidae endemiques de Madagascar. **Mem. Mus. Natl. Hist. nat. (Zool.)**, 40: 4—49.
[Further information on the ecology of Malagasy cichlids.]

Konings, A.
1988. **Tanganyika Cichlids.** Verduijn Cichlids, Zevenhuizen.

1989. **Malawi Cichlids in their natural habitat.** Verduijn Cichlids, Zevenhuizen.

Konings, A., and H. W. Dieckhoff. 1992. **Tanganyika Secrets.** Cichlid Press, St. Leon Rot.
[This and the previous two titles contain much useful information on the natural history of Tanganyikan and Malawian cichlids, although aquarists should be aware that Konings' views on evolutionary processes do not represent mainstream scientific thinking in this field.
All three books are superbly illustrated and well worth buying for their excellent underwater photos of these cichlids in the natural state.]

Kullander, S. O.
1980. A taxonomical study of the genus *Apistogramma* Regan, with a revision of Brazilian

and Peruvian species. **Bonn. Zool. Monogr.,** (14): 1–152.
[An important paper that clarifies much of the confusion that has surrounded the taxonomy of these popular dwarf cichlids ever since their debut as aquarium fish. Includes a comprehensive bibliography.]

1983. **A revision of the South American cichlid genus Cichlasoma (Teleostei: Cichlidae).** Swedish Museum of Natural History, Stockholm.

1986. **Cichlid fishes of the Amazon River drainage of Peru.** Swedish Museum of Natural History, Stockholm.

Kullander, S. O., and H. Nijssen. 1989. **The Cichlids of Suriname.** E. J. Brill, Leiden.
[This paper, together with the two immediately preceding titles, establishes the framework for Kullander's revision of the genus-level taxonomy of the South American cichlids of the *Aequidens, Heros* and *Geophagus* lineages.]

Leibel, W. S. 1993. **A Fishkeeper's Guide to South American Cichlids.** Salamander, London.
[A carefully researched, highly readable guide to the husbandry of the larger South American cichlids.]

Liem, K. F. 1981. A phyletic study of the Lake Tanganyika cichlid genera *Asprotilapia, Ectodus, Lestradea, Cunningtonia, Opthalmochromis* and *Opthalmotilapia.* **Bull. Mus. Comp. Zool.,** 149(3): 191–214.

Loiselle, P. V.
1979. A revision of the genus *Hemichromis* Peters 1858 (Teleostei: Cichlidae). **Ann. Mus. Roy. Afr. centr.** (Sci. Zool.), series *in 8o* (228): 1–124.
[This revision describes a number of new species, corrects the erroneous identifications of several commercially available jewelfishes and presents information on the natural history of these cichlids.]

1988. **A Fishkeeper's Guide to African Cichlids.** Salamander, London. A useful guide to the husbandry of African cichlids.

[The introductory chapters on general husbandry practices and the sections dealing with Tanganyikan and Malawian cichlids form a useful supplement to the present volume.]

Lowe-McConnell, R.
1969. The cichlid fishes of Guyana, South America, with notes on their ecology and breeding behavior. **Zool. J. Linn. Soc., 48:** 255–302.
[The most detailed account of the natural history of South American cichlids to date published.]

1975. **Fish Communities in Tropical Freshwaters.** Longman, London and New York.
[An invaluable source of background information on the ecology of fishes in the tropics.]

1991. Natural history of fishes in Araguaia and Xingu tributaries, Serra do Roncador, Matto Grosso, Brazil. **Ichthyol. Expl. Freshwaters,** 2(2): 63–82.
[This paper presents much useful background information on a portion of the Amazon basin only now opening up as a source of ornamental fishes.]

Marlier, G. 1967. Ecological studies on some lakes of the Amazon valley. **Amazoniana, 1:** 91–115.
[Describes the habitats and provides some information on the natural history of Amazonian cichlids.]

Matthes, H.
1964. Les poissons du Lac Tumba et de la region d'Ikela. **Ann. Mus. Roy. Afr. centr.** (Sci. Zool.), series *in 8o* (126): 1–204.
[Includes much natural history information on cichlids native to the central Zaire basin.]

1973. **A bibliography of African freshwater fish.** United Nations Food and Agriculture Organization, Rome.
[A comprehensive listing of material published on this subject to that date.]

Mayland, H. G. 1984. **Mittelamerika: Cichliden und Lebendgebärende.** Landbuch-Verlag, Hannover.
[Excellent description of fish habitats in Central America, together with a synoptic treat-

ment of the region's native cichlids. Well-illustrated in color.]

McKaye, K. R.
1977a. Competition for breeding sites between the cichlid fishes of Lake Jiloa, Nicaragua. **Ecology, 58**: 291–302.

1977. Defense of a predator's young by an herbivorous fish: an unusual strategy. **Amer. Nat., 111**: 301–315.
[These two papers provide an appreciation of the reproductive ecology of the cichlids of the Nicaraguan Great Lakes based upon extensive underwater observations of their behavior.]

Piparo, A. J.
1983. Culturing wingless fruitflies. **Freshwater and Marine Aquarium, 6** (12): 18–19 *et seq.*

1984. Culturing and feeding red worms. **Freshwater and Marine Aquarium**, (3): 5 *et seq.*

1984. Culturing mealworms. **Freshwater and Marine Aquarium, 7** (6): 18–19 *et seq.*
[Three useful articles on the culture of these versatile live foods under home conditions.]

Poll, M.
1959. Recherches sur la faune ichthyologique de la region du Stanley Pool. **Ann. Mus. Roy. Afr. centr.** (Sci. Zool.), series *in 80* (71): 75–174.
[A useful source of information on the ecology of cichlids found in the Malembo Pool region of Zaire.]

1986. Classification des Cichlidae du lac Tanganyika. Tribus, genres et especes. **Mem. Acad. Roy. Belgique** (Sciences) series *in 80* 45(2): 1–163.
[The final summary of his views on this subject by one of the foremost experts on Tanganyikan cichlids.]

Ribbink, A. J. *et al.* 1983. A preliminary survey of the cichlid fishes of rocky habitats in Lake Malawi. **S. Afr. J. Zool., 13**(3): 149–310.
[A comprehensive treatment of the petricolous cichlids of the Malawian coastline of Lake Malawi, with special emphasis on the *mbuna*. Lavishly illustrated.]

Ringuelet, R. A. 1975. Zoogeografia y ecologia de los peces de aguas continentales de Argentina y consideraciones sobre las areas ictiologicas de America del Sur. **Ecosur, 2**(3): 1–122.
[A useful source of information on the cichlids of the Rio Parana system.]

Roberts, T. R., and D. J. Stewart. 1976. An ecological and systematic survey of fishes in the lower Zaire or Congo River. **Bull. Mus. Comp. Zool., 147**(6): 239–317.
[Detailed habitat descriptions for the Zairean rheophile cichlids with descriptions of numerous new species. Well-illustrated with black and white photos.]

Staeck, W., and H. Linke.
1981. **Afrikanische Cichliden I. Buntbarsche aus Westafrika.** Tetra-Verlag, Melle.

1982. **Afrikanische Cichliden. II. Buntbarsche aus Ostafrika.** Tetra-Verlag, Melle.

1984. **Amerikanische Cichliden I. Kleine Buntbarsche.** Tetra-Verlag, Melle.

1985. **Amerikanische Cichliden II. Grosse Buntbarsche.** Tetra-Verlag, Melle.
[Detailed habitat descriptions for a wide range of Paleotropical and Neotropical cichlids, together with information on their maintenance and breeding in captivity. Well illustrated in color.
English translations of the first and third titles are available through the American Cichlid Association.]

Stawikowski, R., and U. Werner.
1985. **Die Buntbarsche der Neuen Welt. Mittelamerika.** Edition Kernen, Essen.

1988. **Die Buntbarsche der Neuen Welt. Südamerika.** Edition Kernen, Essen.
[Superbly illustrated volumes dealing with the natural history and husbandry of the larger Neotropical cichlids.]

Stiassny, M. L. J., U. K. Schliewen, and W. J. Dominey. 1992. A new species flock of cichlid fishes from Lake Bermin, Cameroon with a description of eight new species of *Tilapia*.

Ichthyol. Explor. Freshwaters, 3(4): 311–346.
[Detailed introduction to the most resently discovered crater lake cichlid community. Well-illustrated in color.]

Thorson, T. B. (Ed.) 1976. **Investigations of the Ichthyofauna of Nicaraguan Lakes.** School of Life Sciences, University of Nebraska.
[Includes an extensive selection of papers dealing with the zoogeography, systematics, general and reproductive ecology and behavior of the cichlids of the San Juan faunal province of Central America. A must for anyone with a serious interest in Mesoamerican cichlids.]

Thys van den Audenaerde, D. F. E. 1968. An annotated bibliography of *Tilapia* (Pisces, Cichlidae). **Mus. Roy. Afr. centr. Documentation Zool.**, (14): i–xi, 1–406.
[As per title, but also includes a synoptic treatment of these cichlids and a complete list of the species known at the date of publication.]

Trewavas, E. 1983. **Tilapiine fishes of the genera Sarotherodon, Oreochromis and Danaki-** lia. British Museum of Natural History, London.
[Presents the author's latest views on the classification of the mouthbrooding tilapias, together with an account of all the known species.]

Trewavas, E., Green, J., and S. A. Corbet. 1972. Ecological studies on crater lakes in West Cameroon: Fishes of Barombi Mbo. **J. Zool. Lond.**, 167: 41–95.
[A well-illustrated and comprehensive account of the natural history of Lake Barombi Mbo's remarkable endemic cichlid fauna.]

Ward, J. A., and R. A. Wyman. 1975. The cichlids of the resplendent isle. **Oceans**, 8: 42–47.
[An excellent account of the natural history of the two *Etroplus* species of Sri Lanka.]

Ziesler, R. 1979. **Bibliography of Latin American freshwater fish.** United Nations Food and Agriculture Organization, Rome.
[A comprehensive listing of material published on this subject to that date.]

List of Currently Active Specialist Cichlid Groups

COUNTRY	GROUP	MAILING ADDRESS
Australia	New South Wales Cichlid Society	P. O. Box 163 Moorebank, New South Wales 2170 Australia
	Queensland Cichlid Group	P.O. Box 163 Wooloongabba, Queensland 4102 Australia
	Victorian Cichlid Society	23 Mangana Dr., Mulgrave, Victoria 3170 Australia
Austria	Deutsche Cichliden Gesellschaft	Victor-Kaplan-Strasse 1-9/1/3/12 A-1220 Wien Ostereich

COUNTRY	GROUP	MAILING ADDRESS
Belgium	Belgische Cichliden Vereninging	Kievitlaan 23 B-2228 Ranst Belgie
Denmark	Dansk Cichlide Selskab	Tollosevej 76 DK-2700 Bronshoj Danmark
France	Association Francaise des Cichlidophiles	15 Rue des Hirondelles F-67350 Dauendorf France
Germany	Deutsche Cichliden Gesellschaft	Ebereschenweg 41 D-46147 Oberhausen Deutschland
Hungary	Hungarian Cichlid Association	Lukas Laszlo Karolina ut 65 H-1113 Budapest Magyar
Netherlands	Nederlandse Cichliden Vereniging	Boeier 31 NL-1625 CJ Hoorn Nederland
Norway	Nordiska Ciklidallskapet	Olaf Flaetensvei N-3280 Tjodlyng Norge
Sweden	Nordiska Ciklid Sallskapet	Skogsglantan 16 S-435 38 Molnlycke Sverige
Switzerland	Deutsche Cichliden Gesellschaft	Am Balsberg 1 CH-8302 Kloten Schweize
Taiwan	Taiwanese Cichlid Association	No17, Lane 239 An-Ho Road Taipei Republic of China
United Kingdom	British Cichlid Association	100 Keighly Rd. Skipton North Yorkshire BD23 2RA United Kingdom
United States	American Cichlid Association	P. O. Box 32130 Raleigh, NC 27622 U.S.A.

COUNTRY	GROUP	MAILING ADDRESS
United States	*Apistogramma* Study Group	1845 Jaynes Rd. Mosinee, WI 54455 U.S.A.
	Cichlasoma Study Group	6432 South Holland Ct. Littleton, CO 80123 U.S.A.
	Ft. Wayne Cichlid Association	9638 Manor Woods Ft. Wayne, IN 46804 U.S.A.
	Greater Chicago Cichlid Association	2633 N. Rhodes River Grove, IL 60171 U.S.A.
	Greater Cincinnati Cichlid Association	15 W. Southern Ave. Covington, K 41015 U.S.A.
	Illinois Cichlids and Scavengers	7807 Sunset Dr. Elmwood Park, IL 60635 U.S.A.
	Michigan Cichlid Association	P. O. Box 59 New Baltimore, MI 48047 U.S.A.
	Ohio Cichlid Association	3896 Boston Rd. Brunswick, OH 44212 U.S.A.
	Pacific Coast Cichlid Association	P. O. Box 28145 San Jose, CA 95128 U.S.A.
	Rocky Mountain Cichlid Association	5065 W. Hinsdale Circle Littleton, CO 80123 U.S.A.
	Southern California Cichlid Association	P. O. Box 574 Midway City, CA 92655 U.S.A.
	Texas Cichlid Association	6845 Winchester Dallas, TX 75231 U.S.A.